FACTS

PLUS™

An Almanac of
Essential Information

Susan C. Anthony

Instructional Resources Company
P.O. Box 111704
Anchorage, Alaska 99511-1704

Attention: Schools and Educational Organizations

Facts Plus is recommended for use by students as a desk reference or text alternative. Contact Instructional Resources Company at one of the addresses below for information on quantity discounts for classroom sets of *Facts Plus*.

Instructional Resources Company
P.O. Box 111704
Anchorage, Alaska 99511-1704
(907) 345-6689

Instructional Resources Company
3235 Garland
Wheat Ridge, CO 80033

Note: Although the author and publisher have exhaustively researched all sources to ensure the accuracy of the information contained in this book, we assume no responsibility for errors, inaccuracies, omissions or any other inconsistency herein. Any slights against people or organizations are unintentional.

Contents

Introduction

The idea for *Facts Plus* came on one of the most frustrating days of my career, as I attempted to teach reference skills using a standard almanac. It was a frustrating day for my students, too, as they struggled to extract information from multi-columned tables with small type, abbreviations and numbers carried to several decimal places.

I couldn't blame them. The almanac was truly too difficult for them. As I analyzed the problem, an idea came. Why not a simplified almanac, "user-friendly" enough for students, yet authoritative enough for people of any age? It seemed a practical idea!

That was the beginning of years of research and writing which led to the initial publication of *Facts Plus*. The more I read and did research for the book, the more I realized that truth can be stranger than fiction. Not only are facts fascinating and useful, they are difficult to remember accurately and they change! A good, up-to-date reference book, kept handy, can be an extension of the mind, freeing it for problem solving and creativity.

Facts Plus is more than a collection of unrelated information. It presents in a concise and understandable format the basic core of information taught in schools and necessary for comprehending books and newspapers intended for the general public. It's arranged to provide a foundation and framework to help learners organize their growing knowledge.

My students use *Facts Plus* as an authentic desk reference. With instant access to maps, charts, statistics and details, they begin to discover that *they* are capable of finding the answer to almost any question they might have in a book or the library. They gain confidence to use reference books of all types. That's power! That's learning *how* to learn.

Students! Improve your grades and impress your teachers!

- Keep *Facts Plus* in your desk or study area at home as a quick source of information for reports, writing, math or other homework.
- Look up answers to questions as they occur to you. Take advantage of an easy opportunity to extend your knowledge.
- Impress others by learning fascinating facts that few people know.
- Use the maps to locate places you hear or read about.
- Review *Facts Plus* to check how well you remember what you've already learned.

Parents & grandparents! Model good habits and invest in the education of those you love!

- Keep *Facts Plus* and other reference sources handy to locate information and answer questions as they arise in the family.
- Play quiz games and challenge each other.
- Teach children to rely on *Facts Plus* and other reference books for help with their homework, rather than you. Assist them at first in using the index, finding the page, and scanning for information.
- Demonstrate the value you place on learning by giving *Facts Plus* to someone special.

Teachers! Conserve planning time and tailor lessons to your students' needs!

- Keep a copy of *Facts Plus* near your desk. Consult it for ideas and fascinating tidbits of information as you plan units and activities. Use it to plan mini-lessons to review or briefly introduce a topic. It can help you teach students how to do an interview, take standardized tests, write a report and more. Have students use the addresses for letter-writing and the statistics for creating their own math problems.

- Use it for instant reference during classroom discussions. Take advantage of "teachable moments" or current events when student interest is high.
- Build background for the enjoyment and understanding of literature. If students are reading a story set in New York City, for example, look up the height of the Empire State Building and the Statue of Liberty. Find the population. Translate the statistics into a mental picture of the traffic, the skyscrapers, the excitement!
- Keep eager learners busy and happy by challenging them to memorize for extra credit or a reward. The preamble to the Constitution, the countries of South America, and the manual alphabet are some possible challenges.
- Use *Facts Plus* as a springboard to the library. Each Indian tribe, notable person, and national park has an individual article in the standard school encyclopedias.
- Order the *Facts Plus Activity Book* for ready-to-use reference activities, including graphs, time lines, puzzles, and games. Students learn to look for patterns, predict, generalize, and hypothesize.
- Consider ordering a set of *Facts Plus* so all or several students can use it at once. Quantity discounts are available to schools ordering 25 or more copies. Contact Instructional Resources Company.

Businesspeople! Time is money! When you need facts, you need them immediately!

- Carry *Facts Plus* in your briefcase and use it for quick information as you plan or write during spare moments that might otherwise be wasted.
- Keep it handy at your desk to easily verify statistics or details that you might other- wise guess or work around.
- Use it to update your information or to brush up on the basics of something you haven't thought about for awhile.

Countless sources were consulted during the preparation of *Facts Plus*. Primary sources of information were used whenever possible. Facts were carefully checked and cross-checked for accuracy, and specialists were asked to comment on sections relating to their areas of expertise. Although I cannot guarantee the accuracy of every fact in this book, I have made every effort to locate and use the most current and reliable sources of information available at the time of publication. Statistics may vary from source to source and even from year to year in the same source. Please call if you have specific questions concerning facts or sources.

A selected bibliography on page 232 lists the books from which most of the substantive information was taken. Numerous other sources were also consulted to ensure accuracy. See pages 229–231 for explanatory notes by page number and sources of specific facts. Information in the notes can be accessed through the index.

To ensure student success in using *Facts Plus*, an exhaustive index containing more than 3,800 entries appears on pages 233–250. Maps, charts, text and even the notes are indexed for easy access. Although it would be impossible to include every fact of importance in any single book, all facts which are included in *Facts Plus* can be easily found using the index.

More thanks than I can express go to Lyle Wheeler, Beverly Wheeler, Dennis Weston, and numerous friends and family members for their assistance. Thanks to my students and colleagues in the Anchorage School District! Special thanks to artists Phyllis Hamann and Joe Nedland. I am deeply grateful to cartographer Susan Peck, who prepared the maps. Thanks also to the librarians at Loussac Public Library. My sincere gratitude to others too numerous to mention who have offered ideas, encouragement and support during the long years it took to make *Facts Plus* a reality.

Time
and
Space

Time and Clocks

Long ago, people began measuring time by keeping track of the regular cycles of nature, such as the movement of the sun, the phases of the moon, and the seasons. The cycle of the sun came to be called a **day**, the cycle of the moon was a **month**, and the cycle of the seasons was a **year**. People tried for hundreds of years to make a calendar which fit both the cycle of the moon and the cycle of the seasons, but nothing worked. The calendar we use today is based on the year. What we call "months" are divisions of the year which have no relation to the phases of the moon. Some groups of people still use calendars based on the moon.

The seven-day **week** is from the Bible, which says God created the universe in six days, and rested on the seventh.

Ancient people divided both the day and night into twelve equal parts, which together made a 24 **hour** day. They also divided the circle into 360 equal degrees. The compass is based on this division, as are the lines of latitude and longitude. Each degree of the circle was further divided into 60 **minutes** and 60 **seconds**. Later, clockmakers borrowed the idea of 60 minutes and 60 seconds. By the 1700's, clocks were correct to the minute.

Conversions

60	seconds	= 1 minute
60	minutes	= 1 hour
24	hours	= 1 day
7	days	= 1 week
365¼	days	= 1 year
52	weeks	= 1 year
12	months	= 1 year
10	years	= 1 decade
100	years	= 1 century
1000	years	= 1 millennium

The short hand is the **hour hand**. The long hand is the **minute hand**.
The narrow sweeping hand is the **second hand**.

Writing Time

8:25 a.m.

hour | minute |
    colon   a.m. or p.m.

The letters **a.m.** stand for *ante meridiem,* from Latin for "before noon." The letters **p.m.** stand for *post meridiem,* from Latin for "after noon."

24 Hour Clock

Because there are two times of the day called 9:00, there must be some way to tell the difference. One way is to use **a.m.** and **p.m.** Another way is to use a **24 hour clock**, as does the military.

Midnight	0000 hours	6:00 a.m.	0600 hours	12:00 noon	1200 hours	6:00 p.m.	1800 hours
1:00 a.m.	0100 hours	7:00 a.m.	0700 hours	1:00 p.m.	1300 hours	7:00 p.m.	1900 hours
2:00 a.m.	0200 hours	8:00 a.m.	0800 hours	2:00 p.m.	1400 hours	8:00 p.m.	2000 hours
3:00 a.m.	0300 hours	9:00 a.m.	0900 hours	3:00 p.m.	1500 hours	9:00 p.m.	2100 hours
4:00 a.m.	0400 hours	10:00 a.m.	1000 hours	4:00 p.m.	1600 hours	10:00 p.m.	2200 hours
5:00 a.m.	0500 hours	11:00 a.m.	1100 hours	5:00 p.m.	1700 hours	11:00 p.m.	2300 hours

Time Zones

Noon is the middle of the day. Because the earth rotates, and half of the earth is always in darkness, the middle of the day comes to different places at different times. A little over a century ago, every place set its own time by the sun. This was confusing for travelers, who didn't know what time it was from place to place. The railroads had a terrible time writing their schedules. It was the railroad companies who first divided the United States into four time zones in 1883. The next year, the entire world was divided into standard time zones, based on the meridians, or lines of longitude. A traveler crossing into a new time zone must change his watch by one hour. It becomes an hour earlier if the person is going from east to west and an hour later if he's going west to east.

A person crossing the international date line in the Pacific Ocean loses or gains not an hour, but a whole day! When a traveler goes from east to west across the Pacific, it becomes a day later. When he goes west to east, it becomes a day earlier. Travelers may arrive in San Francisco earlier than they left Tokyo, Japan!

A few things make using time zones complicated. Many places use Daylight Saving, a plan in which clocks are set one hour ahead of standard time for a certain period, usually in the summer. Time zone maps do not show which places use Daylight Saving and when it is in effect. Lines between time zones are not straight because they are drawn to keep cities, communities, and even states and countries from having two zones. In some places, the time changes by two hours rather than one. A few countries, including India, Afghanistan, Iran and Sri Lanka, use a half hour rather than a full hour change.

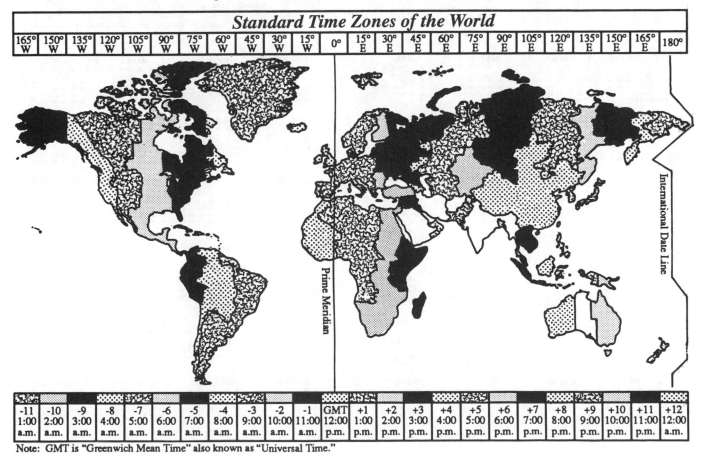

Standard Time Zones of the World

165° W	150° W	135° W	120° W	105° W	90° W	75° W	60° W	45° W	30° W	15° W	0°	15° E	30° E	45° E	60° E	75° E	90° E	105° E	120° E	135° E	150° E	165° E	180°

-11 1:00 a.m.	-10 2:00 a.m.	-9 3:00 a.m.	-8 4:00 a.m.	-7 5:00 a.m.	-6 6:00 a.m.	-5 7:00 a.m.	-4 8:00 a.m.	-3 9:00 a.m.	-2 10:00 a.m.	-1 11:00 a.m.	GMT 12:00 p.m.	+1 1:00 p.m.	+2 2:00 p.m.	+3 3:00 p.m.	+4 4:00 p.m.	+5 5:00 p.m.	+6 6:00 p.m.	+7 7:00 p.m.	+8 8:00 p.m.	+9 9:00 p.m.	+10 10:00 p.m.	+11 11:00 p.m.	+12 12:00 a.m.

Note: GMT is "Greenwich Mean Time" also known as "Universal Time."

Perpetual Calendar

1

JANUARY · **FEBRUARY** · **MARCH** · **APRIL**
MAY · **JUNE** · **JULY** · **AUGUST**
SEPTEMBER · **OCTOBER** · **NOVEMBER** · **DECEMBER**

2

JANUARY · **FEBRUARY** · **MARCH** · **APRIL**
MAY · **JUNE** · **JULY** · **AUGUST**
SEPTEMBER · **OCTOBER** · **NOVEMBER** · **DECEMBER**

3

JANUARY · **FEBRUARY** · **MARCH** · **APRIL**
MAY · **JUNE** · **JULY** · **AUGUST**
SEPTEMBER · **OCTOBER** · **NOVEMBER** · **DECEMBER**

4

JANUARY · **FEBRUARY** · **MARCH** · **APRIL**
MAY · **JUNE** · **JULY** · **AUGUST**
SEPTEMBER · **OCTOBER** · **NOVEMBER** · **DECEMBER**

5

JANUARY · **FEBRUARY** · **MARCH** · **APRIL**
MAY · **JUNE** · **JULY** · **AUGUST**
SEPTEMBER · **OCTOBER** · **NOVEMBER** · **DECEMBER**

6

JANUARY · **FEBRUARY** · **MARCH** · **APRIL**
MAY · **JUNE** · **JULY** · **AUGUST**
SEPTEMBER · **OCTOBER** · **NOVEMBER** · **DECEMBER**

1763—7	1806—4	1849—2	1892—13	1935—3	1978—1	2021—6
1764—8	1807—5	1850—3	1893—1	1936—11	1979—2	2022—7
1765—3	1808—13	1851—4	1894—2	1937—6	1980—10	2023—1
1766—4	1809—1	1852—12	1895—3	1938—7	1981—5	2024—9
1767—5	1810—2	1853—7	1896—11	1939—1	1982—6	2025—4
1768—13	1811—3	1854—1	1897—6	1940—9	1983—7	2026—5
1769—1	1812—11	1855—2	1898—7	1941—4	1984—8	2027—6
1770—2	1813—6	1856—10	1899—1	1942—5	1985—3	2028—14
1771—3	1814—7	1857—5	1900—2	1943—6	1986—4	2029—2
1772—11	1815—1	1858—6	1901—3	1944—14	1987—5	2030—3
1773—6	1816—9	1859—7	1902—4	1945—2	1988—13	2031—4
1774—7	1817—4	1860—8	1903—5	1946—3	1989—1	2032—12
1775—1	1818—5	1861—3	1904—13	1947—4	1990—2	2033—7
1776—9	1819—6	1862—4	1905—1	1948—12	1991—3	2034—1
1777—4	1820—14	1863—5	1906—2	1949—7	1992—11	2035—2
1778—5	1821—2	1864—13	1907—3	1950—1	1993—6	2036—10
1779—6	1822—3	1865—1	1908—11	1951—2	1994—7	2037—5
1780—14	1823—4	1866—2	1909—6	1952—10	1995—1	2038—6
1781—2	1824—12	1867—3	1910—7	1953—5	1996—9	2039—7
1782—3	1825—7	1868—11	1911—1	1954—6	1997—4	2040—8
1783—4	1826—1	1869—6	1912—9	1955—7	1998—5	2041—3
1784—12	1827—2	1870—7	1913—4	1956—8	1999—6	2042—4
1785—7	1828—10	1871—1	1914—5	1957—3	2000—14	2043—5
1786—1	1829—5	1872—9	1915—6	1958—4	2001—2	2044—13
1787—2	1830—6	1873—4	1916—14	1959—5	2002—3	2045—1
1788—10	1831—7	1874—5	1917—2	1960—13	2003—4	2046—2
1789—5	1832—8	1875—6	1918—3	1961—1	2004—12	2047—3
1790—6	1833—3	1876—14	1919—4	1962—2	2005—7	2048—11
1791—7	1834—4	1877—2	1920—12	1963—3	2006—1	2049—6
1792—8	1835—5	1878—3	1921—7	1964—11	2007—2	2050—7
1793—3	1836—13	1879—4	1922—1	1965—6	2008—10	2051—1
1794—4	1837—1	1880—12	1923—2	1966—7	2009—5	2052—9
1795—5	1838—2	1881—7	1924—10	1967—1	2010—6	2053—4
1796—13	1839—3	1882—1	1925—5	1968—9	2011—7	2054—5
1797—1	1840—11	1883—2	1926—6	1969—4	2012—8	2055—6
1798—2	1841—6	1884—10	1927—7	1970—5	2013—3	2056—14
1799—3	1842—7	1885—5	1928—8	1971—6	2014—4	2057—2
1800—4	1843—1	1886—6	1929—3	1972—14	2015—5	2058—3
1801—5	1844—9	1887—7	1930—4	1973—2	2016—13	2059—4
1802—6	1845—4	1888—8	1931—5	1974—3	2017—1	2060—12
1803—7	1846—5	1889—2	1932—13	1975—1	2018—2	2061—7
1804—8	1847—6	1890—4	1933—1	1976—12	2019—3	2062—1
1805—3	1848—14	1891—5	1934—2	1977—7	2020—11	2063—2

Directions: All of the possible calendars are shown on these two pages. Look for the year on the chart to the left, and use the number listed beside it to find the correct calendar.

7

JANUARY	FEBRUARY	MARCH	APRIL
S M T W T F S	S M T W T F S	S M T W T F S	S M T W T F S
1	1 2 3 4 5	1 2 3 4 5	1 2
2 3 4 5 6 7 8	6 7 8 9 10 11 12	6 7 8 9 10 11 12	3 4 5 6 7 8 9
9 10 11 12 13 14 15	13 14 15 16 17 18 19	13 14 15 16 17 18 19	10 11 12 13 14 15 16
16 17 18 19 20 21 22	20 21 22 23 24 25 26	20 21 22 23 24 25 26	17 18 19 20 21 22 23
23 24 25 26 27 28 29	27 28	27 28 29 30 31	24 25 26 27 28 29 30
30 31			

MAY	JUNE	JULY	AUGUST
S M T W T F S	S M T W T F S	S M T W T F S	S M T W T F S
1 2 3 4 5 6 7	1 2 3 4	1 2	1 2 3 4 5 6
8 9 10 11 12 13 14	5 6 7 8 9 10 11	3 4 5 6 7 8 9	7 8 9 10 11 12 13
15 16 17 18 19 20 21	12 13 14 15 16 17 18	10 11 12 13 14 15 16	14 15 16 17 18 19 20
22 23 24 25 26 27 28	19 20 21 22 23 24 25	17 18 19 20 21 22 23	21 22 23 24 25 26 27
29 30 31	26 27 28 29 30	24 25 26 27 28 29 30	28 29 30 31
		31	

SEPTEMBER	OCTOBER	NOVEMBER	DECEMBER
S M T W T F S	S M T W T F S	S M T W T F S	S M T W T F S
1 2 3	1	1 2 3 4 5	1 2 3
4 5 6 7 8 9 10	2 3 4 5 6 7 8	6 7 8 9 10 11 12	4 5 6 7 8 9 10
11 12 13 14 15 16 17	9 10 11 12 13 14 15	13 14 15 16 17 18 19	11 12 13 14 15 16 17
18 19 20 21 22 23 24	16 17 18 19 20 21 22	20 21 22 23 24 25 26	18 19 20 21 22 23 24
25 26 27 28 29 30	23 24 25 26 27 28 29	27 28 29 30	25 26 27 28 29 30 31
	30 31		

8

JANUARY	FEBRUARY	MARCH	APRIL
S M T W T F S	S M T W T F S	S M T W T F S	S M T W T F S
1 2 3 4	1	1 2 3	1 2 3 4 5 6 7
5 6 7 8 9 10 11	2 3 4 5 6 7 8	4 5 6 7 8 9 10	8 9 10 11 12 13 14
12 13 14 15 16 17 18	9 10 11 12 13 14 15	11 12 13 14 15 16 17	15 16 17 18 19 20 21
19 20 21 22 23 24 25	16 17 18 19 20 21 22	18 19 20 21 22 23 24	22 23 24 25 26 27 28
26 27 28 29 30 31	23 24 25 26 27 28 29	25 26 27 28 29 30 31	29 30

MAY	JUNE	JULY	AUGUST
S M T W T F S	S M T W T F S	S M T W T F S	S M T W T F S
1 2 3	1 2	1 2 3 4 5 6 7	1 2 3 4
4 5 6 7 8 9 10	3 4 5 6 7 8 9	8 9 10 11 12 13 14	5 6 7 8 9 10 11
11 12 13 14 15 16 17	10 11 12 13 14 15 16	15 16 17 18 19 20 21	12 13 14 15 16 17 18
18 19 20 21 22 23 24	17 18 19 20 21 22 23	22 23 24 25 26 27 28	19 20 21 22 23 24 25
25 26 27 28 29 30 31	24 25 26 27 28 29 30	29 30 31	26 27 28 29 30 31

SEPTEMBER	OCTOBER	NOVEMBER	DECEMBEER
S M T W T F S	S M T W T F S	S M T W T F S	S M T W T F S
1	1 2 3 4 5 6	1 2 3	1
2 3 4 5 6 7 8	7 8 9 10 11 12 13	4 5 6 7 8 9 10	2 3 4 5 6 7 8
9 10 11 12 13 14 15	14 15 16 17 18 19 20	11 12 13 14 15 16 17	9 10 11 12 13 14 15
16 17 18 19 20 21 22	21 22 23 24 25 26 27	18 19 20 21 22 23 24	16 17 18 19 20 21 22
23 24 25 26 27 28 29	28 29 30 31	25 26 27 28 29 30	23 24 25 26 27 28 29
30			30 31

9

JANUARY	FEBRUARY	MARCH	APRIL
S M T W T F S	S M T W T F S	S M T W T F S	S M T W T F S
1 2 3	1 2 3 4 5 6 7	1 2 3 4 5 6 7	1 2 3 4
7 8 9 10 11 12 13	4 5 6 7 8 9 10	8 9 10 11 12 13 14	5 6 7 8 9 10 11
14 15 16 17 18 19 20	11 12 13 14 15 16 17	15 16 17 18 19 20 21	12 13 14 15 16 17 18
21 22 23 24 25 26 27	18 19 20 21 22 23 24	22 23 24 25 26 27 28	19 20 21 22 23 24 25
28 29 30 31	25 26 27 28	29 30 31	26 27 28 29 30

MAY	JUNE	JULY	AUGUST
S M T W T F S	S M T W T F S	S M T W T F S	S M T W T F S
1 2 3 4	1	1 2 3 4 5 6	1 2 3
5 6 7 8 9 10 11	2 3 4 5 6 7 8	7 8 9 10 11 12 13	4 5 6 7 8 9 10
12 13 14 15 16 17 18	9 10 11 12 13 14 15	14 15 16 17 18 19 20	11 12 13 14 15 16 17
19 20 21 22 23 24 25	16 17 18 19 20 21 22	21 22 23 24 25 26 27	18 19 20 21 22 23 24
26 27 28 29 30 31	23 24 25 26 27 28 29	28 29 30 31	25 26 27 28 29 30 31
	30		

SEPTEMBER	OCTOBER	NOVEMBER	DECEMBER
S M T W T F S	S M T W T F S	S M T W T F S	S M T W T F S
1 2 3 4 5 6 7	1 2 3 4 5	1 2	1 2 3 4 5 6 7
8 9 10 11 12 13 14	6 7 8 9 10 11 12	3 4 5 6 7 8 9	8 9 10 11 12 13 14
15 16 17 18 19 20 21	13 14 15 16 17 18 19	10 11 12 13 14 15 16	15 16 17 18 19 20 21
22 23 24 25 26 27 28	20 21 22 23 24 25 26	17 18 19 20 21 22 23	22 23 24 25 26 27 28
29 30	27 28 29 30 31	24 25 26 27 28 29 30	29 30 31

10

JANUARY	FEBRUARY	MARCH	APRIL
S M T W T F S	S M T W T F S	S M T W T F S	S M T W T F S
1 2	1 2 3 4 5 6	1 2 3 4 5 6	1 2 3
6 7 8 9 10 11 12	3 4 5 6 7 8 9	2 3 4 5 6 7 8	6 7 8 9 10 11 12
13 14 15 16 17 18 19	10 11 12 13 14 15 16	9 10 11 12 13 14 15	13 14 15 16 17 18 19
20 21 22 23 24 25 26	17 18 19 20 21 22 23	16 17 18 19 20 21 22	20 21 22 23 24 25 26
27 28 29 30 31	24 25 26 27 28	23 24 25 26 27 28 29	27 28 29 30
		30 31	

MAY	JUNE	JULY	AUGUST
S M T W T F S	S M T W T F S	S M T W T F S	S M T W T F S
1 2 3	1 2 3 4 5 6 7	1 2 3 4 5	1 2
4 5 6 7 8 9 10	8 9 10 11 12 13 14	6 7 8 9 10 11 12	3 4 5 6 7 8 9
11 12 13 14 15 16 17	15 16 17 18 19 20 21	13 14 15 16 17 18 19	10 11 12 13 14 15 16
18 19 20 21 22 23 24	22 23 24 25 26 27 28	20 21 22 23 24 25 26	17 18 19 20 21 22 23
25 26 27 28 29 30 31	29 30	27 28 29 30 31	24 25 26 27 28 29 30
			31

SEPTEMBER	OCTOBER	NOVEMBER	DECEMBER
S M T W T F S	S M T W T F S	S M T W T F S	S M T W T F S
1 2 3 4 5 6	1 2 3 4	1	1 2 3 4 5 6
7 8 9 10 11 12 13	5 6 7 8 9 10 11	2 3 4 5 6 7 8	7 8 9 10 11 12 13
14 15 16 17 18 19 20	12 13 14 15 16 17 18	9 10 11 12 13 14 15	14 15 16 17 18 19 20
21 22 23 24 25 26 27	19 20 21 22 23 24 25	16 17 18 19 20 21 22	21 22 23 24 25 26 27
28 29 30	26 27 28 29 30 31	23 24 25 26 27 28 29	28 29 30 31
		30	

11

JANUARY	FEBRUARY	MARCH	APRIL
S M T W T F S	S M T W T F S	S M T W T F S	S M T W T F S
1 2 3 4	1 2 3 4 5 6 7	1 2 3 4 5 6 7	1 2 3 4
5 6 7 8 9 10 11	8 9 10 11 12 13 14	8 9 10 11 12 13 14	5 6 7 8 9 10 11
12 13 14 15 16 17 18	15 16 17 18 19 20 21	15 16 17 18 19 20 21	12 13 14 15 16 17 18
19 20 21 22 23 24 25	22 23 24 25 26 27 28	22 23 24 25 26 27 28	19 20 21 22 23 24 25
26 27 28 29 30 31		29 30 31	26 27 28 29 30

MAY	JUNE	JULY	AUGUST
S M T W T F S	S M T W T F S	S M T W T F S	S M T W T F S
1 2	1 2 3 4 5 6	1 2 3 4	1
3 4 5 6 7 8 9	7 8 9 10 11 12 13	5 6 7 8 9 10 11	2 3 4 5 6 7 8
10 11 12 13 14 15 16	14 15 16 17 18 19 20	12 13 14 15 16 17 18	9 10 11 12 13 14 15
17 18 19 20 21 22 23	21 22 23 24 25 26 27	19 20 21 22 23 24 25	16 17 18 19 20 21 22
24 25 26 27 28 29 30	28 29 30	26 27 28 29 30 31	23 24 25 26 27 28 29
31			30 31

SEPTEMBER	OCTOBER	NOVEMBER	DECEMBER
S M T W T F S	S M T W T F S	S M T W T F S	S M T W T F S
1 2 3 4 5	1 2 3	1 2 3 4 5 6 7	1 2 3 4 5
6 7 8 9 10 11 12	4 5 6 7 8 9 10	8 9 10 11 12 13 14	6 7 8 9 10 11 12
13 14 15 16 17 18 19	11 12 13 14 15 16 17	15 16 17 18 19 20 21	13 14 15 16 17 18 19
20 21 22 23 24 25 26	18 19 20 21 22 23 24	22 23 24 25 26 27 28	20 21 22 23 24 25 26
27 28 29 30	25 26 27 28 29 30 31	29 30	27 28 29 30 31

12

JANUARY	FEBRUARY	MARCH	APRIL
S M T W T F S	S M T W T F S	S M T W T F S	S M T W T F S
1 2 3	1 2 3 4 5 6 7	1 2 3 4 5 6	1 2 3
4 5 6 7 8 9 10	8 9 10 11 12 13 14	7 8 9 10 11 12 13	4 5 6 7 8 9 10
11 12 13 14 15 16 17	15 16 17 18 19 20 21	14 15 16 17 18 19 20	11 12 13 14 15 16 17
18 19 20 21 22 23 24	22 23 24 25 26 27 28	21 22 23 24 25 26 27	18 19 20 21 22 23 24
25 26 27 28 29 30 31		28 29 30 31	25 26 27 28 29 30

MAY	JUNE	JULY	AUGUST
S M T W T F S	S M T W T F S	S M T W T F S	S M T W T F S
1	1 2 3 4 5	1 2 3	1 2 3 4 5 6 7
2 3 4 5 6 7 8	6 7 8 9 10 11 12	4 5 6 7 8 9 10	8 9 10 11 12 13 14
9 10 11 12 13 14 15	13 14 15 16 17 18 19	11 12 13 14 15 16 17	15 16 17 18 19 20 21
16 17 18 19 20 21 22	20 21 22 23 24 25 26	18 19 20 21 22 23 24	22 23 24 25 26 27 28
23 24 25 26 27 28 29	27 28 29 30	25 26 27 28 29 30 31	29 30 31
30 31			

SEPTEMBER	OCTOBER	NOVEMBER	DECEMBER
S M T W T F S	S M T W T F S	S M T W T F S	S M T W T F S
1 2 3 4	1 2	1 2 3 4 5 6	1 2 3 4
5 6 7 8 9 10 11	3 4 5 6 7 8 9	7 8 9 10 11 12 13	5 6 7 8 9 10 11
12 13 14 15 16 17 18	10 11 12 13 14 15 16	14 15 16 17 18 19 20	12 13 14 15 16 17 18
19 20 21 22 23 24 25	17 18 19 20 21 22 23	21 22 23 24 25 26 27	19 20 21 22 23 24 25
26 27 28 29 30	24 25 26 27 28 29 30	28 29 30	26 27 28 29 30 31
	31		

13

JANUARY	FEBRUARY	MARCH	APRIL
S M T W T F S	S M T W T F S	S M T W T F S	S M T W T F S
1 2	1 2 3 4 5 6	1 2 3 4 5	1 2
3 4 5 6 7 8 9	7 8 9 10 11 12 13	6 7 8 9 10 11 12	3 4 5 6 7 8 9
10 11 12 13 14 15 16	14 15 16 17 18 19 20	13 14 15 16 17 18 19	10 11 12 13 14 15 16
17 18 19 20 21 22 23	21 22 23 24 25 26 27	20 21 22 23 24 25 26	17 18 19 20 21 22 23
24 25 26 27 28 29 30	28	27 28 29 30 31	24 25 26 27 28 29 30
31			

MAY	JUNE	JULY	AUGUST
S M T W T F S	S M T W T F S	S M T W T F S	S M T W T F S
1 2 3 4 5 6 7	1 2 3 4	1 2	1 2 3 4 5 6
8 9 10 11 12 13 14	5 6 7 8 9 10 11	3 4 5 6 7 8 9	7 8 9 10 11 12 13
15 16 17 18 19 20 21	12 13 14 15 16 17 18	10 11 12 13 14 15 16	14 15 16 17 18 19 20
22 23 24 25 26 27 28	19 20 21 22 23 24 25	17 18 19 20 21 22 23	21 22 23 24 25 26 27
29 30 31	26 27 28 29 30	24 25 26 27 28 29 30	28 29 30 31
		31	

SEPTEMBER	OCTOBER	NOVEMBER	DECEMBER
S M T W T F S	S M T W T F S	S M T W T F S	S M T W T F S
1 2 3	1	1 2 3 4 5	1 2 3
4 5 6 7 8 9 10	2 3 4 5 6 7 8	6 7 8 9 10 11 12	4 5 6 7 8 9 10
11 12 13 14 15 16 17	9 10 11 12 13 14 15	13 14 15 16 17 18 19	11 12 13 14 15 16 17
18 19 20 21 22 23 24	16 17 18 19 20 21 22	20 21 22 23 24 25 26	18 19 20 21 22 23 24
25 26 27 28 29 30	23 24 25 26 27 28 29	27 28 29 30	25 26 27 28 29 30 31
	30 31		

14

JANUARY	FEBRUARY	MARCH	APRIL
S M T W T F S	S M T W T F S	S M T W T F S	S M T W T F S
1	1 2 3 4 5	1 2 3 4	1 2 3 4 5 6 7
2 3 4 5 6 7 8	6 7 8 9 10 11 12	5 6 7 8 9 10 11	8 9 10 11 12 13 14
9 10 11 12 13 14 15	13 14 15 16 17 18 19	12 13 14 15 16 17 18	15 16 17 18 19 20 21
16 17 18 19 20 21 22	20 21 22 23 24 25 26	19 20 21 22 23 24 25	22 23 24 25 26 27 28
23 24 25 26 27 28 29	27 28	26 27 28 29 30 31	29 30
30 31			

MAY	JUNE	JULY	AUGUST
S M T W T F S	S M T W T F S	S M T W T F S	S M T W T F S
1 2 3 4 5 6	1 2 3	1	1 2 3 4
7 8 9 10 11 12 13	4 5 6 7 8 9 10	2 3 4 5 6 7 8	6 7 8 9 10 11 12
14 15 16 17 18 19 20	11 12 13 14 15 16 17	9 10 11 12 13 14 15	13 14 15 16 17 18 19
21 22 23 24 25 26 27	18 19 20 21 22 23 24	16 17 18 19 20 21 22	20 21 22 23 24 25 26
28 29 30 31	25 26 27 28 29 30	23 24 25 26 27 28 29	27 28 29 30 31
		30 31	

SEPTEMBER	OCTOBER	NOVEMBER	DECEMBER
S M T W T F S	S M T W T F S	S M T W T F S	S M T W T F S
1 2	1 2 3 4 5 6 7	1 2 3 4	1 2
3 4 5 6 7 8 9	8 9 10 11 12 13 14	5 6 7 8 9 10 11	3 4 5 6 7 8 9
10 11 12 13 14 15 16	15 16 17 18 19 20 21	12 13 14 15 16 17 18	10 11 12 13 14 15 16
17 18 19 20 21 22 23	22 23 24 25 26 27 28	19 20 21 22 23 24 25	17 18 19 20 21 22 23
24 25 26 27 28 29 30	29 30 31	26 27 28 29 30	24 25 26 27 28 29 30
			31

1995

January
S	M	T	W	T	F	S
1	2	3	4	5	6	7
8	9	10	11	12	13	14
15	**16**	17	18	19	20	21
22	23	24	25	26	27	28
29	30	31				

February
S	M	T	W	T	F	S
			1	**2**	3	4
5	6	7	8	9	10	11
12	13	**14**	15	16	17	18
19	**20**	21	22	23	24	25
26	27	28				

March
S	M	T	W	T	F	S
			1	2	3	4
5	6	7	8	9	10	11
12	13	14	15	16	**17**	18
19	**20**	21	22	23	24	25
26	27	28	29	30	31	

April
S	M	T	W	T	F	S
						1
2	3	4	5	6	7	8
9	10	11	12	13	**14**	15
16	17	18	19	20	21	22
23	24	25	26	27	28	29
30						

May
S	M	T	W	T	F	S
	1	2	3	4	5	6
7	8	9	10	11	12	13
14	15	16	17	18	19	20
21	22	23	24	25	26	27
28	**29**	30	31			

June
S	M	T	W	T	F	S
				1	2	3
4	5	6	7	8	9	10
11	12	13	**14**	15	16	17
18	19	20	**21**	22	23	24
25	26	27	28	29	30	

July
S	M	T	W	T	F	S
						1
2	3	**4**	5	6	7	8
9	10	11	12	13	14	15
16	17	18	19	20	21	22
23	24	25	26	27	28	29
30	31					

August
S	M	T	W	T	F	S
		1	2	3	4	5
6	7	8	9	10	11	12
13	14	15	16	17	18	19
20	21	22	23	24	25	26
27	28	29	30	31		

September
S	M	T	W	T	F	S
					1	2
3	**4**	5	6	7	8	9
10	11	12	13	14	15	16
17	18	19	20	21	22	**23**
24	25	26	27	28	29	30

October
S	M	T	W	T	F	S
1	2	3	4	5	6	7
8	**9**	10	11	12	13	14
15	16	17	18	19	20	21
22	23	24	25	26	27	28
29	30	**31**				

November
S	M	T	W	T	F	S
			1	2	3	4
5	6	**7**	8	9	10	**11**
12	13	14	15	16	17	18
19	20	21	22	**23**	24	25
26	27	28	29	30		

December
S	M	T	W	T	F	S
					1	2
3	4	5	6	7	8	9
10	11	12	13	14	15	16
17	18	19	20	21	**22**	23
24	**25**	26	27	28	29	30
31						

1996

January
S	M	T	W	T	F	S
	1	2	3	4	5	6
7	8	9	10	11	12	13
14	**15**	16	17	18	19	20
21	22	23	24	25	26	27
28	29	30	31			

February
S	M	T	W	T	F	S
				1	**2**	3
4	5	6	7	8	9	10
11	**12**	13	**14**	15	16	17
18	**19**	20	21	22	23	24
25	26	27	28	**29**		

March
S	M	T	W	T	F	S
					1	2
3	4	5	6	7	8	9
10	11	12	13	14	15	16
17	18	19	**20**	21	22	23
24	25	26	27	28	29	30
31						

April
S	M	T	W	T	F	S
	1	2	3	4	**5**	6
7	8	9	10	11	12	13
14	15	16	17	18	19	20
21	22	23	24	25	26	27
28	29	30				

May
S	M	T	W	T	F	S
			1	2	3	4
5	6	7	8	9	10	11
12	13	14	15	16	17	18
19	20	21	22	23	24	25
26	**27**	28	29	30	31	

June
S	M	T	W	T	F	S
						1
2	3	4	5	6	7	8
9	10	11	12	13	**14**	15
16	17	18	19	**20**	21	22
23	24	25	26	27	28	29
30						

July
S	M	T	W	T	F	S
	1	2	3	**4**	5	6
7	8	9	10	11	12	13
14	15	16	17	18	19	20
21	22	23	24	25	26	27
28	29	30	31			

August
S	M	T	W	T	F	S
				1	2	3
4	5	6	7	8	9	10
11	12	13	14	15	16	17
18	19	20	21	22	23	24
25	26	27	28	29	30	31

September
S	M	T	W	T	F	S
1	**2**	3	4	5	6	7
8	9	10	11	12	13	14
15	16	17	18	19	20	21
22	23	24	25	26	27	28
29	30					

October
S	M	T	W	T	F	S
		1	2	3	4	5
6	7	8	9	10	11	12
13	**14**	15	16	17	18	19
20	21	22	23	24	25	26
27	28	29	30	**31**		

November
S	M	T	W	T	F	S
					1	2
3	4	**5**	6	7	8	9
10	**11**	12	13	14	15	16
17	18	19	20	21	22	23
24	25	26	27	**28**	29	30

December
S	M	T	W	T	F	S
1	2	3	4	5	6	7
8	9	10	11	12	13	14
15	16	17	18	19	20	**21**
22	23	24	**25**	26	27	28
29	30	31				

1997

January
S	M	T	W	T	F	S
			1	2	3	4
5	6	7	8	9	10	11
12	13	14	15	16	17	18
19	**20**	21	22	23	24	25
26	27	28	29	30	31	

February
S	M	T	W	T	F	S
						1
2	3	4	5	6	7	8
9	10	11	**12**	13	**14**	15
16	**17**	18	19	20	21	22
23	24	25	26	27	28	

March
S	M	T	W	T	F	S
						1
2	3	4	5	6	7	8
9	10	11	12	13	14	15
16	**17**	18	19	**20**	21	22
23	24	25	26	27	**28**	29
30	31					

April
S	M	T	W	T	F	S
		1	2	3	4	5
6	7	8	9	10	11	12
13	14	15	16	17	18	19
20	21	22	23	24	25	26
27	28	29	30			

May
S	M	T	W	T	F	S
				1	2	3
4	5	6	7	8	9	10
11	12	13	14	15	16	17
18	19	20	21	22	23	24
25	**26**	27	28	29	30	31

June
S	M	T	W	T	F	S
1	2	3	4	5	6	7
8	9	10	11	12	13	**14**
15	16	17	18	19	20	**21**
22	23	24	25	26	27	28
29	30					

July
S	M	T	W	T	F	S
		1	2	3	**4**	5
6	7	8	9	10	11	12
13	14	15	16	17	18	19
20	21	22	23	24	25	26
27	28	29	30	31		

August
S	M	T	W	T	F	S
					1	2
3	4	5	6	7	8	9
10	11	12	13	14	15	16
17	18	19	20	21	22	23
24	25	26	27	28	29	30
31						

September
S	M	T	W	T	F	S
	1	2	3	4	5	6
7	8	9	10	11	12	13
14	15	16	17	18	19	20
21	**22**	23	24	25	26	27
28	29	30				

October
S	M	T	W	T	F	S
			1	2	3	4
5	6	7	8	9	10	11
12	**13**	14	15	16	17	18
19	20	21	22	23	24	25
26	27	28	29	30	**31**	

November
S	M	T	W	T	F	S
						1
2	3	**4**	5	6	7	8
9	10	**11**	12	13	14	15
16	17	18	19	20	21	22
23	24	25	26	**27**	28	29
30						

December
S	M	T	W	T	F	S
	1	2	3	4	5	6
7	8	9	10	11	12	13
14	15	16	17	18	19	20
21	22	23	24	**25**	26	27
28	29	30	31			

Holiday	1995	1996	1997
New Year's Day	Sunday, January 1	Monday, January 1	Wednesday, January 1
Martin Luther King Day	Monday, January 16*	Monday, January 15*	Monday, January 20*
Ground Hog Day	Thursday, February 2	Friday, February 2	Sunday, February 2
Lincoln's Birthday	Sunday, February 12	Monday, February 12	Wednesday, February 12
Valentine's Day	Tuesday, February 14	Wednesday, February 14	Friday, February 14
Washington's Birthday	Monday, February 20*	Monday, February 19*	Monday, February 17*
St. Patrick's Day	Friday, March 17	Sunday, March 17	Monday, March 17
First Day of Spring	Monday, March 20	Wednesday, March 20	Thursday, March 20
Good Friday	Friday, April 14	Friday, April 5	Friday, March 28
Easter	Sunday, April 16	Sunday, April 7	Sunday, March 30
Mother's Day	Sunday, May 14	Sunday, May 12	Sunday, May 11
Memorial Day	Monday, May 29*	Monday, May 27*	Monday, May 26*
Flag Day	Wednesday, June 14	Friday, June 14	Saturday, June 14
Father's Day	Sunday, June 18	Sunday, June 16	Sunday, June 15
First Day of Summer	Wednesday, June 21	Thursday, June 20	Saturday, June 21
Independence Day	Tuesday, July 4	Thursday, July 4	Friday, July 4
Labor Day	Monday, September 4	Monday, September 2	Monday, September 1
First Day of Autumn	Saturday, September 23	Sunday, September 22	Monday, September 22
Columbus Day	Monday, October 9*	Monday, October 14*	Monday, October 13*
Halloween	Tuesday, October 31	Thursday, October 31	Friday, October 31
Election Day	Tuesday, November 7	Tuesday, November 5	Tuesday, November 4
Veterans Day	Saturday, November 11	Monday, November 11	Tuesday, November 11
Thanksgiving	Thursday, November 23	Thursday, November 28	Thursday, November 27
First Day of Winter	Friday, December 22	Saturday, December 21	Sunday, December 21
Christmas	Monday, December 25	Wednesday, December 25	Thursday, December 25

*Date of legal holiday as observed in the United States.

Major Holidays and Special Days

The word "holiday" comes from "holy day." Originally, all holidays were religious celebrations but now the word means any special day, particularly when people do not have to go to work. A "legal holiday" is the day a holiday is celebrated to allow workers to have long weekends. Since 1971, Washington's Birthday, Memorial Day and Columbus Day have been celebrated on Mondays. The holidays listed below are those most commonly observed in the United States. People of various religions celebrate a number of other important holidays.

New Year's Day — January 1. In Roman times, the first day of the new year was the special day of Janus, the god of gates and doors. He had two faces, one looking forward to the future, and one looking back at the past.

P. Hamann

Martin Luther King Day — January 15. This holiday, first celebrated in 1986, honors civil rights leader Dr. Martin Luther King, Jr., who was born on January 15, 1929. He was assassinated on April 4, 1968. The legal holiday is celebrated on the third Monday in January.

Ground Hog Day — February 2. The ground hog, or woodchuck, supposedly awakens from its winter sleep on this day. It sticks its head out of its burrow and looks around. If the day is sunny and it sees its shadow, it is frightened and goes back into its hole to sleep. This means there will be another six weeks of wintery weather. If the day is cloudy and the ground hog cannot see its shadow, it comes out of its hole, and spring weather will come soon. This story is folklore with no scientific basis.

Lincoln's Birthday — February 12. President Abraham Lincoln was born on February 12,

1809. He was president of the United States during the Civil War, and his leadership kept the country from splitting apart. His birthday has been observed as a national holiday since 1866.

Valentine's Day — February 14. The patron saint of this day is St. Valentine. Valentine's Day is usually celebrated by exchanging Valentine's cards and candy with sweethearts and friends. The Valentine's Day colors are red and pink.

Washington's Birthday — February 22. President George Washington, the first president of the United States, was born on February 22, 1732. His birthday has been celebrated since 1796. The legal holiday, President's Day, is observed on the third Monday in February.

Leap Year Day — February 29. A year is the amount of time it takes the earth to revolve around the sun. It takes almost exactly 365¼ days. Because of the ¼ day, every fourth year has an extra day added onto February, the 29th. Years in which February has 29 days can be divided by the number four and are called "leap years." See page 12 for more about leap year.

St. Patrick's Day — March 17. The patron saint of Ireland, St. Patrick, has been honored on this day since the United States began. The day is celebrated by wearing green, and by the St. Patrick's Day Parade in New York City. The shamrock is the symbol of St. Patrick's Day and green is the color.

First Day of Spring — March 20 or 21. On this day, the hours of daylight and the hours of darkness are equal. Between now and the year 2000, the first day of spring each year will be March 20.

Good Friday — The Friday before Easter. This is the day observed by Christians as the anniversary of Christ's death on the Cross.

Easter — Easter is celebrated the Sunday after the first full moon on or after March 21. It is always between March 22 and April 25, but the actual date is different each year. This Christian holiday is to remember the Resurrection of Jesus Christ. It is frequently celebrated with special church services. One common tradition is the dyeing of hard-boiled eggs, which may be hidden by the "Easter bunny." Children search for the eggs on Easter morning. Easter colors are usually pastel pink, blue, and yellow. The flower is the Easter lily. The dates for Easter between 1995 and 2006 are listed below:

1995	April 16	2001	April 15
1996	April 7	2002	March 31
1997	March 30	2003	April 20
1998	April 12	2004	April 11
1999	April 4	2005	March 27
2000	April 23	2006	April 16

Daylight Saving Time Begins — First Sunday in April. Daylight Saving is a period of time during which all clocks are set ahead of standard time by one hour. This means that people must get up an hour earlier, according to the sun. This hour of daylight is "saved" for the evening, when people are more likely to be awake. Daylight Saving was first used during World War I to reduce the use of electricity in the evening. In 1967, a Congressional act went into effect which proclaimed Daylight Saving for the whole country. It begins the first Sunday in April and ends the last Sunday in October. To remember which way to change the clock: "Spring forward, fall back."

Mother's Day — The second Sunday in May. Mother's Day was first observed in 1907, and is a day to honor all mothers.

Memorial Day — May 30. Memorial Day, or Decoration Day, was first observed in 1866 to honor the memory of those who died in the Civil War by decorating their graves with flowers. It is now a special day to remember all loved ones who have passed away, especially those who died in service to their country. The legal holiday is the last Monday in May.

Flag Day — June 14. On this day in 1777, the Stars and Stripes became the official flag of the United States. Flag Day is frequently observed by flying the U.S. flag from homes and businesses.

Father's Day — Third Sunday in June. Father's Day was first celebrated in 1910 as a day to honor all fathers.

First Day of Summer — June 20 or 21. This is the longest day of the year in the northern hemisphere. Summer will begin on June 20 in 1996 and 2000. In all other years until 2000, it will begin on June 21.

Independence Day — July 4. This holiday is also called the Fourth of July. The Declaration of Independence was signed on this date in 1776. People frequently celebrate with picnics and fireworks displays.

Labor Day — First Monday in September. Labor Day honors those who labor, the working people of America. It was first observed in

1882 and was sponsored by the Central Labor Union of New York. It traditionally meant the end of summer and the start of the school year.

First Day of Autumn — September 22 or 23. On this day, the hours of daylight and the hours of darkness are equal. Autumn will begin on September 23 in 1995 and 1999. In all other years until 2000, autumn will begin on September 22.

Columbus Day — October 12. On this holiday, people remember Christopher Columbus' discovery of America, which took place on October 12, 1492. The legal holiday is celebrated the second Monday in October.

Daylight Saving Time Ends — Last Sunday in October. Clocks are moved back one hour on this day. This means that people get an extra hour of sleep.

Halloween — October 31. Halloween is the eve of All Saint's Day, November 1. Halloween is commonly celebrated by wearing costumes, visiting haunted houses, telling ghost stories and partying. Many people hollow out pumpkins and carve them into Jack-o-Lanterns which are lit from inside with a candle. Orange and black are the Halloween colors.

Election Day — First Tuesday after the first Monday in November. Since 1845, presidential elections have been held on this date. Many states also hold elections on this day.

Veterans Day — November 11. In 1918, the Armistice was signed ending World War I, which at that time was thought to be the "war to end all wars." The holiday was called Armistice Day until 1954, when the name was changed to Veterans Day. It is now a day to honor the veterans of all wars.

Thanksgiving — Fourth Thursday in November. Traditionally, Thanksgiving in the United States dates to the time of the Pilgrims in Plymouth Colony, who held a feast in 1621 to celebrate their first harvest after a long and difficult winter. Indians were invited and brought wild turkeys. Thanksgiving is celebrated with large feasts, which usually have turkey as the main dish. The illustration shows a cornucopia, or horn of plenty, which is a symbol of nature's abundance. Thanksgiving is a time to give thanks for food and all the blessings of nature.

First Day of Winter — December 21 or 22. This is the shortest day of the year in the northern hemisphere. Winter will begin on December 22 in 1995 and 1999. In other years through 2000, it will begin on December 21.

Christmas — December 25. Christmas celebrates the birth of Jesus Christ and is the most widely observed Christian holiday. Many people decorate their homes with wreaths, holly and poinsettias. Christmas trees are trimmed with tinsel and ornaments, and gifts are placed underneath to be exchanged and opened Christmas Eve or Christmas Day. Children hang stockings to be filled with candy and small gifts by Santa Claus, a legendary old man who visits homes and delivers gifts on Christmas Eve while children sleep. During the Christmas season, people sing carols and send cards and letters to friends and relatives. Red and dark green are the Christmas colors.

Days

The earth's axis is an imaginary line running from the North Pole to the South Pole through the center of the earth. The earth rotates, or spins, on its axis once every 24 hours. It is **daytime** for the half of the earth facing the sun and **nighttime** for the half facing away from the sun.

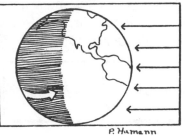

P. Humann

The earth spins very fast. A person standing still on the equator, which is 24,900 miles long, is spinning with the earth at a speed of nearly 1,038 miles per hour (17 miles per minute).

The Names of the Days

Day	Abbrev.	Planet	Latin Name	Anglo-Saxon Name
Sunday	Sun.	Sun	Dies Solis	Sun's Day
Monday	Mon.	Moon	Dies Lunae	Moon's Day
Tuesday	Tues.	Mars	Dies Martis	Tiw's Day
Wednesday	Wed.	Mercury	Dies Mercurii	Woden's Day
Thursday	Thurs.	Jupiter	Dies Jovis	Thor's Day
Friday	Fri.	Venus	Dies Veneris	Frigg's Day
Saturday	Sat.	Saturn	Dies Saturni	Seterne's Day

The Romans named the days of the week for the sun, the moon and the five planets known at that time. The planets had been named after Roman gods. The Anglo-Saxons later renamed the days by substituting the names of Norse gods for the names of Roman gods. For example, Mars is the Roman god of war; Tiw is the Norse god of war. Jupiter is the Roman god of thunder; Thor is the Norse god of thunder. Venus is the Roman goddess of love; Frigg is the Norse goddess of love. The English names of the days are based on the Anglo-Saxon names.

Names of the Days in Foreign Languages

English	French	Italian	Spanish	German
Sunday	dimanche	domenica	domingo	Sonntag
Monday	lundi	lunedì	lunes	Montag
Tuesday	mardi	martedì	martes	Dienstag
Wednesday	mercredi	mercoledì	miércoles	Mittwoch
Thursday	jeudi	giovedì	jueves	Donnerstag
Friday	vendredi	venerdì	viernes	Freitag
Saturday	samedi	sabato	sábado	Samstag

Note: Names of the days are not capitalized in some languages.

Months

The calendar we use was drawn up by Pope Gregory XIII in 1582, and is called the Gregorian calendar. It has 12 months. Before then, people used the Julian calendar, drawn up by Julius Caesar. The Julian calendar was almost the same as the Gregorian calendar. The main change Pope Gregory made was skipping leap year on century years which cannot be divided by 400. The year 2000 will be a leap year, but 1900 was not. England and the American Colonies adopted the Gregorian calendar in 1752.

Month	*Abbrev.*	*Number of Days*	*Flower*	*Gem Birthstone*
January	Jan.	31	Carnation Snowdrop	Garnet
February	Feb.	28*	Primrose	Amethyst
March	Mar.	31	Violet	Aquamarine Bloodstone
April	Apr.	30	Daisy Sweet Pea	Diamond
May	May	31	Lily of the Valley Hawthorne	Emerald
June	June	30	Rose	Pearl Alexandrite
July	July	31	Water Lily	Ruby Star Ruby
August	Aug.	31	Poppy Gladiolus	Sardonyx Peridot
September	Sept.	30	Morning-Glory	Sapphire Star Sapphire
October	Oct.	31	Calendula	Opal Tourmaline
November	Nov.	30	Chrysanthemum	Topaz
December	Dec.	31	Holly Narcissus Poinsettia	Turquoise Zircon Lapis lazuli

*Every fourth year is a "leap year." This means that February has 29 days instead of 28. Leap years are those years evenly divisible by four, except century years unless they are divisible by 400. Read about "leap seconds" on p. 229.

This poem may be helpful in remembering how many days are in each month:

> Thirty days hath September,
> April, June and November.
> All the rest have thirty-one,
> Except February, which has 28.

The Names of the Months

January was named after the Roman god Janus, the god of gates and doors, entrances and exits. Janus had two faces, one looking into the past and one looking into the future.

February is from *februare,* a Latin word meaning "to purify."

March was named after Mars, the Roman god of war.

April is from *Aprilis,* which comes from a Latin word meaning "to open."

May is named after Maia, the Roman goddess of spring and growth.

June is named after Juno, the goddess of marriage.

July was named after the Roman emperor Julius Caesar, who was born during that month. Before then, it was *Quintilis,* or "fifth."*

August was named after the Roman emperor Augustus Caesar. It was originally *Sextilis,* which means "sixth."*

September is from *septum,* the Latin word meaning "seven." *

October is from the Latin word *octo,* meaning "eight."*

November is from the Latin word *novem,* meaning "nine."*

December is from *decem,* the Latin word for "ten."*

* The earliest Latin calendar began on March 1. July was the fifth month, August the sixth, September the seventh, October the eighth, November the ninth, and December the tenth. January and February were the last two months of the year. Julius Caesar changed the calendar in 46 B.C., beginning the year on January 1.

World Calendars

The **Gregorian calendar** is now the most widely used calendar in the world. It dates from what was once thought to be the year of Jesus Christ's birth. The year 1996 is 1,996 years after Christ was born, and may be written 1996 A.D. or A.D. 1996. A.D. stands for *anno Domini,* which is Latin for "in the year of our Lord." The years before Christ was born are counted backwards, and are followed by the letters B.C., which stand for "before Christ." Thus, 10 B.C. is two years earlier than 8 B.C. People of many religions, including those who do not believe in Christ, now use the Gregorian calendar. Instead of the letters B.C. and A.D., non-Christians often use C.E. and B.C.E., which stand for "common era" and "before common era."

The **Hebrew calendar** is used by some people of the Jewish faith. It dates from the Creation of the universe, traditionally 3,760 years and three months before the common era. The year 1996 in the Hebrew calendar is 5756.

The year has 12 or 13 months with Hebrew names. The calendar is based on both sun and moon. Every 19 years, a cycle of years repeats.

The **Islamic calendar** is used in many Moslem countries. It dates from 622 A.D. in the Gregorian calendar, the year that Mohammed, the founder of Islam, escaped from Mecca to Medina. 1996 is the year 1374 in the Islamic countries. The Islamic calendar is based on the moon, and each year has 354 days.

The **Chinese calendar** is also based on the moon. It dates from 2637 B.C. of the Gregorian calendar, when it was supposedly invented. The years are counted in cycles of 60. Each year is assigned one of twelve animal names: *rat, ox, tiger, hare, dragon, snake, horse, sheep, monkey, fowl, dog,* or *pig.* Chinese New Year is the second new moon after winter begins, which is always between January 20 and February 20. The year 1996 is 4633 in China.

Seasons

S easons occur because the earth's axis is tilted at a 23½° angle. As the earth orbits the sun, there is a time when the North Pole is tilted toward the sun and the South Pole is tilted away from it. At this time, the northern hemisphere receives more sunlight and is warmer, while the southern hemisphere receives less sunlight and is cooler. It is **summer** in the north and **winter** in the south.

Six months later, when the earth has traveled halfway around the sun, the opposite is true. The northern hemisphere is tilted away from the sun and has **winter**. The southern hemisphere is tilted toward the sun and has **summer**.

During **spring** and **autumn**, both hemispheres receive about the same amount of sunlight.

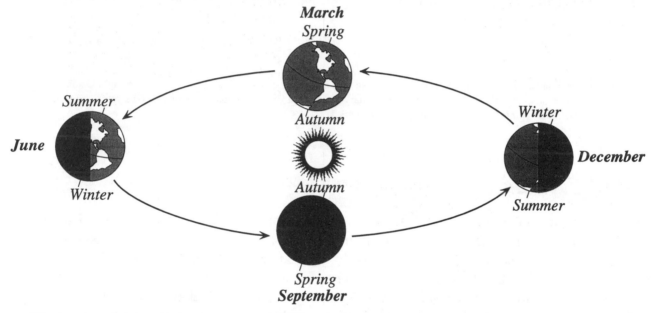

The earth revolves all the way around the sun, a distance of more than 575 million miles, in one year, 365¼ days. Its average speed in orbit is about 18½ miles per second, or 66,600 miles per hour!

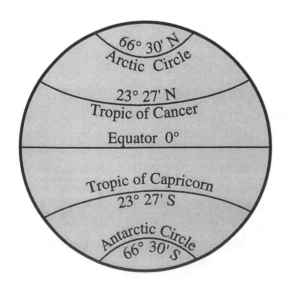

North of the **Arctic Circle** and south of the **Antarctic Circle** the sun stays above the horizon all night at least once a year, the first day of summer. The "midnight sun" dips to the horizon but doesn't set.

Between the **Tropic of Cancer** and the **Tropic of Capricorn** the sun shines down from directly overhead on at least one day each year. On the summer solstice, June 20 or 21, it shines directly over the Tropic of Cancer. On the winter solstice, December 21 or 22, it shines directly over the Tropic of Capricorn. On the vernal and autumnal equinoxes, March 20 or 21 and September 22 or 23 respectively, the sun shines directly over the equator.

The Universe

The **universe** is everything that exists. Many scientists think the universe began 15 to 20 billion years ago with an incredible explosion that is still going on. The universe is expanding outwards in all directions even now.

Astronomy is the scientific study of the universe, especially the stars, galaxies, planets, comets, and so on.

A **light year** is the distance light travels in a year at the speed of 186,282 miles per second— about 5.88 trillion miles. Because space is so vast, the light year is the standard unit used to measure distance in astronomy.

Quasars are the most distant objects astronomers have discovered. Some are as far away as sixteen billion light years and are moving away from us at up to 150,000 miles per second. Quasars give off tremendous amounts of energy, about 100,000 billion times as much as the sun, and more than 100 times as much as all the stars in the sky.

Nebulae are huge clouds of dust and gas, from which scientists think stars and galaxies are born.

Black holes are invisible. They have such strong gravity that all nearby objects are pulled in, and nothing, not even light, can escape.

A **galaxy** is a group of several billion stars. Scientists know about millions of galaxies and think there are many more. Everything we see in the sky belongs to our galaxy, the Milky Way. Three other galaxies can possibly be seen without a telescope, but only on a *very* dark night.

The **Milky Way galaxy** contains our own sun and solar system. It is a spiral galaxy about 100,000 light years across and 10,000 light years thick. Our sun is one of about 100 billion stars in the Milky Way. The sun and solar system travel around the center of the Milky Way every 225 million years at the speed of about 156 miles per second (561,600 mph).

Stars are balls of gas, kept hot by nuclear reactions in their centers. Stars can be as small as ten miles in diameter. Some are as large as 1,000,000,000 miles in diameter. Our sun has a diameter of 865,000 miles and is an average sized star. It looks larger to us than other stars because it is much closer to the earth. The closest star other than our own sun is Proxima Centauri, 25,000,000,000,000 miles away! Some of the brightest stars and their distances from us in light years are listed below:

Sirius	8.8	Betelgeuse	300
Canopus	98	Archernar	114
Alpha Centauri	4.3	Beta Centauri	490
Arcturus	36	Altair	16
Vega	26	Alpha Crucis	370
Capella	46	Aldebaran	68
Rigel	900	Spica	220
Procyon	11	Antares	400

Constellations are groups of stars within a definite region of the sky. They were named by ancient astronomers after figures the stars seemed to form in the sky. Some important constellations are the **Big Dipper**, **Orion**, and the **Southern Cross**.

The Solar System

The **solar system** consists of the sun at the center, nine planets and their moons, comets, asteroids and meteoroids (rocks traveling through space).

Our **sun** is one of billions of stars in the Milky Way galaxy. Like other stars, it is a glowing ball of hot gases. The temperature on the sun's surface is more than 10,000° Fahrenheit. Its energy is produced by **nuclear fusion** as hydrogen atoms **fuse**, or join, to form helium.

The sun is an average distance of 93 million miles away from the earth. Light from the sun takes about eight minutes and twenty seconds to reach the earth, traveling at the speed of 186,282 miles per second.

The sun is 865,000 miles in diameter, about 109 times the diameter of earth. If the earth were one inch in diameter, the sun would be nine feet in diameter. It would take 1.3 million earths to equal the size of the sun.

The sun revolves around the center of the Milky Way at the speed of about 156 miles per second. It rotates completely on its axis about once every 22 days.

Nine **planets** revolve around the sun. Some, such as earth and Mars, are rocky, while others, such as Jupiter and Saturn, are balls of gas. Planets can be seen only because they reflect light from the sun.

Other objects in our solar system include a belt of **asteroids**, which are very small rocky planets between Mars and Jupiter. The largest is Ceres, which is 600 miles in diameter. Only thirty asteroids have diameters greater than 120 miles. Asteroids often collide and break into smaller meteoroids. Some pieces occasionally reach the earth and burn as they fall through the atmosphere, forming "falling stars," or **meteors**.

Some meteoroids are so large that they don't completely burn before reaching the earth. These are called **meteorites.** They form craters on the earth's surface. The moon is covered with craters because it has no atmosphere and is constantly being hit by meteoroids.

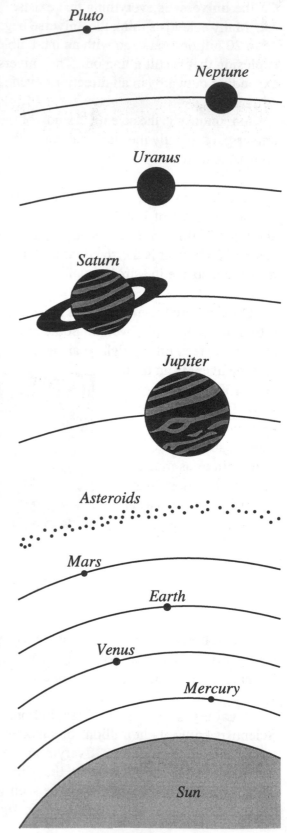

Comets travel in long elliptical orbits around the sun. They are probably like dirty snowballs, made of frozen gases and dust. Comets can be seen when they are close enough to the sun to reflect light. They often have "tails," made of parts of the comet being blown away by the **solar wind**, which consists of gaseous particles flowing from the sun. **Halley's Comet** appears every 76 to 79 years. It last appeared in 1986.

Planets of the Solar System

Planet	Distance from Sun (millions of miles)	Diameter (miles)	Average Speed in Orbit (miles per second)	Length of Year (earth days)	Length of Day (earth time)	Range of Temperatures (degrees Fahrenheit)	Number of Moons
Mercury	36	3,031	30	88	59 days	–279° to 801°	0
Venus	67	7,521	22	225	243 days	864°	0
Earth	93	7,926	19	365	24 hours	–129° to 136°	1
Mars	141	4,223	15	687	24 hours, 37 min.	–225° to 63°	2
Jupiter	484	88,846	8	4,333	9 hours, 55 min.	–250°	16
Saturn	888	74,898	6	10,759	10 hours, 39 min.	–288°	18
Uranus	1,786	31,763	4	30,685	17 hours, 8 min.	–357°	15
Neptune	2,799	30,800	3	60,190	16 hours, 7 min.	–353°	8
Pluto	3,666	1,430	3	90,800	6 days	–387° to –369°	1

Note: See p. 229 for more information. Numbers in the chart above are rounded to the nearest whole unit.

The orbit of Pluto is much longer and narrower than that of any other planet. Every 248 years, Pluto crosses the orbit of Neptune, and is closer to the sun than Neptune. This happened on January 23, 1979. Neptune will be the most distant planet until March 15, 1999, when Pluto will cross outside Neptune's orbit. The distances from the sun given in the chart above are average distances.

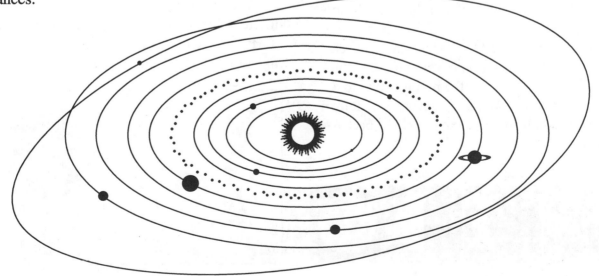

The Moon

The **moon** is the earth's only natural satellite. It is about one-fourth the size of the earth and has a diameter of 2,160 miles. It revolves around the earth every 27⅓ days and is an average distance of 238,857 miles away. The same side of the moon always faces the earth.

The moon has no atmosphere, water, wind or weather. Surface temperatures range from as hot as 260° Fahrenheit during the lunar day to as cold as –400° F in some craters near the poles.

Two major features on the moon's surface are **marias** and **craters**. Marias are large dark areas which are more or less flat. They are also knows as "seas" although they contain no water. Craters are formed when meteoroids, or rocks from space, hit the surface of the moon.

The first man to set foot on the moon was Neil A. Armstrong, on July 20, 1969. His first words became a famous quotation: "That's one small step for man, one giant leap for mankind."

Phases of the Moon

The moon shines because it reflects light from the sun. The moon seems to change size and shape as it goes through **phases** during a 29½ day cycle. Although one-half of the moon is always lit by the sun's rays, we can see only the part of the lighted half which faces the earth. Starting with a new moon, where none of the lighted side faces earth, the moon **waxes** to a crescent, a half moon, and a full moon. It then **wanes** to a half moon, a crescent, and back to a new moon.

| *New* | *Crescent* | *Half* | *Full* |

Tides

Tides are the rise and fall of ocean water. The most important cause of tides is the gravitational pull of the moon and the sun on the waters of the earth. There are two high tides and two low tides each day, approximately six hours apart.

Some high tides are higher than others. These are called **spring tides** and occur when the moon and the sun are lined up in their pull on the water. This can happen in two ways.

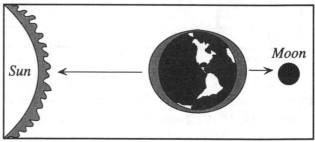

When the moon and sun are pulling in different directions, they cancel each other's effect to some degree, and the tides are not so high or low. These are called **neap tides**.

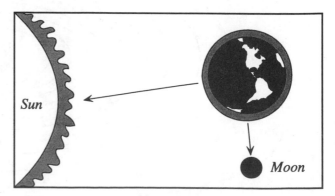

Eclipses

During a **lunar eclipse**, the moon's light is eclipsed (hidden) by the earth's shadow.

During a **solar eclipse**, the sun's light is eclipsed (hidden) by the moon's shadow.

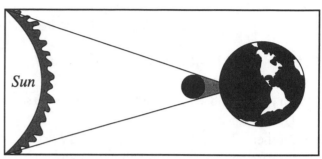

Only a few eclipses are **total eclipses**, where the sun or moon is totally hidden. Most are **partial eclipses**. Another type of solar eclipse is the **annular eclipse**, in which the moon passes directly in front of the sun, but does not completely cover it. A thin outer ring of the sun's disk is not covered by the dark disk of the moon.

Eclipses are usually visible in some parts of the world but not others. A total eclipse can usually be seen best in certain areas, and may appear to be a partial eclipse in other places.

Solar and Lunar Eclipses

April 15, 1995 .... Partial lunar eclipse.
April 29, 1995 .... Annular solar eclipse.
October 24, 1995 .... Total solar eclipse.
April 4, 1996 .... Total lunar eclipse.
April 17, 1996 .... Partial solar eclipse.
September 27, 1996 ..... Total lunar eclipse.
October 12, 1996 .... Partial solar eclipse.
March 9, 1997 .... Total solar eclipse.
March 24, 1997 .... Partial lunar eclipse.
September 2, 1997 .... Partial solar eclipse.
September 16, 1997 ..... Total lunar eclipse.
February 26, 1998 .... Total solar eclipse.
August 22, 1998 .... Annular solar eclipse.
February 16, 1999 .... Annular solar eclipse.
July 28, 1999 .... Partial lunar eclipse.
August 11, 1999 .... Total solar eclipse.
January 21, 2000 .... Total lunar eclipse.
July 16, 2000 .... Total lunar eclipse.
June 21, 2001 .... Total solar eclipse.
December 4, 2002 .... Total solar eclipse.
November 23, 2003 ..... Total solar eclipse.

Facts About the Moon

• Earth's moon is the fifth largest in the solar system. Saturn's Titan is the largest moon, followed by Jupiter's Ganymede, Callisto, and Io. Europa is the sixth largest moon.

• The moon is smaller and has less gravity than earth. A person would weigh about one-sixth as much on the moon as on earth.

• Because the moon has no atmosphere, the sky looks black and stars can be seen even during the moon's daytime.

• The footprints of astronauts who have walked on the moon will probably remain exactly the same for billions of years because there is no weather or erosion.

• To escape from the moon's gravity, a spaceship must travel 5,400 miles per hour, compared to 25,000 mph to escape earth, and 52,200 mph to escape the sun's gravity.

The Space Age

The **space age** began on October 4, 1957, when the Soviet Union launched the first artificial satellite to orbit the earth. This began a "space race" between the United States and Russia.

Notable Events in the Space Age

October 4, 1957—Russia launched *Sputnik I*, the first earth-orbiting satellite.

January 31, 1958—*Explorer I* became the first U.S. earth-orbiting satellite.

September 12, 1959—Russia launched *Luna 2*, the first spacecraft to reach the moon.

April 12, 1961—Russian cosmonaut Yuri A. Gagarin was the first man to orbit the earth.

May 5, 1961—Alan B. Shepard, Jr., became the first American in space.

February 20, 1962—John Glenn, Jr., became the first American to orbit the earth.

July 10, 1962—*Telstar I* relayed the first satellite TV between the U.S. and Europe.

June 16, 1963—Valentina V. Tereshkova of Russia was the first woman in space.

March 18, 1965—Alexei A. Leonov, Soviet cosmonaut, took the first space walk.

January 27, 1967—Three American Apollo astronauts were killed in a spacecraft fire: Virgil I. Grissom, Edward White II, and Roger B. Chaffee.

December 24–25, 1968—U.S. astronauts Frank Borman, William A. Anders and James A. Lovell, Jr. orbited the moon ten times.

July 20, 1969—Americans Neil A. Armstrong and Edwin E. Aldrin, Jr., were the first humans to walk on the moon. Michael Collins piloted the command module.

May 25, 1973—America launched *Skylab*, the first orbiting space station.

July 15, 1975—Apollo and Soyuz spacecraft took off for a U.S.–Soviet linkup in space.

August 20, 1977—*Voyager 2* was launched to photograph planets in the outer solar system, Jupiter, Saturn, Uranus and Neptune.

September 5, 1977—*Voyager 1* was launched to photograph Jupiter and Saturn.

April 12, 1981—U.S. astronauts John W. Young and Robert L. Crippen took off on the maiden voyage of space shuttle *Columbia*.

June 18, 1983—Sally K. Ride became the first American woman in space in the space shuttle *Challenger*.

January 28, 1986—Space shuttle *Challenger* exploded 73 seconds after takeoff, killing all seven people aboard, including American schoolteacher Christa McAuliffe.

September 29, 1988—Space shuttle *Discovery* blasted off on the first U.S. manned space mission after the *Challenger* disaster.

National Aeronautics and Space Administration
600 Independence Avenue
Washington, DC 20546

Science
and
Health

The Atmosphere and Weather

The **atmosphere** is the air that surrounds the earth. 99% of the air is within 25 miles of the earth's surface. The atmosphere is divided into four layers: the troposphere, stratosphere, mesosphere and thermosphere. Above the troposphere, air is too thin to support life.

Air

Air is made up of gases, moisture, and particles such as dust. Water (moisture) gets into the air by the process of **evaporation**. The amount of water in the air is **humidity**.

Nitrogen 78%
Oxygen 21%
Other 1%

Clouds

There are four basic types of **clouds**: cirrus, nimbus, cumulus and stratus. They frequently combine to make clouds with such names as cirrostratus, cumulonimbus, and stratocumulus.

1. **Cirrus** clouds are delicate wispy clouds made of ice crystals which form very high in the atmosphere.
2. **Stratus** clouds look like layers or sheets and are usually near the earth. Drizzle often falls from stratus clouds.
3. **Cumulus** clouds are piled-up heaps of white clouds, often flat on the bottom.
4. **Nimbus** clouds are very dark rain clouds.

Cirrus

Cumulonimbus

Layers of the Atmosphere

To Outer Space

Note: The temperature thirty miles above the earth is higher than that at lower elevations because of the absorption of heat by the ozone layer. There is so little air at this altitude that it would not "feel" warm.

Thermosphere

Aurora Borealis
(Northern Lights)
Aurora Australis
(Southern Lights)

50 miles — –135° Fahrenheit

Mesosphere   Meteors

30 miles — 28° Fahrenheit

Ozone layer
(14–19 miles)

Stratosphere

10 miles — –67° Fahrenheit

Troposphere   Clouds and weather

Earth's Surface   60° Fahrenheit

The Water Cycle

Water circulates from the ocean to clouds to the land and back into the ocean.

Water vapor gets into the air by **evaporating** from oceans, lakes, rivers and other bodies of water. **Transpiration** is the release of moisture into the air by plants.

Clouds form when the air cools. They travel, and may eventually release **precipitation**, rain, snow, sleet or hail. This water soaks into the ground, stands, or runs off toward the ocean in rivers or streams.

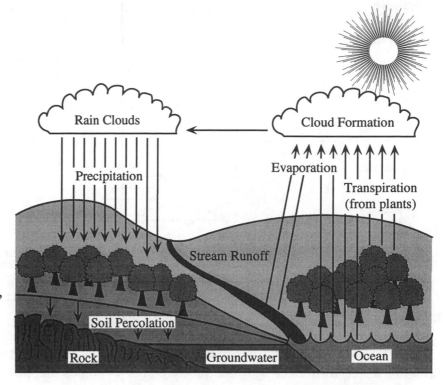

A pint of water weighs about a pound (8⅓ pounds per gallon). If one-half inch of rain falls on a square mile of earth, more than 72,000 *tons* of water, or about 8,685,760 gallons, fall from the sky.

Wind Chill

Wind chill is the freezing effect of the combination of cold temperatures and wind speed. For example, a temperature of 10° Fahrenheit with a wind speed of 15 miles per hour has the same freezing effect as a temperature of –18° Fahrenheit with no wind. Wind has little additional cooling effect at speeds above 45 miles per hour.

Wind Speed (mph)	Thermometer reading (degrees Fahrenheit)													
	35	30	25	20	15	10	5	0	–5	–10	–15	–20	–25	–30
5	32	27	22	16	11	6	0	–5	–10	–15	–21	–26	–31	–36
10	22	16	10	3	–3	–9	–15	–22	–27	–34	–40	–46	–52	–58
15	16	9	2	–5	–11	–18	–25	–31	–38	–45	–51	–58	–65	–72
20	12	4	–3	–10	–17	–24	–31	–39	–46	–53	–60	–67	–74	–81
25	8	1	–7	–15	–22	–29	–36	–44	–51	–59	–66	–74	–81	–88
30	6	–2	–10	–18	–25	–33	–41	–49	–56	–64	–71	–79	–86	–93
35	4	–4	–12	–20	–27	–35	–43	–52	–58	–67	–74	–82	–89	–97
40	3	–5	–13	–21	–29	–37	–45	–53	–60	–69	–76	–84	–92	–100
45	2	–6	–14	–22	–30	–38	–46	–54	–62	–70	–78	–85	–93	–102

Storms

Storms are often the result of a cold mass of air colliding with a warm mass of air. A **cold front** occurs when cold air moves in. It may be accompanied by thundershowers and high winds. A **warm front** moves in more slowly, and may cause rains that last for many days.

Cold Air

Warm Air

Warm Front

Cold Air

Warm Air

Cold Front

Weather maps shows storms and moving fronts that may indicate that storms are coming. The most violent storms are **hurricanes**, **tornados** and **thunderstorms**.

Hurricanes are caused by areas of low pressure which form over warm ocean waters. Hurricanes are 200 to 300 miles in diameter and have winds up to 150 miles per hour. Hurricane-like storms may also be called **cyclones**, or, in the western Pacific Ocean, **typhoons**. They rotate counterclockwise in the northern hemisphere and clockwise in the southern.

Tornados are twisting funnel clouds that extend downward from a mass of dark clouds. Winds may reach up to 280 miles per hour or more. Few tornadoes last more than an hour, but they can cause great damage in populated areas. Tornados may also be called **cyclones**, **twisters** or **waterspouts** (when over lakes or oceans).

Thunderstorms occur in tall cumulonimbus clouds that have built up an electric charge. Lightning is a giant spark that travels within a cloud, between clouds, or between a cloud and the ground. Flashes of lightning between clouds can be up to 90 miles long. The sound of thunder is caused by the quick expansion of heated air hitting other air. Because light travels almost 900,000 times faster than sound, we see lightning before we hear thunder. Light travels 186,282 miles per second (670,615,200 miles per hour). Sound travels only 1,116 feet per second in air (761 miles per hour). Sound travels about one mile every five seconds. To estimate how far lightning is from where you are standing, count the seconds from the time you see the lightning until you hear the thunder and divide by five. The lightning is about that many miles from you.

Common Weather Instruments

Anemometers measure **wind speed.**

Barometers measure **atmospheric pressure**, which can be thought of as the weight of the air. Changing air pressure usually means changing weather, with low pressure bringing cloudy weather and high pressure bringing clear weather. Barometers measure air pressure in inches or millibars of mercury. A simple barometer is a glass tube of mercury upside down in a cup of mercury. The pressure of the atmosphere will hold 29.92 inches (1013 millibars) in the tube when the temperature is 59° Fahrenheit at sea level. Barometric pressure is lower at high altitudes. At 10,000 feet above sea level, the true pressure is 21.03 inches, and at 30,000 feet, it is only 9.07 inches. Pressure altimeters determine the altitude of an airplane by measuring the true barometric pressure and comparing it with the standard value of 29.92 at sea level at 59° F.

Hygrometers measure **relative humidity**, or the amount of water vapor in the air compared to the amount it can hold at a certain temperature. Warm air can hold more moisture than cool air. Relative humidity is written as a percentage. If the air has half the amount of water vapor it can hold, the relative humidity is 50%. When the air can hold no more water vapor, it is **saturated** and the humidity is 100%.

Rain gauges measure rainfall.

Thermometers measure the **temperature.** See page 207 for an illustration.

Weather and Temperature Extremes

Highest recorded temperature on earth: 136° Fahrenheit in the shade at El Azizia, Libya, Africa, on September 13, 1922.

Highest recorded temperature in the United States: 134° Fahrenheit in Death Valley, California, on July 10, 1913.

Lowest recorded temperature on earth: −129° Fahrenheit in Vostok, Antarctica, on July 21, 1983.

Lowest recorded temperature in the United States: −80° F at Prospect Creek, Alaska, on January 23, 1971.

Greatest one-minute rainfall on earth: 1½ inches in Barst, Guadeloupe (near Dominica in the Caribbean Sea) on November 26, 1970.

Greatest 24 hour rainfall on earth: 74 inches on the island of Réunion in the Indian Ocean on March 15–16, 1952.

Greatest 24 hour rainfall in the United States: 19 inches in Alvin, Texas on July 25–26, 1979.

Greatest 12 month rainfall on earth: 1,042 inches in Cherrapunji, India between August 1, 1860 and July 31, 1861.

Greatest 12 month rainfall in the United States: 739 inches at Kukui on the island of Maui, Hawaii between December 1981 and December 1982.

Greatest 24 hour snowfall in the United States: 78 inches at Mile 47 Camp, Copper River Division, Alaska, on February 7, 1963.

Greatest 12 month snowfall in the United States: 1,124½ inches at Rainier Paradise Ranger Station, Washington, 1971–1972.

Largest hailstone on record: 2¼ pounds in Bangladesh on April 14, 1986. A hailstone weighing 1⅔ pounds fell in Kansas in 1970.

Driest place on earth: The Atacama Desert in northern Chile. Little rain fell for 400 years.

Fastest recorded winds: 280 miles per hour in a tornado at Wichita Falls, Texas on April 2, 1958.

Climates

The air in the atmosphere is always moving. The sun's energy heats air at the equator more than air at the poles. Warm air rises, forming areas of low atmospheric pressure. Cooler air moves in underneath. Cold air sinks, forming areas of high pressure. Masses of air are always moving across the surface of the earth, as shown in the wind diagram below.

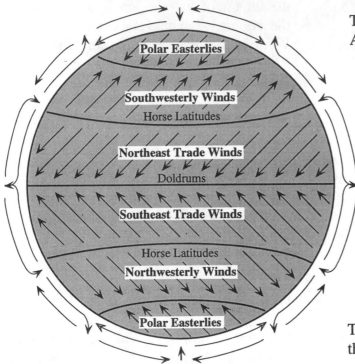

The area between the North Pole and the Arctic Circle is an **arctic zone**.

The area between the Arctic Circle and the Tropic of Cancer is a **temperate zone**.

The area around the equator, between the Tropic of Cancer and the Tropic of Capricorn is the **tropical zone**.

The area between the Tropic of Capricorn and the Antarctic Circle is a **temperate zone**.

The area between the Antarctic Circle and the South Pole is an **arctic zone**.

Climate is the average weather of an area over a long period of time. There are six basic types of climates.

1. The **tropics** are near the equator. They receive the most direct rays of the sun. A **tropical wet** climate has heavy rain throughout the year.

2. A **tropical wet and dry** climate has two seasons. During part of the year, there are heavy **monsoon rains**. The rest of the year is dry.

3. The **temperate zone** has moderate temperatures and four seasons: summer, autumn, winter and spring. Temperature and humidity vary according to seasons. Most of the United States is in the temperate zone.

4. The **arctic** climates are nearly always cold. Summers are short and chilly. Winters are long and very dry. Nearly all precipitation is snow.

5. **Highland** areas, or mountains, usually have a cooler and wetter climate than surrounding areas. The temperature falls by an average of about 1° Fahrenheit for every 275 feet of altitude.

6. A **desert** climate is very dry. Temperatures may change from very hot in the day to very cold at night. Some deserts have so little water that almost nothing can live. Deserts may be located in cool arctic areas.

Geology

Formation of the Earth

Most scientists think that the solar system, of which the earth is part, formed about 4½ billion years ago from a cloud of gas and dust. The central part of the cloud became the sun and swirls in the cloud eventually became the planets.

According to this theory, the earth was first made of gas, but it slowly condensed and became hot and molten. Gradually, as the earth cooled, a thin solid crust formed over the top. The earth is still cooling, and the inside is still molten or partially molten rock.

Inside the Earth

In the very center of the earth is the **core**. The **inner core** is solid iron and nickel, with temperatures as high as 9,000° Fahrenheit. The **outer core** is about 1,400 miles thick and is made of molten iron and nickel.

The **mantle** surrounds the core, and is about 1,800 miles thick. It is mostly solid, with temperatures between 1,600° and 4,000° F.

A solid **crust** covers the mantle. Its thickness ranges from five to 25 miles.

Formation of Continents

Scientists think that long ago, all the land in the world was together in one big land mass called **Pangaea**. The present continents are parts of this land mass which have broken apart. **Tectonic plates** are huge portions of the earth's surface which slide around in relation to each other over a layer of partially molten rock. This movement is sometimes called **continental drift**. The plates move 1½ to 4 inches a year. Most earthquakes and volcanoes occur along the boundaries of the plates, such as along the **Ring of Fire** surrounding the Pacific Ocean.

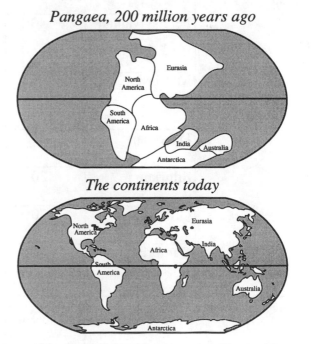

Pangaea, 200 million years ago

The continents today

Crust

Mantle

Core

Geological Periods and Events

Era	Period	Length (millions of yrs.)	Beginning (millions of yrs. ago)	Major Events
Cenozoic *Age of Mammals*	Quaternary			
	Holocene	10,000 years ago to now		Modern times
	Pleistocene	2	2	Early humans, recent ice ages
	Tertiary			
	Pliocene	10	12	Fruits and grasses
	Miocene	13	25	Himalayas and Alps forming
	Oligocene	11	36	First large mammals, apes
	Eocene	18	54	Rocky Mountains forming
	Paleocene	11	65	Much volcanic activity
Mesozoic *Age of Reptiles*	Cretaceous	70	135	Dinosaurs extinct at the end Flowering plants Giant sea turtles South America cut from Africa
	Jurassic	55	190	First birds Dinosaurs reached largest size
	Triassic	35	225	Early dinosaurs First mammals Arizona's Petrified Forest Pangaea began to split
Paleozoic *Age of Fishes*	Permian	55	280	Trilobites became extinct First cone-bearing trees Appalachians forming
	Pennsylvanian	40	320	Extensive formation of coal Many clams and snails Many large insects
	Mississippian	25	345	First known reptiles Dense swampy forests Many amphibians and sharks
	Devonian	55	400	First amphibians and insects First forests
	Silurian	30	430	First land plants First air breathing animals
	Ordovician	70	500	Sea over most of N. America First vertebrates—jawless fish
	Cambrian	100	600	Trilobites, blue-green algae Many marine invertebrates
Precambrian			4,000	Earth formed First life, invertebrates

Forces Which Build the Earth

Volcanoes

Volcanoes begin under the earth as molten rock forms gas and builds up pressure in a chamber of melted rock (magma chamber). This pressure causes a volcano to blast or melt a path to the earth's surface. The explosion caused by this pressure being released is a **volcanic eruption**. Some volcanic eruptions are violent and release huge clouds of gas, dust, rocks and lava. Others are relatively quiet and release a gentle flow of molten rock. Most volcanoes are caused by the movement of tectonic plates.

There are three kinds of volcanoes—shield volcanoes, cinder cones and composite volcanoes. Shield volcanoes are low, broad, dome-shaped mountains consisting mostly of gentle lava flows. Cinder cones are steep and cone-shaped, and made mostly of cinders with little lava. Composite volcanoes are a combination of lava and tephra (ash, dust and rocks) as shown in the diagram.

Some volcanoes are **active** and erupt frequently. Others are **intermittent** and explode fairly regularly. Still others are **dormant**, which means they have not erupted in a very long time but may erupt again. **Extinct** volcanoes have not erupted since the beginning of recorded history and are not likely to erupt again.

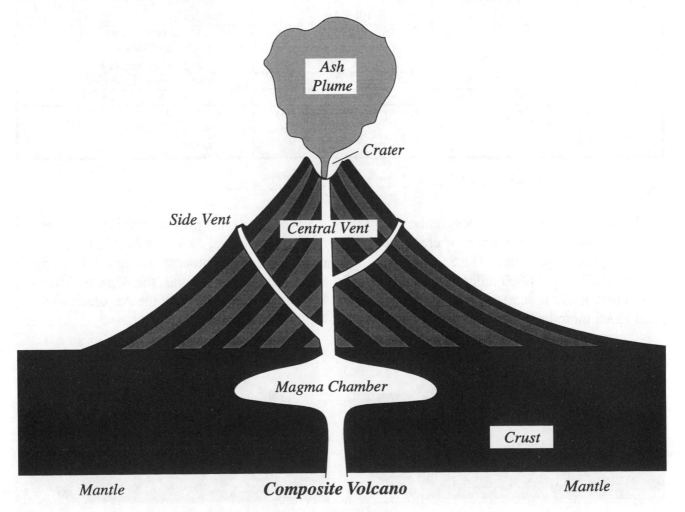

Ash Plume

Crater

Side Vent

Central Vent

Magma Chamber

Crust

Mantle

Composite Volcano

Mantle

Major Volcanoes of the World

Volcano	Location	Last Erupted	Elevation (feet)	Interesting Facts
Aconcagua	Argentina	Extinct	22,831	Highest mountain in the western hemisphere.
Cotopaxi	Ecuador	Active	19,347	Perhaps the highest active volcano in the world.
Katmai	Alaska	Erupted 1912	6,715	Largest eruption of the 20th century.
Kilauea	Hawaii	Active	4,090	On the side of Mauna Loa.
Krakatoa	Indonesia	Active	2,667	1883 explosion caused one of the world's worst disasters.
Lassen Peak	California	Erupted 1921	10,457	In Lassen Volcanic National Park.
Mauna Loa	Hawaii	Active	13,677	Discharges more lava than any other volcano.
Mont Pelée	Martinique	Active	4,583	Eruption in 1902 destroyed the city of St. Pierre and quickly killed 38,000 people.
Mount Etna	Sicily, Italy	Erupted 1992	11,122	In Mediterranean Sea.
Mount Fuji	Japan	Dormant	12,388	Highest mountain in Japan. Considered sacred.
Mt. St. Helens	Washington	Erupted May 18, 1980	8,634	57 people died in 1980 eruption.
Paricutín	Mexico	Erupted 1952	9,213	First appeared in a cornfield in February 1943. A 500 foot cone grew in one week.
Pinatubo	Philippines	Erupted 1991	5,085	Had not erupted since 1380.
Stromboli	Mediterranean	Active	3,031	Erupts constantly.
Vesuvius	Italy	Active	4,190	City of Pompeii buried in 79 A.D. in history's most famous eruption.

Faulting

Faults are zones of weakness in the earth's crust, such as plate boundaries, where sections of rock slip past one another. The San Andreas Fault in California is 600 miles long. One side of a fault may move up and the other down, forming fault-block mountains like the Sierra Nevadas.

Folding

When rocks are pressured from two sides toward the middle, they may **fold**. This forms mountains. Some mountain ranges formed by folding are the Himalayas, the Alps, the Rocky Mountains, the Andes and the Appalachian Mountains.

Earthquakes

Most **earthquakes** occur along the boundaries of tectonic plates. Volcanoes, faulting and folding result in earthquakes. The **Richter Scale** is used to measure the magnitude, or force, of an earthquake. Thousands of earthquakes occur each day with a magnitude of less than five. These are minor. Often people do not even notice them. Each number on the Richter Scale represents ten times more vertical ground movement than the last number. An earthquake with a magnitude of six has ten times more up and down ground movement than one with a magnitude of five! The **epicenter** is the place on the earth's surface directly above the focus of an earthquake. The largest earthquake ever recorded was 9.5, in Chile in 1960. The second largest was the 1964 Alaska earthquake.

The Richter Scale

1   Detected by scientific instruments only.
2   Felt when everything is quiet by a few people and some animals.
3   Felt by most people near the epicenter.
4   Felt by everyone near the epicenter.
5   May cause walls to crack and things to fall off of shelves.
6   Tall structures may fall. Destructive in crowded areas.
7   Lives are lost and buildings destroyed.
8   A major disaster.
9   A different system, moment magnitude, is now used to measure the force of the largest earthquakes.

Some Famous Earthquakes

San Francisco, California, April 18, 1906. Earthquake measuring 7.9 killed 500+ people.
Alaska, March 27, 1964. Strongest earthquake in North America, measuring 9.2, killed 131.
China, July 28, 1976. Earthquake measuring 8.0 killed 242,000 people. This is the highest death toll in modern times.

Forces Which Wear Down the Earth

Mountains are constantly being built by volcanoes, faulting and folding. They are also constantly being worn away, or **eroded**. Three forces that break mountains apart and wear them down are **weathering, erosion**, and **mass movement**.

Weathering breaks rocks into small enough pieces that erosion can occur. Because rocks expand when they are heated by the sun and contract when they cool at night, cracks form. Water which gets into these cracks may freeze and expand, enlarging them. Soil and seeds get into the cracks and plants may sprout. The roots of growing plants cause the cracks to widen, eventually breaking rock apart. Lichens have no roots, but some produce an acid which helps dissolve rock so that they can attach themselves to it with strands. Rainwater may also dissolve minerals in rocks, further wearing them down.

Erosion moves weathered material, called **sediment,** from one place to another. **Wind** and **water** may move sand and soil into creeks, which carry sediment into rivers and lakes or the sea where it settles and piles up in a process called **deposition**. Heat and pressure eventually change it back into rock—sedimentary rock.

Glaciers are rivers of ice which grind through mountains and scrape up underlying rock, moving it to the end of the glacier where it piles up as the glacier melts.

Waves erode the shoreline and **wind** wears down rock by constantly blowing sand against it. Beautiful features formed by wind and water erosion are natural arches, badlands, and canyons such as the Grand Canyon.

Mass movements are landslides and mudslides.

Rocks

Igneous rock is formed when magma (molten rock) from deep inside the earth cools and solidifies. When a volcano erupts, magma comes to the surface of the earth and cools rather quickly. Often, magma slowly rises inside the earth and cools slowly before reaching the surface. *Granite, obsidian* and *pumice* are igneous rocks.

Sedimentary rock is formed when sand, clay, or other eroded material piles up and is changed back into rock by heat and pressure from the weight of the sediment above. *Sandstone, limestone, shale, conglomerate* and *chalk* are sedimentary rocks. Many contain **fossils**, traces of animals or plants buried between layers of sediment as it was deposited.

Metamorphic rocks are rocks which have been changed and partially melted by great heat, often during mountain building. Common metamorphic rocks are *marble, slate* and *schist.*

The basic building blocks of rocks are **minerals**, which were formed into **crystals** as molten rock cooled. Some common minerals are *gold, pyrite, graphite, mica, quartz, salt* and many gems. **Gems** are stones or minerals that are used for ornament. Some well-known gems are *diamonds, opals, rubies, sapphires, emeralds, turquoise* and *jade.* Scientists use **Mohs Hardness Scale** to help identify minerals.

Mohs Hardness Scale

Mineral	Hardness	Easy Tests
Talc	1	Scratched by a fingernail
Gypsum	2	
Calcite	3	Scratched by a copper coin
Fluorite	4	Scratched by window glass or a knife blade
Apatite	5	
Feldspar	6	Scratches window glass or a knife blade
Quartz	7	
Topaz	8	
Corundum	9	
Diamond	10	Scratches all other minerals

Fossil Fuels

There are three primary fossil fuels which people use for energy: **coal, oil** and **natural gas**. These are generally found underground and were formed from the remains of plants and animals that lived long ago. All are **non-renewable**. They are being consumed millions of times faster than they are being replaced.

Coal was formed from plants which lived in swampy areas a million to 440 million years ago. The plants died and their remains piled up. As other things piled on top of them, heat and pressure turned the layer of plant material into **peat**, then **lignite** (soft coal), and finally to **bituminous** and **anthracite** coal. All can be burned. Bituminous coal changes to anthracite under intense pressure. Anthracite is very hard and burns cleanly. Coal is used to heat houses, run factories, and produce electricity.

Natural gas and **oil** (petroleum) were likely formed from the remains of tiny plants and animals that lived in the sea millions of years ago. These animals and plants sank to the bottom of the sea when they died and were covered by sediments. Through millions of years, heat and pressure changed the animal and plant remains into oil and natural gas. Oil and gas move through layers of sedimentary rock until they are trapped by a layer of rock through which they cannot move. Often they form "reservoirs" in folded rock.

Oil shale is a form of oil which is trapped in sedimentary rock. Oil shale has to be heated to more than 900° Fahrenheit in order for the oil to vaporize out of the rock. Because of this, it is quite expensive as a fuel source.

Alternate sources of energy, which do not depend on nonrenewable fossil fuels, include solar, wood, wind, hydroelectric, nuclear, and geothermal.

Energy

Energy is the ability to do work. Energy can be either **potential** (stored), such as the energy in a gallon of gasoline, or **kinetic**, such as the movement of an automobile, the heat of its engine, and the sound of the motor.

There are seven **forms of energy**:

1. Electricity
2. Heat
3. Light
4. Motion
5. Nuclear
6. Sound
7. Chemical

Energy changes from one form to another. For example, *nuclear* energy makes the *light* of the sun, which plants use to make food, stored as *chemical* energy. People eat the food, which then turns into *heat* to warm their bodies, *motion* such as walking, and *sound* as they speak. Another example is the potential energy stored by water in a dam. It changes to kinetic energy as the *motion* of water through turbines creates *hydroelectric* energy, which may travel to homes and be used for *light,* the *heat* of an electric stove, and the *sound* of a radio.

While energy is the ability to do work, a **machine** is a device that works. Although most machines consist of a number of parts that work together, they are all based in some way on six types of **simple machines**: the **lever**, the **wheel and axle**, the **pulley**, the **inclined plane**, the **wedge**, and the **screw**.

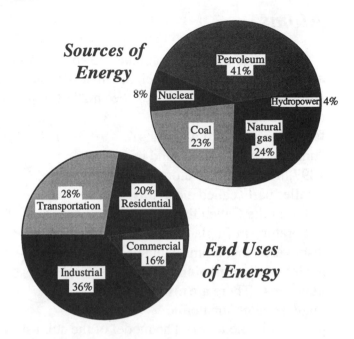

Sources of Energy

Petroleum 41%

8% Nuclear

Hydropower 4%

Coal 23%

Natural gas 24%

28% Transportation

20% Residential

Commercial 16%

Industrial 36%

End Uses of Energy

Decibels

The loudness of sound energy is measured in **decibels** (dB). Each number on the decibel scale below represents a loudness ten times as great as the number just below it. The 120 dB rating for a rock concert is a million times louder than normal conversation. Damage to ears and hearing begins at about 100 dB.

140 Thunder or dynamite at close range
130 Jet plane takeoff nearby
120 Amplified rock and roll band
Impossible to communicate by voice
110 Rock and roll band, loud shout in ear
100 Chain saw, fireworks, screaming near ear
 90 Vacuum cleaner, shouting or screaming
 80 TV on high, loud yelling and laughing
 70 Car horn, louder than average talking
 60 Large store, loud conversation
 50 Soft music, average conversation
 40 Refrigerator, quiet conversation
 30 Turning pages, soft whisper
 20 Cat purring quietly
 10 Soft rustling of leaves
  0 Low threshold of normal hearing

Wheel and Axle   *Pulley*   *Wedge*   *Lever*   *Inclined Plane*   *Screw*

Matter

Atoms

Matter is anything that takes up space. All matter is made of **atoms**. Democritus, an ancient Greek, developed the idea of the atom. He defined an atom as the smallest unit of matter, which could be split no more. In fact, the word "atom" means "uncuttable." It was found in 1897, however, that atoms had smaller parts called **electrons**. Later, at the Cavendish Laboratory in England, it was discovered that atoms contain nuclei made of **protons** and **neutrons**. There are also many smaller subatomic particles in the atom. The model of the atom shown in the illustration was developed by Ernest Rutherford in 1911 and revised in 1913 by Niels Bohr. The revision reflected the theory that electrons could travel only in certain specific orbits.

Atoms are extremely small. More than a million side by side would be only as thick as a hair. The particles which make up atoms, however, are much, much smaller. If a helium atom were enlarged to be a mile in diameter, the nucleus would be less than an inch in diameter. The electrons would be so small they could not be seen. All matter, including our bodies, is mostly empty space! It is the tremendous speed of electrons which makes matter behave as though it were solid.

Elements, Compounds and Mixtures

A substance containing only one kind of atom is known as an **element.** There are about 107 known elements. Each has a name, a chemical symbol, an atomic number, and an atomic weight. The **chemical symbol** is used as an abbreviation. The **atomic number** equals the number of electrons in the atom, which is the same as the number of protons. The **atomic weight** is the relative weight, and is almost the same as the sum of the number of protons and neutrons. Scientists organize the elements into what is known as the **Periodic Table of the Elements**. The alphabetical list shows some of the more common elements.

Elements

Name	Symbol	Atomic Number
Aluminum	Al	13
Argon	Ar	18
Arsenic	As	33
Bromine	Br	35
Cadmium	Cd	48
Calcium	Ca	20
Carbon	C	6
Chlorine	Cl	17
Chromium	Cr	24
Copper	Cu	29
Fluorine	F	9
Gold	Au	79
Helium	He	2
Hydrogen	H	1
Iodine	I	53
Iron	Fe	26
Lead	Pb	82
Magnesium	Mg	12
Manganese	Mn	25
Mercury	Hg	80
Molybdenum	Mo	42
Neon	Ne	10
Nickel	Ni	28
Nitrogen	N	7
Oxygen	O	8
Phosphorous	P	15
Platinum	Pt	78
Plutonium	Pu	94
Potassium	K	19
Radium	Ra	88
Radon	Rn	86
Silver	Ag	47
Sodium	Na	11
Strontium	Sr	38
Sulfur	S	16
Tin	Sn	50
Tungsten	W	74
Uranium	U	92
Zinc	Zn	30

When atoms combine, or join together, they form **molecules**. Oxygen molecules in the air consist of two oxygen atoms combined (O_2).

Compounds are formed when atoms of two or more different elements join together. Some common compounds are: water (H_2O), carbon dioxide (CO_2), salt ($NaCl$), sugar ($C_{12}H_{22}O_{11}$), ammonia (NH_3), baking soda ($NaHCO_3$) and rust ($3Fe_2O_3H_2O$). Rust is formed when water and the oxygen in the air combine with iron.

Mixtures are formed when elements mix but the atoms do not combine. Brass is an **alloy** (mixture) of copper and zinc. Bronze is an alloy of copper and tin.

States of Matter

There are three common **states of matter** on earth: solid, liquid, and gas. In a **solid**, the atoms or molecules are relatively close together and are arranged in regular patterns. Solids are hard and rigid. They take up a fixed amount of space and have a fixed shape. In a **liquid**, the atoms or molecules are further apart and move more freely than in a solid. A liquid takes up a fixed amount of space, but has no shape of its own and takes the shape of the container into which it is poured. In a **gas**, the atoms or molecules are far apart and move freely. A gas has neither a fixed shape nor a fixed volume. It will fill any container into which it is placed, and take the container's shape.

When matter is heated, its molecules gain energy. They move faster and further apart. If enough heat is added, the state of matter may change. A substance **melts** when it changes from solid to liquid, and **boils** or **vaporizes** when it changes from liquid to gas. When ice is heated, it changes from a solid to a liquid at its **melting point** of 32° F (0° C). If it is heated further, it changes from a liquid to a gas, water vapor, at its **boiling point** of 212° F (100° C).

Liquids **evaporate**, or turn to vapor, when fast-moving molecules break away from the surface of the liquid. Different substances melt and boil at different temperatures, and all substances can be in any state depending on the temperature. For example, copper, which is normally solid, will melt at 1981° F (1083° C) and boil at about 4653° F (2567° C). Boiling points depend on atmospheric pressure. At sea level, water boils at 212° F (100° C) but at 10,000 feet above sea level, it boils at about 162°F (72° C). Food must be boiled longer at high altitudes than at sea level in order to be completely cooked.

When matter is cooled, its molecules lose energy. They slow down and move closer together. If cooled enough, the state of matter may change. A substance **condenses** when it changes from a gas to a liquid and **freezes** when it changes from liquid to solid. When water is cooled, it will change from a liquid to a solid at its **freezing point** of 32° F (0° C). Different substances condense and freeze at different temperatures. For example, air, normally a gas, will become liquid at –310° F (–190° C). Liquid air will boil if poured over ice.

Melting Points and Boiling Points

Element	Melting Point	Boiling Point
Aluminum	1220°F	4473°F
Calcium	1542°F	2703°F
Copper	1981°F	4653°F
Gold	1947°F	5086°F
Hydrogen	–434°F	–423°F
Iron	2795°F	4982°F
Mercury	–38°F	675°F
Nickel	2647°F	4950°F
Nitrogen	–346°F	–321°F
Oxygen	–360°F	–297°F
Silver	1764°F	4014°F
Tin	450°F	4118°F
Uranium	2070°F	6904°F

Note: Temperatures are rounded to the nearest degree.

Plants and Animals

Living things have generally been divided into two major groups: **plants** and **animals**. Plants are the basis of all life on earth. They use sunlight to produce food, and they give off oxygen which animals breathe. Animals supply carbon dioxide and water which plants need.

Cells

The basic unit of life is the **cell**. All living things are made up of cells, which are so small they cannot be seen without a microscope. The smallest living things are made up of just a single cell. The human body has more than ten trillion cells (10,000,000,000,000).

Cell
Membrane
Cytoplasm
Nucleus

Cell

Although there are different types and shapes of cells, plant and animal cells have much in common. Every cell has the same basic parts, a cell membrane, cytoplasm, and a nucleus. The **cell membrane** is a thin covering which encloses each cell. The **cytoplasm** is everything in the cell except the nucleus. The **nucleus** is the control center which directs the activities of the cell. It contains **chromosomes**, long, complex **DNA** molecules with **genes** which determine the type of living thing and the thousands of characteristics which make it different from other living things. Each cell performs all the functions of life, such as breathing, taking in food, and giving off wastes. Cells grow, reproduce themselves by dividing in two, and eventually die. About three billion cells in the human body die every minute. During the same minute, about three billion new cells form to replace them. Within a seven year period, nearly all cells in the body are replaced. The only cells which cannot be replaced are nerve cells and brain cells, but these can live for about 100 years. Some cells reproduce fairly quickly. It takes skin cells only ten hours to divide in two.

Plants

Plants make food through a process called **photosynthesis**. Light from the sun is absorbed by pigments such as the green **chlorophyll** in plants. The light causes carbon dioxide to combine with the hydrogen in water to make sugar. Oxygen is given off in the process. The basic chemical formula is:

$$6CO_2 + 6H_2O \xrightarrow[\text{light}]{\text{chlorophyll}} C_6H_{12}O_6 + 6O_2$$

Most plants have the same basic parts. The **root** anchors the plant to the ground and absorbs water and minerals from the soil. The **stem** supports the plant's leaves and flowers. The **leaves**, which can be needles, make food through photosynthesis. The **flowers** contain the reproductive parts of flowering plants. The **seeds** contain all the genetic information needed for the growth of a new plant.

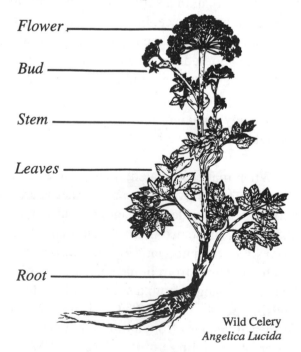

Flower
Bud
Stem
Leaves
Root

Wild Celery
Angelica Lucida

Animals

Animals are divided into two main groups, **vertebrates**, animals with backbones, and **invertebrates**, animals without backbones. Some of the vertebrates are mammals, birds, reptiles, amphibians and fish. Invertebrates include insects, shellfish, jellyfish, crabs and microscopic animals. Over a million species of invertebrates and more than 50,000 species of vertebrates are known.

Animals may be warm-blooded or cold-blooded. **Warm-blooded** animals have about the same body temperature all the time, regardless of the temperature outside. Birds and mammals are warm-blooded. **Cold-blooded** animals have body temperatures which are hot in hot weather and cold in cold weather. Reptiles, amphibians, fish and invertebrates are cold-blooded.

Types of Animals

I. Vertebrates

A. **Mammals** (warm-blooded vertebrates which have hair and nurse their young)
1. Herbivores (plant-eating mammals such as rabbits, cows and beavers)
2. Carnivores (meat-eating mammals such as dogs, lions and seals)
3. Insectivores (insect-eating mammals such as bats and shrews)
4. Omnivores (mammals which eat both plants and animals, such as human beings and bears)

B. **Birds** (warm-blooded vertebrates with wings and feathers which lay eggs)
1. Songbirds (robins, crows)
2. Birds of prey (eagles, hawks, owls)
3. Water birds (loons, ducks, geese)
4. Shorebirds (gulls, sandpipers)
5. Fowl (chickens, pheasants)
6. Flightless birds (ostrich, penguins)

C. **Reptiles** (cold-blooded vertebrates which have scaly skin, produce eggs, and breathe with lungs)
1. Lizards, snakes
2. Turtles
3. Crocodilians (alligators, crocodiles, caymans)

D. **Amphibians** (cold-blooded vertebrates without scaly skins which develop from eggs into adult animals through the process of metamorphosis, and which live part of their lives in water and part on land)
1. Frogs and toads
2. Salamanders
3. Caecilians

E. **Fish** (cold-blooded vertebrates which live in water)
1. Bony fish (bass, catfish, salmon)
2. Fish with skeletons of cartilage (sharks, rays, chimaeras)
3. Lampreys and hagfish

II. Invertebrates

A. **Annelida** (worms with segments)
B. **Mollusca** (animals with shells)
C. **Echinodermata** (starfish, sea urchins)
D. **Arthropoda** (joint-legged animals)
1. Insecta (insects)
2. Arachnida (spiders, scorpions, ticks)
3. Crustacae (crabs, lobsters, shrimp)
E. **Coelenterata** (jellyfish, corals)
F. **Porifera** (sponges)
G. **Protozoa** (one-celled animals)

Animal Information

Animal	Male	Female	Young	Group	Speed (mph)	Gestation Period
Antelope	buck	doe	kid	herd	61	9 months
Bear	boar	sow	cub	sloth	30	7–9 months
Cat	tom	puss	kitten	clowder	30	9 weeks
Cattle	bull	cow	calf	herd	—	9 months
Chicken	rooster	hen	chick	flock	9	21 days
Deer	buck	doe	fawn	herd	35	6–9 months
Dog	dog	bitch	pup	kennel	45	9 weeks
Duck	drake	duck	duckling	brace	72	23–30 days
Elephant	bull	cow	calf	herd	25	18–23 months
Fox	dog	vixen	cub	skulk	42	49–79 days
Goat	billy	nanny	kid	herd	—	151 days
Goose	gander	goose	gosling	gaggle	88	28–32 days
Hog	boar	sow	piglet	herd	11	114 days
Horse	stallion	mare	foal colt (male) filly (female)	herd	45	11 months
Human	man	woman	child	group	20	9 months
Lion	lion	lioness	cub	pride	50	108 days
Rabbit	buck	doe	bunny	warren	40	26–30 days
Seal	bull	cow	pup	herd	10	8–12 months
Sheep	ram	ewe	lamb	flock	—	5 months
Swan	cob	pen	cygnet	flock	55	30–35 days
Whale	bull	cow	calf	pod	30	10–16 months

Amazing Plant and Animal Facts

Smallest plants: Diatoms—as small as one ten-thousandth of an inch.

Largest tree: General Sherman sequoia tree—274.9 feet high and 82 feet around.

Oldest plant: Methuselah, a bristlecone pine—4,700 years old. Oldest living thing on earth.

Largest animal: Blue whale—up to 110 feet long, 2½ times as long as a railroad boxcar. It is the largest animal which ever lived.

Largest land animal: African elephant—6½ tons. The largest weighed 13½ tons.

Largest fish: Whale shark—up to 16½ tons.

Largest bird: African ostrich—up to 9 feet tall and 345 pounds. Egg can weigh 3.88 pounds.

Largest snake: Anaconda—500 pounds.

Largest reptile: Saltwater crocodile—up to 2,465 pounds and 23 feet long.

Largest insects: Goliath beetle—more than four inches long, and Hercules moth, with a wingspread of about 11 inches.

Tallest animal: Giraffe—up to 20 feet tall.

Greatest traveler: Arctic tern—migrates up to 14,000 miles each way from nesting grounds in the Arctic to winter homes in Antarctica.

Highest flying bird: Ruppel's vulture—one hit a jet flying at 37,000 feet above sea level.

Fastest animal: Peregrine falcon—217 mph.

Fastest land animal: Cheetah—63 mph.

Loudest sound: Blue whale—188 decibels, can be detected 530 miles away.

Endangered Species

All animals and plants are classified into **species**. Members of a species are different from all other forms of life in one or more ways, and can breed and produce young of the same species. Scientists know of more than 350,000 species of plants and over a million species of animals. More are discovered every year. A number of species which lived on the earth in the past, such as dinosaurs, are now **extinct**, or no longer in existence. Due to the changes humans have made in the natural environment and the destruction of wildlife habitat, a large number of plant and animal species are now **endangered**, or in danger of becoming extinct. Scientists think that unless this trend is reversed, a different species may disappear permanently from the earth every minute in the 1990's.

Ecology and Environment

Ecology is the study of the relationship living things have to each other and to their **environment**, or surroundings. Animals, for example, depend on plants for food. Plants depend on the soil. The soil is fertilized by the wastes and decaying bodies of both plants and animals. These wastes are decomposed into simple nutrients which can again be used by plants. The diagram below illustrates a very simple food chain. **Producers**, or plants, are eaten by **first-order consumers**, such as rabbits. These, in turn, are eaten by **second-order consumers**, such as wolves. When any living thing produces waste or dies, the waste material is broken down into nutrients by **decomposers** such as mold, yeast and bacteria. These nutrients are then used by plants to make food. The ocean's food chain is similar.

Endangered Large Animals

American crocodile
Blue whale
Brown pelican
California condor
Cheetah
Chimpanzee
Elephant
Florida panther
Giant panda
Gorilla
Gray wolf
Grizzly bear
Indian python
Jaguar
Leopard
Orangutan
Ostrich
Peregrine falcon
Rhinoceros
Snow leopard
Tiger

Food Pyramid

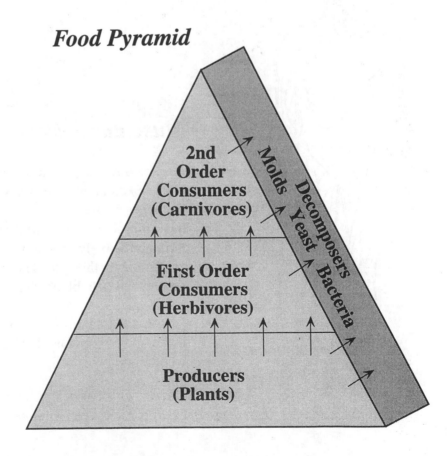

Human Body Systems

The human body consists of nine major **body systems**. Each carries out a different activity, and consists of a number of parts, or **organs**. Only the major parts of the systems are shown in the illustrations in this section. The urinary, endocrine and reproductive systems are not shown.

Skeletal System

The **skeletal system** consists of all the bones in the body. The skeleton gives the body shape, protects and supports vital organs, and, together with the muscles, allows the body to move.

The adult human skeleton has about 206 bones. They are joined to each other by **joints**. Joints may be immovable, such as the joints in the skull, or movable, such as the hinge joint of the elbow, or the ball and socket joint of the shoulder.

Muscular System

The **muscular system** consists of all the muscles in the body. Skeletal muscles are **voluntary muscles**. They move the bones of the skeleton and are controlled by thought. The heart muscle is an **involuntary muscle** which pumps blood through the body. Smooth muscles are also involuntary, not controlled by thought. They move food through the digestive system and help blood circulate.

An adult's body has about 656 skeletal muscles, which make up between one-third and one-half of a person's weight.

Circulatory System

The **circulatory system** consists of the heart, the blood vessels and the blood. Its purpose is to supply all the cells of the body with oxygen and nutrients from food, and to carry away carbon dioxide and other wastes produced by the cells.

The heart of a resting adult beats about 70 times and pumps about five quarts of blood each minute. The number of times a person's heart beats in a minute is called the **pulse**. In ten years, a human heart beats about 368 million times, pumping over six million gallons of blood. That's enough to fill 522 tank trucks! An average adult has about five quarts of blood. It **circulates**, or makes the round trip from the heart to the cells and back, then to the lungs and back, every sixty seconds.

The blood vessels include **arteries**, which carry blood from the heart to the cells, **veins**, which carry blood from the cells to the heart, and **capillaries**, which are tiny vessels connecting the arteries to the veins. There are about 60,000 miles of blood vessels in the circulatory system, enough to wrap around the world almost two and a half times.

Respiratory System

The **respiratory system** consists of the lungs and other organs of breathing. Its purpose is to take in oxygen from the air and transfer it to the blood for circulation to and use in the cells. The lungs also take waste carbon dioxide from the blood and release it into the air.

A resting adult breathes about twelve times each minute, taking in about 2,620 gallons of air each day. In a normal lifetime, that will amount to over 70 million gallons of air!

Digestive System

The **digestive system** consists of the alimentary canal and other organs such as the gall bladder and liver. The **alimentary canal** contains the mouth, esophagus, stomach, small intestine and large intestine. The purpose of the digestive system is to take in food and break it down into simple nutrients which are carried by the blood to the cells for use.

Digestion begins in the **mouth**, where food is chewed and mixed with saliva. Food then passes through a tube called the **esophagus** to the **stomach**, where it is stored and further broken down. The **small intestine**, which is about 22 feet long, finishes digestion and passes the nutrients into the bloodstream. The **large intestine** eliminates indigestible food from the body.

An average American will eat at least 60,000 pounds, or 30 tons, of food in a lifetime. That is about as much as the combined weight of five elephants!

Nervous System

The **nervous system** consists of the brain, the spinal cord, the nerves and the sense organs. Our five **senses** are sight, hearing, smell, taste and touch. The purpose of the nervous system is to control and regulate the activities of all the body systems. The brain receives information brought by the nerves from the sense organs, analyzes it, and decides on a response. Messages then travel from the brain through the spinal cord and nerves to muscles or other organs, directing them to take action.

The brain weighs about three pounds and has two halves, or hemispheres. The right side of the brain controls the left side of the body and vice versa. In general, the left side of the brain is better at logical thinking and understanding time and numbers. The right side of the brain is better at creative thinking.

The spinal cord is a large bundle of nerves which is protected by the backbone. It is about one-half inch wide and weighs one ounce. Nearly 45 miles of nerves travel from the brain to all parts of the body, many of them through the spinal cord.

Nutrition and Health

Good health makes it possible to enjoy life fully. Although illness and injury cannot always be prevented, there are many things people can do to increase their chances for a long healthy life.

Good **nutrition** is necessary for good health. Food is our source of energy, and of the materials that make up our bodies. The amount of energy in food is measured in **calories**. A calorie is a unit of heat that will warm one gram of water $1°$ Centigrade. Our bodies need five important **nutrients** from food: carbohydrates, fats, proteins, minerals and vitamins. Water is also a nutrient.

Carbohydrates are sugars and starches. They are the body's main source of energy. Nearly all foods contain carbohydrates. Foods rich in carbohydrates include fruits, bread, corn, potatoes and rice.

Fats are needed for energy as well as growth and maintenance of the body. Eating too much fat can be harmful to health. Some sources are butter, salad oil, milk, nuts, and meat.

Proteins are necessary for the growth and maintenance of the body. Bones, muscles and skin are made of protein. Good sources are cheese, eggs, fish, meat and milk.

Vitamins and **minerals** are necessary for the correct functioning of parts of the body. The charts on pages 44 and 45 give information about good sources of vitamins and minerals and why they are needed for good health.

Although there is wide debate about the good and bad effects of various foods on health, most people agree that a **balanced diet** is important for good nutrition. Include foods from each of the basic food groups in your diet, preferably foods rich in vitamins and minerals.

Basic Food Groups

Meat, Poultry, Fish, Beans
Sources: meat, poultry and eggs, fish and shellfish, dry beans, dry peas, soybeans, lentils, nuts
Provides: protein, vitamins, minerals

Milk and Cheese
Sources: milk, cheese, cottage cheese, cream cheese, ice cream, yogurt
Provides: calcium, protein, vitamins

Vegetables and Fruits
Sources: all vegetables and fruits, including citrus fruits, green leafy vegetables, tomatoes and potatoes
Provides: vitamins and minerals, fiber

Bread and Cereal
Sources: all breads and cereals, including rice
Provides: protein, iron, vitamins and food energy

Like good nutrition, **exercise** is important for health. Exercising vigorously at least three times a week for twenty minutes at a time without interruption will help your body stay healthy and physically fit. Exercise builds agility, endurance, flexibility and strength.

Rest and **sleep** restore the body's energy and allow it to recover from the effects of stress. **Cleanliness** helps keep disease from spreading. Brushing and flossing teeth every day will help prevent tooth decay and gum disease. Good health habits are a type of insurance.

Vitamins

Vitamin A
Needed for:	eyes, normal growth, skin, bones and teeth
Deficiency:	night blindness, stunted growth, dry, scaly skin
Good sources:	liver, carrots, dark green leafy vegetables, dairy products

Recommended daily allowance: 5000 IU

Vitamin B-1 (Thiamine)
Needed for:	energy, appetite, muscle tone, mental attitude
Deficiency:	tiredness, beriberi
Good sources:	yeast, lean pork, peanuts, whole grains

Recommended daily allowance: 1.4 mg.

Vitamin B-2 (Riboflavin)
Needed for:	chemical reactions during oxidation of foods
Deficiency:	sore mouth and tongue, chapped lips
Good sources:	liver, dairy products, meats, yeast, eggs

Recommended daily allowance: 1.7 mg.

Vitamin B-6
Needed for:	body chemistry
Deficiency:	skin problems, weakness, irritability
Good sources:	meats, whole grain cereals and bread, nuts, bran, sunflower seeds

Recommended daily allowance: 2.2 mg.

Vitamin B-12
Needed for:	bone marrow, nerves, digestive system
Deficiency:	sore tongue, weakness, loss of weight, back pains
Good sources:	meat, fish, eggs, cheese

Recommended daily allowance: 3.0 mcg.

Vitamin C (Ascorbic Acid)
Needed for:	healing wounds, bones
Deficiency:	bleeding gums, brittle bones, scurvy
Good sources:	citrus fruits and juices, rose hips, green leafy vegetables, tomatoes

Recommended daily allowance: 60 mg.

Vitamin D
Needed for:	bones and teeth
Deficiency:	rickets (bowed legs, knocked knees)
Good sources:	sunlight, fatty fish, egg yolks, vitamin D milk

Recommended daily allowance: 400 IU

Vitamin E
Needed for:	intestines and tissue
Deficiency:	often no symptoms
Good sources:	salad and cooking oil, margarine, nuts, oatmeal

Recommended daily allowance: 14.9 IU

Vitamin K
Needed for:	blood clotting
Deficiency:	slow clotting of blood
Good sources:	green tea, green leafy vegetables, beef liver

Recommended daily allowance: 140 mcg.

Niacin
Needed for:	body chemistry
Deficiency:	pellagra, skin problems, anxiety or depression
Good sources:	liver, kidney, lean meats

Recommended daily allowance: 18 mg.

Folic Acid
Needed for:	cell division, hemoglobin
Deficiency:	anemia
Good sources:	liver, kidney, avocados

Recommended daily allowance: 400 mcg.

Minerals

Calcium
Needed for:	bones and teeth
Deficiency:	stunted growth, rickets
Good sources:	cheese, blackstrap molasses, milk, nuts, green leafy vegetables, ice cream, yogurt, cottage cheese

Recommended daily allowance: maximum recommended is 1200 mg.

Phosphorus
Needed for:	bones and teeth, muscles
Deficiency:	weakness, loss of appetite, bone pain
Good sources:	cocoa powder, pumpkin and squash seeds, rice bran, soybean flour, sunflower seeds, wheat bran, meat, cheese, nuts

Recommended daily allowance: 1200 mg.

Sodium
Needed for:	balanced body chemistry
Deficiency:	poor growth, loss of weight, muscle cramps, headache, nausea
Good sources:	bacon, bologna, bran cereal, butter and margarine

Recommended daily allowance: 900-2,700 mg.

Magnesium
Needed for:	bones and teeth, relaxation of nerves
Deficiency:	muscle spasms, rapid heartbeat, confusion
Good sources:	instant coffee, cocoa powder, sesame seeds, wheat germ

Recommended daily allowance: 400 mg.

Potassium
Needed for:	cells, relaxing heart
Deficiency:	rapid, irregular heartbeat, weakness, irritability
Good sources:	dehydrated fruits, molasses, rice bran, seaweed, soybean flour, spices, sunflower seeds, wheat bran, meat

Recommended daily allowance: 1,875-5,625 mg.

Iodine
Needed for:	thyroid gland
Deficiency:	goiter, obesity, high blood cholesterol
Good sources:	iodized salt, seafood

Recommended daily allowance: 150 mcg.

Iron
Needed for:	blood, red blood cells which carry oxygen
Deficiency:	anemia
Good sources:	kidneys, blackstrap molasses, chicken giblets, cocoa powder, liver, oysters, spices, wheat bran

Recommended daily allowance: 18 mg.

Zinc
Needed for:	normal skin, bones, hair
Deficiency:	loss of appetite, stunted growth, skin changes
Good sources:	beef, liver, oysters, spices, wheat bran

Recommended daily allowance: 15 mg.

Abbreviations
IU	International Units
mg.	milligrams
mcg.	micrograms

Drugs and Alcohol

A **drug** is any chemical substance which affects the functioning of the body. Drugs can be helpful or harmful depending on their use. Even the safest and most helpful drugs can cause sickness or death if misused or abused.

Drugs are a very valuable tool for doctors. They are used to prevent and treat diseases, some of which might otherwise result in death. Many people live longer and healthier lives than would otherwise be possible because of helpful drugs.

Alcohol, although legal, is one of the most widely abused drugs. Many people who use alcohol become addicted to it. **Addiction** means a person's body needs a drug so badly that pain or sickness results when the drug is not used regularly. Addicts often need larger and larger doses of a drug as they become accustomed to using it. An adult can become an **alcoholic**, or a person addicted to alcohol, in one to eighteen years. A teenager can become addicted in one to eighteen months.

There are many other kinds of drugs, both helpful and harmful. They are classified according to the effect they have on the body. The outline lists some major classifications of drugs with examples of each.

Types of Drugs

A. **Narcotics.** These depress or numb the nervous system and are addicting.
   1. Natural—opium, morphine, codeine
   2. Semisynthetic—heroin
   3. Synthetic—Methadone (used to treat heroin addicts), Demerol, Darvon

B. **Nonprescription analgesics.**
   1. Aspirin
   2. Tylenol

C. **Stimulants**, or "uppers." These speed up the nervous system, creating alertness and/or edginess.
   1. Amphetamines—diet pills, pep pills
   2. Cocaine
   3. Caffeine—in coffee, tea, chocolate, cola drinks
   4. Nicotine—in cigarettes, cigars, snuff and chewing tobacco

D. **Sedatives**, also called depressants or "downers." These slow down, sedate and depress the nervous system.
   1. Alcohol—beer, wine, distilled spirits
   2. Tranquilizers—Valium, Benadryl
   3. Barbiturates—sleeping pills

E. **Cannabis** is legally a narcotic, but it sometimes acts as a hallucinogen or depressant.
   1. THC
   2. Hashish
   3. Marijuana

F. **Hallucinogens**, or psychedelic drugs. These distort sight and sound, and are mind-altering.
   1. L.S.D. (lysergic acid diethylamide-25)
   2. Mescaline
   3. Peyote

G. **Volatile Inhalants.** These depress the body's breathing mechanism.
   1. Gasoline
   2. Aerosol Spray
   3. Glue
   4. Paint

The Earth and its People

Waters of the World

Water covers more than 70% of the earth's surface. There are four oceans as well as seas, bays, gulfs, channels, lakes and rivers.

The Oceans

Ocean	Area (square miles)	Average Depth (feet)	Deepest Point (feet)
Pacific	63,800,000	14,040	36,198
Atlantic	31,830,000	12,890	28,374
Indian	28,360,000	10,040	25,344
Arctic	5,440,000	3,950	17,880

From *Encyclopædia Britannica*. Marginal seas not included.

The deepest place in any ocean is the Mariana Trench, east of the Philippines. There the bottom of the ocean is 36,198 feet below the surface of the Pacific Ocean. No light shines into the deepest parts of the ocean, but some unusual fish live there, eating remains of dead plants and animals that drift down from above.

The deeper into the ocean you go, the more pressure there is from the weight of the water above. The pressure would crush an unprotected human. Fish which live deep in the ocean must have pressure inside their bodies to equal the pressure outside. Scientists have gone as deep as 35,000 feet (6.6 miles) into the ocean in a special submarine called a **bathyscaph.**

Depth & Pressure Chart

Depth	Pounds per sq. in. pressure
Surface	14.7 (from atmosphere)
600 feet	282 pounds
1,200 feet	549 pounds
3,000 feet	1,351 pounds
7,200 feet	3,222 pounds
18,000 feet	8,033 pounds
30,000 feet	13,378 pounds
36,198 feet	16,139 pounds

Lakes of the World

Lake	Location	Area (square miles)	Length (miles)	Greatest Depth (feet)
Caspian Sea*	Asia	143,250	746	3,264
Lake Superior	North America	31,700	350	1,333
Lake Victoria	Africa	26,828	260	270
Lake Huron	North America	23,000	206	750
Lake Michigan	North America	22,300	307	923
Aral Sea*	Asia	15,500	220	177
Lake Tanganyika	Africa	12,700	420	4,708
Lake Baikal	Asia	12,162	395	5,315
Great Bear Lake	North America	12,096	211	1,299
Lake Nyasa	Africa	11,100	350	2,300
Great Slave Lake	North America	11,030	298	2,015
Lake Erie	North America	9,910	241	210
Lake Winnipeg	North America	9,416	258	70
Lake Ontario	North America	7,320	193	802
Lake Chad	Africa	6,300	Varies	22
Great Salt Lake*	North America	1,700	75	44

*Salt water.

Seas of the World

Sea	Area (sq. mi.)	Location
Adriatic	41,440	Mediterranean, east of Italy
Aegean	69,110	Mediterranean, east of Greece
Arabian	1,492,000	Indian Ocean, near Saudi Arabia
Azov	14,000	Southern Russia, near Black Sea
Baltic	162,930	Between Russia and northern Europe
Banda	285,020	Near Indonesia
Barents	529,096	North of eastern Norway and Russia
Bering	956,700	Between Alaska and Russia (Siberia)
Black	175,960	Between Russia and Turkey
Caribbean	758,400	East of Central America
Dead	395	Middle East, between Israel and Jordan
East China	281,850	Between Korea, Japan and China
Ionian	—	Mediterranean, between southern Italy & Greece
Irish	40,000	Separates Ireland from Great Britain
Japan	389,200	Separates Japan and Korea
Java	120,000	Near Indonesia
Marmara	4,300	Between Mediterranean and Black Seas
Mediterranean	967,230	Between Europe and Africa
North	222,000	Between Great Britain and mainland of Europe
Okhotsk	589,961	East of Russia
Red	169,112	Between Africa and Asia
South China	894,980	East of Southeast Asia
Sulu	100,386	Between Philippines and Borneo
Tasman	888,030	Between Australia and New Zealand
Timor	173,745	Northwest of Australia
Tyrrhenian	60,000	Mediterranean, west of Italy
White	36,680	North of Russia
Yellow	180,000	Between China and Korea

Waterfalls of the World

Waterfall	Location	Height (feet)	Waterfall	Location	Height (feet)
Angel	Venezuela	3,212	Takakkaw	Canada	1,200
Tugela	South Africa	2,014	Silver Strand	California	1,170
Cuquenán	Venezuela	2,000	Vettisfoss	Norway	900
Sutherland	New Zealand	1,904	Bridalveil	California	620
Ribbon	California	1,612	Multnomah	Oregon	620
King George VI	Guyana	1,600	Victoria	Southeast Africa	355
Upper Yosemite	California	1,430	Lower Yellowstone	Wyoming	308
Gavarnie	France	1,385	Niagara	New York	167

Important Rivers of the World

River	Location	Length (miles)	Other Facts
Amazon	South America	4,000	Most water of any river
Arkansas	North America	1,459	Carved Royal Gorge
Colorado	North America	1,450	Carved Grand Canyon
Congo (Zaire)	Central Africa	2,900	Explored by Stanley in 1877
Danube	Europe	1,777	Second longest in Europe
Ganges	Asia	1,560	Sacred river for Hindus
Indus	Asia	1,800	Used heavily for irrigation
MacKenzie	North America	1,071	Longest Canadian river
Mekong	Southeast Asia	2,600	Longest river in Southeast Asia
Mississippi	North America	2,340	Longest river in United States
Missouri	North America	2,315	Second longest U.S. river
Niger	Africa	2,600	Source is 150 miles from ocean
Nile	Northern Africa	4,145	Longest river in the world
Paraná	South America	2,485	Second longest in South America
Rhine	Europe	700	Very important inland waterway
Rio Grande	North America	1,885	Border of U.S. and Mexico
Saint Lawrence	North America	800	Links Atlantic and Great Lakes
Seine	Europe	475	Flows through Paris, France
Thames	Great Britain	215	Flows through London, England
Volga	Europe (Russia)	2,194	Longest river in Europe
Yangtze Kiang	Asia	3,915	Longest river in China, 3rd in world
Yellow (Huang He)	Asia	2,903	Many terrible floods
Yukon	North America	1,979	Famous for Klondike Gold Rush

The Continents and Oceans

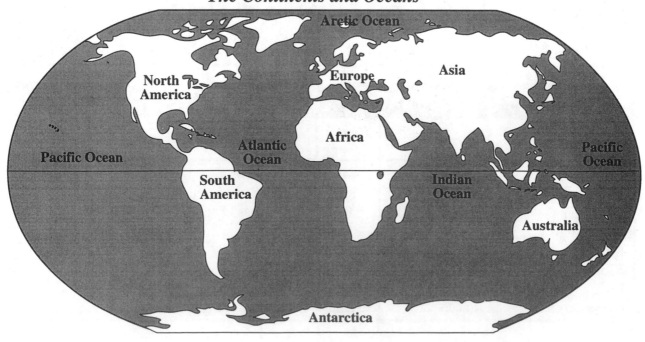

Land Areas of the World

About 30% of the earth's surface is **land**. Seven **continents** make up most of the land area. There are also thousands of islands.

Continent	Area (square miles)	Population	Population Density	Highest Point	Lowest Point
Continents					
Africa	11,678,000	699,602,000	60	Kilimanjaro 19,340	Lake Assali −509
Antarctica	5,400,000	—	0	Vinson Massif 16,864	sea level
Asia	17,005,000	3,391,776,000	200	Mt. Everest 29,028	Dead Sea −1,310
Australia	2,941,290	17,843,000	6	Mt. Kosciusko 7,310	Lake Eyre −52
Europe	4,069,000	728,026,000	181	Mt. Elbrus 18,481	Caspian Sea −92
North America	9,351,000	428,885,000	46	Mt. McKinley 20,320	Death Valley −282
South America	6,885,000	311,131,000	45	Aconcagua 22,831	Valdés Peninsula −131

% of Land Area

% of Population

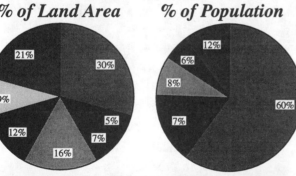

- ■ Africa
- ■ Asia
- ■ Australia
- ■ Europe
- ▨ North America
- ■ South America
- ☐ Antarctica

Note: Australia has less than 1% of the world's population.

Deserts of the World

Desert	Location	Approximate Size
Sahara	Africa	3,500,000 sq. mi.
Australian	Australia	660,000 sq. mi.
Arabian	E. of Africa	500,000 sq. mi.
Gobi	Asia	500,000 sq. mi.
Kalahari	Africa	190,000 sq. mi.
Atacama	S. America	51,000 sq. mi.

Islands of the World

Island	Location	Area (sq. miles)
Greenland	North Atlantic	840,004
New Guinea	SW Pacific	311,737
Borneo	W. mid-Pacific	288,151
Madagascar	Indian Ocean	226,658
Baffin	North Atlantic	195,927
Sumatra	NE Indian Ocean	182,860
Honshu	Sea of Japan	87,805
Great Britain	West of Europe	84,550
Victoria	Arctic Ocean	83,896
Ellesmere	Arctic Ocean	75,767

Mountain Ranges of the World

Range	Location	Tallest Peak	Length (miles)
Alaska	Alaska	Mount McKinley	600
Alps	Europe	Mont Blanc	750
Andes	West coast of South America	Aconcagua	4,500
Appalachian	Eastern United States	Mount Mitchell	1,500
Atlas	Northern Africa	Jebel Toubkal	1,500
Cascades	West coast of North America	Mount Rainier	700
Himalayas	Asia	Mount Everest	1,500
Rockies	Western United States	Mount Elbert	3,000

Of the 100 tallest peaks in the world, 59 are in the Himalayas and 14 others are in nearby mountain ranges. The remaining 27 are in the Andes of South America.

Important Mountain Peaks

Peak	Location	Height (feet)	Other Information
Aconcagua	Andes	22,831	Highest in western hemisphere
Annapurna	Himalayas	26,504	Highest climbed before Mt. Everest
Cook	New Zealand	12,349	Highest in New Zealand
Cotopaxi	Andes	19,347	Highest active volcano in world
Elbert	Rockies	14,433	Highest in Rocky Mountains
Elbrus	Russia	18,481	Highest in Europe
Everest	Himalayas	29,028	Highest mountain in the world
Fuji	Japan	12,388	Considered sacred by Japanese
Godwin Austen (K-2)	Himalayas	28,250	2nd highest in the world
Jebel Toubkal	Atlas	13,665	Highest in Atlas Mountains
Kanchenjunga	Himalayas	28,208	3rd highest in the world
Kenya	Africa	17,058	Second highest in Africa
Kilimanjaro	Africa	19,340	Highest in Africa
Kosciusko	Australia	7,310	Highest in Australia
Logan	Canada	19,524	Highest in Canada
Matterhorn	Alps	14,692	Steep and pyramid-shaped
Mauna Kea	Hawaii	13,796	Highest island peak in world
McKinley (Denali)	Alaska	20,320	Highest in North America, 103rd in world
Mitchell	Appalachians	6,684	Highest in Appalachians
Mont Blanc	Alps	15,771	Highest in Alps
Pikes Peak	Rockies	14,110	Gold rush slogan, "Pikes Peak or Bust"
Rainier	Cascades	14,410	Highest in Cascades
Vinson Massif	Antarctica	16,864	Highest in Antarctica

Countries of the World

Refer to page 230 for information on these statistics including sources.

Afghanistan
Capital: Kabul
Area: 251,770 sq. mi.
Language: Pashtu and Dari Persian
Currency: afghani
Population: 17,846,000
Population Growth Rate: 2.8%
Population Density: 71
Per Capita GNP: $200
Average Life Expectancy: 42
Infant Mortality Rate: 168
Location: South Central Asia
Latitude-Longitude: 33°N 65°E

Albania
Capital: Tiranë
Area: 10,580 sq. mi.
Language: Albanian
Currency: lek
Population: 3,403,000
Population Growth Rate: 1.8%
Population Density: 322
Per Capita GNP: $760
Average Life Expectancy: 72
Infant Mortality Rate: 33
Location: Southern Europe
Latitude-Longitude: 41°N 20°E

Algeria
Capital: Algiers
Area: 919,590 sq. mi.
Language: Arabic, French
Currency: Algerian dinar
Population: 27,895,000
Population Growth Rate: 2.5%
Population Density: 30
Per Capita GNP: $1,830
Average Life Expectancy: 67
Infant Mortality Rate: 58
Location: Northern Africa
Latitude-Longitude: 28°N 3°E

Andorra
Capital: Andorra la Vella
Area: 180 sq. mi.
Language: Catalan, French, Spanish
Currency: French franc and
Spanish peseta

Population: 64,000
Population Growth Rate: 0.9%
Population Density: 356
Per Capita GNP: $14,000
Average Life Expectancy: 78
Infant Mortality Rate: 11
Location: Southern Europe
Latitude-Longitude: 42°N 1°E

Angola
Capital: Luanda
Area: 481,350 sq. mi.
Language: Portuguese, Bantu
Currency: new kwanza
Population: 11,206,000
Population Growth Rate: 2.7%
Population Density: 23
Per Capita GNP: $950
Average Life Expectancy: 46
Infant Mortality Rate: 137
Location: Central Africa
Latitude-Longitude: 12°S 18°E

Antigua and Barbuda
Capital: St. John's
Area: 170 sq. mi.
Language: English
Currency: East Caribbean dollar
Population: 65,000
Population Growth Rate: 1.2%
Population Density: 383
Per Capita GNP: $6,600
Average Life Expectancy: 73
Infant Mortality Rate: 20
Location: Caribbean Sea
Latitude-Longitude: 17°N 61°W

Argentina
Capital: Buenos Aires (12,232,000)
Area: 1,056,640 sq. mi.
Language: Spanish, English
Currency: peso
Population: 33,913,000
Population Growth Rate: 1.3%
Population Density: 32
Per Capita GNP: $6,050
Average Life Expectancy: 71
Infant Mortality Rate: 26

Location: South America
Latitude-Longitude: 34°S 64°W

Armenia
Capital: Yerevan
Area: 11,500 sq. mi.
Language: Armenian, Russian
Currency: ruble
Population: 3,676,000
Population Growth Rate: 1.4%
Population Density: 320
Per Capita GNP: $780
Average Life Expectancy: 70
Infant Mortality Rate: 18
Location: Western Asia
Latitude-Longitude: 39°N 43°E

Australia
Capital: Canberra
Area: 2,941,290 sq. mi.
Language: English
Currency: Australian dollar
Population: 17,843,000
Population Growth Rate: 0.8%
Population Density: 6
Per Capita GNP: $17,070
Average Life Expectancy: 77
Infant Mortality Rate: 7
Location: Oceania
Latitude-Longitude: 25°S 135°E

Austria
Capital: Vienna (2,474,000)
Area: 31,940 sq. mi.
Language: German
Currency: Austrian schilling
Population: 7,984,000
Population Growth Rate: 0.2%
Population Density: 250
Per Capita GNP: $22,110
Average Life Expectancy: 76
Infant Mortality Rate: 7
Location: Western Europe
Latitude-Longitude: 47°N 14°E

Azerbaijan
Capital: Baku
Area: 33,400 sq. mi.

Language: Azeri
Currency: manat
Population: 7,386,000
Population Growth Rate: 1.9%
Population Density: 221
Per Capita GNP: $870
Average Life Expectancy: 71
Infant Mortality Rate: 25
Location: Western Asia
Latitude-Longitude: 40°N 47°E

Bahamas

Capital: Nassau
Area: 3,860 sq. mi.
Language: English
Currency: Bahamian dollar
Population: 272,000
Population Growth Rate: 1.5%
Population Density: 70
Per Capita GNP: $12,020
Average Life Expectancy: 72
Infant Mortality Rate: 24
Location: Caribbean Sea
Latitude-Longitude: 24°N 76°W

Bahrain

Capital: Manama
Area: 260 sq. mi.
Language: Arabic, English
Currency: Bahraini dinar
Population: 564,000
Population Growth Rate: 2.4%
Population Density: 2,148
Per Capita GNP: $7,150
Average Life Expectancy: 71
Infant Mortality Rate: 25
Location: Western Asia
Latitude-Longitude: 26°N 50°E

Bangladesh

Capital: Dhaka (5,296,000)
Area: 50,260 sq. mi.
Language: Bangla, English
Currency: taka
Population: 116,602,000
Population Growth Rate: 2.4%
Population Density: 2,320
Per Capita GNP: $220
Average Life Expectancy: 53
Infant Mortality Rate: 116
Location: South Central Asia
Latitude-Longitude: 24°N 90°E

Barbados

Capital: Bridgetown
Area: 170 sq. mi.
Language: English
Currency: Barbadian dollar
Population: 260,000
Population Growth Rate: 0.7%
Population Density: 1,566
Per Capita GNP: $6,530
Average Life Expectancy: 76
Infant Mortality Rate: 9
Location: Caribbean Sea
Latitude-Longitude: 13°N 59°W

Belarus

Capital: Minsk
Area: 80,200 sq. mi.
Language: Byelorussian, Russian
Currency: rubel
Population: 10,330,000
Population Growth Rate: 0.1%
Population Density: 129
Per Capita GNP: $2,910
Average Life Expectancy: 71
Infant Mortality Rate: 12
Location: Eastern Europe
Latitude-Longitude: 54°N 28°E

Belgium

Capital: Brussels
Area: 11,750 sq. mi.
Language: Dutch, French
Currency: Belgian franc
Population: 10,137,000
Population Growth Rate: 0.2%
Population Density: 863
Per Capita GNP: $20,880
Average Life Expectancy: 76
Infant Mortality Rate: 8
Location: Western Europe
Latitude-Longitude: 50°N 4°E

Belize

Capital: Belmopan
Area: 8,800 sq. mi.
Language: English, Spanish
Currency: Belizean dollar
Population: 207,000
Population Growth Rate: 3.3%
Population Density: 24
Per Capita GNP: $2,210
Average Life Expectancy: 68
Infant Mortality Rate: 23

Location: Central America
Latitude-Longitude: 17°N 89°W

Benin

Capital: Porto-Novo
Area: 42,710 sq. mi.
Language: French, African languages
Currency: CFA franc
Population: 5,265,000
Population Growth Rate: 3.1%
Population Density: 123
Per Capita GNP: $410
Average Life Expectancy: 46
Infant Mortality Rate: 87
Location: Western Africa
Latitude-Longitude: 9°N 2°E

Bhutan

Capital: Thimphu
Area: 18,150 sq. mi.
Language: Dzongkha
Currency: ngultrum
Population: 804,000
Population Growth Rate: 2.3%
Population Density: 44
Per Capita GNP: $180
Average Life Expectancy: 49
Infant Mortality Rate: 130
Location: South Central Asia
Latitude-Longitude: 27°N 90°E

Bolivia

Capital: La Paz
Area: 418,680 sq. mi.
Language: Spanish, Quechua, Aymara
Currency: boliviano
Population: 8,214,000
Population Growth Rate: 2.7%
Population Density: 20
Per Capita GNP: $680
Average Life Expectancy: 61
Infant Mortality Rate: 75
Location: South America
Latitude-Longitude: 17°S 65°W

Bosnia-Herzegovina

Capital: Sarajevo
Area: 19,740 sq. mi.
Language: Serbo-Croatian
Currency: dinar
Population: 4,600,000

Population Growth Rate: 0.7%
Population Density: 233
Per Capita GNP: $3,200
Average Life Expectancy: 72
Infant Mortality Rate: 15
Location: Southern Europe
Latitude-Longitude: 44°N 18°E

Botswana

Capital: Gaborone
Area: 218,810 sq. mi.
Language: English, Setswana
Currency: pula
Population: 1,439,000
Population Growth Rate: 2.7%
Population Density: 7
Per Capita GNP: $2,790
Average Life Expectancy: 62
Infant Mortality Rate: 43
Location: Southern Africa
Latitude-Longitude: 22°S 24°E

Brazil

Capital: Brasília
Area: 3,265,060 sq. mi.
Language: Portuguese, Spanish
Currency: real
Population: 155,254,000
Population Growth Rate: 1.7%
Population Density: 48
Per Capita GNP: $2,770
Average Life Expectancy: 67
Infant Mortality Rate: 66
Location: South America
Latitude-Longitude: 9°S 53°W

Brunei

Capital: Bandar Seri Begawan
Area: 2,030 sq. mi.
Language: Malay, Chinese, English
Currency: Bruneian dollar
Population: 285,000
Population Growth Rate: 2.6%
Population Density: 140
Per Capita GNP: $8,800
Average Life Expectancy: 71
Infant Mortality Rate: 9
Location: Southeast Asia
Latitude-Longitude: 4°N 115°E

Bulgaria

Capital: Sofia
Area: 42,680 sq. mi.
Language: Bulgarian
Currency: lev
Population: 8,393,000
Population Growth Rate: −0.2%
Population Density: 197
Per Capita GNP: $1,330
Average Life Expectancy: 72
Infant Mortality Rate: 16
Location: Eastern Europe
Latitude-Longitude: 43°N 25°E

Burkina Faso

Capital: Ouagadougou
Area: 105,710 sq. mi.
Language: French, African languages
Currency: CFA franc
Population: 10,069,000
Population Growth Rate: 3.1%
Population Density: 95
Per Capita GNP: $290
Average Life Expectancy: 48
Infant Mortality Rate: 123
Location: Western Africa
Latitude-Longitude: 13°N 2°W

Burma

Capital: Rangoon (3,075,000)
Area: 253,880 sq. mi.
Language: Burmese
Currency: kyat
Population: 45,423,000
Population Growth Rate: 1.9%
Population Density: 179
Per Capita GNP: $660
Average Life Expectancy: 59
Infant Mortality Rate: 98
Location: Southeast Asia
Latitude-Longitude: 22°N 98°E

Burundi

Capital: Bujumbura
Area: 9,900 sq. mi.
Language: Kirundi, French
Currency: Burundi franc
Population: 6,039,000
Population Growth Rate: 2.9%
Population Density: 610
Per Capita GNP: $210
Average Life Expectancy: 48
Infant Mortality Rate: 105
Location: Eastern Africa
Latitude-Longitude: 3°S 30°E

Cambodia

Capital: Phnom Penh
Area: 68,150 sq. mi.
Language: Khmer, French
Currency: riel
Population: 10,265,000
Population Growth Rate: 2.9%
Population Density: 151
Per Capita GNP: $200
Average Life Expectancy: 49
Infant Mortality Rate: 112
Location: Southeast Asia
Latitude-Longitude: 13°N 105°E

Cameroon

Capital: Yaoundé
Area: 179,690 sq. mi.
Language: French, English, African languages
Currency: CFA franc
Population: 13,132,000
Population Growth Rate: 2.9%
Population Density: 73
Per Capita GNP: $820
Average Life Expectancy: 56
Infant Mortality Rate: 81
Location: Central Africa
Latitude-Longitude: 6°N 12°E

Canada

Capital: Ottawa, Ontario
Area: 3,560,220 sq. mi.
Language: English, French
Currency: Canadian dollar
Population: 29,112,000
Population Growth Rate: 0.7%
Population Density: 8
Per Capita GNP: $20,320
Average Life Expectancy: 77
Infant Mortality Rate: 7
Location: North America
Latitude-Longitude: 60°N 95°W

Cape Verde

Capital: Praia
Area: 1,560 sq. mi.
Language: Portuguese, Crioulo
Currency: Cape Verdean escudo
Population: 407,000
Population Growth Rate: 2.9%
Population Density: 262
Per Capita GNP: $850
Average Life Expectancy: 68

Infant Mortality Rate: 40
Location: Atlantic Ocean west of
Africa
Latitude-Longitude: 16°N 24°W

Central African Republic

Capital: Bangui
Area: 240,530 sq. mi.
Language: French, Sangho, Arabic,
Hunsa, Swahili
Currency: CFA franc
Population: 3,142,000
Population Growth Rate: 2.4%
Population Density: 13
Per Capita GNP: $410
Average Life Expectancy: 44
Infant Mortality Rate: 142
Location: Central Africa
Latitude-Longitude: 7°N 21°E

Chad

Capital: N'Djamena
Area: 486,180 sq. mi.
Language: French, Arabic, tribal
languages
Currency: CFA franc
Population: 6,494,000
Population Growth Rate: 2.6%
Population Density: 13
Per Capita GNP: $220
Average Life Expectancy: 48
Infant Mortality Rate: 122
Location: Central Africa
Latitude-Longitude: 15°N 19°E

Chile

Capital: Santiago (5,812,000)
Area: 289,110 sq. mi.
Language: Spanish
Currency: Chilean peso
Population: 14,030,000
Population Growth Rate: 1.7%
Population Density: 49
Per Capita GNP: $2,730
Average Life Expectancy: 72
Infant Mortality Rate: 15
Location: South America
Latitude-Longitude: 30°S 71°W

China

Capital: Beijing (5,865,000)
Area: 3,600,930 sq. mi.
Language: Chinese (many dialects)

Currency: Renminbi yuan
Population: 1,191,976,000
Population Growth Rate: 1.2%
Population Density: 331
Per Capita GNP: $380
Average Life Expectancy: 70
Infant Mortality Rate: 31
Location: East Asia
Latitude-Longitude: 35°N 105°E

Colombia

Capital: Bogotá (6,801,000)
Area: 401,040 sq. mi.
Language: Spanish
Currency: Colombian peso
Population: 35,578,000
Population Growth Rate: 2.0%
Population Density: 89
Per Capita GNP: $1,290
Average Life Expectancy: 71
Infant Mortality Rate: 33
Location: South America
Latitude-Longitude: 4°N 72°W

Comoros

Capital: Moroni
Area: 860 sq. mi.
Language: Comoran, Arabic,
French
Currency: Comoran franc
Population: 530,000
Population Growth Rate: 3.5%
Population Density: 616
Per Capita GNP: $510
Average Life Expectancy: 56
Infant Mortality Rate: 86
Location: East of Africa
Latitude-Longitude: 12°S 44°E

Congo

Capital: Brazzaville
Area: 131,850 sq. mi.
Language: French, African
languages
Currency: CFA franc
Population: 2,447,000
Population Growth Rate: 2.6%
Population Density: 19
Per Capita GNP: $1,030
Average Life Expectancy: 49
Infant Mortality Rate: 116
Location: Central Africa
Latitude-Longitude: 1°S 15°E

Costa Rica

Capital: San José
Area: 19,710 sq. mi.
Language: Spanish
Currency: Costa Rican colón
Population: 3,248,000
Population Growth Rate: 2.3%
Population Density: 165
Per Capita GNP: $2,000
Average Life Expectancy: 76
Infant Mortality Rate: 14
Location: Central America
Latitude-Longitude: 10°N 84°W

Croatia

Capital: Zagreb
Area: 21,830 sq. mi.
Language: Serbo-Croatian
Currency: kuna
Population: 4,800,000
Population Growth Rate: − 0.1%
Population Density: 220
Per Capita GNP: $5,600
Average Life Expectancy: 71
Infant Mortality Rate: 11
Location: Southern Europe
Latitude-Longitude: 45°N 15°E

Cuba

Capital: Havana (2,218,000)
Area: 42,400 sq. mi.
Language: Spanish
Currency: Cuban peso
Population: 11,064,000
Population Growth Rate: 0.8%
Population Density: 261
Per Capita GNP: $1,370
Average Life Expectancy: 77
Infant Mortality Rate: 10
Location: Caribbean Sea
Latitude-Longitude: 21°N 80°W

Cyprus

Capital: Nicosia
Area: 3,570 sq. mi.
Language: Greek, Turkish,
English
Currency: Cypriot pound
Population: 741,000
Population Growth Rate: 1.1%
Population Density: 208
Per Capita GNP: $9,820

Average Life Expectancy: 76
Infant Mortality Rate: 10
Location: Mediterranean Sea
Latitude-Longitude: 35°N 33°E

Czech Republic

Capital: Prague
Area: 30,590 sq. mi.
Language: Czech, Slovak
Currency: koruna
Population: 10,342,000
Population Growth Rate: 0.0%
Population Density: 338
Per Capita GNP: $2,440
Average Life Expectancy: 72
Infant Mortality Rate: 9
Location: Eastern Europe
Latitude-Longitude: 50°N 14°E

Denmark

Capital: Copenhagen
Area: 16,360 sq. mi.
Language: Danish
Currency: Danish krone
Population: 5,214,000
Population Growth Rate: 0.1%
Population Density: 319
Per Capita GNP: $25,930
Average Life Expectancy: 75
Infant Mortality Rate: 7
Location: Northern Europe
Latitude-Longitude: 56°N 10°E

Djibouti

Capital: Djibouti
Area: 8,950 sq. mi.
Language: French, Arabic, Afar, Somali
Currency: Djiboutian franc
Population: 569,000
Population Growth Rate: 3.0%
Population Density: 64
Per Capita GNP: $1,030
Average Life Expectancy: 49
Infant Mortality Rate: 112
Location: Eastern Africa
Latitude-Longitude: 11°N 43°E

Dominica

Capital: Roseau
Area: 290 sq. mi.

Language: English and French patois
Currency: East Caribbean dollar
Population: 75,000
Population Growth Rate: 1.3%
Population Density: 259
Per Capita GNP: $2,520
Average Life Expectancy: 76
Infant Mortality Rate: 18
Location: Caribbean Sea
Latitude-Longitude: 15°N 61°W

Dominican Republic

Capital: Santo Domingo
Area: 18,680 sq. mi.
Language: Spanish
Currency: Dominican peso
Population: 7,769,000
Population Growth Rate: 2.2%
Population Density: 416
Per Capita GNP: $1,040
Average Life Expectancy: 68
Infant Mortality Rate: 43
Location: Caribbean Sea
Latitude-Longitude: 19°N 71°W

Ecuador

Capital: Quito
Area: 106,890 sq. mi.
Language: Spanish, Quechua
Currency: sucre
Population: 10,566,000
Population Growth Rate: 2.5%
Population Density: 99
Per Capita GNP: $1,070
Average Life Expectancy: 69
Infant Mortality Rate: 53
Location: South America
Latitude-Longitude: 2°S 77°W

Egypt

Capital: Cairo (11,155,000)
Area: 384,340 sq. mi.
Language: Arabic
Currency: Egyptian pound
Population: 58,873,000
Population Growth Rate: 2.3%
Population Density: 153
Per Capita GNP: $630
Average Life Expectancy: 62
Infant Mortality Rate: 62
Location: Northern Africa
Latitude-Longitude: 27°N 30°E

El Salvador

Capital: San Salvador
Area: 8,000 sq. mi.
Language: Spanish, Nahua
Currency: Salvadoran colón
Population: 5,237,000
Population Growth Rate: 2.7%
Population Density: 655
Per Capita GNP: $1,170
Average Life Expectancy: 66
Infant Mortality Rate: 45
Location: Central America
Latitude-Longitude: 14°N 89°W

Equatorial Guinea

Capital: Malabo
Area: 10,830 sq. mi.
Language: Spanish, Fang, Bubi
Currency: CFA franc
Population: 389,000
Population Growth Rate: 2.6%
Population Density: 36
Per Capita GNP: $330
Average Life Expectancy: 51
Infant Mortality Rate: 110
Location: Central Africa
Latitude-Longitude: 2°N 9°E

Eritrea

Capital: Asmara
Area: 48,260 sq. mi.
Language: Tigre, Kunama
Currency: Ethiopian birr
Population: 3,482,000
Population Growth Rate: 2.6%
Population Density: 72
Per Capita GNP: $115
Average Life Expectancy: 52
Infant Mortality Rate: 110
Location: Eastern Africa
Latitude-Longitude: 15°N 39°E

Estonia

Capital: Tallinn
Area: 17,410 sq. mi.
Language: Estonian, Russian
Currency: Estonian kroon
Population: 1,542,000
Population Growth Rate: −0.4%
Population Density: 89
Per Capita GNP: $2,750
Average Life Expectancy: 70
Infant Mortality Rate: 13

Location: Northern Europe
Latitude-Longitude: 59°N 26°E

Ethiopia

Capital: Addis Ababa
Area: 376,830 sq. mi.
Language: Amharic, Tigrinya,
Orominga, native languages
Currency: birr
Population: 55,228,000
Population Growth Rate: 3.1%
Population Density: 147
Per Capita GNP: $130
Average Life Expectancy: 52
Infant Mortality Rate: 110
Location: Eastern Africa
Latitude-Longitude: 9°N 39°E

Fiji

Capital: Suva
Area: 7,050 sq. mi.
Language: English, Fijian,
Hindustani
Currency: Fijian dollar
Population: 764,000
Population Growth Rate: 2.0%
Population Density: 108
Per Capita GNP: $2,010
Average Life Expectancy: 64
Infant Mortality Rate: 15
Location: Oceania
Latitude-Longitude: 18°S 178°E

Finland

Capital: Helsinki
Area: 117,610 sq. mi.
Language: Finnish, Swedish
Currency: markka
Population: 5,095,000
Population Growth Rate: 0.3%
Population Density: 43
Per Capita GNP: $22,980
Average Life Expectancy: 75
Infant Mortality Rate: 4
Location: Northern Europe
Latitude-Longitude: 64°N 26°E

France

Capital: Paris (8,764,000)
Area: 212,390 sq. mi.
Language: French
Currency: French franc
Population: 57,999,000
Population Growth Rate: 0.4%

Population Density: 273
Per Capita GNP: $22,300
Average Life Expectancy: 77
Infant Mortality Rate: 7
Location: Western Europe
Latitude-Longitude: 46°N 2°E

Gabon

Capital: Libreville
Area: 99,490 sq. mi.
Language: French, African
languages
Currency: CFA franc
Population: 1,139,000
Population Growth Rate: 2.7%
Population Density: 11
Per Capita GNP: $4,450
Average Life Expectancy: 54
Infant Mortality Rate: 94
Location: Central Africa
Latitude-Longitude: 1°S 12°E

Gambia

Capital: Banjul
Area: 3,860 sq. mi.
Language: English, African
languages
Currency: dalasi
Population: 1,061,000
Population Growth Rate: 2.7%
Population Density: 275
Per Capita GNP: $390
Average Life Expectancy: 45
Infant Mortality Rate: 90
Location: Western Africa
Latitude-Longitude: 13°N 16°W

Georgia, Republic of

Capital: Tbilisi
Area: 26,900 sq. mi.
Language: Georgian, Russian
Currency: lari
Population: 5,450,000
Population Growth Rate: 0.8%
Population Density: 203
Per Capita GNP: $850
Average Life Expectancy: 73
Infant Mortality Rate: 16
Location: Western Asia
Latitude-Longitude: 42°N 44°E

Germany

Capital: Berlin (3,018,000)
Area: 134,930 sq. mi.

Language: German
Currency: deutsche mark
Population: 81,175,000
Population Growth Rate: −0.1%
Population Density: 602
Per Capita GNP: $23,030
Average Life Expectancy: 76
Infant Mortality Rate: 6
Location: Western Europe
Latitude-Longitude: 51°N 9°E

Ghana

Capital: Accra
Area: 88,810 sq. mi.
Language: English, African
languages
Currency: cedi
Population: 16,944,000
Population Growth Rate: 3.0%
Population Density: 191
Per Capita GNP: $450
Average Life Expectancy: 56
Infant Mortality Rate: 81
Location: Western Africa
Latitude-Longitude: 8°N 2°W

Greece

Capital: Athens (3,670,000)
Area: 50,520 sq. mi.
Language: Greek
Currency: drachma
Population: 10,380,000
Population Growth Rate: 0.1%
Population Density: 205
Per Capita GNP: $7,180
Average Life Expectancy: 77
Infant Mortality Rate: 8
Location: Southern Europe
Latitude-Longitude: 39°N 22°E

Grenada

Capital: St. George's
Area: 130 sq. mi.
Language: English
Currency: East Caribbean dollar
Population: 94,000
Population Growth Rate: 2.5%
Population Density: 716
Per Capita GNP: $2,310
Average Life Expectancy: 70
Infant Mortality Rate: 13
Location: Caribbean Sea
Latitude-Longitude: 12°N 62°W

Guatemala

Capital: Guatemala City
Area: 41,860 sq. mi.
Language: Spanish, Indian dialects
Currency: quetzal
Population: 10,322,000
Population Growth Rate: 3.1%
Population Density: 247
Per Capita GNP: $980
Average Life Expectancy: 65
Infant Mortality Rate: 57
Location: Central America
Latitude-Longitude: 15°N 90°W

Guinea

Capital: Conakry
Area: 94,930 sq. mi.
Language: French, African languages
Currency: Guinean franc
Population: 6,392,000
Population Growth Rate: 2.5%
Population Density: 67
Per Capita GNP: $510
Average Life Expectancy: 43
Infant Mortality Rate: 147
Location: Western Africa
Latitude-Longitude: 11°N 10°W

Guinea-Bissau

Capital: Bissau
Area: 10,860 sq. mi.
Language: Portuguese, African languages
Currency: Guinea-Bissau peso
Population: 1,050,000
Population Growth Rate: 2.1%
Population Density: 97
Per Capita GNP: $210
Average Life Expectancy: 44
Infant Mortality Rate: 140
Location: Western Africa
Latitude-Longitude: 12°N 15°W

Guyana

Capital: Georgetown
Area: 76,000 sq. mi.
Language: English, Amerindian dialects
Currency: Guyanese dollar
Population: 825,000
Population Growth Rate: 1.8%
Population Density: 11

Per Capita GNP: $330
Average Life Expectancy: 65
Infant Mortality Rate: 48
Location: South America
Latitude-Longitude: 5°N 59°W

Haiti

Capital: Port-au-Prince
Area: 10,640 sq. mi.
Language: French, Creole
Currency: gourde
Population: 7,035,000
Population Growth Rate: 2.3%
Population Density: 661
Per Capita GNP: $380
Average Life Expectancy: 46
Infant Mortality Rate: 111
Location: Caribbean Sea
Latitude-Longitude: 19°N 72°W

Honduras

Capital: Tegucigalpa
Area: 43,200 sq. mi.
Language: Spanish, Indian dialects
Currency: lempira
Population: 5,315,000
Population Growth Rate: 3.1%
Population Density: 123
Per Capita GNP: $580
Average Life Expectancy: 66
Infant Mortality Rate: 50
Location: Central America
Latitude-Longitude: 15°N 86°W

Hungary

Capital: Budapest (2,313,000)
Area: 35,650 sq. mi.
Language: Hungarian
Currency: forint
Population: 10,262,000
Population Growth Rate: – 0.3%
Population Density: 288
Per Capita GNP: $3,010
Average Life Expectancy: 69
Infant Mortality Rate: 13
Location: Eastern Europe
Latitude-Longitude: 47°N 20°E

Iceland

Capital: Reykjavik
Area: 38,710 sq. mi.
Language: Icelandic
Currency: króna

Population: 267,000
Population Growth Rate: 1.1%
Population Density: 7
Per Capita GNP: $23,670
Average Life Expectancy: 78
Infant Mortality Rate: 4
Location: Northern Europe
Latitude-Longitude: 65°N 18°W

India

Capital: New Delhi
Area: 1,147,950 sq. mi.
Language: Hindi, English, Bengali, Telgu, Marathi, Tamil, Urdu, Gujarati, Malayalam, Kannada, Oriya, Punjabi, Assamese, Kashmiri, Sindhi, Sanskrit
Currency: Indian rupee
Population: 911,576,000
Population Growth Rate: 1.9%
Population Density: 794
Per Capita GNP: $310
Average Life Expectancy: 57
Infant Mortality Rate: 79
Location: South Central Asia
Latitude-Longitude: 20°N 77°E

Indonesia

Capital: Jakarta (11,151,000)
Area: 705,190 sq. mi.
Language: Bahasa Indonesia, Dutch, English, regional languages
Currency: Indonesian rupiah
Population: 199,717,000
Population Growth Rate: 1.6%
Population Density: 283
Per Capita GNP: $670
Average Life Expectancy: 60
Infant Mortality Rate: 68
Location: Southeast of Asia
Latitude-Longitude: 5°S 120°E

Iran

Capital: Teheran (11,681,000)
Area: 631,660 sq. mi.
Language: Farsi (Persian), Turkic
Currency: Iranian rial
Population: 61,168,000
Population Growth Rate: 3.6%
Population Density: 97
Per Capita GNP: $2,190
Average Life Expectancy: 65
Infant Mortality Rate: 66

Location: South Central Asia
Latitude-Longitude: 32°N 53°E

Iraq
Capital: Baghdad (4,566,000)
Area: 168,870 sq. mi.
Language: Arabic, Kurdish
Currency: Iraqi dinar
Population: 19,890,000
Population Growth Rate: 3.7%
Population Density: 118
Per Capita GNP: $1,940
Average Life Expectancy: 64
Infant Mortality Rate: 79
Location: Western Asia
Latitude-Longitude: 33°N 44°E

Ireland
Capital: Dublin
Area: 26,600 sq. mi.
Language: Irish, English
Currency: Irish pound
Population: 3,604,000
Population Growth Rate: 0.6%
Population Density: 135
Per Capita GNP: $12,100
Average Life Expectancy: 74
Infant Mortality Rate: 6
Location: Northern Europe
Latitude-Longitude: 53°N 8°W

Israel
Capital: Jerusalem
Area: 7,850 sq. mi.
Language: Hebrew, Arabic, English
Currency: new Israeli shekel
Population: 5,432,000
Population Growth Rate: 1.5%
Population Density: 692
Per Capita GNP: $13,230
Average Life Expectancy: 76
Infant Mortality Rate: 8
Location: Western Asia
Latitude-Longitude: 31°N 35°E

Italy
Capital: Rome (3,079,000)
Area: 113,540 sq. mi.
Language: Italian
Currency: Italian lira
Population: 57,150,000
Population Growth Rate: 0.0%

Population Density: 503
Per Capita GNP: $20,510
Average Life Expectancy: 77
Infant Mortality Rate: 8
Location: Southern Europe
Latitude-Longitude: 43°N 13°E

Ivory Coast
Capital: Abidjan
Area: 122,780 sq. mi.
Language: French and African
languages
Currency: CFA franc
Population: 13,896,000
Population Growth Rate: 3.5%
Population Density: 113
Per Capita GNP: $670
Average Life Expectancy: 52
Infant Mortality Rate: 91
Location: Western Africa
Latitude-Longitude: 8°N 5°W

Jamaica
Capital: Kingston
Area: 4,180 sq. mi.
Language: English, Creole
Currency: Jamaican dollar
Population: 2,452,000
Population Growth Rate: 1.9%
Population Density: 586
Per Capita GNP: $1,340
Average Life Expectancy: 74
Infant Mortality Rate: 13
Location: Caribbean Sea
Latitude-Longitude: 18°N 77°W

Japan
Capital: Tokyo (28,447,000)
Area: 145,370 sq. mi.
Language: Japanese
Currency: yen
Population: 125,023,000
Population Growth Rate: 0.3%
Population Density: 860
Per Capita GNP: $28,220
Average Life Expectancy: 79
Infant Mortality Rate: 4
Location: East Asia
Latitude-Longitude: 38°N 137°E

Jordan
Capital: Amman
Area: 34,340 sq. mi.

Language: Arabic, English
Currency: Jordanian dinar
Population: 4,224,000
Population Growth Rate: 3.3%
Population Density: 123
Per Capita GNP: $1,120
Average Life Expectancy: 67
Infant Mortality Rate: 34
Location: Western Asia
Latitude-Longitude: 31°N 36°E

Kazakhstan
Capital: Alma-Ata
Area: 1,049,200 sq. mi.
Language: Kazakh, Russian
Currency: ruble
Population: 17,087,000
Population Growth Rate: 1.2%
Population Density: 16
Per Capita GNP: $1,680
Average Life Expectancy: 69
Infant Mortality Rate: 27
Location: South Central Asia
Latitude-Longitude: 48°N 68°E

Kenya
Capital: Nairobi
Area: 219,960 sq. mi.
Language: Swahili, English,
African languages
Currency: Kenyan shilling
Population: 26,975,000
Population Growth Rate: 3.3%
Population Density: 123
Per Capita GNP: $330
Average Life Expectancy: 59
Infant Mortality Rate: 66
Location: Eastern Africa
Latitude-Longitude: 1°N 38°E

Kiribati
Capital: Tarawa
Area: 280 sq. mi.
Language: English, Gilbertese
Currency: Australian dollar
Population: 78,000
Population Growth Rate: 2.3%
Population Density: 281
Per Capita GNP: $700
Average Life Expectancy: 60
Infant Mortality Rate: 65
Location: Oceania
Latitude-Longitude: 0° 174°E

Korea, North
Capital: P'yongyang
Area: 46,490 sq. mi.
Language: Korean
Currency: North Korean won
Population: 23,067,000
Population Growth Rate: 1.9%
Population Density: 496
Per Capita GNP: $1,100
Average Life Expectancy: 69
Infant Mortality Rate: 30
Location: East Asia
Latitude-Longitude: 40°N 127°E

Korea, South
Capital: Seoul (19,065,000)
Area: 38,120 sq. mi.
Language: Korean
Currency: South Korean won
Population: 44,454,000
Population Growth Rate: 1.0%
Population Density: 1,166
Per Capita GNP: $6,790
Average Life Expectancy: 71
Infant Mortality Rate: 15
Location: East Asia
Latitude-Longitude: 38°N 127°E

Kuwait
Capital: Kuwait
Area: 6,880 sq. mi.
Language: Arabic and English
Currency: Kuwaiti dinar
Population: 1,272,000
Population Growth Rate: 3.3%
Population Density: 185
Per Capita GNP: $11,100
Average Life Expectancy: 76
Infant Mortality Rate: 16
Location: Western Asia
Latitude-Longitude: 29°N 48°E

Kyrgyzstan
Capital: Bishkek
Area: 76,600 sq. mi.
Language: Kirghiz
Currency: som
Population: 4,519,000
Population Growth Rate: 2.1%
Population Density: 59
Per Capita GNP: $810
Average Life Expectancy: 69
Infant Mortality Rate: 52

Location: South Central Asia
Latitude-Longitude: 41°N 75°E

Laos
Capital: Vientiane
Area: 89,110 sq. mi.
Language: Lao, French, English
Currency: kip
Population: 4,702,000
Population Growth Rate: 2.9%
Population Density: 53
Per Capita GNP: $250
Average Life Expectancy: 51
Infant Mortality Rate: 107
Location: Southeast Asia
Latitude-Longitude: 18°N 105°E

Latvia
Capital: Riga
Area: 24,900 sq. mi.
Language: Latvian, Russian
Currency: lat
Population: 2,549,000
Population Growth Rate: -0.2%
Population Density: 102
Per Capita GNP: $1,930
Average Life Expectancy: 69
Infant Mortality Rate: 17
Location: Northern Europe
Latitude-Longitude: 57°N 25°E

Lebanon
Capital: Beirut
Area: 3,950 sq. mi.
Language: Arabic, French, Armenian, English
Currency: Lebanese pound
Population: 3,620,000
Population Growth Rate: 2.0%
Population Density: 917
Per Capita GNP: $1,400
Average Life Expectancy: 75
Infant Mortality Rate: 28
Location: Western Asia
Latitude-Longitude: 34°N 36°E

Lesotho
Capital: Maseru
Area: 11,720 sq. mi.
Language: Sesotho, English
Currency: maloti
Population: 1,929,000
Population Growth Rate: 1.9%

Population Density: 165
Per Capita GNP: $590
Average Life Expectancy: 61
Infant Mortality Rate: 79
Location: Southern Africa
Latitude-Longitude: 29°S 28°E

Liberia
Capital: Monrovia
Area: 37,190 sq. mi.
Language: English, African languages
Currency: Liberian dollar
Population: 2,941,000
Population Growth Rate: 3.3%
Population Density: 79
Per Capita GNP: $400
Average Life Expectancy: 55
Infant Mortality Rate: 126
Location: Western Africa
Latitude-Longitude: 6°N 10°W

Libya
Capital: Tripoli
Area: 679,360 sq. mi.
Language: Arabic
Currency: Libyan dinar
Population: 5,057,000
Population Growth Rate: 3.4%
Population Density: 7
Per Capita GNP: $5,800
Average Life Expectancy: 63
Infant Mortality Rate: 68
Location: Northern Africa
Latitude-Longitude: 27°N 17°E

Liechtenstein
Capital: Vaduz
Area: 60 sq. mi.
Language: German
Currency: Swiss franc
Population: 31,000
Population Growth Rate: 0.8%
Population Density: 502
Per Capita GNP: $22,300
Average Life Expectancy: 77
Infant Mortality Rate: 3
Location: Western Europe
Latitude-Longitude: 47°N 9°E

Lithuania
Capital: Vilnius
Area: 25,210 sq. mi.

Language: Lithuanian, Russian
Currency: litas
Population: 3,726,000
Population Growth Rate: 0.3%
Population Density: 148
Per Capita GNP: $1,310
Average Life Expectancy: 71
Infant Mortality Rate: 17
Location: Northern Europe
Latitude-Longitude: 56°N 24°E

Luxembourg

Capital: Luxembourg
Area: 990 sq. mi.
Language: Luxembourgisch,
 German, French
Currency: Luxembourg franc
Population: 402,000
Population Growth Rate: 0.3%
Population Density: 407
Per Capita GNP: $35,260
Average Life Expectancy: 76
Infant Mortality Rate: 9
Location: Western Europe
Latitude-Longitude: 50°N 6°E

Macedonia

Capital: Skopje
Area: 9,930 sq. mi.
Language: Macedonian, Albanian
Currency: denar
Population: 2,090,000
Population Growth Rate: 0.8%
Population Density: 211
Per Capita GNP: $3,110
Average Life Expectancy: 72
Infant Mortality Rate: 24
Location: Southern Europe
Latitude-Longitude: 42°N 22°E

Madagascar

Capital: Antananarivo
Area: 224,530 sq. mi.
Language: Malagasy, French
Currency: Malagasy franc
Population: 13,702,000
Population Growth Rate: 3.3%
Population Density: 61
Per Capita GNP: $230
Average Life Expectancy: 56
Infant Mortality Rate: 93
Location: East of Africa
Latitude-Longitude: 19°S 46°E

Malawi

Capital: Lilongwe
Area: 36,320 sq. mi.
Language: English and Chichewa
Currency: Malawian kwacha
Population: 9,532,000
Population Growth Rate: 2.7%
Population Density: 263
Per Capita GNP: $210
Average Life Expectancy: 44
Infant Mortality Rate: 134
Location: Eastern Africa
Latitude-Longitude: 13°S 34°E

Malaysia

Capital: Kuala Lumpur
Area: 126,850 sq. mi.
Language: Malay, English,
 Chinese, tribal languages
Currency: ringgit
Population: 19,486,000
Population Growth Rate: 2.3%
Population Density: 154
Per Capita GNP: $2,790
Average Life Expectancy: 71
Infant Mortality Rate: 14
Location: Southeast of Asia
Latitude-Longitude: 4°N 102°E

Maldives

Capital: Malé
Area: 120 sq. mi.
Language: Divehi
Currency: rufiyaa
Population: 244,000
Population Growth Rate: 3.2%
Population Density: 2,107
Per Capita GNP: $500
Average Life Expectancy: 61
Infant Mortality Rate: 38
Location: South of Asia
Latitude-Longitude: 3°N 73°E

Mali

Capital: Bamako
Area: 471,120 sq. mi.
Language: French, Bambara,
 African languages
Currency: CFA franc
Population: 9,113,000
Population Growth Rate: 3.0%
Population Density: 19
Per Capita GNP: $300

Average Life Expectancy: 45
Infant Mortality Rate: 110
Location: Western Africa
Latitude-Longitude: 17°N 4°W

Malta

Capital: Valletta
Area: 120 sq. mi.
Language: Maltese and English
Currency: Maltese lira
Population: 365,000
Population Growth Rate: 0.7%
Population Density: 2,954
Per Capita GNP: $7,300
Average Life Expectancy: 75
Infant Mortality Rate: 8
Location: Mediterranean Sea
Latitude-Longitude: 36°N 14°E

Mauritania

Capital: Nouakchott
Area: 395,840 sq. mi.
Language: Arabic
Currency: ouguiya
Population: 2,270,000
Population Growth Rate: 2.9%
Population Density: 6
Per Capita GNP: $530
Average Life Expectancy: 48
Infant Mortality Rate: 117
Location: Western Africa
Latitude-Longitude: 20°N 12°W

Mauritius

Capital: Port Louis
Area: 710 sq. mi.
Language: English, Creole, French,
 Hindi, Urdu, Hakka, Bojpoori
Currency: Mauritian rupee
Population: 1,100,000
Population Growth Rate: 1.5%
Population Density: 1,540
Per Capita GNP: $2,700
Average Life Expectancy: 69
Infant Mortality Rate: 19
Location: Eastern Africa
Latitude-Longitude: 18°S 58°E

Mexico

Capital: Mexico City (23,913,000)
Area: 736,950 sq. mi.
Language: Spanish
Currency: new peso

Population: 91,840,000
Population Growth Rate: 2.2%
Population Density: 125
Per Capita GNP: $3,470
Average Life Expectancy: 70
Infant Mortality Rate: 35
Location: North America
Latitude-Longitude: 23°N 102°W

Moldova

Capital: Kishinëv
Area: 14,170 sq. mi.
Language: Moldovan, Romanian, Russian
Currency: Moldovan lei
Population: 4,352,000
Population Growth Rate: 0.6%
Population Density: 307
Per Capita GNP: $1,260
Average Life Expectancy: 69
Infant Mortality Rate: 19
Location: Eastern Europe
Latitude-Longitude: 47°N 29°E

Monaco

Capital: Monaco
Area: 1 sq. mi.
Language: French, English, Italian, Monegasque
Currency: French franc
Population: 31,000
Population Growth Rate: 0.3%
Population Density: 31,000
Per Capita GNP: $16,000
Average Life Expectancy: 77
Infant Mortality Rate: 4
Location: Western Europe
Latitude-Longitude: 44°N 7°E

Mongolia

Capital: Ulaanbaatar
Area: 604,830 sq. mi.
Language: Khalkha Mongol
Currency: tugrik
Population: 2,369,000
Population Growth Rate: 2.7%
Population Density: 4
Per Capita GNP: $800
Average Life Expectancy: 65
Infant Mortality Rate: 48
Location: East Asia
Latitude-Longitude: 47°N 104°E

Morocco

Capital: Rabat
Area: 172,320 sq. mi.
Language: Arabic, Berber, French
Currency: Moroccan dirham
Population: 28,559,000
Population Growth Rate: 2.3%
Population Density: 166
Per Capita GNP: $1,040
Average Life Expectancy: 67
Infant Mortality Rate: 57
Location: Northern Africa
Latitude-Longitude: 32°N 6°W

Mozambique

Capital: Maputo
Area: 302,740 sq. mi.
Language: Portuguese, African languages
Currency: metical
Population: 15,823,000
Population Growth Rate: 2.7%
Population Density: 52
Per Capita GNP: $60
Average Life Expectancy: 47
Infant Mortality Rate: 147
Location: Eastern Africa
Latitude-Longitude: 18°S 35°E

Namibia

Capital: Windhoek
Area: 317,870 sq. mi.
Language: English, Afrikaans, German
Currency: South African rand
Population: 1,635,000
Population Growth Rate: 3.3%
Population Density: 5
Per Capita GNP: $1,610
Average Life Expectancy: 59
Infant Mortality Rate: 66
Location: Southern Africa
Latitude-Longitude: 22°S 17°E

Nauru

Capital: Yaren
Area: 8 sq. mi.
Language: Nauruan, English
Currency: Australian dollar
Population: 10,000
Population Growth Rate: 1.9%
Population Density: 1,250
Per Capita GNP: $10,000

Average Life Expectancy: 56
Infant Mortality Rate: 26
Location: Oceania
Latitude-Longitude: 1°S 167°E

Nepal

Capital: Kathmandu
Area: 52,820 sq. mi.
Language: Nepali, native languages
Currency: Nepalese rupee
Population: 22,050,000
Population Growth Rate: 2.4%
Population Density: 417
Per Capita GNP: $170
Average Life Expectancy: 51
Infant Mortality Rate: 90
Location: South Central Asia
Latitude-Longitude: 28°N 84°E

Netherlands

Capital: Amsterdam
Area: 13,100 sq. mi.
Language: Dutch
Currency: Netherlands guilder
Population: 15,378,000
Population Growth Rate: 0.4%
Population Density: 1,174
Per Capita GNP: $20,590
Average Life Expectancy: 77
Infant Mortality Rate: 6
Location: Western Europe
Latitude-Longitude: 52°N 5°E

New Zealand

Capital: Wellington
Area: 103,470 sq. mi.
Language: English, Maori
Currency: New Zealand dollar
Population: 3,498,000
Population Growth Rate: 0.9%
Population Density: 34
Per Capita GNP: $12,060
Average Life Expectancy: 75
Infant Mortality Rate: 7
Location: Oceania
Latitude-Longitude: 41°S 174°E

Nicaragua

Capital: Managua
Area: 45,850 sq. mi.
Language: Spanish
Currency: gold córdoba
Population: 4,275,000

Population Growth Rate: 2.9%
Population Density: 93
Per Capita GNP: $410
Average Life Expectancy: 63
Infant Mortality Rate: 57
Location: Central America
Latitude-Longitude: 13°N 85°W

Niger

Capital: Niamey
Area: 489,070 sq. mi.
Language: French, Hausa, Djerma
Currency: CFA franc
Population: 8,813,000
Population Growth Rate: 3.4%
Population Density: 18
Per Capita GNP: $300
Average Life Expectancy: 47
Infant Mortality Rate: 123
Location: Western Africa
Latitude-Longitude: 16°N 8°E

Nigeria

Capital: Lagos (9,799,000)
Area: 351,650 sq. mi.
Language: English, African
  languages
Currency: naira
Population: 98,091,000
Population Growth Rate: 3.1%
Population Density: 279
Per Capita GNP: $320
Average Life Expectancy: 54
Infant Mortality Rate: 87
Location: Western Africa
Latitude-Longitude: 10°N 8°E

Norway

Capital: Oslo
Area: 118,470 sq. mi.
Language: Norwegian
Currency: Norwegian krone
Population: 4,336,000
Population Growth Rate: 0.4%
Population Density: 37
Per Capita GNP: $25,800
Average Life Expectancy: 77
Infant Mortality Rate: 6
Location: Northern Europe
Latitude-Longitude: 62°N 10°E

Oman

Capital: Muscat
Area: 82,030 sq. mi.
Language: Arabic, English
Currency: Omani rial
Population: 1,922,000
Population Growth Rate: 4.9%
Population Density: 23
Per Capita GNP: $6,490
Average Life Expectancy: 71
Infant Mortality Rate: 24
Location: Western Asia
Latitude-Longitude: 21°N 57°E

Pakistan

Capital: Islamabad
Area: 297,640 sq. mi.
Language: Urdu, English, Punjabi,
  Sindhi, Pashtu, others
Currency: Pakistani rupee
Population: 126,415,000
Population Growth Rate: 2.8%
Population Density: 425
Per Capita GNP: $410
Average Life Expectancy: 60
Infant Mortality Rate: 109
Location: South Central Asia
Latitude-Longitude: 30°N 70°E

Panama

Capital: Panama City
Area: 29,340 sq. mi.
Language: Spanish, English
Currency: balboa
Population: 2,531,000
Population Growth Rate: 1.8%
Population Density: 86
Per Capita GNP: $2,440
Average Life Expectancy: 72
Infant Mortality Rate: 21
Location: Central America
Latitude-Longitude: 9°N 80°W

Papua New Guinea

Capital: Port Moresby
Area: 174,850 sq. mi.
Language: English, Melanesian
  pidgin, 715 native tongues
Currency: kina
Population: 4,041,000
Population Growth Rate: 2.3%
Population Density: 23
Per Capita GNP: $950
Average Life Expectancy: 55
Infant Mortality Rate: 72
Location: Oceania
Latitude-Longitude: 6°S 150°E

Paraguay

Capital: Asunción
Area: 153,400 sq. mi.
Language: Spanish, Guarani
Currency: guaraní
Population: 4,771,000
Population Growth Rate: 2.7%
Population Density: 31
Per Capita GNP: $1,340
Average Life Expectancy: 67
Infant Mortality Rate: 48
Location: South America
Latitude-Longitude: 23°S 58°W

Peru

Capital: Lima (7,853,000)
Area: 494,210 sq. mi.
Language: Spanish and Quechua
Currency: nuevo sol
Population: 22,914,000
Population Growth Rate: 2.0%
Population Density: 46
Per Capita GNP: $950
Average Life Expectancy: 65
Infant Mortality Rate: 81
Location: South America
Latitude-Longitude: 10°S 76°W

Philippines

Capital: Manila (11,342,000)
Area: 115,120 sq. mi.
Language: Pilipino, English
Currency: Philippine peso
Population: 68,726,000
Population Growth Rate: 2.4%
Population Density: 597
Per Capita GNP: $770
Average Life Expectancy: 64
Infant Mortality Rate: 40
Location: Southeast of Asia
Latitude-Longitude: 13°N 122°E

Poland

Capital: Warsaw
Area: 117,550 sq. mi.
Language: Polish
Currency: zloty
Population: 38,564,000
Population Growth Rate: 0.3%
Population Density: 328
Per Capita GNP: $1,960
Average Life Expectancy: 71
Infant Mortality Rate: 14

Location: Eastern Europe
Latitude-Longitude: 52°N 19°E

Portugal

Capital: Lisbon (2,551,000)
Area: 35,500 sq. mi.
Language: Portuguese
Currency: Portuguese escudo
Population: 9,860,000
Population Growth Rate: 0.2%
Population Density: 278
Per Capita GNP: $7,450
Average Life Expectancy: 74
Infant Mortality Rate: 9
Location: Southern Europe
Latitude-Longitude: 39°N 8°W

Qatar

Capital: Doha
Area: 4,250 sq. mi.
Language: Arabic
Currency: Qatari riyal
Population: 513,000
Population Growth Rate: 1.0%
Population Density: 121
Per Capita GNP: $16,240
Average Life Expectancy: 73
Infant Mortality Rate: 20
Location: Western Asia
Latitude-Longitude: 25°N 51°E

Romania

Capital: Bucharest (2,214,000)
Area: 88,930 sq. mi.
Language: Romanian, Hungarian, German
Currency: leu
Population: 22,728,000
Population Growth Rate: –0.1%
Population Density: 256
Per Capita GNP: $1,090
Average Life Expectancy: 70
Infant Mortality Rate: 23
Location: Eastern Europe
Latitude-Longitude: 46°N 25°E

Russia

Capital: Moscow (10,769,000)
Area: 6,592,800 sq. mi.
Language: Russian
Currency: ruble
Population: 147,820,000
Population Growth Rate: –0.2%
Population Density: 22

Per Capita GNP: $2,680
Average Life Expectancy: 68
Infant Mortality Rate: 18
Location: Europe, Northern Asia
Latitude-Longitude: 60°N 100°E

Rwanda

Capital: Kigali
Area: 9,530 sq. mi.
Language: Kinyarwanda, French
Currency: Rwandan franc
Population: 7,664,000
Population Growth Rate: 2.3%
Population Density: 805
Per Capita GNP: $250
Average Life Expectancy: 46
Infant Mortality Rate: 117
Location: Eastern Africa
Latitude-Longitude: 2°S 30°E

St. Kitts and Nevis

Capital: Basseterre
Area: 140 sq. mi.
Language: English
Currency: East Caribbean dollar
Population: 41,000
Population Growth Rate: 1.3%
Population Density: 295
Per Capita GNP: $3,990
Average Life Expectancy: 69
Infant Mortality Rate: 21
Location: Caribbean Sea
Latitude-Longitude: 17°N 63°W

St. Lucia

Capital: Castries
Area: 240 sq. mi.
Language: English, French patois
Currency: East Caribbean dollar
Population: 139,000
Population Growth Rate: 2.0%
Population Density: 590
Per Capita GNP: $2,900
Average Life Expectancy: 72
Infant Mortality Rate: 19
Location: Caribbean Sea
Latitude-Longitude: 14°N 61°W

St. Vincent and the Grenadines

Capital: Kingstown
Area: 150 sq. mi.
Language: English

Currency: East Caribbean dollar
Population: 110,000
Population Growth Rate: 1.7%
Population Density: 731
Per Capita GNP: $1,990
Average Life Expectancy: 71
Infant Mortality Rate: 21
Location: Caribbean Sea
Latitude-Longitude: 14°N 61°W

San Marino

Capital: San Marino
Area: 20 sq. mi.
Language: Italian
Currency: Italian lira
Population: 24,000
Population Growth Rate: 0.3%
Population Density: 1,036
Per Capita GNP: $20,000
Average Life Expectancy: 76
Infant Mortality Rate: 8
Location: Southern Europe
Latitude-Longitude: 44°N 12°E

São Tomé and Príncipe

Capital: São Tomé
Area: 370 sq. mi.
Language: Portuguese
Currency: dobra
Population: 137,000
Population Growth Rate: 2.5%
Population Density: 370
Per Capita GNP: $370
Average Life Expectancy: 63
Infant Mortality Rate: 72
Location: Central Africa
Latitude-Longitude: 1°N 7°E

Saudi Arabia

Capital: Riyadh
Area: 830,000 sq. mi.
Language: Arabic
Currency: Saudi riyal
Population: 17,999,000
Population Growth Rate: 3.2%
Population Density: 22
Per Capita GNP: $7,940
Average Life Expectancy: 70
Infant Mortality Rate: 24
Location: Western Asia
Latitude-Longitude: 25°N 45°E

Senegal

Capital: Dakar

Area: 74,340 sq. mi.
Language: French, Wolof, Pulaar, Diola, Mandingo
Currency: CFA franc
Population: 8,165,000
Population Growth Rate: 2.7%
Population Density: 110
Per Capita GNP: $780
Average Life Expectancy: 49
Infant Mortality Rate: 80
Location: Western Africa
Latitude-Longitude: 14°N 14°W

Seychelles

Capital: Victoria
Area: 100 sq. mi.
Language: English, French, Creole
Currency: Seychelles rupee
Population: 72,000
Population Growth Rate: 1.5%
Population Density: 691
Per Capita GNP: $5,480
Average Life Expectancy: 69
Infant Mortality Rate: 12
Location: East of Africa
Latitude-Longitude: 8°S 55°E

Sierra Leone

Capital: Freetown
Area: 27,650 sq. mi.
Language: English, Mende, Temne, Krio
Currency: leone
Population: 4,616,000
Population Growth Rate: 2.7%
Population Density: 167
Per Capita GNP: $170
Average Life Expectancy: 43
Infant Mortality Rate: 143
Location: Western Africa
Latitude-Longitude: 8°N 11°W

Singapore

Capital: Singapore (2,816,000)
Area: 240 sq. mi.
Language: Chinese, Malay, Tamil, English
Currency: Singapore dollar
Population: 2,930,000
Population Growth Rate: 1.2%
Population Density: 12,440
Per Capita GNP: $15,750
Average Life Expectancy: 74

Infant Mortality Rate: 5
Location: Southeast Asia
Latitude-Longitude: 1°N 104°E

Slovakia

Capital: Bratislava
Area: 18,790 sq. mi.
Language: Slovak, Hungarian
Currency: koruna
Population: 5,342,000
Population Growth Rate: 0.4%
Population Density: 284
Per Capita GNP: $1,920
Average Life Expectancy: 71
Infant Mortality Rate: 16
Location: Eastern Europe
Latitude-Longitude: 49°N 19°E

Slovenia

Capital: Ljubljana
Area: 7,820 sq. mi.
Language: Slovenian
Currency: tolar
Population: 1,992,000
Population Growth Rate: 0.1%
Population Density: 255
Per Capita GNP: $6,330
Average Life Expectancy: 73
Infant Mortality Rate: 7
Location: Southern Europe
Latitude-Longitude: 46°N 15°E

Solomon Islands

Capital: Honiara
Area: 10,810 sq. mi.
Language: Melanesian pidgin, English, 120 native languages
Currency: Solomon Islands dollar
Population: 361,000
Population Growth Rate: 3.7%
Population Density: 33
Per Capita GNP: $710
Average Life Expectancy: 61
Infant Mortality Rate: 43
Location: Oceania
Latitude-Longitude: 8°S 159°E

Somalia

Capital: Mogadishu
Area: 242,220 sq. mi.
Language: Somali, Arabic, Italian, English
Currency: Somali shilling

Population: 9,845,000
Population Growth Rate: 3.2%
Population Density: 41
Per Capita GNP: $210
Average Life Expectancy: 47
Infant Mortality Rate: 122
Location: Eastern Africa
Latitude-Longitude: 10°N 49°E

South Africa

Capital: Cape Town, Pretoria, Bloemfontein
Area: 471,440 sq. mi.
Language: Afrikaans, English, African languages
Currency: rand
Population: 41,155,000
Population Growth Rate: 2.6%
Population Density: 87
Per Capita GNP: $2,670
Average Life Expectancy: 65
Infant Mortality Rate: 49
Location: Southern Africa
Latitude-Longitude: 30°S 26°E

Spain

Capital: Madrid (4,772,000)
Area: 192,830 sq. mi.
Language: Castilian Spanish, Catalan, Galician, Basque
Currency: peseta
Population: 39,193,000
Population Growth Rate: 0.1%
Population Density: 203
Per Capita GNP: $14,020
Average Life Expectancy: 77
Infant Mortality Rate: 8
Location: Southern Europe
Latitude-Longitude: 40°N 4°W

Sri Lanka

Capital: Colombo
Area: 24,950 sq. mi.
Language: Sinhala, Tamil, English
Currency: Sri Lankan rupee
Population: 17,899,000
Population Growth Rate: 1.5%
Population Density: 717
Per Capita GNP: $540
Average Life Expectancy: 73
Infant Mortality Rate: 19
Location: South of Asia
Latitude-Longitude: 8°N 81°E

Sudan

Capital: Khartoum
Area: 917,370 sq. mi.
Language: Arabic, tribal languages and dialects, English
Currency: Sudanese pound
Population: 28,175,000
Population Growth Rate: 3.1%
Population Density: 31
Per Capita GNP: $184
Average Life Expectancy: 53
Infant Mortality Rate: 85
Location: Northern Africa
Latitude-Longitude: 15°N 30°E

Suriname

Capital: Paramaribo
Area: 60,230 sq. mi.
Language: Dutch, Surinamese, English
Currency: Surinamese guilder
Population: 423,000
Population Growth Rate: 1.6%
Population Density: 7
Per Capita GNP: $3,700
Average Life Expectancy: 69
Infant Mortality Rate: 27
Location: South America
Latitude-Longitude: 4°N 56°W

Swaziland

Capital: Mbabane
Area: 6,640 sq. mi.
Language: English, siSwati
Currency: lilangeni
Population: 836,000
Population Growth Rate: 3.2%
Population Density: 126
Per Capita GNP: $1,080
Average Life Expectancy: 56
Infant Mortality Rate: 98
Location: Southern Africa
Latitude-Longitude: 26°S 31°E

Sweden

Capital: Stockholm
Area: 158,930 sq. mi.
Language: Swedish
Currency: Swedish krona
Population: 8,821,000
Population Growth Rate: 0.3%
Population Density: 56
Per Capita GNP: $26,780

Average Life Expectancy: 78
Infant Mortality Rate: 5
Location: Northern Europe
Latitude-Longitude: 62°N 15°E

Switzerland

Capital: Bern
Area: 15,360 sq. mi.
Language: German, French, Italian
Currency: Swiss franc
Population: 7,012,000
Population Growth Rate: 0.3%
Population Density: 457
Per Capita GNP: $36,230
Average Life Expectancy: 78
Infant Mortality Rate: 6
Location: Western Europe
Latitude-Longitude: 46°N 8°E

Syria

Capital: Damascus
Area: 71,070 sq. mi.
Language: Arabic, Kurdish, Armenian, Aramaic
Currency: Syrian pound
Population: 13,966,000
Population Growth Rate: 3.7%
Population Density: 197
Per Capita GNP: $1,170
Average Life Expectancy: 66
Infant Mortality Rate: 44
Location: Western Asia
Latitude-Longitude: 35°N 38°E

Taiwan

Capital: Taipei (7,477,000)
Area: 13,900 sq. mi.
Language: Mandarin Chinese, Taiwanese, Hakka
Currency: new Taiwan dollar
Population: 21,050,000
Population Growth Rate: 1.0%
Population Density: 1,514
Per Capita GNP: $10,000
Average Life Expectancy: 74
Infant Mortality Rate: 6
Location: East Asia
Latitude-Longitude: 23°N 121°E

Tajikistan

Capital: Dushanbe
Area: 55,300 sq. mi.

Language: Tajik
Currency: ruble
Population: 5,882,000
Population Growth Rate: 2.9%
Population Density: 106
Per Capita GNP: $482
Average Life Expectancy: 69
Infant Mortality Rate: 40
Location: South Central Asia
Latitude-Longitude: 39°N 71°E

Tanzania

Capital: Dar es Salaam
Area: 342,100 sq. mi.
Language: Swahili, English
Currency: Tanzanian shilling
Population: 29,755,000
Population Growth Rate: 3.4%
Population Density: 87
Per Capita GNP: $110
Average Life Expectancy: 51
Infant Mortality Rate: 102
Location: Eastern Africa
Latitude-Longitude: 6°S 35°E

Thailand

Capital: Bangkok (6,657,000)
Area: 197,250 sq. mi.
Language: Thai, English
Currency: baht
Population: 59,396,000
Population Growth Rate: 1.4%
Population Density: 301
Per Capita GNP: $1,840
Average Life Expectancy: 69
Infant Mortality Rate: 39
Location: Southeast Asia
Latitude-Longitude: 15°N 100°E

Togo

Capital: Lomé
Area: 21,000 sq. mi.
Language: French, Ewe, Mina, Dagomba, Kabyè
Currency: CFA franc
Population: 4,255,000
Population Growth Rate: 3.6%
Population Density: 203
Per Capita GNP: $400
Average Life Expectancy: 56
Infant Mortality Rate: 94
Location: Western Africa
Latitude-Longitude: 8°N 1°E

Tonga

Capital: Nuku'alofa
Area: 288 sq. mi.
Language: Tongan, English
Currency: pa'anga
Population: 105,000
Population Growth Rate: 2.5%
Population Density: 365
Per Capita GNP: $1,350
Average Life Expectancy: 69
Infant Mortality Rate: 26
Location: Oceania
Latitude-Longitude: 20°S 175°W

Trinidad and Tobago

Capital: Port-of-Spain
Area: 1,980 sq. mi.
Language: English, Hindi, French, Spanish
Currency: Trinidad and Tobago dollar
Population: 1,287,000
Population Growth Rate: 1.2%
Population Density: 650
Per Capita GNP: $3,940
Average Life Expectancy: 71
Infant Mortality Rate: 17
Location: Caribbean Sea
Latitude-Longitude: 11°N 61°W

Tunisia

Capital: Tunis
Area: 59,980 sq. mi.
Language: Arabic, French
Currency: Tunisian dinar
Population: 8,696,000
Population Growth Rate: 1.9%
Population Density: 145
Per Capita GNP: $1,740
Average Life Expectancy: 68
Infant Mortality Rate: 43
Location: Northern Africa
Latitude-Longitude: 34°N 9°E

Turkey

Capital: Ankara (3,263,000)
Area: 297,150 sq. mi.
Language: Turkish, Kurdish, Arabic
Currency: Turkish lira
Population: 61,799,000
Population Growth Rate: 2.2%
Population Density: 208

Per Capita GNP: $1,950
Average Life Expectancy: 67
Infant Mortality Rate: 57
Location: Western Asia
Latitude-Longitude: 39°N 35°E

Turkmenistan

Capital: Ashkhabad
Area: 188,500 sq. mi.
Language: Turkmen, Russian
Currency: manat
Population: 4,055,000
Population Growth Rate: 2.6%
Population Density: 22
Per Capita GNP: $1,270
Average Life Expectancy: 66
Infant Mortality Rate: 45
Location: South Central Asia
Latitude-Longitude: 40°N 60°E

Tuvalu

Capital: Funafuti
Area: 10 sq. mi.
Language: Tuvaluan, English
Currency: Tuvaluan dollar or Australian dollar
Population: 10,000
Population Growth Rate: 2.0%
Population Density: 1,000
Per Capita GNP: $530
Average Life Expectancy: 67
Infant Mortality Rate: 41
Location: Oceania
Latitude-Longitude: 8°S 178°E

Uganda

Capital: Kampala
Area: 77,050 sq. mi.
Language: English, Swahili, Luganda, native languages
Currency: Ugandan shilling
Population: 19,823,000
Population Growth Rate: 3.0%
Population Density: 257
Per Capita GNP: $170
Average Life Expectancy: 42
Infant Mortality Rate: 104
Location: Eastern Africa
Latitude-Longitude: 1°N 32°E

Ukraine

Capital: Kiev (2,983,000)
Area: 233,100 sq. mi.

Language: Ukrainian, Russian
Currency: karbovanet
Population: 51,482,000
Population Growth Rate: −0.2%
Population Density: 221
Per Capita GNP: $1,670
Average Life Expectancy: 69
Infant Mortality Rate: 14
Location: Eastern Europe
Latitude-Longitude: 49°N 32°E

United Arab Emirates

Capital: Abu Dhabi
Area: 32,280 sq. mi.
Language: Arabic, Persian, English
Currency: Emirian dirham
Population: 1,686,000
Population Growth Rate: 1.9%
Population Density: 52
Per Capita GNP: $22,220
Average Life Expectancy: 72
Infant Mortality Rate: 23
Location: Western Asia
Latitude-Longitude: 24°N 54°E

United Kingdom

Capital: London (8,897,000)
Area: 93,280 sq. mi.
Language: English, Welsh, Gaelic
Currency: Pound sterling (£)
Population: 58,370,000
Population Growth Rate: 0.3%
Population Density: 626
Per Capita GNP: $17,760
Average Life Expectancy: 76
Infant Mortality Rate: 7
Location: Northern Europe
Latitude-Longitude: 54°N 2°W

United States

Capital: Washington, D.C. (2,637,000 in metro area)
Area: 3,539,230 sq. mi.
Language: English
Currency: U.S. dollar
Population: 260,750,000
Population Growth Rate: 0.7%
Population Density: 74
Per Capita GNP: $23,120
Average Life Expectancy: 76
Infant Mortality Rate: 8
Location: North America
Latitude-Longitude: 38°N 97°W

Uruguay
Capital: Montevideo
Area: 67,490 sq. mi.
Language: Spanish
Currency: Uruguayan peso
Population: 3,174,000
Population Growth Rate: 0.8%
Population Density: 47
Per Capita GNP: $3,340
Average Life Expectancy: 73
Infant Mortality Rate: 21
Location: South America
Latitude-Longitude: 33°S 56°W

Uzbekistan
Capital: Tashkent (2,640,000)
Area: 172,700 sq. mi.
Language: Uzbek, Russian
Currency: ruble
Population: 22,118,000
Population Growth Rate: 2.7%
Population Density: 128
Per Capita GNP: $860
Average Life Expectancy: 69
Infant Mortality Rate: 35
Location: South Central Asia
Latitude-Longitude: 41°N 64°E

Vanuatu
Capital: Port-Vila
Area: 4,710 sq. mi.
Language: English, French, Bislama
Currency: vatu
Population: 170,000
Population Growth Rate: 2.9%
Population Density: 36
Per Capita GNP: $1,220
Average Life Expectancy: 63
Infant Mortality Rate: 63
Location: Oceania
Latitude-Longitude: 16°S 167°E

Venezuela
Capital: Caracas (3,338,000)
Area: 340,560 sq. mi.
Language: Spanish, Amerindian dialects
Currency: bolívar
Population: 21,328,000
Population Growth Rate: 2.6%
Population Density: 63
Per Capita GNP: $2,900
Average Life Expectancy: 70
Infant Mortality Rate: 20
Location: South America
Latitude-Longitude: 8°N 65°W

Vietnam
Capital: Hanoi
Area: 125,670 sq. mi.
Language: Vietnamese, French, Chinese, English, Khmer, tribal languages
Currency: dong
Population: 73,104,000
Population Growth Rate: 2.3%
Population Density: 582
Per Capita GNP: $230
Average Life Expectancy: 65
Infant Mortality Rate: 36
Location: Southeast Asia
Latitude-Longitude: 13°N 108°E

Western Samoa
Capital: Apia
Area: 1,090 sq. mi.
Language: Samoan, English
Currency: tala
Population: 212,000
Population Growth Rate: 2.6%
Population Density: 194
Per Capita GNP: $940
Average Life Expectancy: 67
Infant Mortality Rate: 21
Location: Oceania
Latitude-Longitude: 14°S 172°W

Yemen
Capital: Sana
Area: 203,850 sq. mi.
Language: Arabic
Currency: rial
Population: 12,920,000
Population Growth Rate: 3.4%
Population Density: 63
Per Capita GNP: $520
Average Life Expectancy: 54
Infant Mortality Rate: 115
Location: Western Asia
Latitude-Longitude: 14°N 45°E

Yugoslavia
Capital: Belgrade
Area: 26,940 sq. mi.
Language: Serbo-Croatian
Currency: Yugoslav new dinar
Population: 10,517,000
Population Growth Rate: 0.4%
Population Density: 390
Per Capita GNP: $3,000
Average Life Expectancy: 72
Infant Mortality Rate: 17
Location: Southern Europe
Latitude-Longitude: 45°N 21°E

Zaire
Capital: Kinshasa (4,520,000)
Area: 875,520 sq. mi.
Language: French, African languages
Currency: new zaire
Population: 42,476,000
Population Growth Rate: 3.3%
Population Density: 49
Per Capita GNP: $235
Average Life Expectancy: 52
Infant Mortality Rate: 93
Location: Central Africa
Latitude-Longitude: 1°S 25°E

Zambia
Capital: Lusaka
Area: 287,020 sq. mi.
Language: English, about 70 African languages
Currency: Zambian kwacha
Population: 9,132,000
Population Growth Rate: 2.8%
Population Density: 32
Per Capita GNP: $290
Average Life Expectancy: 44
Infant Mortality Rate: 107
Location: Eastern Africa
Latitude-Longitude: 15°S 30°E

Zimbabwe
Capital: Harare
Area: 149,290 sq. mi.
Language: English, Sindebele, Shona
Currency: Zimbabwean dollar
Population: 11,215,000
Population Growth Rate: 3.0%
Population Density: 75
Per Capita GNP: $570
Average Life Expectancy: 56
Infant Mortality Rate: 59
Location: Eastern Africa
Latitude-Longitude: 20°S 30°E

Regions and Groups of Countries

Balkans — countries of the Balkan Peninsula in Europe: Albania, Bosnia-Herzegovina, Bulgaria, Croatia, Greece, Macedonia, Romania, Slovenia, Yugoslavia (consisting of the republics of Serbia and Montenegro), and a small part of Turkey.

Baltic States — Estonia, Latvia and Lithuania.

Central America — the bridge of land between Mexico and South America. The Central American countries are Belize, Costa Rica, El Salvador, Guatemala, Honduras, Nicaragua, and Panama.

Commonwealth of Independent States — nine republics of the former Soviet Union: Armenia, Belarus, Kazakhstan, Kyrgyzstan, Russia, Tajikistan, Turkmenistan, Ukraine and Uzbekistan. The three Baltic states, the Republic of Georgia, Azerbaijan and Moldova were part of the Soviet Union but are not members of the Commonwealth.

European Community (Common Market) — twelve countries working to achieve a single European market: Belgium, Denmark, France, Germany, Greece, Ireland, Italy, Luxembourg, Netherlands, Portugal, Spain, and the United Kingdom.

European Free Trade Association — seven countries working to reduce obstacles to trade in Western Europe: Austria, Finland, Iceland, Liechtenstein, Norway, Sweden, and Switzerland.

Far East — the easternmost region of Asia, including China, Japan, North Korea, South Korea, Mongolia and eastern Russia.

Low Countries — Netherlands, Belgium and Luxembourg. Much of the land in Belgium and the Netherlands is at or below sea level.

Middle East — a region which covers parts of Africa, Asia and Europe. It includes Bahrain, Cyprus, Egypt, Iran, Iraq, Israel, Jordan, Kuwait, Lebanon, Oman, Qatar, Saudi Arabia, Sudan, Syria, Turkey, United Arab Emirates, and Yemen.

Oceania — Pacific Islands. The main groups are Melanesia, Micronesia and Polynesia. Countries include Fiji, Kiribati, Nauru, Solomon Islands, Tonga, Tuvalu, Vanuatu, Western Samoa, Papua New Guinea, and New Zealand.

Scandinavia — Norway, Sweden and Denmark.

Southeast Asia — the peninsula and islands east of India and south of China. It includes Brunei, Burma, Cambodia, Laos, Malaysia, Philippines, Singapore, Thailand, Vietnam and some of Indonesia.

Third World — approximately 120 developing countries, many of which are in Asia, Africa and South America.

United Kingdom of Great Britain — England, Scotland, Wales, and Northern Ireland. England, Scotland and Wales are on the island of Great Britain. Northern Ireland occupies one-sixth of the island of Ireland, to the west of Great Britain.

United Nations — an organization of 184 nations, begun in 1945 for the purpose of maintaining world peace. Of the countries listed on pages 53–69, only Kiribati, Switzerland, Taiwan, Tonga, Tuvalu and Yugoslavia are not members. The U.N. Security Council has five permanent members: China, France, Russia, the United Kingdom and the United States. Ten other members are elected by the General Assembly for two-year terms.

History

History is the study of past events. Many scientists think people have lived on the earth for about three million years. Until the ancient Egyptian civilization, which began about 5,000 years ago, no written records were kept. Things which happened before writing are **prehistoric**.

A **generation** is the time it takes for an average person to grow up and have children. If a generation is considered to be 30 years, there may have been 100,000 generations since the first people. Of that, 90,000 generations were spent in caves. If a generation is 30 years, it has been:

16,000 generations since man learned to control fire
8,300 generations since people crossed the Bering Strait from Asia into North America
250 generations since farming began
170 generations since written history began
67 generations since the birth of Jesus Christ
17 generations since Christopher Columbus came to America
7 generations since the United States began
4 generations since slavery was outlawed after the American Civil War
3 generations since electric lights were invented and cars were first manufactured
1 generation since man first set foot on the moon

In the past 100 years, more change has taken place on the earth than in all the years before, due to man's technology and exploding population. In 1994, the world population was growing by more than 89,000,000 per year. After deaths are taken into account, that amounts to a net growth of about:

3 .... per second
170 .... per minute
10,212 .... per hour
245,092 .... per day, nearly as many as live in Anchorage, the largest city in Alaska
1,720,357 .... per week, more than live in Houston, the fourth largest city in the U.S.
7,454,880 .... per month, more than live in New York City, the largest city in the U.S.
89,458,558 .... per year, nearly many people as live in Mexico, the eleventh most populous country in the world

World Population Growth

World population began to grow rapidly in about 1630 A.D.
It reached:
1 billion in 1800
2 billion in 1930
3 billion in 1960
4 billion in 1975
5 billion in 1987

The estimated population of the world at the end of June 1994 was 5,606,989,000.

World population is expected to reach:
6 billion in 1998
7 billion by 2008
8 billion by 2019

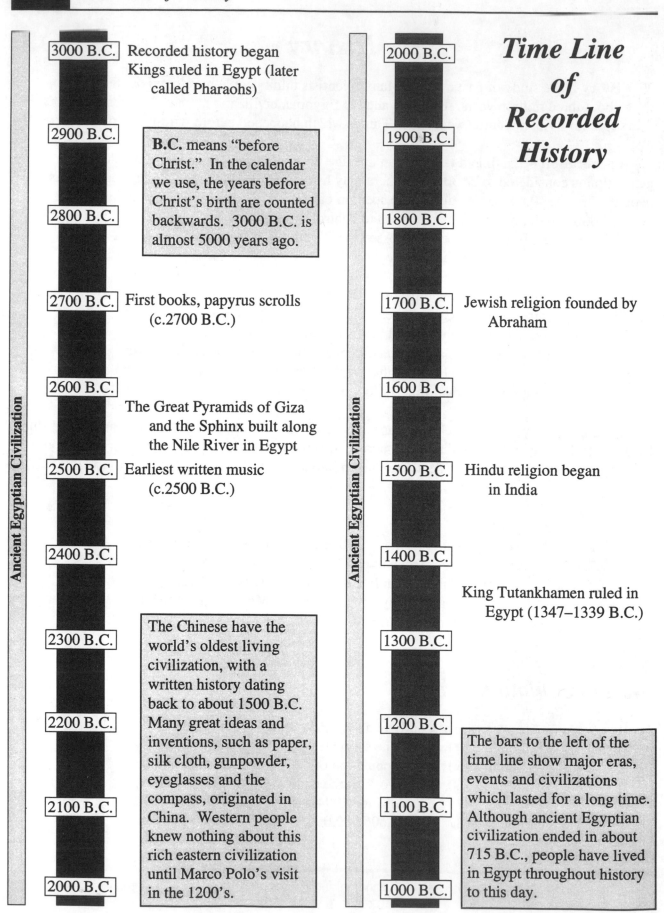

Time Line of Recorded History

Ancient Egyptian Civilization

3000 B.C. — Recorded history began Kings ruled in Egypt (later called Pharaohs)

2900 B.C.

B.C. means "before Christ." In the calendar we use, the years before Christ's birth are counted backwards. 3000 B.C. is almost 5000 years ago.

2800 B.C.

2700 B.C. — First books, papyrus scrolls (c.2700 B.C.)

2600 B.C.

The Great Pyramids of Giza and the Sphinx built along the Nile River in Egypt

2500 B.C. — Earliest written music (c.2500 B.C.)

2400 B.C.

The Chinese have the world's oldest living civilization, with a written history dating back to about 1500 B.C. Many great ideas and inventions, such as paper, silk cloth, gunpowder, eyeglasses and the compass, originated in China. Western people knew nothing about this rich eastern civilization until Marco Polo's visit in the 1200's.

2300 B.C.

2200 B.C.

2100 B.C.

2000 B.C.

Ancient Egyptian Civilization

2000 B.C.

1900 B.C.

1800 B.C.

1700 B.C. — Jewish religion founded by Abraham

1600 B.C.

1500 B.C. — Hindu religion began in India

1400 B.C.

King Tutankhamen ruled in Egypt (1347–1339 B.C.)

1300 B.C.

1200 B.C.

The bars to the left of the time line show major eras, events and civilizations which lasted for a long time. Although ancient Egyptian civilization ended in about 715 B.C., people have lived in Egypt throughout history to this day.

1100 B.C.

1000 B.C.

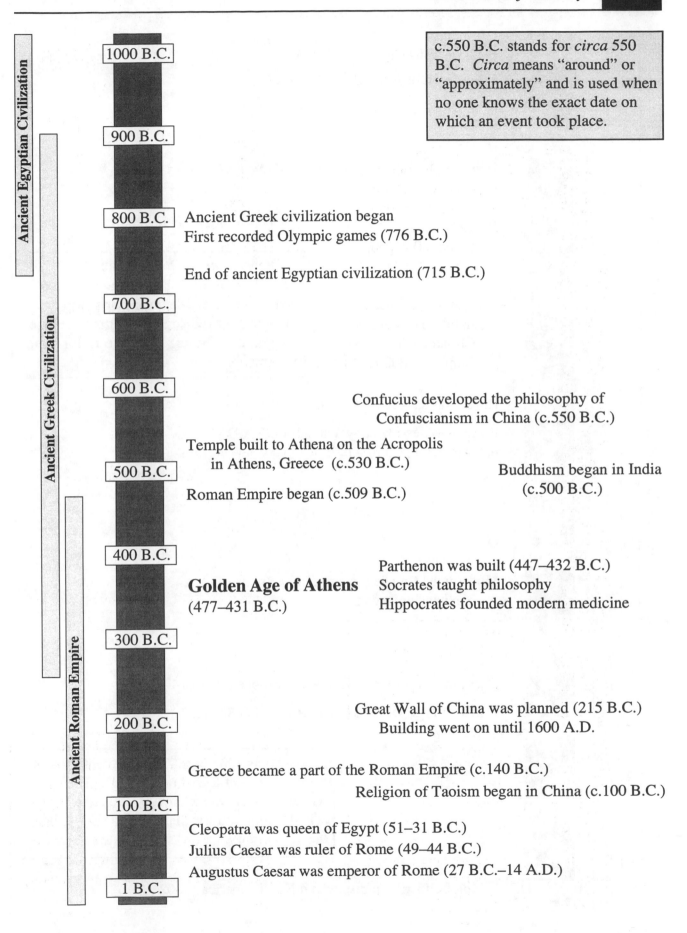

Ancient Egyptian Civilization

Ancient Greek Civilization

Ancient Roman Empire

1000 B.C.

900 B.C.

800 B.C.

700 B.C.

600 B.C.

500 B.C.

400 B.C.

300 B.C.

200 B.C.

100 B.C.

1 B.C.

c.550 B.C. stands for *circa* 550 B.C. *Circa* means "around" or "approximately" and is used when no one knows the exact date on which an event took place.

Ancient Greek civilization began
First recorded Olympic games (776 B.C.)

End of ancient Egyptian civilization (715 B.C.)

Confucius developed the philosophy of
    Confuscianism in China (c.550 B.C.)

Temple built to Athena on the Acropolis
    in Athens, Greece (c.530 B.C.)

Roman Empire began (c.509 B.C.)

Buddhism began in India
    (c.500 B.C.)

Golden Age of Athens
(477–431 B.C.)

Parthenon was built (447–432 B.C.)
Socrates taught philosophy
Hippocrates founded modern medicine

Great Wall of China was planned (215 B.C.)
    Building went on until 1600 A.D.

Greece became a part of the Roman Empire (c.140 B.C.)

Religion of Taoism began in China (c.100 B.C.)

Cleopatra was queen of Egypt (51–31 B.C.)
Julius Caesar was ruler of Rome (49–44 B.C.)
Augustus Caesar was emperor of Rome (27 B.C.–14 A.D.)

Ancient Roman Empire

Middle Ages

Arab Civilization

1 A.D.	Birth of Jesus Christ (c.4 B.C.) Beginning of Christian religion
	Crucifixion of Jesus Christ (c.30 A.D.)
	Colosseum was built in Rome (71–80 A.D.)
100 A.D.	Paper was invented in China (105 A.D.)

Roman Empire at greatest power (27 B.C.–180 A.D.)

200 A.D.	Bubonic plague in Rome killed 5,000 people a day (262 A.D.)

Mayan civilization began in North America

> **A.D.** means *anno Domini,* Latin for "in the year of our Lord." The calendar we use counts time from the year Christ was thought to have been born. It is called the Gregorian calendar. See page 13 for more information.

300 A.D.	Constantine granted freedom of religion to Christians in Roman Empire (c.300 A.D.)
400 A.D.	Rome was sacked (410 A.D.)
	Rome was destroyed by Vandals (455 A.D.)
	Fall of Roman Empire (476 A.D.) Middle Ages began
500 A.D.	
600 A.D.	
	Mohammed founded Islam religion (622 A.D.) Arab expansion began
700 A.D.	
	Charlemagne's empire in western Europe (768–814 A.D.)

Golden Age of Arab Culture (786–809 A.D.)

800 A.D.	

> A **century** is 100 years. The first century was from the birth of Christ to 100 A.D. The second century was from 100–200 A.D. 1995 is in the 20th century. The year 2000 will begin the 21st century.

900 A.D.	
1000 A.D.	Viking Leif Ericson discovered North America (1002 A.D.)

Middle Ages

Arab Civilization

Crusades

Renaissance

Inquisition

1000 A.D.

1100 A.D.

1200 A.D.

1300 A.D.

1400 A.D.

1500 A.D.

Orthodox churches and the Roman Catholic Church separated in the first major division in Christian history (1054 A.D.)

Crusades began in an attempt by Christians to recapture the Holy Land, present-day Israel, from the Moslems (1096 A.D.)

Children's Crusade (1212 A.D.)

Genghis Khan ruled in China (1206–1227 A.D

Inquisition began (1231 A.D.)

Marco Polo traveled to China (1271–1292 A.D.)

End of Crusades (1291 A.D.)

Renaissance began (c.1325 A.D.)

Aztecs built their capital city in present-day Mexico (c.1325 A.D.

The Black Death, bubonic plague, killed about a fourth of Europe's people, as well as thousands in China, India, Persia and Russia (1347–1351 A.D.)

Middle Ages ended

Inca civilization in present-day Peru

Johannes Gutenberg invented movable type and printed the Bible

Christopher Columbus first came to America (1492 A.D.)

1500 A.D.

Martin Luther began the Reformation, during which Christian Protestants broke away from the Roman Catholic Church (1517 A.D.)

Ferdinand Magellan's ship circled the globe (1519–1522 A.D.)

Hernando Cortés conquered the Aztec Empire in Mexico (1521 A.D.)

Francisco Pizarro conquered the Inca Empire in Peru (1533 A.D.)

Nicolaus Copernicus said that the earth went around the sun (1543 A.D.)

St. Augustine, Florida, was the first permanent settlement established by Europeans in the present-day United States (1565 A.D.)

Renaissance ended (c.1568 A.D.)

Pope Gregory XIII worked out the modern calendar (1582 A.D.)

Spanish established first permanent settlement in present-day New Mexico (1598 A.D.)

1600 A.D.   Age of Reason began. William Shakespeare wrote plays in England.

Jamestown, Virginia, was the first permanent English colony in the present-day United States (1607 A.D.)

The Pilgrims came to America on the Mayflower (1620 A.D.)

First Thanksgiving in Plymouth Colony, Massachusetts (1621 A.D.)

French and Indian Wars (1689–1763 A.D.)

1700 A.D.

Arab civilization declined

Arab Civilization

Renaissance

Inquisition

Age of Reason

Original Thirteen American Colonies

with dates of first permanent settlement

Virginia	1607
Massachusetts	1620
New Hampshire	1623
New York	1624
Connecticut	1633
Maryland	1634
Rhode Island	1636
Delaware	1638
Pennsylvania	1643
North Carolina	1653
New Jersey	1660
South Carolina	1670
Georgia	1733

Age of Reason

Inquisition

Industrial Revolution

Space Age

First English dictionary was published by Samuel Johnson (1755 A.D.)

Industrial Revolution began (c.1765 A.D.)
James Watt invented the steam engine (1769 A.D.)

American Revolutionary War (1775–1781 A.D.)
United States Constitution signed (1787 A.D.)

French Revolution (1789–1799 A.D.)   Age of Reason ended

1800 A.D. Louisiana Purchase added 827,987 square miles to the U.S. (1803 A.D.)
Lewis and Clark began exploring northwest U.S. (1804–1806 A.D.)

War of 1812 (1812 –1815 A.D.)
Napoleon Bonaparte was defeated at Waterloo (1815 A.D.)

First railroad which carried passengers built in England (1825 A.D.)

Inquisition ended (1834 A.D.)   Mexican War (1846–
                                  1848 A.D.)
Famine in Ireland, potato blight (1845–1848 A.D.)
California Gold Rush (1849 A.D.)
                                First oil well (1859 A.D.)
Civil War ended slavery in the United States (1861–1865 A.D.)
    (See list of Confederate States on page 101.)

Custer's Last Stand (1876 A.D.)   First telephone (1876 A.D.)

Spanish-American War (1898 A.D.)
"Gay Nineties" (1890–1899 A.D.)

1900 A.D.
Wright brothers flew first successful airplane (1903 A.D.)

World War I (1914–1918 A.D.)

Stock Market Crash (October 29, 1929)   First TV broadcast
Great Depression (1929–1942 A.D.)   (1936 A.D.)
World War II (1939–1945 A.D.) Pearl Harbor bombed by Japanese
    (December 7, 1941) Atomic bomb dropped on Hiroshima (1945 A.D.)

Korean War (1950–1953 A.D.)
Space Age began (1957 A.D.) See *The Space Age*, page 20.

Neil Armstrong was the first man on the moon (1969 A.D.)

Vietnam War (1957–1975 A.D.)

Iraq's invasion of Kuwait (1990 A.D.) led to Persian Gulf War (1991 A.D.)
Collapse of Communist governments and Soviet Union (1989–1991 A.D.)

2000 A.D.

Notable People

Aaron, Henry, American baseball player (1934-)

Abernathy, Ralph David, American civil rights leader (1926-1990)

Abraham, founder of Jewish religion (c.1700 B.C.)

Adams, Ansel, American photographer (1902-1984)

Adams, John, second U.S. president (1735-1826)

Adams, John Quincy, sixth U.S. president (1767-1848)

Adams, Samuel, American patriot and politician (1722-1803)

Addams, Jane, American social worker (1860-1935)

Aesop, Greek writer of fables (c. 600 B.C.)

Alcott, Louisa May, American author and war nurse (1832-1888)

Alexander the Great, Macedonian king & conqueror (356-323 B.C.)

Ali, Muhammad (Cassius Clay), American heavyweight boxing champion (1942-)

Allen, Ethan, American patriot and soldier (1738-1789)

Amundsen, Roald, Norwegian explorer of South Pole (1872-1928)

Andersen, Hans Christian, Danish author of fairy tales (1805-1875)

Anderson, Marian, American opera singer (1897-1993)

Anthony, Susan Brownell, American woman suffragist (1820-1906)

Antony, Mark, Roman general and statesman (83?-30 B.C.)

Appleseed, Johnny (John Chapman), American apple tree planter (1774-1845)

Archimedes, Greek inventor and mathematician (287?-212 B.C.)

Aristotle, ancient Greek philosopher and scientist (384-322 B.C.)

Armstrong, Louis, American jazz musician (1901?-1971)

Armstrong, Neil Alden, American astronaut (1930-)

Arnold, Benedict, American general and traitor (1741-1801)

Arthur, Chester A., twenty-first U.S. president (1829-1886)

Arthur, King, medieval English king (c. 500 A.D.)

Astaire, Fred, American dancer and actor (1899-1987)

Atahualpa, last Inca emperor (1500?- 1533)

Attucks, Crispus, American patriot (1723?-1770)

Audubon, John James, American naturalist and painter (1785-1851)

Augustus Caesar (Octavian), Roman emperor (63 B.C.-14 A.D.)

Austin, Stephen, American pioneer and colonizer (1793-1836)

Baca, Elfego, Mexican-American frontiersman (1865-1945)

Bach, Johann Sebastian, German composer (1685-1750)

Baden-Powell, Lord, English founder of Boy Scouts (1857-1941)

Balboa, Vasco Núñez de, Spanish explorer (1475?-1519)

Banneker, Benjamin, American astronomer (1731-1806)

Bannister, Sir Roger, British athlete and doctor (1929-)

Bañuelos, Romana Acosta, former Mexican-American treasurer of U.S. (1925-)

Barnum, P. T., American circus showman (1810-1891)

Barton, Clara, founder of American Red Cross (1821-1912)

Bass, Sam, American outlaw (1851-1878)

Bean, Judge Roy, American frontiersman (1825?-1904)

Beethoven, Ludwig van, German composer (1770-1827)

Bell, Alexander Graham, American inventor of telephone (1847-1922)

Bernhardt, Sarah, French actress (1844-1923)

Bethune, Mary McLeod, American educator (1875-1955)

Billy the Kid, American outlaw (1859-1881)

Black Hawk, American Indian chief, Sauk tribe (1767-1838)

Black Kettle, Cheyenne Indian chief (1803?-1868)

Blackbeard, British pirate (?-1718)

Blackwell, Antoinette Brown, first female American minister (1825-1921)

Blackwell, Elizabeth, first woman doctor in the U.S. (1821-1910)

Bloomer, Amelia, American women's rights champion (1818-1894)

Bluford, Guion S., Jr., American astronaut (1942-)

Bly, Nellie, American journalist (1867?-1922)

Bogart, Humphrey, American actor (1899-1957)

Bolívar, Simón, South American general (1783-1830)

Bonaparte, Napoleon, French emperor (1769-1821)

Boone, Daniel, American pioneer (1734-1820)

Booth, John Wilkes, American actor who assassinated Abraham Lincoln (1838-1865)

Brahms, Johannes, German composer (1833-1897)

Braille, Louis, French inventor of Braille (1809-1852)

Brando, Marlon, American actor (1924-)

Brant, Joseph, American Indian leader, Mohawk tribe (1742-1807)

Brezhnev, Leonid, Soviet head of Communist Party (1906-1982)

Bridger, Jim, American frontiersman (1804-1881)

Brown, John, American abolitionist (1800-1859)

Browning, Elizabeth Barrett, English poet (1806-1861)

Bryan, William Jennings, American lawyer and statesman (1860-1925)

Buchanan, James, fifteenth U.S. president (1791-1868)

Buddha, Siddhartha Gautama, founder of Buddhism (563 B.C.?-483 B.C.?)

Buffalo Bill Cody, American frontiersman and Wild West showman (1846-1917)

Burbank, Luther, American plant breeder (1849-1926)

Burns, Robert, Scottish poet (1759-1796)

Burr, Aaron, American revolutionary officer and vice president (1756-1836)

Bush, George Herbert Walker, forty-first U.S. president (1924-)

Byrd, Richard E., American polar explorer (1888-1957)

Cabot, John, Italian-English explorer (1450?-1498?)

Caesar, Augustus (Octavian), Roman emperor (63 B.C.-A.D. 14)

Caesar, Julius, Roman general and ruler (100?-44 B.C.)

Calamity Jane, American frontierswoman (1852-1903)

Calvin, John, French religious leader of Protestant Reformation (1509-1564)

Capone, Al, American gangster (1899-1947)

Captain Jack, American Indian leader, Modoc tribe (1837-1873)

Carnegie, Andrew, American industrialist (1835-1919)

Carson, Kit, American frontiersman (1809-1868)

Carter, James Earl, Jr., thirty-ninth U.S. president (1924-)

Carver, George Washington, American scientist (1864-1943)

Castro, Fidel, Cuban dictator (1926-)

Castro, Raul Hector, American governor and ambassador (1916-)

Catherine the Great, empress of Russia (1729-1796)

Champlain, Samuel de, French explorer of America (1570?-1635)

Chaplin, Charlie, English screen actor-director (1889-1977)

Charlemagne, Frankish ruler (742-814)

Charles, Prince, British heir to the throne (1948-)

Chavez, Cesar Estrada, Mexican-American labor union organizer (1927-1993)

Chiang Kai-shek, Nationalist Chinese leader (1887-1975)

Chopin, Frédéric François, Polish composer (1810?-1849)

Churchill, Sir Winston, British statesman (1874-1965)

Cisneros, Henry Gabriel, Mexican-American mayor of San Antonio (1947-)

Clark, William, American explorer, leader of Lewis & Clark expedition (1770-1838)

Clay, Henry, American lawyer and statesman (1777-1852)

Clemens, Samuel L., also known as Mark Twain, American author (1835-1910)

Cleopatra, ancient Egyptian queen (69-30 B.C.)

Cleveland, Grover, twenty-second and twenty-fourth U.S. president (1837-1908)

Clinton, William J., forty-second U.S. president (1946-)

Cochise, Apache Indian chief (1800?-1874)

Cody, William Frederick, American frontiersman and Wild West showman, also known as Buffalo Bill (1846-1917)

Columbus, Christopher, Italian explorer and discoverer of America (1451-1506)

Confucius, Chinese philosopher (c. 551?-479? B.C.)

Cook, James, British explorer of the Pacific Ocean (1728-1779)

Coolidge, Calvin, thirtieth U.S. president (1872-1933)

Copernicus, Nicolaus, Polish astronomer (1473-1543)

Cornwallis, Charles, English military leader (1738-1805)

Cortés, Hernando, Spanish conquistador who conquered the Aztecs in Mexico (1485-1547)

Cortina, Juan Nepomuceno, Mexican-American civil rights leader (1824-1894)

Cosby, Bill, American entertainer, author & TV producer (1937-)

Cousteau, Jacques-Yves, French oceanographer (1910-)

Crazy Horse, American Indian chief, Oglala Sioux (1844?-1877)

Crockett, David, American frontiersman (1786-1836)

Curie, Marie, Polish-French scientist (1867-1934)

Curie, Pierre, French physicist (1859-1906)

Custer, George Armstrong, American army officer (1839-1876)

Dali, Salvador, Spanish artist (1904-1989)

Darwin, Charles, English scientist (1809-1882)

Da Vinci, Leonardo, Italian Renaissance artist and scientist (1452-1519)

Davis, Jefferson, president of Confederate States of America during Civil War (1808-1889)

De Gaulle, Charles, French military and political leader (1890-1970)

Deloria, Vine, Jr., American Indian rights leader, Sioux tribe (1933-)

Demosthenes, Greek orator (384?-322 B.C.)

De Soto, Hernando, Spanish explorer of America, discovered Mississippi River (1500?-1542)

Dickens, Charles, English novelist (1812-1870)

Dickinson, Emily, American poet (1830-1886)

Diesel, Rudolf, German inventor of diesel engine (1858-1913)

Dillinger, John, American criminal (1903-1934)

Disney, Walt, American cartoonist and motion-picture producer (1901-1966)

Dix, Dorothea, American social reformer (1802-1887)

Dorion, Marie, American Indian explorer, Iowa tribe (1790?-1850)

Douglas, Stephen A., American political leader (1813-1861)

Douglass, Frederick, American abolitionist (1818?-1895)

Drake, Sir Francis, English explorer and sea captain (1543?-1596)

Earhart, Amelia, American aviator (1897-1937?)

Earp, Wyatt Berry Stapp, American frontiersman (1848-1929)

Eastman, George, American photographic pioneer (1854-1932)

Eddy, Mary Baker, American founder of Christian Science (1821-1910)

Edison, Thomas Alva, American inventor (1847-1931)

Einstein, Albert, German-American scientist (1879-1955)

Eisenhower, Dwight D., thirty-fourth U.S. president (1890-1969)

Ellington, Duke, American jazz composer (1899-1974)

Emerson, Ralph Waldo, American philosopher & author (1803-1882)

Ericson, Leif, Norse explorer (980?-1025?)

Fahrenheit, Gabriel, German physicist (1686-1736)

Faraday, Michael, English scientist and pioneer in electricity (1791-1867)

Fermi, Enrico, Italian-American physicist (1901-1954)

Fields, W. C., American entertainer (1879-1946)

Fillmore, Millard, thirteenth U.S. president (1800-1874)

Fink, Mike, American frontiersman (1770-1823)

Ford, Gerald R., thirty-eighth U.S. president (1913-)

Ford, Henry, American automobile pioneer (1863-1947)

Forten, James, American abolitionist (1766-1842)

Foster, Stephen, American songwriter (1826-1864)

Franco, Francisco, dictator of Spain (1892-1975)

Frank, Anne, young German-Jewish writer (1929-1945)

Franklin, Benjamin, American statesman and inventor (1706-1790)

Freud, Sigmund, Austrian founder of psychoanalysis (1856-1939)

Friedan, Betty, American feminist (1921-)

Frost, Robert, American poet (1874-1963)

Fulton, Robert, American inventor (1765-1815)

Gagarin, Yuri, Soviet cosmonaut, first man in space (1934-1968)

Galarza, Ernesto, Mexican-American historian (1905-1984)

Galileo, Italian astronomer and physicist (1564-1642)

Gall, Sioux Indian leader (1840-1894)

Gamio, Manuel, Mexican anthropologist (1883-1960)

Gandhi, Indira, prime minister of India (1917-1984)

Gandhi, Mohandas (Mahatma Gandhi), leader of India (1869-1948)

Garfield, James A., twentieth U.S. president (1831-1881)

Gauguin, Paul, French artist (1848-1903)

Gautama, Siddhartha (Buddha), founder of Buddhism (563 B.C.?-483 B.C.?)

Gehrig, Lou, American baseball player (1903-1941)

Genghis Khan, Mongol conqueror (1162-1227)

Geronimo, Apache Indian chief (1829-1909)

Giovanni, Nikki, American poet (1943-)

Glenn, John, Jr., American astronaut and senator (1921-)

Goddard, Robert, American rocket scientist (1882-1945)

Gonzales, Rodolfo (Corky), Mexican-American leader (1928-)

Gorbachev, Mikhail S., leader of the Soviet Union from 1985 to 1991 (1931-)

Gore, Al, vice president of U.S. (1948-)

Goya, Francisco, Spanish painter (1746-1828)

Grant, Ulysses S., Civil War general and eighteenth U.S. president (1822-1885)

Greaves, Captain, Scotch-Irish pirate (c. 1670)

Greco, El, Greek-Spanish painter (1541?-1614)

Greeley, Horace, American publisher (1811-1872)

Gutenberg, Johannes, German inventor of movable type (1395?-1468?)

Guthrie, Woody, American folk singer and composer (1912-1967)

Haile Selassie I, emperor of Ethiopia (1892-1975)

Hale, Nathan, American patriot (1755-1776)

Halley, Edmond, English astronomer (1656-1742)

Hamilton, Alexander, American statesman & political leader (1755 or 1757-1804)

Hancock, John, American revolutionary leader (1737-1793)

Handel, George Frideric, German composer (1685-1759)

Handy, W. C., American composer, father of the Blues (1873-1958)

Hannibal, Carthaginian general and political leader (247-183 B.C.)

Harding, Warren G., twenty-ninth U.S. president (1865-1923)

Harrison, Benjamin, twenty-third U.S. president (1833-1901)

Harrison, William Henry, ninth U.S. president (1773-1841)

Hawthorne, Nathaniel, American author (1804-1864)

Haydn, Joseph, Austrian composer (1732-1809)

Hayes, Rutherford B., nineteenth U.S. president (1822-1893)

Hemingway, Ernest, American author (1899-1961)

Henry, Patrick, American patriot (1736-1799)

Herschel, Sir William, British astronomer (1738-1822)

Hickok, Wild Bill, American frontiersman (1837-1876)

Hillary, Sir Edmund, New Zealand mountain climber (1919-)

Hippocrates, Greek father of modern medicine (460?-380? B.C.)

Hirohito, emperor of Japan (1901-1989)

Hitchcock, Alfred, English-American director of suspense thriller films (1899-1980)

Hitler, Adolf, German dictator (1889-1945)

Ho Chi Minh, Vietnamese revolutionary leader (1890-1969)

Hogan, Ben, American golfer (1912-)

Holmes, Oliver Wendell, Jr., American judge (1841-1935)

Homer, Winslow, American artist (1836-1910)

Hoover, Herbert, thirty-first U.S. president (1874-1964)

Hoover, J. Edgar, American director of FBI (1895-1972)

Hope, Bob, American comedian and actor (1903-)

Houdini, Harry (Ehrich Weiss), American magician and escape artist (1874-1926)

Houston, Samuel, American, political leader and soldier in Texas (1793-1863)

Howe, Elias, American inventor of sewing machine (1819-1867)

Howe, Julia Ward, American composer of "Battle Hymn of the Republic" (1819-1910)

Hudson, Henry, English explorer and sea captain (?-1611)

Hughes, Howard, rich American businessman (1905-1976)

Hughes, Langston, American author and poet (1902-1967)

Irving, Washington, American author (1783-1859)

Jackson, Andrew, seventh U.S. president (1767-1845)

Jackson, Jesse, American politician and minister (1941-)

Jackson, Stonewall, Confederate general during U.S. Civil War (1824-1863)

James, Jesse, American outlaw (1847-1882)

Jefferson, Thomas, third U.S. president, author of Declaration of Independence (1743-1826)

Joan of Arc, French heroine and saint (1412?-1431)

Johnson, Andrew, seventeenth U.S. president (1808-1875)

Johnson, Lyndon B., thirty-sixth U.S. president (1908-1973)

Johnson, Samuel, English writer of first dictionary (1709-1784)

Jones, Casey, American railroad engineer (1863-1900)

Jones, John Paul, Scottish-American naval hero (1747-1792)

Joseph, Chief, Nez Perce Indian chief (1840?-1904)

Kamehameha I, Hawaiian king (1758?-1819)

Keats, John, English poet (1795-1821)

Keller, Helen, American author and educator (1880-1968)

Kennedy, John F., thirty-fifth U.S. president (1917-1963)

Kepler, Johannes, German astronomer and mathematician (1571-1630)

Key, Francis Scott, American composer of national anthem (1779-1843)

Kidd, William, Scottish pirate (1645?-1701)

King, Martin Luther, Jr., American civil rights leader (1929-1968)

Kirkpatrick, Jeane, U.S. ambassador to United Nations (1926-)

Kublai Khan, Chinese ruler (1216-1294)

Lafayette, Marquis de, French soldier and statesman (1757-1834)

Laffite, Jean, French-American pirate (1780?-1826?)

Landers, Ann, American advice columnist (1918-)

Laozi, legendary Chinese philosopher (c. 500 B.C.)

La Salle, Sieur de, French explorer of Mississippi Valley (1643-1687)

Lee, Robert E., Confederate general during U.S. Civil War (1807-1870)

Leeuwenhoek, Anton van, Dutch naturalist and "father of the microscope" (1632-1723)

Lenin, V. I., Soviet Communist leader (1870-1924)

Lewis, Meriwether, American explorer; leader of Lewis & Clark expedition (1774-1809)

Lincoln, Abraham, sixteenth U.S. president (1809-1865)

Lindbergh, Charles, American aviator (1902-1974)

Lister, Sir Joseph, English surgeon (1827-1912)

Liszt, Franz, Hungarian composer (1811-1886)

Livingstone, David, British explorer of Africa (1813-1873)

Lloyd George, David, British prime minister (1863-1945)

Longfellow, Henry Wadsworth, American poet (1807-1882)

Low, Juliette Gordon, U.S. founder of Girl Scouts (1860-1927)

Luther, Martin, German religious leader of Reformation (1483-1546)

MacArthur, Douglas, five-star U.S. general during WWII (1880-1964)

Madison, James, fourth U.S. president (1751-1836)

Magellan, Ferdinand, Portuguese sea captain and explorer (1480?-1521)

Mandela, Nelson, South African president (1918-)

Mann, Horace, American educator (1796-1859)

Mao Tse-tung, Chinese Communist leader (1893-1976)

Marconi, Guglielmo, Italian inventor of the radio (1874-1937)

Marshall, Thurgood, U.S. Supreme Court justice (1908-1993)

Marx, Karl, German philosopher and "father of communism" (1818-1883)

Massasoit, Wampanoag Indian chief (1580?-1661)

Maximilian, emperor of Mexico (1832-1867)

McCormick, Cyrus Hall, American inventor of the reaper (1809-1884)

McKinley, William, twenty-fifth U.S. president (1843-1901)

Meir, Golda, prime minister of Israel (1898-1978)

Mendel, Gregor, Austrian botanist (1822-1884)

Mendelssohn, Felix, German composer (1809-1847)

Michelangelo Buonarroti, Italian Renaissance artist and architect (1475-1564)

Milton, John, English poet (1608-1674)

Mohammed, founder of Islamic religion (570?-632 A.D.)

Monet, Claude, French painter (1840-1926)

Monroe, James, fifth U.S. president (1758-1831)

Monroe, Marilyn, American motion-picture actress (1926-1962)

Montessori, Maria, Italian educator and physician (1870-1952)

Montezuma II, Aztec emperor (1480?-1520)

Montgolfier, Jacques, French co-inventor of balloon (1745-1799)

Montgolfier, Joseph, French co-inventor of balloon (1740-1810)

Morse, Samuel F. B., American inventor of telegraph (1791-1872)

Moses, Grandma (Anna Mary Moses), American folk artist (1860-1961)

Mott, Lucretia, American abolitionist and women's rights leader (1793-1880)

Mozart, Wolfgang Amadeus, Austrian composer (1756-1791)

Muir, John, American naturalist and conservationist (1838-1914)

Mussolini, Benito, Italian fascist dictator (1883-1945)

Nader, Ralph, American lawyer and consumer advocate (1934-)

Napoleon Bonaparte, French emperor (1769-1821)

Nash, Ogden, American poet (1902-1971)

Nation, Carry, American temperance leader (1846-1911)

Nero, Roman emperor (37-68 A.D.)

Newton, Sir Isaac, English astronomer and mathematician who discovered gravity (1642-1727)

Nicholas II, last czar of Russia (1868-1918)

Nightingale, Florence, English founder of nursing (1820-1910)

Nixon, Richard M., thirty-seventh U.S. president (1913-1994)

Nobel, Alfred, Swedish industrialist, inventor of dynamite, and founder of Nobel prizes (1833-1896)

Oakley, Annie, American sharpshooter (1860-1926)

O'Keeffe, Georgia, American artist (1887-1986)

Osceola, Seminole Indian leader (1804?-1838)

Owens, Jesse, American track and field athlete (1913-1980)

Paine, Thomas, American revolutionary writer (1737-1809)

Parker, Ely, American Indian political leader, Seneca Iroquois (1828-1895)

Parks, Rosa Lee, American civil rights leader (1913-)

Pasteur, Louis, French scientist (1822-1895)

Patton, George Smith, Jr., American general (1885-1945)

Peale, Norman Vincent, American clergyman (1898-1993)

Peary, Robert, American arctic explorer (1856-1920)

Penn, William, English founder of Pennsylvania (1644-1718)

Perot, H. Ross, American businessman (1930-)

Philip, King, Wampanoag Indian chief (?-1676)

Picasso, Pablo, Spanish-born French painter (1881-1973)

Picotte, Susan La Flesche, American Indian doctor, Omaha tribe (1865-1915)

Pierce, Franklin, fourteenth U.S. president (1804-1869)

Pitcher, Molly, American Revolutionary War heroine (1754?-1832)

Pizarro, Francisco, Spanish conquistador who conquered the Incas in Peru (1478?-1541)

Plato, ancient Greek philosopher (427?-347? B.C.)

Pocahontas, Powhatan Indian princess (1595?-1617)

Poe, Edgar Allan, American writer (1809-1849)

Polk, James K., eleventh U.S. president (1795-1849)

Polo, Marco, Italian explorer of the Far East (1254-1324?)

Ponce de León, Juan, Spanish explorer of Florida (1474-1521)

Pontiac, Ottawa Indian chief (1720?-1769)

Post, Wiley, American aviator (1899-1935)

Powell, Colin L., chairman of U.S. Joint Chiefs of Staff (1937-)

Powhatan, Powhatan Indian chief (?-1618)

Presley, Elvis, American singer of rock music (1935-1977)

Priestley, Joseph, English scientist (1733-1804)

Ptolemy, ancient Egyptian astronomer (100?-165? A.D.)

Quayle, J. Danforth, former vice president of U.S. (1947-)

Raleigh, Sir Walter, English explorer (1552?-1618)

Ramses II, ancient Egyptian pharaoh (reigned 1290-1224 B.C.)

Raphael, Italian Renaissance painter (1483-1520)

Reagan, Ronald, fortieth U.S. president (1911-)

Reed, Walter, American army medical officer (1851-1902)

Rembrandt (Rembrandt Harmenszoon van Rijn), Dutch artist (1606-1669)

Remington, Frederic, American artist (1861-1909)

Renoir, Pierre, French painter (1841-1919)

Revere, Paul, American patriot (1735-1818)

Rickenbacker, Eddie, American aviator (1890-1973)

Ride, Sally K., American astronaut (1951-)

Robin Hood, legendary English outlaw (c. 1300)

Robinson, Jackie, American baseball player (1919-1972)

Rockefeller, John D., American businessman and philanthropist (1839-1937)

Rockwell, Norman, American illustrator (1894-1978)

Roentgen, Wilhelm Conrad, German discoverer of X rays (1845-1923)

Rogers, Will, American humorist and author (1879-1935)

Roosevelt, Eleanor, American first lady and humanitarian (1884-1962)

Roosevelt, Franklin D., thirty-second U.S. president (1882-1945)

Roosevelt, Theodore, twenty-sixth U.S. president (1858-1919)

Ross, Betsy, American flagmaker (1752-1836)

Ruth, Babe (George Herman Ruth), American baseball hero (1895-1948)

Sacagawea, Shoshone Indian guide of Lewis & Clark expedition (1787?-1812)

Salk, Jonas, American research scientist who developed the polio vaccine (1914-)

Samoset, Pemaquid Indian, friend of Pilgrims (1590?-1655)

Sandburg, Carl, American poet, historian and author (1878-1967)

Schubert, Franz, Austrian composer (1797-1828)

Schulz, Charles, American cartoonist (1922-)

Schumann, Robert, German composer (1810-1856)

Schwarzkopf, H. Norman, U.S. general during Persian Gulf War (1934-)

Schweitzer, Albert, German missionary (1875-1965)

Sequoyah, Cherokee Indian who invented a system of writing (1760?-1843)

Seward, William H., American political leader and diplomat who purchased Alaska (1801-1872)

Shackleton, Sir Ernest Henry, Irish explorer (1874-1922)

Shakespeare, William, English playwright and poet (1564-1616)

Sinatra, Frank, American singer (1915-)

Sitting Bull, Sioux Indian chief (1834?-1890)

Smith, John, English soldier who helped found Jamestown, Virginia, the first permanent English colony in America (1580?-1631)

Smith, Joseph, American founder of Mormon Church (1805-1844)

Socrates, ancient Greek philosopher (470?-399 B.C.)

Sousa, John Philip, American composer and bandmaster (1854-1932)

Squanto, Patuxet Indian friend of Pilgrims (1585?-1622)

Stalin, Joseph, Soviet dictator (1879-1953)

Stanley, Henry Morton, British explorer of Africa (1841-1904)

Stanton, Elizabeth Cady, American reformer and women's rights leader (1815-1902)

Stowe, Harriet Beecher, American author and abolitionist (1811-1896)

Strauss, Johann, Austrian composer of waltzes (1825-1899)

Strauss, Richard, German composer (1864-1949)

Stravinsky, Igor, Russian composer (1882-1971)

Taft, William H., twenty-seventh U.S. president (1857-1930)

Taylor, Zachary, twelfth U.S. president (1784-1850)

Tchaikovsky, Peter Ilich, Russian composer (1840-1893)

Teasdale, Sara, American poet (1884-1933)

Tecumseh, American Indian leader, Shawnee tribe (1765?-1813)

Temple, Shirley, American child motion-picture star (1928-)

Tennyson, Lord, English poet (1809-1892)

Teresa, Mother, Roman Catholic nun and humanitarian (1910-)

Tereshkova, Valentina, Soviet cosmonaut, first woman in space (1937-)

Thatcher, Margaret, former British prime minister (1925-)

Thoreau, Henry David, American writer (1817-1862)

Thorpe, Jim, American athlete (1887-1953)

Tito, Josip Broz, communist dictator of Yugoslavia (1892-1980)

Trevino, Lee, American golfer (1939-)

Trotsky, Leon, Russian revolutionist (1879-1940)

Truman, Harry S., thirty-third U.S. president (1884-1972)

Truth, Sojourner, American abolitionist (1797?-1883)

Tubman, Harriet, American abolitionist (1820?-1913)

Tutankhamen, ancient Egyptian pharaoh (1347?-1339 B.C.)

Tutu, Desmond, South African civil rights leader & archbishop (1931-)

Twain, Mark, pen name for Samuel Langhorne Clemens, American author (1835-1910)

Tyler, John, tenth U.S. president (1790-1862)

Van Buren, Martin, eighth U.S. president (1782-1862)

Van Gogh, Vincent, Dutch painter (1853-1890)

Vespucci, Amerigo, Italian explorer after whom America was named (1454-1512)

Villa, Pancho, Mexican bandit leader (1877-1923)

Von Braun, Wernher, American rocket engineer (1912-1977)

Wagner, Richard, German composer of operas (1813-1883)

Walesa, Lech, Polish president and labor union leader (1943-)

Washington, Booker T., American educator (1856-1915)

Washington, George, first U.S. president, Revolutionary War general (1732-1799)

Watie, Stand, Confederate army general, Cherokee (1806-1871)

Watt, James, Scottish engineer and inventor (1736-1819)

Webster, Daniel, American statesman and orator (1782-1852)

Webster, Noah, American writer of the dictionary (1758-1843)

Wellington, Duke of, British general who defeated Napoleon (1769-1852)

Westinghouse, George, American inventor and manufacturer (1846-1914)

Westmoreland, William, American general in Vietnam War (1914-)

Wheatley, Phillis, black American poet (1753?-1784)

Whistler, James McNeill, American artist (1834-1903)

Whitman, Walt, American.poet (1819-1892)

Whitney, Eli, American inventor of cotton gin (1765-1825)

Wilkins, Roy, American civil rights leader (1901-1981)

Williams, Daniel Hale, American surgeon (1856-1931)

Williams, Hank, American singer and composer (1923-1953)

Wilson, Woodrow, twenty-eighth U.S. president (1856-1924)

Wonder, Stevie, American composer and musician (1950-)

Wordsworth, William, English poet (1770-1850)

Wright, Frank Lloyd, American architect (1867-1959)

Wright, Orville, American aviation pioneer (1871-1948)

Wright, Wilbur, American aviation pioneer (1867-1912)

Wyeth, Andrew, American painter (1917-)

Yeltsin, Boris N., president of Russia (1931-)

Young, Brigham, American Mormon leader (1801-1877)

Inventions and Discoveries

Inventions start with ideas for doing something better or solving a problem. Some inventions are new combinations or uses of things which already exist. Others are new processes, or ways of doing things. Many are new devices, or things. Inventions often build upon one another as people improve on older ideas. It is difficult to give credit for the invention of the computer to a single person, for example. The first computers were nothing like those of today, which are the result of ideas from hundreds of people.

Some inventions were ahead of their time. Barthélemy Thimonnier invented the first sewing machine in France in the early 1800's, but a group of angry tailors destroyed his shop. They were afraid that the machines would put them out of work. Elias Howe is usually given credit for inventing the sewing machine in 1846, but it wasn't until Isaac Singer's improved machine in 1851 that sewing machines became popular.

Inventors who think they have an idea which could sell may get a **patent** to keep others from copying the idea. Some inventors never patented or sold their good ideas, and so did not receive credit for them. Occasionally, it is the person who sold an idea to the public who is remembered. Johannes Gutenberg is given credit for movable type, although the Chinese invented it almost 400 years earlier. Robert Fulton is often given credit for inventing the steamship, but patents were issued to three others before he launched the first successful steamship on the Mississippi River in 1807.

Discoveries are not inventions. People who discover something find out about it. For example, Sir Isaac Newton discovered gravity, but it existed before he learned about it.

Some Important Discoveries

Discovery	Date	Discoverer	Country
Atomic structure, theory of	1911	Ernest Rutherford	England
Atomic theory, modern	1803	John Dalton	England
Bacteria	1674	Anton van Leeuwenhoek	Netherlands
Blood, circulation of	1628	William Harvey	England
Earth goes around sun	1543	Nicolaus Copernicus	Poland
Electromagnetic induction	1831	Michael Faraday	England
Electron	1897	Sir Joseph J. Thomson	England
Falling bodies, law of	1590	Galileo Galilei	Italy
Gravity	1665	Sir Isaac Newton	England
Heredity, laws of	1865	Gregor Mendel	Austria
Light, speed of	1675	Olaus Roemer	Denmark
Neutron	1932	Sir James Chadwick	England
Ozone	1840	Christian Schönbein	Germany
Penicillin	1928	Sir Alexander Fleming	England
Planetary orbits	1609	Johannes Kepler	Germany
Proton	1902	Wilhelm Wien	Germany
Relativity, theory of ($e=mc^2$)	1905	Albert Einstein	Switzerland
X rays	1895	Wilhelm Roentgen	Germany

Important Inventions

Invention	Date	Inventor	Country
Accordion	1829	Cyrillys Damian	Austria
Adding machine (printing)	1885	William Burroughs	United States
Airplane	1903	Wilbur and Orville Wright	United States
Aluminum manufacture	1886	Charles M. Hall	United States
		Paul L. T. Héroult	France
Anesthetic (on man)	1842	Crawford W. Long	United States
Antiseptic for surgery	1865	Sir Joseph Lister	England
Aspirin	1853	Charles Gerhardt	France
Automobile with gasoline engine	1885	Karl Benz	Germany
Balloon, hot air	1783	Joseph and Jacques Montgolfier	France
Barbed wire, machine for manufacture	1874	Joseph Glidden	United States
Barometer	1643	Evangelista Torricelli	Italy
Basketball	1891	James Naismith	United States
Battery, electric	c.1800	Alessandro Volta	Italy
Bicycle	1790	Comte Mede de Sivrac	France
Braille	1824	Louis Braille	France
Brake, air	1868	George Westinghouse	United States
Camera, hand-held	1888	George Eastman	United States
Cash register	1879	James Ritty	United States
Cereal, Corn Flakes	1894	John Harvey Kellogg	United States
Cereal, Grape Nuts	1897	C. W. Post	United States
Clock, pendulum	1656	Christiaan Huygens	Netherlands
Compass, magnetic	c.1088	Unknown	China, Europe
Computer, analog	1930	Vannevar Bush	United States
Computer, electronic digital	1946	J. Presper Eckert, John Mauchly	United States
Cotton gin	1793	Eli Whitney	United States
Denim jeans	1873	Levi Strauss	United States
Dyes, chemical	1856	William Perkin	England
Dynamite	1867	Alfred Nobel	Sweden
Earmuffs	1873	Chester Greenwood	United States
Electromagnet	1825	William Sturgeon	England
Elevator with brake	1854	Elisha Otis	United States
Engine, diesel	1892	Rudolf Diesel	Germany
Engine, 4-cycle gasoline	1866	Nikolaus Otto, Eugen Langen	Germany
Eyeglasses, bifocal	1784	Benjamin Franklin	United States
Ferris wheel	1893	George W. G. Ferris, Jr.	United States
Food, canned	1810	Nicolas Appert	France
Food, quick frozen	1925	Clarence Birdseye	United States
Frisbee	1948	Walter Frederick Morrison	United States

Invention	Date	Inventor	Country
Geiger counter	1912	Hans Geiger	Germany
Generator, electric	1832	Hippolyte Pixii	France
Glider	1809	Sir George Cayley	England
Gum, chewing	1870	Thomas Adams	United States
Gyroscope	1852	Jean Foucault	France
Helicopter, single rotor	1939	Igor Sikorsky	United States
Jet engine	1930	Frank Whittle	England
Jigsaw puzzles	1767	John Spilsbury	England
Laser	1960	Theodore H. Maiman	United States
Lawn mower	1830	Edwin Budding	England
Life Savers candy	1913	Clarence Crane	United States
Light bulb, incandescent (practical)	1879	Thomas A. Edison	United States
Light, fluorescent	1867	A. E. Becquerel	France
Lightning rod	1752	Benjamin Franklin	United States
Locomotive, steam	1804	Richard Trevithick	England
Loom, power	1785	Edmund Cartwright	England
Machine gun	1862	Richard Jordan Gatling	United States
Match	1816	François Derosne	France
Microscope, compound	1590	Zacharias Janssen	Netherlands
Motion pictures, commercial	1893	Thomas A. Edison	United States
Motor, electric (AC)	1887	Nikola Tesla	United States
Motor, outboard	1905	Cameron B. Waterman	United States
Motorcycle	1885	Gottlieb Daimler	Germany
Nuclear reactor	1942	Enrico Fermi and others	United States
Nylon	1935	Wallace H. Carothers	United States
Paper	105	Ts'ai Lun	China
Parachute	1783	Sebastian Lenormand	France
Pen, ball-point	1888	John H. Loud	United States
Pencil, wooden	1683	J. Pettus	Germany
Phonograph	1877	Thomas A. Edison	United States
Photography, daguerreotype	1837	Louis Daguerre	France
Piano	1709	Bartolommeo Cristofori	Italy
Pin, safety	1849	Walter Hunt	United States
Plastic (celluloid)	1869	John Wesley Hyatt	United States
Potato chips	1853	George Crum	United States
Pressure cooker	1679	Denis Papin	France
Printing, movable type	1045	Bi Sheng	China
Printing, movable type	1456	Johannes Gutenberg	Germany
Propeller, screw (successful)	1836	John Ericsson	Sweden/U.S.
Radio, wireless	1895	Guglielmo Marconi	Italy
Reaper	1834	Cyrus Hall McCormick	United States
Revolver	1835	Samuel Colt	United States

Invention	Date	Inventor	Country
Rocket, modern	1926	Robert Goddard	United States
Roller skate (4-wheeled)	1863	James L. Plimpton	United States
Rubber bands	1821	Thomas Hancock	England
Rubber, vulcanized	1839	Charles Goodyear	United States
Saxophone	1840	Adolphe Sax	Belgium
Scuba gear (aqualung)	1943	Jacques-Yves Cousteau, Émile Gagnan	France
Seed drill	1700	Jethro Tull	England
Seismograph	132	Chang Heng	China
Sewing machine	1846	Elias Howe	United States
Shopping cart	1937	Sylvan N. Goldman	United States
Shuttle, flying	1733	John Kay	England
Spinning jenny	1764	James Hargreaves	England
Spinning mule	1779	Samuel Crompton	England
Spinning wheel	c.500 B.C.	Unknown	India
Steam engine, modern	1769	James Watt	England
Steamship	1783	Claude de Jouffroy d'Abbans	France
Stethoscope	1816	René Laënnec	France
Straws, drinking	1888	Marvin Stone	United States
Submarine	1891	John P. Holland	United States
Synthesizer (successful)	1964	Robert A. Moog	United States
		Donald Buchla	United States
Tape recorder, magnetic	1898	Valdemar Poulsen	Denmark
Telegraph	1837	Samuel F. B. Morse	United States
Telephone	1876	Alexander Graham Bell	United States
Telescope	1608	Hans Lippershey	Netherlands
Television	1925	John Baird	Scotland
Television camera	1927	Philo T. Farnsworth	United States
Thermometer, Celsius scale	1742	Anders Celsius	Sweden
Thermometer, mercury, Fahrenheit scale	1714	Gabriel D. Fahrenheit	Germany
Tire, pneumatic	1845	Robert W. Thomson	Scotland
Toothbrush	1770	William Addis	England
Tractor	1892	John Froehlich	United States
Trampoline, modern	1936	George Nissen	United States
Typewriter	1867	C. Latham Sholes and others	United States
Vaccine, polio	1953	Jonas E. Salk	United States
Vaccine, smallpox	1796	Edward Jenner	United States
Vacuum cleaner, home	1908	James Murray Spangler	United States
Velcro	1956	George de Mestral	Switzerland
Water skis	1922	Ralph Samuelson*	United States
Xerography (copy machine)	1938	Chester F. Carlson	United States
Zipper	1893	Whitcomb Judson	United States

*Patented by Fred Walker

Man-Made Structures

Important Canals

Canal	Location	Length (miles)	Number of Locks	Year Opened
Albert	Belgium	80.8	6	1939
Amsterdam-Rhine	Netherlands	45	4	1952
Chesapeake and Delaware	Maryland–Del.	14	0	1829
Chicago Sanitary and Ship	Illinois	30	1	1900
Houston Ship Channel	Texas	50.6	0	1914
Kiel (Nord-Ostsee)	Germany	61.3	8	1895
New York State Barge System*	New York	524	57	1918
North Sea	Netherlands	15.3	4	1876
Panama	Panama	50.7	12	1914
Sabine-Neches Waterway	Texas	93	0	1916
Saint Lawrence Seaway	N.Y.–Canada	182	7	1959
Soo	Michigan	1.8	4	1855
Suez	Egypt	117.9	0	1869
Welland Ship	Canada	26	8	1932

*The Erie Canal, (83 locks, 363 miles, opened in 1825), is part of the present-day New York State Barge System.

Important Bridges

Bridge	Location	Type	Main Span*	Year Opened
Humber	England	Suspension	4,626	1981
Verrazano-Narrows	New York	Suspension	4,260	1964
Golden Gate	California	Suspension	4,200	1937
Mackinac	Michigan	Suspension	3,800	1957
Minami Bisan-seto	Japan	Suspension	3,609	1988
Second Bosporus	Turkey	Suspension	3,576	1988
First Bosporus	Turkey	Suspension	3,524	1973
George Washington	New York–N.J.	Suspension	3,500	1931
25th of April	Portugal	Suspension	3,323	1966
San Fran.-Oakland Bay	California	Combination	2,310	1936
Quebec	Canada	Cantilever	1,800	1917
Forth	Scotland	Cantilever	1,710	1890
New River Gorge	West Virginia	Steel Arch	1,700	1977
Bayonne	New York–N.J.	Steel Arch	1,675	1931
Osaka Port	Japan	Cantilever	1,673	1974
Sydney Harbour	Australia	Steel Arch	1,650	1932
Commodore John Barry	Penn.–N.J.	Cantilever	1,644	1974
Brooklyn	New York	Suspension	1,595	1883

*In feet.

Important Railroad Tunnels

Tunnel	Location	Length (miles)	Year Opened
Seikan	Japan	33.5	1988
Channel	England–France	30.6	1994
Rogers Pass	Canada	22.0	1989
Ooshimizu	Japan	13.8	1982
Simplon I	Italy–Switzerland	12.3	1906
Simplon II	Italy–Switzerland	12.3	1922
Shin Kanmon	Japan	11.6	1975
Apennine	Italy	11.5	1934
Rokko	Japan	10.1	1972
Furka Base	Switzerland	9.5	1982
St. Gotthard	Switzerland	9.3	1882
Moffat	Colorado, USA	6.2	1928

The **Taj Mahal** is at Agra in northern India. An Indian ruler, Shah Jahan, had it built as a tomb for his wife Mumtaz Mahal, who died in 1629.

Important Motor Vehicle Tunnels

Tunnel	Location	Length (miles)	Year Opened
St. Gotthard	Switzerland	10.1	1980
Arlberg	Austria	8.6	1978
Fréjus	France–Italy	8.0	1980
Mont Blanc	France–Italy	7.3	1965
Gran Sasso	Italy	6.2	1976
Seelisberg	Switzerland	5.8	1980
Ena	Japan	5.3	1976
Rokko II	Japan	4.3	1974
San Bernardino	Switzerland	4.1	1967
Tauern	Austria	4.0	1974
Lincoln	United States	2.5	1937

The **Golden Gate Bridge** (below) is at the entrance to San Francisco Bay in California. It was the longest single span suspension bridge in the world between 1937 and 1964.

The **Arc de Triomphe** (Arch of Triumph) is in Paris, France. Napoleon Bonaparte began building the arc as a monument to his troops in 1806. The names of 386 of his generals are on the inner walls.

Important Dams

Dam	Location	Capacity*	Height (feet)	Year Completed
Afsluitdijk	Netherlands	37,739	62	1932
Aswan, High	Egypt	1,062,347	364	1970
Chicoasén	Mexico	10,145	856	1980
Dworshak	Idaho	26,788	718	1973
Fort Peck	Montana	139,124	249	1937
Glen Canyon	Arizona	209,475	709	1966
Grand Coulee	Washington	74,188	551	1942
Hoover	Arizona–Nevada	219,212	725	1936
Inguri	Rep. of Georgia	6,919	892	1980
New Cornelia Tailings	Arizona	157	98	1973
Nurek	Tajikistan	66,043	984	1980
Oahe Tailings	South Dakota	183,102	246	1960
Oroville	California	27,027	755	1968
Owen Falls	Uganda	16,982,460	102	1954
Rogun	Tajikistan	83,654	1,099	1985
Tarbela	Pakistan	86,107	469	1976

*In millions of gallons.

Tallest Skyscrapers

Skyscraper	Location	Stories	Height
Sears Tower	Chicago	110	1,454 ft.
World Trade Center	New York City	110	1,350 ft.
Empire State Building	New York City	102	1,250 ft.
AMOCO Building	Chicago	80	1,136 ft.
John Hancock Center	Chicago	100	1,127 ft.
Chrysler	New York City	77	1,048 ft.
First Interstate World Center	Los Angeles	73	1,018 ft.
Texas Commerce Tower	Houston	75	1,002 ft.
Bank of China	Hong Kong	73	1,001 ft.
Allied Bank Plaza	Houston	71	992 ft.
First Canadian Place	Toronto, Canada	72	980 ft.
311 South Wacker	Chicago	65	970 ft.
Columbia Seafirst	Seattle	76	954 ft.
AIG Tower	New York City	67	952 ft.
One Liberty Place	Philadelphia	61	945 ft.
40 Wall Tower	New York City	70	927 ft.
NCNB Plaza	Dallas	72	921 ft.

Empire State Building

Major World Religions

Religion is an organized system of beliefs, ceremonies, traditions and values that center on the worship of divine power. The eight major world religions are listed in order of their founding.

Judaism

Abraham founded Judaism in about 1700 B.C. Jews practice **monotheism**, or the worship of one God. The Holy Books are the **Torah**, the first five books of the Bible, and the **Talmud**, a guide to Jewish laws. The Jewish holy day is the **Sabbath**, Saturday, which they believe is the day God rested after creating the universe and the earth. Jewish groups worship in a **synagogue**, and are led by a **rabbi**. About 12,810,000 people are Jews. They live scattered throughout the world, with many in Israel, the United States, and the republics of the former Soviet Union. The Jewish symbol is the **Star of David**.

Hinduism

Hinduism began about 1500 B.C. in India and developed gradually over thousands of years. Hindus are **polytheistic**, which means they worship many gods. All of the gods are considered part of the universal spirit **Brahman**. Hindus believe that a person's soul never dies, and if he lives a good life, he will be **reincarnated**, or reborn, into a higher state of life. This is called **karma**. A person who lives a bad life may be reincarnated into a lower state, perhaps as an animal. Hindus do not kill animals. Reincarnation is thought to continue until a person reaches spiritual perfection. **Gurus** or **yogis** are considered near spiritual perfection and are followed by others. About 689,205,000 people are Hindu, and most live in

India. A symbol is the Sanskrit word **om**, which is used in meditation.

Buddhism

Buddhism was begun in India about 500 B.C. by Siddhartha Gautama, the **Buddha**, or *Enlightened One*. Buddhists believe that life is filled with suffering, and the way to find **nirvana**, or a state of happiness and peace, is to become free from all desires and worldly attachments. Like Hindus, Buddhists believe in reincarnation and karma. Buddha is honored, but is not considered to be God. The book of scriptures is called the **Tripitika** and the spiritual leaders are **monks**. About 311,438,000 Buddhists live mostly in Sri Lanka, Southeast Asia and Japan. A symbol of Buddhism is the **Wheel of Life**, which represents the **Noble Eightfold Path**: right knowledge, right intention, right speech, right conduct, right livelihood, right effort, right mindfulness and right concentration.

Confucianism

Confucianism was begun about 500 B.C. by **Confucius** in China. It does not teach the worship of a God or gods, but rather a way of living. Confucius stressed the importance of self-discipline, duty, moral living and respect for ancestors and authority. He taught that leaders must govern by high moral standards and serve as examples of good living for others to follow. His teachings are recorded in the **Five Classics**

and **Four Books**. For 2000 years, Confucianism was the basis of Chinese thought and government. Chinese communists opposed it until 1977 because they thought it looked too much to the past instead of the future. About 170,236,000 people practice Confucianism, mostly in China and Taiwan.

Taoism

Taoism was begun about 100 B.C. in reaction to Confucianism in China. It is based on the teachings in two books, the **Tao Te Ching** and **Chuang Tzu**. Taoists try to live simple, reflective lives close to nature, and to find their own unique way of being. **Tao** means "way." **Priests** are the spiritual leaders. About 29 million people, mostly in China, are Taoist. The symbol stands for what Taoists consider the two basic forces of the universe, **yin**, or female energy, and **yang**, or male energy. Yin is shown as white and yang as black.

Shintoism

Shintoism developed in Japan from native folk beliefs. Shintos worship spirits and demons they believe to live in animals, plants, mountains, and other parts of nature. The sun goddess is considered the highest god, and until the 1940's, the emperor of Japan was worshipped as a descendent of the sun goddess. About 3,205,000 Shintos live in Japan.

Christianity

Christianity began with **Jesus Christ** in Palestine, present-day Israel. The first Christians were Jews who believed that Jesus was God's promised Messiah, or Savior. Christians believe Christ was God in human form, that He died on the Cross to pay the penalty for human sin, or wrongdoing, and that He rose from the dead three days later. Christianity teaches that those who repent, or feel sorry about and turn away from their sin, and accept Jesus' gift of salvation will have eternal life with God in Heaven after death. Christ told his followers to love God and one another, and to spread His teachings throughout the world. The Orthodox and Roman Catholic churches split in 1054 A.D. In the 1500's, the Reformation led by Martin Luther divided Catholic and Protestant churches. Many Protestant churches now exist, including Congregationalist, Baptist, Episcopal, Lutheran, Methodist and Presbyterian. The book of scriptures is the **Bible**, including the **New Testament**. The spiritual leaders are **priests**, **ministers**, or **preachers** who lead worship on **Sunday**, the anniversary of the Resurrection of Christ. About 1,553,754,000 Christians live throughout the world, mostly in Europe and the Americas.

Islam

Islam was founded in the early 600's by **Mohammed**, who was believed by his followers to be a prophet of **Allah**, or God. Mohammed said he had visions in which he was commanded to preach the message of Allah to the Arabs, who at that time worshipped many gods. He wrote his message in the **Koran**, the Holy Book. Believers pray five times daily facing the Holy City of **Mecca**, give alms to the poor, fast during the daylight hours of the month of **Ramadan**, and make a pilgrimage, or **hajj**, to Mecca during their lifetime. Moslems gather for worship on **Fridays** in **mosques**, and are led by an **imam**. About 924,612,000 Moslems live mostly in the Middle East, North Africa, Bangladesh, Pakistan and Indonesia. Two major Moslem groups are the Shiites and Sunnites. The symbol is a crescent and star.

The United States

States of the Union

Alabama

Capital: Montgomery (187,106)
Governor: Fob James, Jr.
(to Jan. 1999)
Entered Union (rank): Dec. 14, 1819 (22nd)
Motto: *Audemus jura nostra defendere* (We dare maintain our rights)
State Song: "Alabama"
State Flower: Camellia
State Bird: Yellowhammer
State Tree: Southern Longleaf Pine
Nickname: The Heart of Dixie
Origin of Name: May come from Choctaw meaning "thicket-clearers" or "vegetation-gatherers"
Population (rank): 4,040,587 (22nd)
Population Density: 77 per sq. mi.
Per Capita Income: $16,220
Area (rank): 52,423 sq. mi. (30th)
Highest Point: 2,405 feet
Lowest Point: Sea level

Alaska

Capital: Juneau (26,751)
Governor: Tony Knowles
(to Jan. 1999)
Entered Union (rank): Jan. 3, 1959 (49th)
Motto: North to the Future
State Song: "Alaska's Flag"
State Flower: Forget-Me-Not
State Bird: Willow Ptarmigan
State Tree: Sitka Spruce
Nicknames: The Last Frontier, Land of the Midnight Sun
Origin of Name: From Aleut word meaning "great land"
Population (rank): 550,043 (49th)
Population Density: 0.8 per sq. mi.
Per Capita Income: $21,603
Area (rank): 656,424 sq. mi. (1st)
Highest Point: 20,320 feet
Lowest Point: Sea level

Arizona

Capital: Phoenix (983,403)
Governor: J. Fife Symington 3rd
(to Jan. 1999)
Entered Union (rank): Feb. 14, 1912 (48th)
Motto: *Ditat Deus* (God enriches)
State Song: "Arizona"
State Flower: Blossom of the Giant Saguaro Cactus
State Bird: Cactus Wren
State Tree: Palo Verde
Nickname: Grand Canyon State
Origin of Name: From Indian word "Arizonac," meaning "little spring"
Population (rank): 3,665,228 (24th)
Population Density: 32 per sq. mi.
Per Capita Income: $17,119
Area (rank): 114,006 sq. mi. (6th)
Highest Point: 12,633 feet
Lowest Point: 70 feet

Arkansas

Capital: Little Rock (175,795)
Governor: Jim Guy Tucker
(to Jan. 1999)
Entered Union (rank): June 15, 1836 (25th)
Motto: *Regnat Populus* (The people rule)
State Song: "Arkansas"
State Flower: Apple Blossom
State Bird: Mockingbird
State Tree: Pine
Nickname: Land of Opportunity
Origin of Name: From the Quapaw Indians
Population (rank): 2,350,725 (33rd)
Population Density: 44 per sq. mi.
Per Capita Income: $15,439
Area (rank): 53,182 sq. mi. (29th)
Highest Point: 2,753 feet
Lowest Point: 55 feet

California

Capital: Sacramento (369,365)
Governor: Pete Wilson
(to Jan. 1999)
Entered Union (rank): Sept. 9, 1850 (31st)
Motto: *Eureka* (I have found it)
State Song: "I Love You, California"
State Flower: Golden Poppy
State Bird: California Valley Quail
State Tree: California Redwood
Nickname: Golden State
Origin of Name: From a book by Garcia Ordóñez de Montalvo
Population (rank): 29,760,021 (1st)
Population Density: 182 per sq. mi.
Per Capita Income: $21,278
Area (rank): 163,707 sq. mi. (3rd)
Highest Point: 14,494 feet
Lowest Point: –282 feet

Colorado

Capital: Denver (467,610)
Governor: Roy Romer
(to Jan. 1999)
Entered Union (rank): Aug. 1, 1876 (38th)
Motto: *Nil sine Numine* (Nothing without Providence)
State Song: "Where the Columbines Grow"
State Flower: Rocky Mountain Columbine
State Bird: Lark Bunting
State Tree: Colorado Blue Spruce
Nickname: Centennial State
Origin of Name: From Spanish meaning "reddish"
Population (rank): 3,294,394 (26th)
Population Density: 32 per sq. mi.
Per Capita Income: $20,124
Area (rank): 104,100 sq. mi. (8th)
Highest Point: 14,433 feet
Lowest Point: 3,350 feet

Connecticut

Capital: Hartford (139,739)
Governor: John Rowland
(to Jan. 1999)
Entered Union (rank): Jan. 9, 1788 (5th)
Motto: *Qui transtulit sustinet* (He who transplanted still sustains)
State Song: "Yankee Doodle"
State Flower: Mountain Laurel
State Bird: American Robin
State Tree: White Oak

Nickname: Constitution State
Origin of Name: From a Quinnehtukqut Indian word meaning "beside the long tidal river"
Population (rank): 3,287,116 (27th)
Population Density: 593 per sq. mi.
Per Capita Income: $26,979
Area (rank): 5,544 sq. mi. (48th)
Highest Point: 2,380 feet
Lowest Point: Sea level

Delaware

Capital: Dover (27,630)
Governor: Thomas R. Carper (to Jan. 1997)
Entered Union (rank): Dec. 7, 1787 (1st)
Motto: Liberty and Independence
State Song: "Our Delaware"
State Flower: Peach Blossom
State Bird: Blue Hen Chicken
State Tree: American Holly
Nicknames: First State
Origin of Name: From Delaware River and Bay, named after Sir Thomas West, Lord De La Warr
Population (rank): 666,168 (46th)
Population Density: 277 per sq. mi.
Per Capita Income: $21,451
Area (rank): 2,489 sq. mi. (49th)
Highest Point: 442 feet
Lowest Point: Sea level

Florida

Capital: Tallahassee (124,773)
Governor: Lawton Chiles (to Jan. 1999)
Entered Union (rank): March 3, 1845 (27th)
Motto: In God We Trust
State Song: "Swanee River"
State Flower: Orange Blossom
State Bird: Mockingbird
State Tree: Sabal Palm
Nickname: Sunshine State
Origin of Name: From Spanish word meaning "feast of flowers"
Population (rank): 12,937,926 (4th)
Population Density: 197 per sq. mi.
Per Capita Income: $19,397
Area (rank): 65,758 sq. mi. (22nd)
Highest Point: 345 feet
Lowest Point: Sea level

Georgia

Capital: Atlanta (394,017)
Governor: Zell Miller (to Jan. 1999)
Entered Union (rank): Jan. 2, 1788 (4th)
Motto: Wisdom, Justice, and Moderation
State Song: "Georgia On My Mind"
State Flower: Cherokee Rose
State Bird: Brown Thrasher
State Tree: Live Oak
Nicknames: Empire State of the South, Peach State
Origin of Name: In honor of George II of England
Population (rank): 6,478,216 (11th)
Population Density: 109 per sq. mi.
Per Capita Income: $18,130
Area (rank): 59,441 sq. mi. (24th)
Highest Point: 4,784 feet
Lowest Point: Sea level

Hawaii

Capital: Honolulu (365,272)
Governor: Ben Cayetano (to Dec. 1998)
Entered Union (rank): Aug. 21, 1959 (50th)
Motto: *Ua Mau Ke Ea O Ka Aina I Ka Pono* (The life of the land is perpetuated in righteousness)
State Song: "Hawaii Ponoi"
State Flower: Hibiscus
State Bird: Nene (Hawaiian goose)
State Tree: Kukui Tree
Nickname: Aloha State
Origin of Name: Uncertain. Hawaii Loa is the traditional discoverer of the islands.
Population (rank): 1,108,229 (41st)
Population Density: 101 per sq. mi.
Per Capita Income: $21,218
Area (rank): 10,932 sq. mi. (43rd)
Highest Point: 13,796 feet
Lowest Point: Sea level

Idaho

Capital: Boise (125,738)
Governor: Phil Batt (to Jan. 1999)
Entered Union (rank): July 3, 1890 (43rd)
Motto: *Esto perpetua* (Let it be perpetual)
State Song: "Here We Have Idaho"
State Flower: Syringa
State Bird: Mountain Bluebird
State Tree: Western White Pine
Nicknames: Gem State, Spud State, Panhandle State
Origin of Name: Means "Gem of the Mountains"
Population (rank): 1,006,749 (42nd)
Population Density: 12 per sq. mi.
Per Capita Income: $16,067
Area (rank): 83,574 sq. mi. (14th)
Highest Point: 12,662 feet
Lowest Point: 710 feet

Illinois

Capital: Springfield (105,227)
Governor: Jim Edgar (to Jan. 1999)
Entered Union (rank): Dec. 3, 1818 (21st)
Motto: State Sovereignty, National Union
State Song: "Illinois"
State Flower: Native Violet
State Bird: Cardinal
State Tree: White Oak
Nickname: Prairie State
Origin of Name: From Indian and French meaning "tribe of superior men"
Population (rank): 11,430,602 (6th)
Population Density: 197 per sq. mi.
Per Capita Income: $21,608
Area (rank): 57,918 sq. mi. (25th)
Highest Point: 1,235 feet
Lowest Point: 279 feet

Indiana

Capital: Indianapolis (731,327)
Governor: Evan Bayh (to Jan. 1997)
Entered Union (rank): Dec. 11, 1816 (19th)
Motto: Crossroads of America
State Song: "On the Banks of the Wabash, Far Away"
State Flower: Peony
State Bird: Cardinal
State Tree: Tulip Poplar
Nickname: Hoosier State

Origin of Name: Meaning is "land of Indians"
Population (rank): 5,544,159 (14th)
Population Density: 152 per sq. mi.
Per Capita Income: $18,043
Area (rank): 36,420 sq. mi. (38th)
Highest Point: 1,257 feet
Lowest Point: 320 feet

Iowa

Capital: Des Moines (193,187)
Governor: Terry E. Branstad (to Jan. 1999)
Entered Union (rank): Dec. 28, 1846 (29th)
Motto: Our liberties we prize and our rights we will maintain
State Song: "The Song of Iowa"
State Flower: Wild Rose
State Bird: Eastern Goldfinch
State Tree: Oak
Nickname: Hawkeye State
Origin of Name: Probably from an Indian word meaning "this is the place" or "the beautiful land"
Population (rank): 2,776,755 (30th)
Population Density: 49 per sq. mi.
Per Capita Income: $18,287
Area (rank): 56,276 sq. mi. (26th)
Highest Point: 1,670 feet
Lowest Point: 480 feet

Kansas

Capital: Topeka (119,883)
Governor: Bill Graves (to Jan. 1999)
Entered Union (rank): Jan. 29, 1861 (34th)
Motto: *Ad astra per aspera* (To the stars through difficulties)
State Song: "Home on the Range"
State Flower: Wild Sunflower
State Bird: Western Meadowlark
State Tree: Cottonwood
Nicknames: Sunflower State, Jayhawk State
Origin of Name: From Siouan meaning "people of the south wind"
Population (rank): 2,477,574 (32)
Population Density: 30 per sq. mi.
Per Capita Income: $19,376
Area (rank): 82,282 sq. mi. (15th)
Highest Point: 4,039 feet
Lowest Point: 679 feet

Kentucky

Capital: Frankfort (25,968)
Governor: Brereton C. Jones (to Dec. 1995)
Entered Union (rank): June 1, 1792 (15th)
Motto: United we stand, divided we fall
State Song: "My Old Kentucky Home"
State Flower: Goldenrod
State Bird: Kentucky Cardinal
State Tree: Kentucky Coffee Tree
Nickname: Bluegrass State
Origin of Name: From Iroquois word meaning "land of tomorrow"
Population (rank): 3,685,296 (23rd)
Population Density: 91 per sq. mi.
Per Capita Income: $16,534
Area (rank): 40,411 sq. mi. (37th)
Highest Point: 4,139 feet
Lowest Point: 257 feet

Louisiana

Capital: Baton Rouge (219,531)
Governor: Edwin Edwards (to Jan. 1996)
Entered Union (rank): April 30, 1812 (18th)
Motto: Union, Justice, and Confidence
State Song: "Give Me Louisiana" and "You Are My Sunshine"
State Flower: Magnolia
State Bird: Eastern Brown Pelican
State Tree: Bald Cypress
Nicknames: Pelican State, Sportsman's Paradise, Creole State, Sugar State
Origin of Name: In honor of Louis XIV of France
Population (rank): 4,219,973 (21st)
Population Density: 81 per sq. mi.
Per Capita Income: $15,712
Area (rank): 51,843 sq. mi. (31st)
Highest Point: 535 feet
Lowest Point: –8 feet

Maine

Capital: Augusta (21,325)
Governor: Angus King (to Jan. 1999)
Entered Union (rank): March 15, 1820 (23rd)
Motto: *Dirigo* (I direct)
State Song: "State of Maine Song"
State Flower: White Pine Cone and Tassel
State Bird: Chickadee
State Tree: White Pine
Nickname: Pine Tree State
Origin of Name: Name first used to distinguish the mainland from offshore islands
Population (rank): 1,227,928 (38th)
Population Density: 37 per sq. mi.
Per Capita Income: $18,226
Area (rank): 35,387 sq. mi. (39th)
Highest Point: 5,267 feet
Lowest Point: Sea level

Maryland

Capital: Annapolis (33,187)
Governor: Parris Glendening (to Jan. 1999)
Entered Union (rank): April 28, 1788 (7th)
Motto: *Fatti maschii, parole femine* (Manly deeds, womanly words)
State Song: "Maryland! My Maryland!"
State Flower: Black-Eyed Susan
State Bird: Baltimore Oriole
State Tree: White Oak
Nicknames: Old Line State, Free State
Origin of Name: In honor of Henrietta Maria, Queen of England
Population (rank): 4,781,468 (19th)
Population Density: 385 per sq. mi.
Per Capita Income: $22,974
Area (rank): 12,407 sq. mi. (42nd)
Highest Point: 3,360 feet
Lowest Point: Sea level

Massachusetts

Capital: Boston (574,283)
Governor: William F. Weld (to Jan. 1999)
Entered Union (rank): Feb. 6, 1788 (6th)
Motto: *Ense petit placidam sub libertate quietem* (By the sword we seek peace, but peace only under liberty)
State Song: "All Hail to Massachusetts"

State Flower: Mayflower
State Bird: Chickadee
State Tree: American Elm
Nicknames: Bay State, Old Colony State
Origin of Name: From Indian words meaning "great mountain place"
Population (rank): 6,016,425 (13th)
Population Density: 570 per sq. mi.
Per Capita Income: $24,059
Area (rank): 10,555 sq. mi. (44th)
Highest Point: 3,487 feet
Lowest Point: Sea level

Michigan

Capital: Lansing (127,321)
Governor: John Engler (to Jan. 1999)
Entered Union (rank): Jan. 26, 1837 (26th)
Motto: *Si quaeris peninsulam amoenam circumspice* (If you seek a pleasant peninsula, look about you)
State Song: "Michigan, My Michigan"
State Flower: Apple Blossom
State Bird: Robin
State Tree: White Pine
Nickname: Wolverine State, Great Lake State
Origin of Name: From Indian words meaning "great lake"
Population (rank): 9,295,297 (8th)
Population Density: 96 per sq. mi.
Per Capita Income: $19,508
Area (rank): 96,705 sq. mi. (11th)
Highest Point: 1,979 feet
Lowest Point: 571 feet

Minnesota

Capital: Saint Paul (272,235)
Governor: Arne Carlson (to Jan. 1999)
Entered Union (rank): May 11, 1858 (32nd)
Motto: *L'Etoile du Nord* (The Star of the North)
State Song: "Hail! Minnesota"
State Flower: Pink and White Lady's Slipper
State Bird: Common Loon
State Tree: Red Pine

Nicknames: North Star State, Gopher State, Land of 10,000 Lakes
Origin of Name: From Dakota Indian word meaning "sky-tinted water"
Population (rank): 4,375,099 (20th)
Population Density: 50 per sq. mi.
Per Capita Income: $20,049
Area (rank): 86,943 sq. mi. (12th)
Highest Point: 2,301 feet
Lowest Point: 600 feet

Mississippi

Capital: Jackson (196,637)
Governor: Kirk Fordice (to Jan. 1996)
Entered Union (rank): Dec. 10, 1817 (20th)
Motto: *Virtute et armis* (By valor and arms)
State Song: "Go, Mississippi"
State Flower: Magnolia
State Bird: Mockingbird
State Tree: Magnolia
Nickname: Magnolia State
Origin of Name: From Indian word meaning "Father of Waters"
Population (rank): 2,573,216 (31st)
Population Density: 53 per sq. mi.
Per Capita Income: $14,088
Area (rank): 48,434 sq. mi. (32nd)
Highest Point: 806 feet
Lowest Point: Sea level

Missouri

Capital: Jefferson City (35,481)
Governor: Mel Carnahan (to Jan. 1997)
Entered Union (rank): Aug. 10, 1821 (24th)
Motto: *Salus populi suprema lex esto* (The welfare of the people shall be the supreme law)
State Song: "Missouri Waltz"
State Flower: White Hawthorn
State Bird: Bluebird
State Tree: Flowering Dogwood
Nickname: Show-Me State
Origin of Name: Named after Missouri Indian tribe. "Missouri" means "town of the large canoes."
Population (rank): 5,117,073 (15th)

Population Density: 73 per sq. mi.
Per Capita Income: $18,835
Area (rank): 69,709 sq. mi. (21st)
Highest Point: 1,772 feet
Lowest Point: 230 feet

Montana

Capital: Helena (24,569)
Governor: Marc Racicot (to Jan. 1997)
Entered Union (rank): Nov. 8, 1889 (41st)
Motto: *Oro y plata* (Gold and silver)
State Song: "Montana"
State Flower: Bitterroot
State Bird: Western Meadowlark
State Tree: Ponderosa Pine
Nickname: Treasure State
Origin of Name: Chosen from Latin dictionary
Population (rank): 799,065 (44th)
Population Density: 5 per sq. mi.
Per Capita Income: $16,062
Area (rank): 147,046 sq. mi. (4th)
Highest Point: 12,799 feet
Lowest Point: 1,800 feet

Nebraska

Capital: Lincoln (191,972)
Governor: Ben Nelson (to Jan. 1999)
Entered Union (rank): March 1, 1867 (37th)
Motto: Equality before the law
State Song: "Beautiful Nebraska"
State Flower: Goldenrod
State Bird: Western Meadowlark
State Tree: Western Cottonwood
Nicknames: Cornhusker State, Beef State, Tree Planters State
Origin of Name: From Oto Indian language, means "flat water"
Population (rank): 1,578,385 (36th)
Population Density: 20 per sq. mi.
Per Capita Income: $19,084
Area (rank): 77,358 sq. mi. (16th)
Highest Point: 5,424 feet
Lowest Point: 840 feet

Nevada

Capital: Carson City (40,443)
Governor: Robert J. Miller (to Jan. 1999)

Entered Union (rank): Oct. 31, 1864 (36th)
Motto: All for Our Country
State Song: "Home Means Nevada"
State Flower: Sagebrush
State Bird: Mountain Bluebird
State Trees: Bristlecone Pine and Single-Leaf Piñon
Nicknames: Silver State, Sagebrush State, Battle-born State
Origin of Name: Spanish meaning "snowcapped"
Population (rank): 1,201,833 (39th)
Population Density: 11 per sq. mi.
Per Capita Income: $20,266
Area (rank): 110,567 sq. mi. (7th)
Highest Point: 13,140 feet
Lowest Point: 479 feet

New Hampshire

Capital: Concord (36,006)
Governor: Steve Merrill (to Jan. 1997)
Entered Union (rank): June 21, 1788 (9th)
Motto: Live free or die
State Songs: "Old New Hampshire"
State Flower: Purple Lilac
State Bird: Purple Finch
State Tree: White Birch
Nickname: Granite State
Origin of Name: From the English county of Hampshire
Population (rank): 1,109,252 (40th)
Population Density: 119 per sq. mi.
Per Capita Income: $22,934
Area (rank): 9,351 sq. mi. (46th)
Highest Point: 6,288 feet
Lowest Point: Sea level

New Jersey

Capital: Trenton (88,675)
Governor: James Florio (to Jan. 1998)
Entered Union (rank): Dec. 18, 1787 (3rd)
Motto: Liberty and Prosperity
State Song: None
State Flower: Purple Violet
State Bird: Eastern Goldfinch
State Tree: Red Oak
Nickname: Garden State
Origin of Name: From the Channel Isle of Jersey
Population (rank): 7,730,188 (9th)

Population Density: 886 per sq. mi.
Per Capita Income: $26,457
Area (rank): 8,722 sq. mi. (47th)
Highest Point: 1,803 feet
Lowest Point: Sea level

New Mexico

Capital: Santa Fe (55,859)
Governor: Gary Johnson (to Jan. 1999)
Entered Union (rank): Jan. 6, 1912 (47th)
Motto: *Crescit eundo* (It grows as it goes)
State Song: "O Fair New Mexico"
State Flower: Yucca
State Bird: Chaparral Bird (Roadrunner)
State Tree: Piñon
Nicknames: Land of Enchantment, Sunshine State
Origin of Name: From the country of Mexico
Population (rank): 1,515,069 (37th)
Population Density: 12 per sq. mi.
Per Capita Income: $15,353
Area (rank): 121,598 sq. mi. (5th)
Highest Point: 13,161 feet
Lowest Point: 2,842 feet

New York

Capital: Albany (101,082)
Governor: George Pataki (to Jan. 1999)
Entered Union (rank): July 26, 1788 (11th)
Motto: *Excelsior* (Ever upward)
State Song: "I Love New York"
State Flower: Rose
State Bird: Bluebird
State Tree: Sugar Maple
Nickname: Empire State
Origin of Name: In honor of the English Duke of York
Population (rank): 17,990,455 (2nd)
Population Density: 330 per sq. mi.
Per Capita Income: $23,534
Area (rank): 54,556 sq. mi. (27th)
Highest Point: 5,344 feet
Lowest Point: Sea level

North Carolina

Capital: Raleigh (207,951)

Governor: James B. Hunt (to Jan. 1997)
Entered Union (rank): Nov. 21, 1789 (12th)
Motto: *Esse quam videri* (To be rather than to seem)
State Song: "The Old North State"
State Flower: Dogwood
State Bird: Cardinal
State Tree: Pine
Nickname: Tar Heel State, Old North State
Origin of Name: In honor of Charles I of England
Population (rank): 6,628,637 (10th)
Population Density: 123 per sq. mi.
Per Capita Income: $17,667
Area (rank): 53,821 sq. mi. (28th)
Highest Point: 6,684 feet
Lowest Point: Sea level

North Dakota

Capital: Bismarck (49,256)
Governor: Edward Schafer (to Jan. 1997)
Entered Union (rank): Nov. 2, 1889 (39th)
Motto: Liberty and union, now and forever, one and inseparable
State Song: "North Dakota Hymn"
State Flower: Wild Prairie Rose
State Bird: Western Meadowlark
State Tree: American Elm
Nicknames: Peace Garden State, Sioux State, Flickertail State
Origin of Name: From the Dakotah tribe, meaning "allies"
Population (rank): 638,800 (47th)
Population Density: 9 per sq. mi.
Per Capita Income: $16,854
Area (rank): 70,704 sq. mi. (19th)
Highest Point: 3,506 feet
Lowest Point: 750 feet

Ohio

Capital: Columbus (632,910)
Governor: George G. Voinovich (to Jan. 1999)
Entered Union (rank): March 1, 1803 (17th)
Motto: With God, all things are possible
State Song: "Beautiful Ohio"
State Flower: Scarlet Carnation

State Bird: Cardinal
State Tree: Buckeye
Nickname: Buckeye State
Origin of Name: From Iroquois word meaning "great river"
Population (rank): 10,847,115 (7th)
Population Density: 242 per sq. mi.
Per Capita Income: $18,624
Area (rank): 44,828 sq. mi. (34th)
Highest Point: 1,549 feet
Lowest Point: 455 feet

Oklahoma

Capital: Oklahoma City (444,719)
Governor: Frank Keating (to Jan. 1999)
Entered Union (rank): Nov. 16, 1907 (46th)
Motto: *Labor omnia vincit* (Labor conquers all things)
State Song: "Oklahoma"
State Flower: Mistletoe
State Bird: Scissor-Tailed Flycatcher
State Tree: Redbud
Nickname: Sooner State
Origin of Name: From Choctaw Indian words meaning "red people"
Population (rank): 3,145,585 (28th)
Population Density: 45 per sq. mi.
Per Capita Income: $16,198
Area (rank): 69,903 sq. mi. (20th)
Highest Point: 4,973 feet
Lowest Point: 289 feet

Oregon

Capital: Salem (107,786)
Governor: John Kitzhaber (to Jan. 1999)
Entered Union (rank): Feb. 14, 1859 (33rd)
Motto: *Alis volat Propriis* (She flies with her own wings)
State Song: "Oregon, My Oregon"
State Flower: Oregon Grape
State Bird: Western Meadowlark
State Tree: Douglas Fir
Nickname: Beaver State
Origin of Name: Unknown, possibly taken from the writings of Major Robert Rogers, an English army officer
Population (rank): 2,842,321 (29th)

Population Density: 29 per sq. mi.
Per Capita Income: $18,202
Area (rank): 98,386 sq. mi. (9th)
Highest Point: 11,239 feet
Lowest Point: Sea level

Pennsylvania

Capital: Harrisburg (52,376)
Governor: Thomas Ridge (to Jan. 1999)
Entered Union (rank): Dec. 12, 1787 (2nd)
Motto: Virtue, Liberty, and Independence
State Song: None
State Flower: Mountain Laurel
State Bird: Ruffed Grouse
State Tree: Hemlock
Nickname: Keystone State
Origin of Name: In honor of Sir William Penn, William Penn's father. It means "Penn's Woodland."
Population (rank): 11,881,643 (5th)
Population Density: 258 per sq. mi.
Per Capita Income: $20,253
Area (rank): 46,058 sq. mi. (33rd)
Highest Point: 3,213 feet
Lowest Point: Sea level

Rhode Island

Capital: Providence (160,728)
Governor: Lincoln Almond (to Jan. 1997)
Entered Union (rank): May 29, 1790 (13th)
Motto: Hope
State Song: "Rhode Island"
State Flower: Violet
State Bird: Rhode Island Red
State Tree: Red Maple
Nickname: Little Rhody, Ocean State
Origin of Name: From the Greek Island of Rhodes
Population (rank): 1,003,464 (43rd)
Population Density: 649 per sq. mi.
Per Capita Income: $20,299
Area (rank): 1,545 sq. mi. (50th)
Highest Point: 812 feet
Lowest Point: Sea level

South Carolina

Capital: Columbia (98,052)

Governor: David Beasley (to Jan. 1999)
Entered Union (rank): May 23, 1788 (8th)
Mottos: *Animis opibusque parati* (Prepared in mind and resources) and *Dum spiro spero* (While I breathe, I hope)
State Songs: "Carolina" and "South Carolina on My Mind"
State Flower: Yellow Jessamine
State Bird: Carolina Wren
State Tree: Palmetto Tree
Nickname: Palmetto State
Origin of Name: In honor of Charles I of England
Population (rank): 3,486,703 (25th)
Population Density: 109 per sq. mi.
Per Capita Income: $15,989
Area (rank): 32,008 sq. mi. (40th)
Highest Point: 3,560 feet
Lowest Point: Sea level

South Dakota

Capital: Pierre (12,906)
Governor: William Janklow (to Jan. 1999)
Entered Union (rank): Nov. 2, 1889 (40th)
Motto: Under God the People Rule
State Song: "Hail! South Dakota"
State Flower: American Pasque Flower
State Bird: Ring-Necked Pheasant
State Tree: Black Hills Spruce
Nicknames: Coyote State, Sunshine State
Origin of Name: From the Dakotah tribe, meaning "allies"
Population (rank): 696,004 (45th)
Population Density: 9 per sq. mi.
Per Capita Income: $16,558
Area (rank): 77,121 sq. mi. (17th)
Highest Point: 7,242 feet
Lowest Point: 966 feet

Tennessee

Capital: Nashville (488,374)
Governor: Don Sundquist (to Jan. 1999)
Entered Union (rank): June 1, 1796 (16th)
Motto: Agriculture and Commerce
State Song: "Tennessee Waltz"

State Flower: Iris
State Bird: Mockingbird
State Tree: Tulip Poplar
Nickname: Volunteer State
Origin of Name: From Cherokee, meaning is not known
Population (rank): 4,877,185 (17th)
Population Density: 116 per sq. mi.
Per Capita Income: $17,341
Area (rank): 42,146 sq. mi. (36th)
Highest Point: 6,643 feet
Lowest Point: 178 feet

Texas

Capital: Austin (465,622)
Governor: George W. Bush (to Jan. 1999)
Entered Union (rank): Dec. 29, 1845 (28th)
Motto: Friendship
State Song: "Texas, Our Texas"
State Flower: Bluebonnet
State Bird: Mockingbird
State Tree: Pecan
Nickname: Lone Star State
Origin of Name: From an Indian word meaning "friends"
Population (rank): 16,986,510 (3rd)
Population Density: 63 per sq. mi.
Per Capita Income: $17,892
Area (rank): 268,601 sq. mi. (2nd)
Highest Point: 8,749 feet
Lowest Point: Sea level

Utah

Capital: Salt Lake City (159,936)
Governor: Mike Leavitt (to Jan. 1997)
Entered Union (rank): Jan. 4, 1896 (45th)
Motto: Industry
State Song: "Utah, We Love Thee"
State Flower: Sego Lily
State Bird: Seagull
State Tree: Blue Spruce
Nickname: Beehive State
Origin of Name: From Ute, meaning "people of the mountains"
Population (rank): 1,722,850 (35th)
Population Density: 20 per sq. mi.
Per Capita Income: $15,325
Area (rank): 84,904 sq. mi. (13th)
Highest Point: 13,528 feet
Lowest Point: 2,000 feet

Vermont

Capital: Montpelier (8,247)
Governor: Howard Dean (to Jan. 1997)
Entered Union (rank): March 4, 1791 (14th)
Motto: Freedom and Unity
State Song: "Hail, Vermont!"
State Flower: Red Clover
State Bird: Hermit Thrush
State Tree: Sugar Maple
Nickname: Green Mountain State
Origin of Name: From French "vert mont," meaning "green mountain"
Population (rank): 562,758 (48th)
Population Density: 59 per sq. mi.
Per Capita Income: $18,834
Area (rank): 9,615 sq. mi. (45th)
Highest Point: 4,393 feet
Lowest Point: 95 feet

Virginia

Capital: Richmond (203,056)
Governor: Douglas Wilder (to Jan. 1998)
Entered Union (rank): June 25, 1788 (10th)
Motto: *Sic semper tyrannis* (Thus always to tyrants)
State Song: "Carry Me Back to Old Virginia"
State Flower: American Dogwood
State Bird: Cardinal
State Tree: Flowering Dogwood
Nicknames: The Old Dominion, Mother of Presidents
Origin of Name: In honor of Elizabeth "Virgin Queen" of England
Population (rank): 6,187,358 (12th)
Population Density: 145 per sq. mi.
Per Capita Income: $20,629
Area (rank): 42,769 sq. mi. (35th)
Highest Point: 5,729 feet
Lowest Point: Sea level

Washington

Capital: Olympia (33,840)
Governor: Mike Lowry (to Jan. 1997)
Entered Union (rank): Nov. 11, 1889 (42nd)
Motto: *Alki* (Chinook Indian word meaning "by and by")

State Song: "Washington, My Home"
State Flower: Coast Rhododendron
State Bird: Willow Goldfinch
State Tree: Western Hemlock
Nicknames: Evergreen State, Chinook State
Origin of Name: In honor of George Washington
Population (rank): 4,866,692 (18th)
Population Density: 68 per sq. mi.
Per Capita Income: $20,398
Area (rank): 71,302 sq. mi. (18th)
Highest Point: 14,410 feet
Lowest Point: Sea level

West Virginia

Capital: Charleston (57,287)
Governor: Gaston Caperton (to Jan. 1997)
Entered Union (rank): June 20, 1863 (35th)
Motto: *Montani semper liberi* (Mountaineers are always free)
State Songs: "West Virginia, My Home Sweet Home," "The West Virginia Hills," and "This Is My West Virginia"
State Flower: Big Rhododendron
State Bird: Cardinal
State Tree: Sugar Maple
Nickname: Mountain State
Origin of Name: In honor of Elizabeth "Virgin Queen" of England
Population (rank): 1,793,477 (34th)
Population Density: 74 per sq. mi.
Per Capita Income: $15,065
Area (rank): 24,231 sq. mi. (41st)
Highest Point: 4,861 feet
Lowest Point: 240 feet

Wisconsin

Capital: Madison (191,262)
Governor: Tommy G. Thompson (to Jan. 1999)
Entered Union (rank): May 29, 1848 (30th)
Motto: Forward
State Song: "On, Wisconsin!"
State Flower: Wood Violet
State Bird: Robin
State Tree: Sugar Maple
Nickname: Badger State

Origin of Name: French version of Indian word, uncertain meaning
Population (rank): 4,891,769 (16th)
Population Density: 75 per sq. mi.
Per Capita Income: $18,727
Area (rank): 65,499 sq. mi. (23rd)
Highest Point: 1,951 feet
Lowest Point: 579 feet

Wyoming

Capital: Cheyenne (50,008)
Governor: Jim Geringer (to Jan. 1999)
Entered Union (rank): July 10, 1890 (44th)
Motto: Equal rights
State Song: "Wyoming"
State Flower: Indian Paintbrush
State Bird: Western Meadowlark
State Tree: Cottonwood
Nickname: Equality State, Cowboy State
Origin of Name: From Delaware Indian word meaning "mountains and valleys alternating"
Population (rank): 453,588 (50th)
Population Density: 5 per sq. mi.
Per Capita Income: $17,423
Area (rank): 97,818 sq. mi. (10th)
Highest Point: 13,804 feet
Lowest Point: 3,099 feet

Confederate States of America

These states seceded from the United States during the Civil War of 1861–1865.
1. South Carolina
2. Mississippi
3. Florida
4. Alabama
5. Georgia
6. Louisiana
7. Texas
8. Virginia
9. Arkansas
10. North Carolina
11. Tennessee

Chart of States and Their Abbreviations

P.O. means Post Office abbreviation. Trad. means traditional abbreviation.

State	P.O.	Trad.	State	P.O.	Trad.
Alabama	AL	Ala.	New Mexico	NM	N.M.
Alaska	AK	Alas.	New York	NY	N.Y.
Arizona	AZ	Ariz.	North Carolina	NC	N.C.
Arkansas	AR	Ark.	North Dakota	ND	N. Dak.
California	CA	Calif.	Ohio	OH	O.
Colorado	CO	Colo.	Oklahoma	OK	Okla.
Connecticut	CT	Conn.	Oregon	OR	Oreg.
Delaware	DE	Del.	Pennsylvania	PA	Penn.
Florida	FL	Fla.	Rhode Island	RI	R.I.
Georgia	GA	Ga.	South Carolina	SC	S.C.
Hawaii	HI		South Dakota	SD	S. Dak.
Idaho	ID	Ida.	Tennessee	TN	Tenn.
Illinois	IL	Ill.	Texas	TX	Tex.
Indiana	IN	Ind.	Utah	UT	Ut.
Iowa	IA	Ia.	Vermont	VT	Vt.
Kansas	KS	Kan.	Virginia	VA	Va.
Kentucky	KY	Ky.	Washington	WA	Wash.
Louisiana	LA	La.	West Virginia	WV	W. Va.
Maine	ME	Me.	Wisconsin	WI	Wisc.
Maryland	MD	Md.	Wyoming	WY	Wyo.
Massachusetts	MA	Mass.			
Michigan	MI	Mich.			
Minnesota	MN	Minn.	***Districts and Territories***		
Mississippi	MS	Miss.			
Missouri	MO	Mo.	Canal Zone	CZ	
Montana	MT	Mont.	District of		
Nebraska	NE	Neb.	Columbia	DC	D.C.
Nevada	NV	Nev.	Guam	GU	
New Hampshire	NH	N.H.	Puerto Rico	PR	
New Jersey	NJ	N.J.	Virgin Islands	VI	

Largest state: Alaska
Smallest state: Rhode Island
Largest population: California
Smallest population: Wyoming

Northernmost point in U.S.: Point Barrow, Alaska— 71°23'N, 156°29'W
Easternmost point: West Quoddy Head, Maine— 44°49'N, 66°57'W
Southernmost point: Ka Lae (South Cape), Hawaii— 18°55'N, 155°41'W
Westernmost point: Pochnoi Point, Alaska—51°17'N, 172°09'E

State Information

Students may contact the following agencies to request information. Allow 4–6 weeks.

Alabama Bureau of Tourism, 401 Adams Avenue, P.O. Box 4309, Montgomery, AL 36103	1-800-ALABAMA
Alaska Division of Tourism, P.O. Box 110801, Juneau, AK 99811-0801	1-907-465-2010
Arizona Office of Tourism, 1100 West Washington, Phoenix, AZ 85007	1-800-842-8257
Arkansas Tourism Division, #1 Capitol Mall, Little Rock, AR 72201	1-800-NATURAL
California Office of Tourism, 801 K Street, Suite 1600, Sacramento, CA 95814-3908	1-800-862-2543
Connecticut Tourism Division, 865 Brook Street, Rocky Hill, CT 06067	1-800-CT BOUND
Delaware State Travel Service, P.O. Box 1401, 99 Kings Highway, Dover, DE 19903	1-800-441-8846
District of Columbia. Washington Visitor's & Convention Assn., 1212 New York Avenue NW, 6th Floor, Washington, DC 20005	1-202-789-7000
Florida Division of Tourism, 126 West Van Buren Street, Tallahassee, FL 32399-2000	1-904-487-1462
Georgia Tourist Division, P.O. Box 1776, Atlanta, GA 30301	1-800-VISIT GA
Hawaii Division of Tourism, 220 S. King Street, 11th Floor, Honolulu, HI 96813	1-808-586-2550
Idaho Department of Commerce, 700 West State Street, Boise, ID 83720-2700	1-800-635-7820
Central **Illinois** Tourism Council, 629 E. Washington, Springfield, IL 62701	1-800-262-2482
Indiana Tourism Development, 1 North Capitol, Indianapolis, IN 46204	1-800-289-6646
Iowa Department of Tourism, 200 E. Grand, Des Moines, IA 50309	1-800-345-IOWA
Kansas Division of Travel & Tourism, 700 SW Harrison, Suite 1300, Topeka, KS 66603-3712	1-800-2KANSAS
Kentucky Dept. of Travel Development, 2200 Capital Plaza Tower, Frankfort, KY 40601	1-800-225-TRIP
Louisiana Office of Tourism, P.O. Box 94291, Baton Rouge, LA 70804-9291	1-800-33-GUMBO
Maine Publicity Bureau, P.O. Box 2300, Hallowell, ME 04347	1-800-533-9595
Maryland Office of Tourism, 217 E. Redwood Street, 9th Floor, Baltimore, MD 21202	1-800-445-4558
Massachusetts Division of Tourism, 100 Cambridge St., 13th Floor, Boston, MA 02202	1-617-727-3201
Michigan Travel Bureau, P.O. Box 3393, Lavonia, MI 48151	1-800-543-2937
Minnesota Office of Tourism, 100 Metro Square Bldg., 121–7th Place East, St. Paul, MN 55101	1-800-657-3700
Mississippi Division of Tourism, P.O. Box 849, Jackson, MS 39205-0849	1-800-927-6378
Missouri Division of Tourism, P.O. Box 1055, Jefferson City, MO 65101	1-800-877-1234
Montana Promotion Bureau, 1424 Ninth Avenue, Helena, MT 59620	1-800-541-1447
Nebraska Division of Travel & Tourism, P.O. Box 94666, Lincoln, NE 68509-4666	1-800-228-4307
Nevada Commission on Tourism, Capitol Complex, Carson City, NV 89710	1-800-638-2328
New Hampshire Vacation Travel Promotion Office, P.O. Box 1856, Concord, NH 03302-1856	1-800-FUN IN NH
New Jersey Division of Travel & Tourism, 20 West State Street, CN 826, Trenton, NJ 08625	1-800-JERSEY-7
New Mexico Tourism & Travel Division, 495 Old Santa Fe Trail, Santa Fe, NM 87503	1-800-545-2040
New York Division of Tourism, 1 Commerce Plaza, Albany, NY 12245	1-800-CALL NYS
North Carolina Travel and Tourism, 430 North Salisbury Street, Raleigh, NC 27611	1-800-VISIT NC
North Dakota Tourism Division, 604 East Boulevard, Bismarck, ND 58505	1-800-437-2077
Ohio Office of Travel & Tourism, 30 E. Broad Street, 14th Floor, Columbus, OH 43266	1-800-BUCKEYE
Oklahoma State Dept. of Tourism, Literature Dist., P.O. Box 60789, Oklahoma City, OK 73146	1-800-652-6552
Oregon Division of Tourism, 775 Summer Street NE, Salem, OR 97310	1-800-547-7842
Pennsylvania Department of Commerce, 453 Forum Building, Harrisburg, PA 17120	1-800-VISIT PA
Rhode Island Division of Tourism, 7 Jackson Walkway, Providence, RI 02903	1-800-556-2484
South Carolina Division of Tourism, 1205 Pendleton Street, Suite 106, Columbia, SC 29201	1-800-346-3634
South Dakota Department of Tourism, Capitol Lake Plaza, Pierre, SD 57501	1-800-732-5682
Tennessee Education Department, Tennessee Tower, 8th Avenue North, Nashville, TN 37243	1-615-741-7010
Texas Dept. of Travel and Information, P.O. Box 5064, Austin, TX 78763	1-800-888-8839
Utah Travel Council, Council Hall & Capitol Hill, Salt Lake City, UT 84114	1-800-UTAH FUN
Vermont Travel Division, 134 State Street, Montpelier, VT 05601-1471	1-800-VERMONT
Virginia Tourism Development Group, 901 E. Byrd Street, Richmond, VA 23219	1-800-VISIT VA
Washington Tourism Division, 101 GA Building, P.O. Box 42500, Olympia, WA 98504-2500	1-800-544-1800
West Virginia Tourism, State Capitol Complex, Bldg. 6, Room B-564, Charleston, WV 25305	1-800-CALL WVA
Wisconsin Division of Tourism Development, P.O. Box 7970, Madison, WI 53707	1-800-372-2737
Wyoming Division of Tourism, I-25 at College Drive, Cheyenne, WY 82002	1-800-CALL WYO

Note: Colorado does not have a state tourism office.

Largest Cities of the United States

Albuquerque
State: New Mexico
Population (rank): 384,736 (38)
Area: 132.2 sq. mi.
Altitude: 4,958 feet
Latitude: 35°05' N
Longitude: 106°40' W

Atlanta
State: Georgia
Population (rank): 394,017 (36)
Area: 131.8 sq. mi.
Altitude: 940 to 1,050 feet
Latitude: 33°45' N
Longitude: 84°23' W

Austin
State: Texas
Population (rank): 465,622 (27)
Area: 217.8 sq. mi.
Altitude: 425 to 1000 feet
Latitude: 30°16' N
Longitude: 97°45' W

Baltimore
State: Maryland
Population (rank): 736,014 (12)
Area: 80.8 sq. mi.
Altitude: Sea level to 490 feet
Latitude: 39°17' N
Longitude: 76°37' W

Boston
State: Massachusetts
Population (rank): 574,283 (20)
Area: 48.4 sq. mi.
Altitude: Sea level to 330 feet
Latitude: 42°21' N
Longitude: 71°04' W

Buffalo
State: New York
Population (rank): 328,123 (50)
Area: 40.6 sq. mi.
Altitude: 572 to 705 feet
Latitude: 42°54' N
Longitude: 78°53' W

Charlotte
State: North Carolina
Population (rank): 395,934 (35)
Area: 174.3 sq. mi.
Altitude: 765 feet
Latitude: 35°14' N
Longitude: 80°50' W

Chicago
State: Illinois
Population (rank): 2,783,726 (3)
Area: 227.2 sq. mi.
Altitude: 579 to 672 feet
Latitude: 41°53' N
Longitude: 87°38' W

Cincinnati
State: Ohio
Population (rank): 364,040 (45)
Area: 77.2 sq. mi.
Altitude: 441 to 960 feet
Latitude: 39°06' N
Longitude: 84°31' W

Cleveland
State: Ohio
Population (rank): 505,616 (23)
Area: 77 sq. mi
Altitude: 573 to 1048 feet
Latitude: 41°30' N
Longitude: 81°41' W

Columbus
State: Ohio
Population (rank): 632,910 (16)
Area: 190.9 sq. mi.
Altitude: 702 to 902 feet
Latitude: 39°57' N
Longitude: 83°00' W

Dallas
State: Texas
Population (rank): 1,006,877 (8)
Area: 342.4 sq. mi.
Altitude: 375 to 750 feet
Latitude: 32°47' N
Longitude: 96°48' W

Denver
State: Colorado
Population (rank): 467,610 (26)
Area: 153.3 sq. mi.
Altitude: 5,130 to 5,470 feet
Latitude: 39°43' N
Longitude: 105°01' W

Detroit
State: Michigan
Population (rank): 1,027,974 (7)
Area: 138.7 sq. mi.
Altitude: 574 to 685 feet
Latitude: 42°20' N
Longitude: 83°03' W

El Paso
State: Texas
Population (rank): 515,342 (22)
Area: 245.4 sq. mi.
Altitude: 4,000 feet
Latitude: 31°45' N
Longitude: 106°29' W

Fort Worth
State: Texas
Population (rank): 447,619 (28)
Area: 281.1 sq. mi.
Altitude: 520 to 780 feet
Latitude: 32°45' N
Longitude: 97°20' W

Fresno
State: California
Population (rank): 354,202 (47)
Area: 99.1 sq. mi.
Altitude: 322 feet
Latitude: 36°45' N
Longitude: 119°45' W

Honolulu
State: Hawaii
Population (rank): 365,272 (44)
Area: 82.8 sq. mi.
Altitude: Sea level to 4,025 feet
Latitude: 21°19' N
Longitude: 157°52' W

Houston
State: Texas
Population (rank): 1,630,553 (4)
Area: 539.9 sq. mi.
Altitude: Sea level to 120 feet
Latitude: 29°46' N
Longitude: 95°22' W

Indianapolis
State: Indiana
Population (rank): 731,327 (13)
Area: 361.7 sq. mi.
Altitude: 700 to 840 feet
Latitude: 39°46' N
Longitude: 86°09' W

Jacksonville
State: Florida
Population (rank): 635,230 (15)
Area: 758.7 sq. mi.
Altitude: Sea level to 71 feet
Latitude: 30°20' N
Longitude: 81°40' W

Kansas City
State: Missouri
Population (rank): 435,146 (31)
Area: 311.5 sq. mi.
Altitude: 722 to 1,014 feet
Latitude: 39°05' N
Longitude: 94°35' W

Long Beach
State: California
Population (rank): 429,433 (32)
Area: 50 sq. mi.
Altitude: Sea level to 170 feet
Latitude: 33°46' N
Longitude: 118°11' W

Los Angeles
State: California
Population (rank): 3,485,398 (2)
Area: 469.3 sq. mi.
Altitude: Sea level to 5,081 feet
Latitude: 34°03' N
Longitude: 118°15' W

Memphis
State: Tennessee
Population (rank): 610,337 (18)
Area: 256 sq. mi.
Altitude: 331 feet
Latitude: 35°08' N
Longitude: 90°03' W

Miami
State: Florida
Population (rank): 358,548 (46)
Area: 35.6 sq. mi.
Altitude: 12 feet
Latitude: 25°46' N
Longitude: 80°12' W

Milwaukee
State: Wisconsin
Population (rank): 628,088 (17)
Area: 96.1 sq. mi.
Altitude: 581 feet
Latitude: 43°02' N
Lngitude: 87°54' W

Minneapolis
State: Minnesota
Population (rank): 368,383 (42)
Area: 54.9 sq. mi.
Altitude: 695 to 945 feet
Latitude: 44°59' N
Longitude: 93°13' W

Nashville–Davidson
State: Tennessee
Population (rank): 488,374 (25)
Area: 473.3 sq. mi.
Altitude: 400 to 1,100 feet
Latitude: 36°09' N
Longitude: 86°48' W

New Orleans
State: Louisiana
Population (rank): 496,938 (24)
Area: 180.6 sq. mi.
Altitude: −4 to 15 feet
Latitude: 29°58' N
Longitude: 90°07' W

New York
State: New York
Population (rank): 7,322,564 (1)
Area: 308.9 sq. mi.
Altitude: Sea level to 410 feet
Latitude: 40°43' N
Longitude: 74°01' W

Oakland
State: California
Population (rank): 372,242 (39)
Area: 56.1 sq. mi.
Altitude: Sea level to 1,700 feet
Latitude: 37°47' N
Longitude: 122°13' W

Oklahoma City
State: Oklahoma
Population (rank): 444,719 (29)
Area: 608.2 sq. mi.
Altitude: 1,140 to 1,320 feet
Latitude: 35°28' N
Longitude: 97°32' W

Omaha
State: Nebraska
Population (rank): 335,795 (48)
Area: 100.7 sq. mi.
Altitude: 1,270 feet
Latitude: 41°16' N
Longitude: 95°57' W

Philadelphia
State: Pennsylvania
Population (rank): 1,585,577 (5)
Area: 135.1 sq. mi.
Altitude: Sea level to 440 feet
Latitude: 39°57' N
Longitude: 75°07' W

Phoenix
State: Arizona
Population (rank): 983,403 (9)
Area: 419.9 sq. mi.
Altitude: 1,017 to 2,740 feet
Latitude: 33°27' N
Longitude: 112°05' W

Pittsburgh
State: Pennsylvania
Population (rank): 369,879 (40)
Area: 55.6 sq. mi.
Altitude: 715 to 1,240 feet
Latitude: 40°26' N
Longitude: 80°00' W

Portland
State: Oregon
Population (rank): 437,319 (30)
Area: 124.7 sq. mi.
Altitude: Sea level to 1,073 feet
Latitude: 45°33' N
Longitude: 122°36' W

Sacramento
State: California
Population (rank): 369,365 (41)
Area: 96.3 sq. mi.
Altitude: 22 feet
Latitude: 38°35' N
Longitude: 121°30' W

St. Louis
State: Missouri
Population (rank): 396,685 (34)
Area: 61.9 sq. mi.
Altitude: 413 to 616 feet
Latitude: 38°38' N
Longitude: 90°11' W

San Antonio
State: Texas
Population (rank): 935,933 (10)
Area: 333 sq. mi.
Altitude: 700 feet
Latitude: 29°28' N
Longitude: 98°31' W

San Diego
State: California
Population (rank): 1,110,549 (6)
Area: 324 sq. mi.
Altitude: Sea level to 1,591 feet
Latitude: 32°43' N
Longitude: 117°09' W

San Francisco
State: California
Population (rank): 723,959 (14)
Area: 46.7 sq. mi.
Altitude: Sea level to 925 feet

Latitude: 37°48' N
Longitude: 122°24' W

San Jose
State: California
Population (rank): 782,248 (11)
Area: 171.3 sq. mi.
Altitude: Sea level to 4,372 feet
Latitude: 37°20' N
Longitude: 121°53' W

Seattle
State: Washington
Population (rank): 516,259 (21)
Area: 83.9 sq. mi.
Altitude: Sea level to 540 feet
Latitude: 47°36' N
Longitude: 122°20' W

Toledo
State: Ohio
Population (rank): 332,943 (49)
Area: 80.6 sq. mi.
Altitude: 630 feet
Latitude: 41°39' N
Longitude: 83°32' W

Tucson
State: Arizona

Population (rank): 405,390 (33)
Area: 156.3 sq. mi.
Altitude: 2,500 feet
Latitude: 32°13' N
Longitude: 110°58' W

Tulsa
State: Oklahoma
Population (rank): 367,302 (43)
Area: 183.5 sq. mi.
Altitude: 674 feet
Latitude: 36°09' N
Longitude: 95°58' W

Virginia Beach
State: Virginia
Population (rank): 393,069 (37)
Area: 248.3 sq. mi.
Altitude: 12 feet
Latitude: 36°51' N
Longitude: 75°59' W

Washington, D.C.
State: District of Columbia
Population (rank): 606,900 (19)
Area: 61.4 sq. mi.
Altitude: Sea level to 420 feet
Latitude: 38°54' N
Longitude: 77°01' W

Largest Urban Areas of the World*

Tokyo–Yokohama, Japan
Population (rank): 28,447,000 (1)
Location: 35°40' N, 139°46' E

Mexico City, Mexico
Population (rank): 23,813,000 (2)
Location: 19°24' N, 99°09' W

São Paulo, Brazil
Population (rank): 21,539,000 (3)
Location: 23°32' S, 46°37' W

Seoul, South Korea
Population (rank): 19,065,000 (4)
Location: 37°34' N, 127°00' E

New York City, United States
Population (rank): 14,638,000 (5)
Location: 40°43' N, 74°01' W

Osaka–Kobe–Kyoto, Japan
Population (rank): 14,060,000 (6)
Location: 34°40' N, 135°30' E

Bombay, India
Population (rank): 13,532,000 (7)
Location: 18°58' N, 72°50' E

Calcutta, India
Population (rank): 12,885,000 (8)
Location: 22°30' N, 88°22' E

Rio de Janeiro, Brazil
Population (rank): 12,786,000 (9)
Location: 22°54' S, 43°15' W

Buenos Aires, Argentina
Population (rank): 12,232,000 (10)
Location: 34°36' S, 58°27' W

Manila, Philippines
Population (rank): 11,342,000 (11)
Location: 14°35' N, 121°00' E

Moscow, Russia
Population (rank): 10,769,000 (12)
Location: 55°45' N, 37°35' E

Cairo, Egypt
Population (rank): 11,155,000 (13)
Location: 30°03' N, 31°15' E

Jakarta, Indonesia
Population (rank): 11,151,000 (14)
Location: 6°10' S, 106°46' E

Teheran, Iran
Population (rank): 11,681,000 (15)
Location: 35°40' N, 51°26' E

*Metropolitan areas. A definition of "urban area" appears on page 231.

National Parks

On March 1, 1872, the United States Congress established Yellowstone National Park "as a public park or pleasuring ground for the benefit and enjoyment of the people." This began a worldwide national park movement. Today, more than 100 nations of the world have some 1,200 national parks or preserves. The United States contains 51 national parks, as well as many national monuments, preserves, lakeshores, scenic trails and historic sites.

National Park	Date Established and Acreage	Outstanding Features
Acadia National Park P.O. Box 177 Bar Harbor, Maine 04609	February 26, 1919 41,818.99 acres	Rugged coastal area, highest land on the eastern seaboard.
Arches National Park P.O. Box 907 Moab, Utah 84532	November 12, 1971 73,378.98 acres	Giant eroded arches, windows, and towers.
Badlands National Park P.O. Box 6 Interior, South Dakota 57750	November 10, 1978 242,755.94 acres	Eroded landscape, animal fossils 40 million years old.
Big Bend National Park Texas 79834	June 20, 1935 801,163.21 acres	The big bend of the Rio Grande River, mountains and desert.
Biscayne National Park P.O. Box 1369 Homestead, Florida 33090	June 28, 1980 172,924.07 acres	Coral reef and islands.
Bryce Canyon National Park Bryce Canyon, Utah 84717	June 7, 1924 35,835.08 acres	Some of the most colorful and unusual eroded forms in the world.
Canyonlands National Park 125 West 200 South Moab, Utah 84532	September 12, 1964 337,570.43 acres	Geological wonderland of rocks, spires and mesas.
Capitol Reef National Park HC 70, Box 15 Torrey, Utah 84775	December 18, 1971 241,904.26 acres	Narrow high-walled gorges, white dome-shaped rock.
Carlsbad Caverns National Park 3225 National Parks Highway Carlsbad, New Mexico 88220	May 14, 1930 46,766.45 acres	Large underground caverns with magnificent limestone formations.
Channel Islands National Park 1901 Spinnaker Drive Ventura, California 93001	March 5, 1980 249,353.77 acres	Five islands with nesting sea birds, sea lion rookeries and unique plants.
Crater Lake National Park P.O. Box 7 Crater Lake, Oregon 97604	May 22, 1902 183,224.05 acres	Deep lake in ancient volcano crater. Colorful lava walls 500–2,000 feet above water.
Denali National Park P.O. Box 9 McKinley Park, Alaska 99755	February 26, 1917 4,741,910 acres	Mt. McKinley, North America's highest mountain (20,320 feet), large glaciers, wildlife.

National Park	*Date Established and Acreage*	*Outstanding Features*
Dry Tortugas National Park c/o Everglades National Park P.O. Box 279 Homestead, Florida 33030	October 26, 1992 64,700 acres	Fort Jefferson, the largest all-masonry fortification in the Western world. Bird refuge and marine life.
Everglades National Park P.O. Box 279 Homestead, Florida 33030	December 6, 1947 1,507,400 acres	Subtropical wilderness with abundant wildlife.
Gates of the Arctic National Park P.O. Box 74680 Fairbanks, Alaska 99707	December 2, 1980 7,523,888 acres	Often called the greatest remaining wilderness in North America. Jagged peaks, arctic valleys, wild rivers and many lakes.
Glacier Bay National Park P.O. Box 140 Gustavus, Alaska 99826	December 2, 1980 3,225,284 acres	Huge glaciers that break up into the sea, whales and other wild animals.
Glacier National Park West Glacier, Montana 59936	May 11, 1910 1,013,572.42 acres	Ruggedly beautiful land, towering peaks, many glaciers.
Grand Canyon National Park P.O. Box 129 Grand Canyon, Arizona 86023	February 26, 1919 1,217,158.32 acres	The one-mile deep Grand Canyon of the Colorado River.
Grand Teton National Park P.O. Drawer 170 Moose, Wyoming 83012	February 26, 1929 309,993.72 acres	Blue-gray mountain peaks rising more than a mile above the flats, winter feeding ground for elk.
Great Basin National Park Baker, Nevada 89311	October 27, 1986 77,180 acres	Peaks, ancient bristlecone pine forest, Lehman Caves.
Great Smoky Mountains National Park Gatlinburg, Tennessee 37738	June 15, 1934 521,053.41 acres	One of the oldest mountain ranges on earth, extraordinary plant life.
Guadalupe Mountains National Park H. C. 60, Box 400 Salt Flat, Texas 79847	September 30, 1972 86,415.97 acres	Limestone fossil reef, geological fault.
Haleakala National Park P.O. Box 369 Makawao, Hawaii 96768	August 1, 1916 28,099 acres	Inactive volcano on the island of Maui. Originally part of Hawaii Volcanoes National Park.
Hawaii Volcanoes National Park Hawaii 96718	August 1, 1916 209,695.38 acres	Active volcanoes on the island of Hawaii.
Hot Springs National Park P.O. Box 1860 Hot Springs, Arkansas 71902	March 4, 1921 5,549.46 acres	47 thermal hot springs.
Isle Royale National Park 800 E. Lakeshore Drive Houghton, Michigan 49931	March 3, 1931 571,790.11 acres	Largest island in Lake Superior, wilderness forest with much wildlife.

National Park	Date Established and Acreage	Outstanding Features
Katmai National Park P.O. Box 7 King Salmon, Alaska 99613	December 2, 1980 3,674,540.87 acres	Valley of Ten Thousand Smokes, Alaska brown bear feeding on spawning salmon.
Kenai Fjords National Park P.O. Box 1727 Seward, Alaska 99664	December 2, 1980 669,541 acres	One of the major icecaps in the United States, coastal fjords, breeding birds and sea mammals.
Kings Canyon National Park Three Rivers, California 93271	October 1, 1890 461,901.2 acres	Two enormous canyons, summit peaks of High Sierra, giant sequoia trees.
Kobuk Valley National Park P.O. Box 1029 Kotzebue, Alaska 99752	December 2, 1980 1,750,736.86 acres	Arctic wildlife, Great Kobuk Sand Dunes, archeological sites, arctic wildlife.
Lake Clark National Park 4230 University Dr., Suite 311 Anchorage, Alaska 99508	December 2, 1980 2,636,839 acres	Jagged peaks, granite spires, two active volcanoes, glaciers, lakes, spawning salmon.
Lassen Volcanic National Park P.O. Box 100 Mineral, California 96063	August 9, 1916 106,372.36 acres	Lassen Peak volcano which last erupted in 1921. Hot springs, fumaroles, mud pots, sulfur vents.
Mammoth Cave National Park Mammoth Cave Kentucky 42259	July 1, 1941 52,830.19 acres	Longest recorded cave system in the world. Underground river, beautiful limestone formations.
Mesa Verde National Park Colorado 81321	June 29, 1906 52,121.93 acres	Well-preserved prehistoric Indian cliff dwelling.
Mount Rainier National Park Tahoma Woods, Star Route Ashford, Washington 98304	March 2, 1899 235,612.5 acres	Greatest single-peak glacial system in the United States.
North Cascades National Park 2105 Highway 20 Sedro Woolley, WA 98284	October 2, 1968 504,780.94 acres	High jagged peaks, glaciers, lakes, waterfalls.
Olympic National Park 600 East Park Avenue Port Angeles, Washington 98362	June 29, 1938 922,651.01 acres	Mountain wilderness with Pacific Northwest rain forest, active glaciers, wild ocean coastline.
Petrified Forest National Park Arizona 86028	December 9, 1962 93,532.57 acres	Petrified trees, Indian ruins and rock carvings, part of the Painted Desert.
Redwood National Park 1111 Second Street Crescent City, California 95531	October 2, 1968 110,232.4 acres	Coastal redwood forest containing the world's tallest trees, scenic Pacific coastline.
Rocky Mountain National Park Estes Park, Colorado 80517	January 26, 1915 265,727.15 acres	14,000 foot Rocky Mountain peaks, wildlife and wildflowers.
Sequoia National Park Three Rivers, California 93271	September 25, 1890 402,482.38 acres	Great groves of giant sequoia trees, Mount Whitney.
Shenandoah National Park Route 4, Box 348 Luray, Virginia 22835	December 26, 1935 196,466.19 acres	Hardwood forests, Blue Ridge Mountains, Shenandoah Valley.

National Park	*Date Established and Acreage*	*Outstanding Features*
Theodore Roosevelt Natl. Park P.O. Box 7 Medora, North Dakota 58645	November 10, 1978 70,446.59 acres	Scenic badlands and part of Theodore Roosevelt's Elkhorn Ranch.
Virgin Islands National Park 6310 Estate Nazareth St. Thomas, Virgin Islands 00802	August 2, 1956 14,688.87 acres	Quiet coves, blue-green waters and white sandy beaches.
Voyageurs National Park 3131 Highway 53 Intl. Falls, Minnesota 56649	April 8, 1975 218,035.33 acres	Numerous interconnected lakes surrounded by northern forest.
Wind Cave National Park R.R. 1, Box 190 Hot Springs South Dakota 57747	January 9, 1903 28,295.03 acres	Limestone caverns in the scenic Black Hills, wildlife.
Wrangell-St. Elias National Park P.O. Box 29 Glennallen, Alaska 99588	December 2, 1980 8,323,617.68 acres	The continent's greatest collection of peaks over 16,000 feet. Glaciers, rivers, remote mountains, wildlife.
Yellowstone National Park P.O. Box 168 Yellowstone National Park Wyoming 82190	March 1, 1872 2,219,790.71 acres	Earth's greatest geyser area, with some 10,000 geysers and hot springs including Old Faithful. Lakes, waterfalls and canyons.
Yosemite National Park P.O. Box 577 Yosemite National Park California 95389	October 1, 1890 761,236.2 acres	Nation's highest waterfalls. Granite peaks and domes, mountains, giant sequoia trees.
Zion National Park Springdale, Utah 84767-1099	November 19, 1919 146,597.64 acres	Colorful canyon and mesa scenery.

In addition to the 51 National Parks, the National Park System includes the the Statue of Liberty and the U.S. Capitol Building, as well as the areas listed below with their respective acreages. Altogether, the National Park System manages 80,322,346 acres of land. That's about 125,400 square miles, an area nearly half as large as Texas!

11 National Battlefields 13,098.39	76 National Monuments 4,788,605.95
3 National Battlefield Parks 8,727.65	51 National Parks 47,458,461.62
1 National Battlefield Site 1.00	4 National Parkways 170,706.51
1 National Capital Park 6,613.76	14 National Preserves 22,239,219.85
72 National Historic Sites 23,108.06	18 National Recreation Areas.... 3,700,634.47
36 National Historical Parks 160,627.85	15 National Rivers 415,928.16
4 National Lakeshores 228,819.79	3 National Scenic Trails 184,122.54
1 National Mall 146.35	10 National Seashores 592,627.66
26 National Memorials 8,050.00	11 Parks (other than Natl. Parks).... 38,769.27
9 National Military Parks 38,016.35	1 White House 18.07

Indians of the United States and Canada

Eskimos

Location: arctic coastlines of eastern Russia, Alaska, Canada and Greenland
Staple foods: sea mammals such as whale and seal, caribou, fish
Clothing: caribou skins, fur, seal skins
Shelter: tents of caribou or sealskin, sod houses, snowhouses or igloos (seldom used)
Transportation: dogsleds, kayaks, umiaks
Tools: soapstone, wood, bones, ulu (knife)
Art: carved and decorated bone, ivory, antler and stone

Indians of the Far North

Location: most of Canada from Rocky Mountains to Hudson Bay
Major tribes: Algonquin, Beothuk, Cree, Micmac, Montagnais, Naskapi
Staple foods: caribou, moose, wild plants, fish
Clothing: caribou or moose skin
Shelter: caribou-skin tents, bark lodges, teepees
Transportation: canoes, toboggans, snowshoes
Tools: containers of bark or spruce roots, utensils of wood
Art: quill work, embroidery

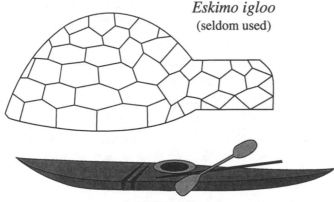

Eskimo igloo
(seldom used)

Eskimo kayak

Kwakiutl plank house
with totem pole

Indians of the Northwest

Location: along the Pacific Ocean from southern Alaska to northern California
Major tribes: Bella Coola, Chinook, Haida, Kwakiutl, Nootka, Tlingit, Tsimshian
Staple foods: primarily salmon, but also seal, whale, elk and other game, bulbs, berries
Clothing: varied, some woven blankets of wool or dog hair
Shelter: plank houses, often with totem poles
Transportation: dugout canoes, cedar planked canoes
Art: copper shields, weaving, wooden boxes, rattles and masks
Customs: potlatch, slaves

Indians of the Plateau Area
(California–Intermountain)

Location: California and the Great Basin area west of the Rocky Mountains and east of the coastal ranges, from north of the Canadian border to the Southwest
Major tribes: Bannock, Klamath, Kutenai, Maidu, Nez Percé, Paiute, Pomo, Shoshone, Ute
Staple foods: wild plants, seeds, nuts, acorns, roots, fruit, small game, insects
Clothing: skins
Shelter: wickiup, brush shelters, lean-tos
Transportation: foot
Art: baskets

Indians of the Southwest

Location: Arizona, New Mexico, parts of Colorado and Utah
Major tribes: Apache, Navajo, Pima, Yaqui
    Pueblo Indian tribes: Hopi, Zuni
Staple foods of the Pueblo Indians: corn, beans, squash
Staple foods of the Apache and Navajo: antelope, rabbit,
    cactus fruit, piñon nuts, roots
Clothing of the Pueblo Indians: cotton
Clothing of the Apache and Navajo: skins
Shelter of the Pueblo Indians: adobe
Shelter of the Navajo: hogans or teepees
Transportation: foot, horses
Tools: atlatl (spear thrower)
Art: pottery, Navajo sand paintings
Customs: rain dances

Navajo hogan

Indians of the Plains

Location: from just north of the Canadian border south to Texas
    between the Mississippi River and the Rocky Mountains
Major tribes: Arapahoe, Arikana, Assiniboine, Blackfeet,
    Caddo, Cheyenne, Comanche, Crow, Gros Ventre, Iowa,
    Kansa, Kiowa, Mandan, Osage, Pawnee, Sioux
Staple food: buffalo (jerky, pemmican)
Clothing: buffalo hides and deerskins
Shelter: teepees made with buffalo hides
Transportation: before 1700 A.D., foot and dog-drawn travois;
    after Europeans arrived, horses were used
Tools: travois, tools from buffalo horns and bone
Art: bead and feather work, decorated hides
Customs: sign language, counting coup, sun dance

Sioux Teepee

Indians of the Eastern Woodlands

Location: eastern U.S. from the Atlantic Ocean to the Mississippi River, including the Great Lakes
Major tribes of the Northeast: Cayuga, Chippewa, Delaware, Illinois, Iroquois, Kickapoo, Sauk,
    Mahican, Menominee, Miami, Mohawk, Mohegan, Munsee, Narraganset, Potawatomi, Seneca
Major tribes of the Southeast: Cherokee, Chickasaw, Choctaw, Creek, Lumbee, Natchez,
    Powhatan, Seminole, Shawnee
Staple foods: corn, beans, squash, deer, wild
    rice, maple sugar
Clothing: deerskin, feather robes
Shelter: wigwams, Iroquois longhouses
Transportation: foot, birchbark canoes
Art: wicker baskets, pottery and wooden bowls
Customs: peace pipe, wampum belts

Iroquois longhouse

The Declaration of Independence

The Declaration of Independence was adopted in Philadelphia by the Second Continental Congress, a meeting of delegates from the original thirteen colonies. It lists the complaints of the American colonists against the British government, and proclaims a new nation, the United States of America. Thomas Jefferson wrote the Declaration. The date it was signed, July 4, 1776, is considered the birthdate of the nation, and is celebrated yearly as the "Fourth of July" or "Independence Day."

The Declaration of Independence in Congress, July 4, 1776

The unanimous Declaration of the thirteen united States of America.

When in the Course of human events it becomes necessary for one people to dissolve the political bands which have connected them with another, and to assume among the powers of the earth, the separate and equal station to which the Laws of Nature and of Nature's God entitle them, a decent respect to the opinions of mankind requires that they should declare the causes which impel them to the separation.

We hold these truths to be self-evident, that all men are created equal, that they are endowed by their Creator with certain unalienable Rights, that among these are Life, Liberty and the pursuit of Happiness.—That to secure these rights, Governments are instituted among Men, deriving their just powers from the consent of the governed,—That whenever any Form of Government becomes destructive of these ends, it is the Right of the People to alter or to abolish it, and to institute new Government, laying its foundation on such principles and organizing its powers in such form, as to them shall seem most likely to effect their Safety and Happiness. Prudence, indeed, will dictate that Governments long established should not be changed for light and transient causes; and accordingly all experience hath shewn that mankind are more disposed to suffer, while evils are sufferable, than to right themselves by abolishing the forms to which they are accustomed. But when a long train of abuses and usurpations, pursuing invariably the same Object evinces a design to reduce them under absolute Despotism, it is their right, it is their duty, to throw off such Government, and to provide new Guards for their future security.—Such has been the patient sufferance of these Colonies; and such is now the necessity which constrains them to alter their former Systems of Government. The history of the present King of Great Britain is a history of repeated injuries and usurpations, all having in direct object the establishment of an absolute Tyranny over these States. To prove this, let Facts be submitted to a candid world.

He has refused his Assent to Laws, the most wholesome and necessary for the public good.

He has forbidden his Governors to pass Laws of immediate and pressing importance, unless suspended in their operation till his Assent should be obtained; and when so suspended, he has utterly neglected to attend to them.

He has refused to pass other Laws for the accommodation of large districts of people, unless those people would relinquish the right of Representation in the Legislature, a right inestimable to them and formidable to tyrants only.

He has called together legislative bodies at places unusual, uncomfortable, and distant from the depository of their Public Records, for the sole purposes of fatiguing them into compliance with his measures.

He has dissolved Representative Houses repeatedly, for opposing with manly firmness his invasions on the rights of the people.

He has refused for a long time, after such dissolutions, to cause others to be elected; whereby the Legislative Powers, incapable of Annihilation, have returned to the People at large for their exercise; the State remaining in the mean time exposed to all the dangers of invasion from without, and convulsions within.

He has endeavored to prevent the population of these States; for that purpose obstructing the Laws for Naturalization of Foreigners; refusing to pass others to encourage their migrations hither, and raising the conditions of new Appropriations of Lands.

He has obstructed the Administration of Justice, by refusing his Assent to Laws for establishing Judiciary Powers.

He has made Judges dependent on his Will alone, for the tenure of their offices, and the amount and payment of their salaries.

He has erected a multitude of New Offices, and sent hither swarms of Officers to harass our people, and eat out their substance.

He has kept among us, in times of peace, Standing Armies without the Consent of our legislatures.

He has affected to render the Military independent of and superior to the Civil Power.

He has combined with others to subject us to a jurisdiction foreign to our constitution, and unacknowledged by our laws; giving his Assent to their Acts of pretended Legislation:

For quartering large bodies of armed troops among us:

For protecting them, by a mock Trial, from punishment for any Murders which they should commit on the Inhabitants of these States:

For cutting off our Trade with all parts of the world:

For imposing Taxes on us without our Consent:

For depriving us in many cases, of the benefits of Trial by Jury:

For transporting us beyond Seas to be tried for pretended offences:

For abolishing the free System of English Laws in a neighbouring Province, establishing therein an Arbitrary government, and enlarging its Boundaries so as to render it at once an example and fit instrument for introducing the same absolute rule into these Colonies:

For taking away our Charters, abolishing our most valuable Laws and altering fundamentally the Forms of our Governments:

For suspending our own Legislatures, and declaring themselves invested with power to legislate for us in all cases whatsoever.

He has abdicated Government here, by declaring us out of his Protection and waging War against us.

He has plundered our seas, ravaged our Coasts, burnt our towns, and destroyed the lives of our people.

He is at this time transporting large Armies of foreign Mercenaries to compleat the works of death, desolation, and tyranny, already begun with circumstances of Cruelty & Perfidy scarcely paralleled in the most barbarous ages, and totally unworthy the Head of a civilized nation.

He has constrained our fellow Citizens taken Captive on the high Seas to bear Arms against their Country, to become the executioners of their friends and Brethren, or to fall themselves by their Hands.

He has excited domestic insurrections amongst us, and has endeavoured to bring on the inhabitants of our frontiers, the merciless Indian Savages, whose known rule of warfare, is an undistinguished destruction of all ages, sexes and conditions.

In every stage of these Oppressions We have Petitioned for Redress in the most humble terms: Our repeated Petitions have been answered only by repeated injury. A Prince, whose character is thus marked by every act which may define a Tyrant, is unfit to be the ruler of a free people.

Nor have We been wanting in attentions to our Brittish brethren. We have warned them from time to time of attempts by their legislature to extend an unwarrantable jurisdiction over us. We have reminded them of the circumstances of our emigration and settlement here. We have appealed to their native justice and magnanimity, and we have conjured them by the ties of our common kindred to disavow these usurpations, which would inevitably interrupt our connections and correspondence. They too have been deaf to the voice of justice and of consanguinity. We must, therefore, acquiesce in the necessity, which denounces our Separation, and hold them, as we hold the rest of mankind, Enemies in War, in Peace Friends.

We, therefore, the Representatives of the United States of America, in General Congress, Assembled, appealing to the Supreme Judge of the world for the rectitude of our intentions, do, in the Name, and by Authority of the good People of these Colonies, solemnly publish and declare, That these United Colonies are, and of Right ought to be Free and Independent States; that they are Absolved from all Allegiance to the British Crown, and that all political connection between them and the State of Great Britain, is and ought to be totally dissolved; and that as Free and Independent States, they have full Power to levy War, conclude Peace, contract Alliances, establish Commerce, and to do all other Acts and Things which Independent States may of right do.—And for the support of this Declaration, with a firm reliance on the protection of Divine Providence, we mutually pledge to each other our Lives, our Fortunes and our sacred Honor.

—John Hancock

New Hampshire	*New York*	*Pennsylvania*	John Adams	Charles Carroll of	Joseph Hewes
Josiah Bartlett	Wm. Floyd	Robt. Morris	Robt. Treat Paine	Carrollton	John Penn
Wm. Whipple	Phil. Livingston	Benjamin Rush	Elbridge Gerry	*Virginia*	*South Carolina*
Matthew Thornton	Frans. Lewis	Benj. Franklin	*Delaware*	George Wythe	Edward Rutledge
Rhode Island	Lewis Morris	John Morton	Caesar Rodney	Richard Henry Lee	Thos. Heyward, Junr.
Step. Hopkins	*New Jersey*	Geo. Clymer	Geo. Read	Th. Jefferson	Thomas Lynch, Junr.
William Ellery	Richd. Stockton	Jas. Smith	Tho. M'Kean	Benj. Harrison	Arthur Middleton
Connecticut	Jno. Witherspoon	Geo. Taylor	*Maryland*	Ths. Nelson, Jr.	*Georgia*
Roger Sherman	Fras. Hopkinson	James Wilson	Samuel Chase	Francis Lightfoot Lee	Button Gwinnett
Sam'el Huntington	John Hart	Geo. Ross	Wm. Paca	Carter Braxton	Lyman Hall
Wm. Williams	Abra. Clark	*Massachusetts-Bay*	Thos. Stone	*North Carolina*	Geo. Walton
Oliver Wolcott		Saml. Adams		Wm. Hooper	

The United States Constitution

The Constitution of the United States outlines the organization of the national government, defines the process of making and enforcing rules (laws), and describes the rights of the people. It was signed on September 17, 1787, at Independence Hall in Philadelphia and is currently the oldest written national constitution still in force. The first ten amendments are called the Bill of Rights and were added by the First Congress in 1791 to safeguard individual rights. The additional amendments have been added since that time. Sections in parentheses have been amended.

Constitution of the United States of America

(Preamble)

We the people of the United States, in order to form a more perfect Union, establish justice, insure domestic tranquility, provide for the common defence, promote the general welfare, and secure the blessings of liberty to ourselves and our posterity, do ordain and establish this Constitution for the United States of America.

Article 1

Section 1. All legislative powers herein granted shall be vested in a Congress of the United States, which shall consist of a Senate and House of Representatives.

Section 2. The House of Representatives shall be composed of members chosen every second year by the people of the several States, and the electors in each State shall have the qualifications requisite for electors of the most numerous branch of the State Legislature.

No Person shall be a Representative who shall not have attained to the age of twenty-five years, and been seven years a citizen of the United States, and who shall not, when elected, be an inhabitant of that State in which he shall be chosen.

(Representatives and direct taxes shall be apportioned among the several States which may be included within this Union, according to their respective numbers, which shall be determined by adding to the whole number of free persons, including those bound to service for a term of years, and excluding Indians not taxed, three fifths of all other persons.) The actual enumeration shall be made within three years after the first meeting of the Congress of the United States, and within every subsequent term of ten years, in such manner as they shall by law direct. The number of Representatives shall not exceed one for every thirty thousand, but each State shall have at least one Representative; and until such enumeration shall be made, the State of New Hampshire shall be entitled to choose three, Massachusetts eight, Rhode-Island and Providence Plantations one, Connecticut five, New York six, New Jersey four, Pennsylvania eight, Delaware one, Maryland six, Virginia ten, North Carolina five, South Carolina five, and Georgia three.

When vacancies happen in the representation from any State, the Executive Authority thereof shall issue writs of election to fill such vacancies.

The House of Representatives shall choose their Speaker and other officers and shall have the sole power of impeachment.

Section 3. The Senate of the United States shall be composed of two Senators from each State, chosen by the Legislature thereof, for six years; and each Senator shall have one vote

Immediately after they shall be assembled in consequence of the first election, they shall be divided as equally as may be into three classes. The seats of the Senators of the first class shall be vacated at the expiration of the second year, of the second class at the expiration of the fourth year, and of the third class at the expiration of the sixth year, so that one-third may be chosen every second year; and if vacancies happen by resignation, or otherwise, during the recess of the Legislature of any State, the Executive thereof may make temporary appointments (until the next meeting of the Legislature, which shall then fill such vacancies).

No person shall be a Senator who shall not have attained to the age of thirty years, and been nine years a citizen of the United States, and who shall not, when elected, be an inhabitant of that State for which he shall be chosen.

The Vice President of the United States shall be President of the Senate, but shall have no vote, unless they be equally divided.

The Senate shall choose their other officers, and also a President *pro tempore,* in the absence of the Vice President, or when he shall exercise the office of President of the United States.

The Senate shall have the sole power to try all impeachments. When sitting for that purpose, they shall be on oath or affirmation. When the President of the United States is tried, the Chief Justice shall preside: and no person shall be convicted without the concurrence of two thirds of the members present.

Judgment in cases of impeachment shall not extend further than to removal from office, and disqualification to hold and enjoy any office of honor, trust, or profit under the United States: but the party convicted shall nevertheless be liable and subject to indictment, trial, judgment and punishment, according to Law.

Section 4. The times, places, and manner of holding elections for Senators and Representatives, shall be prescribed in each

State by the Legislature thereof; but the Congress may at any time by law make or alter such regulations, except as to the places of choosing Senators.

The Congress shall assemble at least once in every year, and such meeting shall be on the first Monday in December, unless they shall by law appoint a different day.

Section 5. Each House shall be the judge of the elections, returns, and qualifications of its own members, and a majority of each shall constitute a quorum to do business; but a smaller number may adjourn from day to day, and may be authorized to compel the attendance of absent members, in such manner, and under such penalties as each House may provide.

Each House may determine the rules of its proceedings, punish its members for disorderly behavior, and, with the concurrence of two thirds, expel a member.

Each House shall keep a journal of its proceedings, and from time to time publish the same, excepting such parts as may in their judgment require secrecy; and the yeas and nays of the members of either House on any question shall, at the desire of one fifth of those present, be entered on the journal.

Neither House, during the session of Congress, shall, without the consent of the other, adjourn for more than three days, nor to any other place than that in which the two Houses shall be sitting.

Section 6. The Senators and Representatives shall receive a compensation for their services, to be ascertained by law, and paid out of the Treasury of the United States. They shall in all cases, except treason, felony, and breach of the peace, be privileged from arrest during their attendance at the session of their respective Houses, and in going to and returning from the same; and for any speech or debate in either House, they shall not be questioned in any other place.

No Senator or Representative shall, during the time for which he was elected, be appointed to any civil office under the authority of the United States, which shall have been created, or the emoluments whereof shall have been increased during such time; and no person holding any office under the United States shall be a member of either House during his continuance in office.

Section 7. All bills for raising revenue shall originate in the House of Representatives; but the Senate may propose or concur with amendments as on other bills.

Every bill which shall have passed the House of Representatives and the Senate, shall, before it becomes a law, be presented to the President of the United States; if he approve he shall sign it, but if not he shall return it, with his objections to that House in which it shall have originated, who shall enter the objections at large on their journal, and proceed to reconsider it. If after such reconsideration two thirds of that House shall agree to pass the bill, it shall be sent, together with the objections, to the other

House, by which it shall likewise be reconsidered, and if approved by two thirds of that House, it shall become a law. But in all such cases the votes of both Houses shall be determined by yeas and nays, and the names of the persons voting for and against the bill shall be entered on the journal of each house, respectively. If any bill shall not be returned by the President within ten days (Sundays excepted) after it shall have been presented to him, the same shall be a law, in like manner as if he had signed it, unless the Congress by their adjournment prevent its return, in which case it shall not be a law.

Every order, resolution, or vote to which the concurrence of the Senate and House of Representatives may be necessary (except on a question of adjournment) shall be presented to the President of the United States; and before the same shall take effect, shall be approved by him, or being disapproved by him, shall be repassed by two thirds of the Senate and House of Representatives, according to the rules and limitations prescribed in the case of a bill.

Section 8. The Congress shall have power to lay and collect taxes, duties, imposts and excises, to pay the debts and provide for the common defense and general welfare of the United States; but all duties, imposts and excises shall be uniform throughout the United States;

To borrow money on the credit of the United States;

To regulate commerce with foreign nations, and among the several States, and with the Indian tribes;

To establish a uniform rule of naturalization, and uniform laws on the subject of bankruptcies throughout the United States;

To coin money, regulate the value thereof, and of foreign coin, and fix the standard of weights and measures;

To provide for the punishment of counterfeiting the securities and current coin of the United States;

To establish post offices and post roads;

To promote the progress of science and useful arts, by securing for limited times to authors and inventors the exclusive right to their respective writings and discoveries;

To constitute tribunals inferior to the Supreme Court;

To define and punish piracies and felonies committed on the high seas, and offences against the law of nations;

To declare war, grant letters of marque and reprisal, and make rules concerning captures on land and water;

To raise and support armies, but no appropriation of money to that use shall be for a longer term than two years;

To provide and maintain a navy;

To make rules for the government and regulation of the land and naval forces;

To provide for calling forth the militia to execute the laws of the Union, suppress insurrections, and repel invasions.

To provide for organizing, arming, and disciplining, the militia, and for governing such part of them as may be employed in the service of the United States, reserving to the States, respectively, the appointment of the officers, and the authority of training the militia according to the discipline prescribed by Congress;

To exercise exclusive legislation in all cases whatsoever, over such district (not exceeding ten miles square) as may, by cession of particular States, and the acceptance of Congress, become the seat of the Government of the United States, and to exercise like authority over all places purchased by the consent of the Legislature of the State in which the same shall be, for the erection of forts, magazines, arsenals, dockyards, and other needful buildings;—And

To make all laws which shall be necessary and proper for carrying into execution the foregoing powers, and all other powers vested by this Constitution in the Government of the United States, or in any department or officer thereof.

Section 9. The migration or importation of such persons as any of the States now existing shall think proper to admit, shall not be prohibited by the Congress prior to the year one thousand eight hundred and eight, but a tax or duty may be imposed on such importation, not exceeding ten dollars for each person.

The privilege of the writ of habeas corpus shall not be suspended, unless when in cases of rebellion or invasion the public safety may require it.

No bill of attainder or ex post facto law shall be passed.

No capitation, or other diréct, tax shall be laid, unless in proportion to the census or enumeration herein before directed to be taken.

No tax or duty shall be laid on articles exported from any State.

No preference shall be given by any regulation of commerce or revenue to the ports of one State over those of another: nor shall vessels bound to, or from, one State, be obliged to enter, clear, or pay duties in another.

No money shall be drawn from the Treasury, but in consequence of appropriations made by law; and a regular statement and account of the receipts and expenditures of all public money shall be published from time to time.

No title of nobility shall be granted by the United States: and no person holding any office of profit or trust under them, shall, without the consent of the Congress, accept of any present, emolument, office, or title, of any kind whatever, from any king, prince, or foreign state.

Section 10. No State shall enter into any treaty, alliance, or confederation; grant letters of marque and reprisal; coin money; emit bills of credit; make any thing but gold and silver coin a tender in payment of debts; pass any bill of attainder, ex post facto law, or law impairing the obligation of contracts, or grant any title of nobility.

No State shall, without the consent of the Congress, lay any imposts or duties on imports or exports, except what may be absolutely necessary for executing its inspection laws; and the net produce of all duties and imposts, laid by any State on imports or exports, shall be for the use of the Treasury of the United States; and all such laws shall be subject to the revision and control of the Congress.

No State shall, without the consent of Congress, lay any duty of tonnage, keep troops, or ships of war in time of peace, enter into any agreement or compact with another state, or with a foreign power, or engage in war, unless actually invaded, or in such imminent danger as will not admit of delay.

Article 2

Section 1. The executive power shall be vested in a President of the United States of America. He shall hold his office during the term of four years, and, together with the Vice President, chosen for the same term, be elected, as follows:

Each State shall appoint, in such manner as the Legislature thereof may direct, a number of electors, equal to the whole number of Senators and Representatives to which the State may be entitled in the Congress: but no Senator or Representative, or person holding an office of trust or profit under the United States, shall be appointed an elector.

(The electors shall meet in their respective States, and vote by ballot for two persons, of whom one at least shall not be an inhabitant of the same State with themselves. And they shall make a list of all the persons voted for, and of the number of votes for each; which list they shall sign and certify, and transmit sealed to the seat of the Government of the United States, directed to the President of the Senate. The President of the Senate shall, in the presence of the Senate and House of Representatives, open all the certificates, and the votes shall then be counted. The person having the greatest number of votes shall be the President, if such number be a majority of the whole number of electors appointed; and if there be more than one who have such majority, and have an equal number of votes, then the House of Representatives shall immediately choose by ballot one of them for President; and if no person have a majority, then from the five highest on the list the said House shall in like manner choose the President. But in choosing the President, the votes shall be taken by States, the representative from each State having one vote; A quorum for this purpose shall consist of a member or members from two thirds of the States, and a majority of all the states shall be necessary to a choice. In every case, after the choice of the President, the person having the greatest number of votes of the electors shall be the Vice President. But if there should remain two or more who have equal votes, the Senate should choose from them by ballot the Vice President.)

The Congress may determine the time of choosing the electors, and the day on which they shall give their votes; which day shall be the same throughout the United States.

No person except a natural born citizen, or a citizen of the United States, at the time of the adoption of this Constitution, shall be eligible to the office of President; neither shall any person be eligible to that office who shall not have attained to the age of thirty-five years, and been fourteen years a resident within the United States.

In case of the removal of the President from office, or of his death, resignation, or inability to discharge the powers and duties of the said office, the same shall devolve on the Vice President, and the Congress may by law provide for the case of removal, death, resignation or inability, both of the President and Vice President, declaring what officer shall then act as President, and such officer shall act accordingly, until the disability be removed, or a President shall be elected.

The President shall, at stated times, receive for his services, a compensation, which shall neither be increased nor diminished during the period for which he shall have been elected, and he shall not receive within that period any other emolument from the United States, or any of them.

Before he enter on the execution of his office, he shall take the following oath or affirmation—"I do solemnly swear (or affirm) that I will faithfully execute the office of President of the United States, and will to the best of my ability, preserve, protect, and defend the Constitution of the United States."

Section 2. The President shall be Commander in Chief of the Army and Navy of the United States, and of the militia of the several States, when called into the actual service of the United States; he may require the opinion, in writing, of the principal officer in each of the executive departments, upon any subject relating to the duties of their respective offices, and he shall have power to grant reprieves and pardons for offences against the United States, except in cases of impeachment.

He shall have power, by and with the advice and consent of the Senate, to make treaties, provided two thirds of the Senators present concur; and he shall nominate, and by and with the advice and consent of the Senate, shall appoint ambassadors, other public ministers and consuls, judges of the Supreme Court, and all other officers of the United States, whose appointments are not herein otherwise provided for, and which shall be established by law: but the Congress may by law vest the appointment of such inferior officers, as they think proper, in the President alone, in the courts of law, or in the heads of departments.

The President shall have power to fill up all vacancies that may happen during the recess of the Senate, by granting commissions which shall expire at the end of their session.

Section 3. He shall from time to time give to the Congress information of the state of the Union, and recommend to their consideration such measures as he shall judge necessary and expedient; he may, on extraordinary occasions, convene both Houses, or either of them, and in case of disagreement between them, with respect to the time of adjournment, he may adjourn them to such time as he shall think proper; he shall receive ambassadors and other public ministers: he shall take care that the laws be faithfully executed, and shall commission all the officers of the United States.

Section 4. The President, Vice President, and all civil officers of the United States shall be removed from office on impeachment for, and conviction of, treason, bribery, or other high crimes and misdemeanors.

Article 3

Section 1. The judicial Power of the United States, shall be vested in one Supreme Court, and in such inferior courts as the Congress may from time to time ordain and establish. The judges, both of the supreme and inferior courts, shall hold their offices during good behavior, and shall, at stated times, receive for their services, a compensation, which shall not be diminished during their continuance in office.

Section 2. The judicial power shall extend to all cases, in law and equity, arising under this Constitution, the laws of the United States, and treaties made, or which shall be made, under their authority; to all cases affecting ambassadors, other public ministers and consuls; to all cases of admiralty and maritime jurisdiction; to controversies to which the United States, shall be a party; to controversies between two or more States; between a State and citizens of another State; between citizens of different States; between citizens of the same State claiming lands under grants of different states, and between a State, or the citizens thereof, and foreign states, citizens, or subjects.

In all cases affecting ambassadors, other public ministers and consuls, and those in which a State shall be party, the Supreme Court shall have original jurisdiction. In all the other cases before mentioned, the Supreme Court shall have appellate jurisdiction, both as to law and fact, with such exceptions, and under such regulations, as the Congress shall make.

The trial of all crimes, except in cases of impeachment, shall be by jury; and such trial shall be held in the State where the said crimes shall have been committed; but when not committed within any State, the trial shall be at such place or places as the Congress may by law have directed.

Section 3. Treason against the United States, shall consist only in levying war against them, or, in adhering to their enemies, giving them aid and comfort. No person shall be convicted of treason unless on the testimony of two witnesses to the same overt act, or on confession in open court.

The Congress shall have power to declare the punishment of treason, but no attainder of treason shall work corruption of blood, or forfeiture except during the life of the person attained.

Article 4

Section 1. Full faith and credit shall be given in each State to the public acts, records, and judicial proceedings of every other State. And the Congress may by general laws prescribe the manner in which such acts, records, and proceedings shall be proved, and the effect thereof.

Section 2. The citizens of each State shall be entitled to all privileges and immunities of citizens in the several States.

A person charged in any State with treason, felony, or other crime, who shall flee from justice, and be found in another State, shall on demand of the Executive authority of the State from which he fled, be delivered up, to be removed to the State having jurisdiction of the crime.

No person held to service or labor in one State, under the laws thereof, escaping into another, shall, in consequence of any law or regulation therein, be discharged from such service or labor, but shall be delivered up on claim of the party to whom such service or labor may be due.

Section 3. New States may be admitted by the Congress into this Union; but no new State shall be formed or erected within the jurisdiction of any other State; nor any State be formed by the junction of two or more States, or parts of States, without the consent of the Legislatures of the States concerned as well as of the Congress.

The Congress shall have power to dispose of and make all needful rules and regulations respecting the territory or other property belonging to the United States; and nothing in this Constitution shall be so construed as to prejudice any claims of the United States, or of any particular State.

Section 4. The United States shall guarantee to every State in this Union a Republican form of government, and shall protect each of them against invasion; and on application of the Legislature, or of the Executive (when the Legislature cannot be convened) against domestic violence.

Article 5

The Congress, whenever two-thirds of both houses shall deem it necessary, shall propose amendments to this Constitution, or, on the application of the legislatures of two-thirds of the several states, shall call a convention for proposing amendments, which, in either case, shall be valid to all intents and purposes, as part of this Constitution, when ratified by the legislatures of three-fourths of the several states, or by conventions in three-fourths thereof, as the one or the other mode of ratification may be proposed by the Congress; provided (that no amendment which may be made prior to the year one thousand eight hundred and eight shall in any manner affect the first and fourth clauses in the ninth section of the first article; and) that no state, without its consent, shall be deprived of its equal suffrage in the Senate.

Article 6

All debts contracted and engagements entered into, before the adoption of this Constitution, shall be as valid against the United States under this Constitution, as under the Confederation.

This Constitution, and the laws of the United States which shall be made in pursuance thereof; and all treaties made, or which shall be made, under the authority of the United States, shall be the supreme law of the land; and the judges in every State shall be bound thereby, any thing in the Constitution or laws of any State to the contrary notwithstanding.

The Senators and Representatives before mentioned, and the members of the several State Legislatures, and all executive and judicial officers, both of the United States and of the several States, shall be bound by oath or affirmation, to support this Constitution; but no religious test shall ever be required as a qualification to any office or public trust under the United States.

Article 7

The ratification of the conventions of nine States shall be sufficient for the establishment of this Constitution between the States so ratifying the same.

Done in convention by the unanimous consent of the States present the seventeenth day of September in the year of our Lord one thousand seven hundred and eighty seven and of the independence of the United States of America the Twelfth. In witness whereof we have hereunto subscribed our names

George Washington, President and Deputy from Virginia

New Hampshire
John Langdon
Nicholas Gilman

Massachusetts
Nathaniel Gorham
Rufus King

Connecticut
Wm. Saml. Johnson
Roger Sherman

New York
Alexander Hamilton

New Jersey
Wil. Livingston
David Brearley
Wm. Paterson
Jona. Dayton

Pennsylvania
B. Franklin
Robt. Morris
Thos. FitzSimons
James Wilson
Thomas Mifflin
Geo. Clymer

Jared Ingersoll
Gouv. Morris

Delaware
Geo. Read
John Dickinson
Jaco. Broom
Gunning Bedford
Jun.
Richard Bassett

Maryland
James McHenry
Danl. Carrol
Dan. of St. Thos.
Jenifer

Virginia
John Blair
James Madison, Jr.

North Carolina
Wm. Blount
Hu. Williamson
Richd Dobbs Spaight

South Carolina
J. Rutledge
Charles Pinckney
Charles Cotesworth
Pinckney
Pierce Butler

Georgia
William Few
Abr. Baldwin
Attest:
    William Jackson,
Secretary

Amendments to the Constitution of the United States

The first ten amendments are known as the Bill of Rights. They were ratified (officially approved) December 15, 1791.

Amendment 1

Congress shall make no law respecting an establishment of religion, or prohibiting the free exercise thereof; or abridging the freedom of speech, or of the press; or the right of the people peaceably to assemble, and to petition the Government for a redress of grievances.

Amendment 2

A well regulated militia, being necessary to the security of a free State, the right of the people to keep and bear arms, shall not be infringed.

Amendment 3

No soldier shall, in time of peace be quartered in any house, without the consent of the owner, nor in time of war, but in a manner to be prescribed by law.

Amendment 4

The right of the people to be secure in their persons, houses, papers, and effects, against unreasonable searches and seizures, shall not be violated, and no warrants shall issue, but upon probable cause, supported by oath or affirmation, and particularly describing the place to be searched, and the persons or things to be seized.

Amendment 5

No person shall be held to answer for a capital, or otherwise infamous crime, unless on a presentment or indictment of a Grand Jury, except in cases arising in the land or naval forces, or in the militia, when in actual service in time of war or public danger; nor shall any person be subject for the same offence to be twice put in jeopardy of life or limb; nor shall be compelled in any criminal case to be a witness, against himself, nor be deprived of life, liberty, or property, without due process of law; nor shall private property be taken for public use, without just compensation.

Amendment 6

In all criminal prosecutions, the accused shall enjoy the right to a speedy and public trial, by an impartial jury of the State and district wherein the crime shall have been committed, which district shall have been previously ascertained by law, and to be informed of the nature and cause of the accusation; to be confronted with the witnesses against him; to have compulsory process for obtaining witnesses in his favor, and to have the assistance of counsel for his defense.

Amendment 7

In suits at common law, where the value in controversy shall exceed twenty dollars, the right of trial by jury shall be preserved, and no fact tried by a jury, shall be otherwise re-examined in any court of the United States, than according to the rules of the common law.

Amendment 8

Excessive bail shall not be required, nor excessive fines imposed, nor cruel and unusual punishments inflicted.

Amendment 9

The enumeration in the Constitution, of certain rights, shall not be construed to deny or disparage others retained by the people.

Amendment 10

The powers not delegated to the United States by the Constitution, nor prohibited by it to the States, are reserved to the States, respectively, or to the people.

Amendment 11
(Ratified February 7, 1795)

The judicial power of the United States shall not be construed to extend to any suit in law or equity, commenced or prosecuted against one of the United States by citizens of another State, or by citizens or subjects of any foreign state.

Amendment 12
(Ratified July 27, 1804)

The electors shall meet in their respective states, and vote by ballot for President and Vice President, one of whom, at least, shall not be an inhabitant of the same state with themselves; they shall name in their ballots the person voted for as President, and in distinct ballots the person voted for as Vice President, and they shall make distinct lists of all persons voted for as President, and of all persons voted for as Vice President, and of the number of votes for each, which lists they shall sign and certify, and transmit sealed to the seat of the government of the United States, directed to the President of the Senate; the President of the Senate shall, in the presence of the Senate and House of Representatives, open all the certificates and the votes shall then be counted; the person having the greatest number of votes for President, shall be the President, if such number be a majority of the whole number of electors appointed; and if no person have such majority, then from the persons having the highest numbers not exceeding three on the list of those voted for as President, the House of Representatives shall choose immediately, by ballot, the President. But in choosing the President, the votes shall be taken by states, the representation from each State having one vote; a quorum for this purpose shall consist of a member or members from two thirds of the states, and a majority of all the states shall be necessary to a choice. And if the House of Representatives shall not choose a President whenever the right of choice shall devolve upon them, before the fourth day of March next following, then the Vice President shall act as President, as in the case of the death or other constitutional disability of the President. The person having the greatest number of votes as Vice President, shall be the Vice President, if such number be a majority of the whole number of electors appointed, and if no person have a majority, then from the two highest numbers on the list, the Senate shall choose the Vice President; a quorum for the purpose shall consist of two thirds of the whole number of Senators, and a majority of the whole number shall be necessary to a choice. But no person constitutionally ineligible to the office of President shall be eligible to that of Vice President of the United States.

Amendment 13
(Ratified December 6, 1865)

Section 1. Neither slavery nor involuntary servitude, except as a punishment for crime whereof the party shall have been duly convicted, shall exist within the United States, or any place subject to their jurisdiction.

Section 2. Congress shall have power to enforce this article by appropriate legislation.

Amendment 14
(Ratified July 9, 1868)

Section 1. All persons born or naturalized in the United States, and subject to the jurisdiction thereof, are citizens of the United States and of the State wherein they reside. No State shall make or enforce any law which shall abridge the privileges or immunities of citizens of the United States; nor shall any State deprive any person of life, liberty, or property, without due process of law; nor deny to any person within its jurisdiction the equal protection of the laws.

Section 2. Representatives shall be apportioned among the several States according to their respective numbers, counting the whole number of persons in each State, excluding Indians not taxed. But when the right to vote at any election for the choice of electors for President and Vice President of the United States, Representatives in Congress, the executive and judicial officers of a State, or the members of the Legislature thereof, is denied to any of the male inhabitants of such State, being twenty-one years of age, and citizens of the United States, or in any way abridged, except for participation in rebellion, or other crime, the basis of representation therein shall be reduced in the proportion which the number of such male citizens shall bear to the whole number of male citizens twenty-one years of age in such State.

Section 3. No person shall be a Senator or Representative in Congress, or elector of President and Vice President, or hold any office, civil or military, under the United States, or under any State, who, having previously taken an oath, as a member of Congress, or as an officer of the United States, or as a member of any State Legislature, or as an executive or judicial officer of any State, to support the Constitution of the United States, shall have engaged in insurrection or rebellion against the same, or given aid or comfort to the enemies thereof. But Congress may by a vote of two thirds of each House, remove such disability.

Section 4. The validity of the public debt of the United States, authorized by law, including debts incurred for payment of pensions and bounties for services in suppressing insurrection or rebellion, shall not be questioned. But neither the United States nor any State shall assume or pay any debt or obligation incurred in aid of insurrection or rebellion against the United States, or any claim for the loss or emancipation of any slave; but all such debts, obligations, and claims shall be held illegal and void.

Section 5. The Congress shall have power to enforce, by appropriate legislation, the provisions of this article.

Amendment 15
(Ratified February 3, 1870)

Section 1. The right of citizens of the United States to vote shall not be denied or abridged by the United States or by any State on account of race, color, or previous condition of servitude.

Section 2. The Congress shall have power to enforce this article by appropriate legislation.

Amendment 16
(Ratified February 3, 1913)

The Congress shall have power to lay and collect taxes on incomes, from whatever source derived, without apportionment among the several States, and without regard to any census or enumeration.

Amendment 17
(Ratified April 8, 1913)

The Senate of the United States shall be composed of two Senators from each State, elected by the people thereof, for six years; and each Senator shall have one vote. The electors in each State shall have the qualifications requisite for electors of the most numerous branch of the State Legislatures.

When vacancies happen in the representation of any State in the Senate, the executive authority of such State shall issue writs of election to fill such vacancies: Provided, that the legislature of any State may empower the executive thereof to make temporary appointment until the people fill the vacancies by election as the legislature may direct.

This amendment shall not be so construed as to affect the election or term of any Senator chosen before it becomes valid as part of the Constitution.

Amendment 18
(Ratified January 16, 1919. Repealed December 5, 1933 by Amendment 21)

Section 1. After one year from the ratification of this article the manufacture, sale, or transportation of intoxicating liquors within, the importation thereof into, or the exportation thereof from the United States and all territory subject to the jurisdiction thereof for beverage purposes is hereby prohibited.

Section 2. The Congress and the several States shall have concurrent power to enforce this article by appropriate legislation.

Section 3. This article shall be inoperative unless it shall have been ratified as an amendment to the Constitution by the legislatures of the several States, as provided in the Constitution, within seven years from the date of the submission hereof to the States by Congress.

Amendment 19
(Ratified August 18, 1920)

The right of citizens of the United States to vote shall not be denied or abridged by the United States or by any State on account of sex.

Congress shall have power to enforce this article by appropriate legislation.

Amendment 20
(Ratified January 23, 1933)

Section 1. The terms of the President and Vice President shall end at noon on the twentieth day of January, and the terms of Senators and Representatives at noon on the third day of January, of the years in which such terms would have ended if this article had not been ratified; and the terms of their successors shall then begin.

Section 2. The Congress shall assemble at least once in every year, and such meetings shall begin at noon on the third day of January, unless they shall by law appoint a different day.

Section 3. If, at the time fixed for the beginning of the term of the President, the President-elect shall have died, the Vice President-elect shall become President. If a President shall not have been chosen before the time fixed for the beginning of his term, or if the President-elect shall have failed to qualify, then the Vice President shall have qualified; and the Congress may by law provide for the case wherein neither a President-elect nor a Vice President-elect shall have qualified, declaring who shall then act as President, or the manner in which one who is to act shall be selected, and such person shall act accordingly until a President or Vice President shall have qualified.

Section 4. The Congress may by law provide for the case of the death of any of the persons from whom the House of Representatives may choose a President whenever the right of choice shall have devolved upon them, and for the case of the death of any of the persons from whom the Senate may choose a Vice President whenever the right of choice shall have devolved upon them.

Section 5. Sections 1 and 2 shall take effect on the 15th day of October following the ratification of this article.

Section 6. This article shall be inoperative unless it shall have been ratified as an amendment to the Constitution by the legislatures of three fourths of the several States within seven years from the date of its submission.

Amendment 21
(Ratified December 5, 1933)

Section 1. The eighteenth article of amendment to the Constitution of the United States is hereby repealed.

Section 2. The transportation or importation into any State, territory, or possession of the United States for delivery or use therein of intoxicating liquors, in violation of the laws thereof, is hereby prohibited.

Section 3. This article shall be inoperative unless it shall have been ratified as an amendment to the Constitution, within seven years from the date of the submission thereof to the States by the Congress.

Amendment 22
(Ratified February 27, 1951)

Section 1. No person shall be elected to the office of the President more than twice, and no person who has held the office of President, or acted as President, for more than two years of a term to which some other person was elected President shall be elected to the office of the President more than once. But this article shall not apply to any person holding the office of President when this article was proposed by the Congress, and shall not prevent any person who may be holding the office of President, or acting as President, during the term within which this article becomes operative from holding the office of President or acting as President during the remainder of such term.

Section 2. This article shall be inoperative unless it shall have been ratified as an amendment to the Constitution by the legislatures of three fourths of the several States within seven years from the date of its submission to the States by the Congress.

Amendment 23
(Ratified March 29, 1961)

Section 1. The District constituting the seat of Government of the United States shall appoint in such manner as the Congress may direct:

A number of electors of President and Vice President equal to the whole number of Senators and Representatives in Congress to which the District would be entitled if it were a State, but in no event more than the least populous State; they shall be in addition to those appointed by the States, but they shall be considered, for the purposes of the election of President and Vice President, to be electors appointed by a State; and they shall meet in the District and perform such duties as provided by the twelfth article of amendment.

Section 2. The Congress shall have the power to enforce this article by appropriate legislation.

Amendment 24
(Ratified January 23, 1964)

Section 1. The right of citizens of the United States to vote in any primary or other election for President or Vice President, or for Senator or Representative in Congress, shall not be denied or abridged by the United States or any State by reasons of failure to pay any poll tax or other tax.

Section 2. The Congress shall have the power to enforce this article by appropriate legislation.

Amendment 25
(Ratified February 10, 1967)

Section 1. In case of the removal of the President from office or of his death or resignation, the Vice President shall become President.

Section 2. Whenever there is a vacancy in the office of the Vice President, the President shall nominate a Vice President who shall take office upon confirmation by a majority vote of both Houses of Congress.

Section 3. Whenever the President transmits to the President pro tempore of the Senate and the Speaker of the House of Representatives his written declaration that he is unable to discharge the powers and duties of his office, and until he transmits to them a written declaration to the contrary, such powers and duties shall be discharged by the Vice President as Acting President.

Section 4. Whenever the Vice President and a majority of either the principal officers of the executive departments or of such other body as Congress may by law provide, transmit to the President pro tempore of the Senate and the Speaker of the House of Representatives their written declaration that the President is unable to discharge the powers and duties of his office, the Vice President shall immediately assume the powers and duties of the office as Acting President.

Thereafter, when the President transmits to the President pro tempore of the Senate and the Speaker of the House of Representatives his written declaration that no inability exists, he shall resume the powers and duties of his office unless the Vice President and a majority of either the principal officers of the executive department or of such other body as Congress may by law provide, transmit within four days to the President pro tempore of the Senate and the Speaker of the House of Representatives their written declaration that the President is unable to discharge the powers and duties of his office. Thereupon Congress shall decide the issue, assembling within forty-eight hours for that purpose if not in session. If the Congress, within twenty-one days after receipt of the latter written declaration, or, if Congress is not in session, within twenty-one days after Congress is required to assemble, determines by two thirds vote of both Houses that the President is unable to discharge the powers and duties of his office, the Vice President shall continue to discharge the same as Acting President; otherwise, the President shall resume the powers and duties of his office.

Amendment 26
(Ratified July 1, 1971).

Section 1. The right of citizens of the United States, who are 18 years of age or older, to vote shall not be denied or abridged by the United States or by any state on account of age.

Section 2. The Congress shall have power to enforce this article by appropriate legislation.

Amendment 27
(Ratified May 7, 1992)

No law varying the compensation for the services of the senators and representatives shall take effect, until an election of representatives shall have intervened.

Facts About the Constitution

- The United States has the world's oldest written Constitution still in effect. All countries in the world now have one, except Israel, Libya, New Zealand, Oman and the United Kingdom.
- Until 1789, the United States was organized under the Articles of Confederation.
- The Constitutional Convention was supposed to begin May 14, 1787, but almost no one showed up! It finally began 11 days late, on May 25.
- Rhode Island did not send anyone to the convention and no one from Rhode Island signed the Constitution because it did not want a national government interfering with the state's affairs. Rhode Island and North Carolina would not sign without a Bill of Rights.

Forms of Government

When people live together in groups, they must share resources such as food and space. To keep things running smoothly, rules called **laws** are made to govern the members. Without rules, life would be unsafe and nothing much would be accomplished. Because not everyone follows the rules willingly, there must be a "power structure"—people with the power to make and enforce the rules.

"Government" is the process of making and enforcing rules. People have many different ideas and so there are many kinds of governments. The success of any form of government depends on how good the rules are and how well people follow them. Some governments allow people freedom and depend on them to be responsible citizens; others use force to make people follow the rules.

Forms of Government

A. **Rule by one person—autocracy**
1. **Monarchy.** The leader usually inherits the throne and holds power for life. Kings, queens and emperors are monarchs.
2. **Dictatorship.** The leader generally comes to power when a country is having many problems, and may seize power by force. The dictator has complete authority. Famous dictators are Adolf Hitler, Joseph Stalin, and Benito Mussolini.

B. **Rule by a few persons**
1. **Aristocracy.** Leaders may be members of a royal family or wealthy landowners. They are generally the powerful upper-class citizens.
2. **Oligarchy.** A small group of people holds power and rules as in a dictatorship.

C. **Rule by many**
1. **Democracy.** All the people meet and decide on every issue.
2. **Representative Democracy (Republic).** People elect representatives to rule because it is not possible for everyone to get together. The United States is a republic.

Some Theories of How Government Should Run

A. **Anarchism.** Private individuals govern themselves. There is little or no public government.
B. **Socialism.** The government works to own the country's main resources, factories, etc., generally in a peaceful way.
C. **Communism.** The government takes control of factories, land, and other means of production. The government may rule strictly and allow little or no criticism. The stated goal of communism is common ownership of means of production and common sharing of labor and products.

Governmental Systems

A. **Authoritarianism.** Government power is used without the consent of the people. People are expected to obey without question. There is little individual freedom.
B. **Capitalism.** An economic system in which individual people and private businesses own most of a country's resources and industries. Capitalism is often called a *free-enterprise system.*
C. **Fascism.** A system of government with a rigid, one-party dictatorship.
D. **Totalitarianism.** The government controls all of the activities of the people.

Speeches and Quotes

I know not what course others may take, but as for me, give me liberty or give me death!

> —Patrick Henry, 1775, urging the colonies to revolt against England.

These are the times that try men's souls.

> —Thomas Paine, 1776, in pamphlets trying to stir up the revolutionary spirit of Americans against the British.

We must indeed all hang together, or most assuredly, we shall all hang separately.

> —Benjamin Franklin, 1776, at the signing of the Declaration of Independence.

I only regret that I have but one life to lose for my country.

> —Nathan Hale, 1776, in a speech just before he was hanged by the British for spying during the American Revolution.

I have not yet begun to fight!

> —John Paul Jones, 1779. Jones' ship was badly damaged. The British commander asked if he would surrender. He answered, "I have not yet begun to fight!" As Jones' ship sank, his crew captured the British ship.

Go west, young man!

> —John Soule, later Horace Greeley, 1851, urging young people to take advantage of the opportunities on the American frontier.

Speak softly and carry a big stick.

> —Proverb quoted in 1902 by President Theodore Roosevelt. He believed the United States should negotiate with other countries carefully, but backed by the threat of force.

The world must be made safe for democracy.

> —President Woodrow Wilson, 1917, to justify his call for a declaration of war on Germany during World War I.

The business of America is business.

> —President Calvin Coolidge, 1925.

The only thing we have to fear is fear itself.

> — President Franklin D. Roosevelt, 1933, at first inaugural address. It was the worst point of the Great Depression.

I shall return.

> —General Douglas MacArthur, 1942, commander of the U.S. forces in the Far East during World War II. He was promising to return to his men in the Philippines after he was ordered to leave.

The buck stops here.

> —On President Harry Truman's desk.

Ask not what your country can do for you; ask what you can do for your country.

> —President John F. Kennedy, 1961, from his Inaugural Address.

Gettysburg Address

The **Gettysburg Address** is a short speech delivered by President Abraham Lincoln on November 19, 1863 during the Civil War. Its purpose was to dedicate a part of the battlefield of the Battle of Gettysburg as a cemetery for people who had lost their lives in the battle. The Gettysburg Address is engraved on a tablet on the wall of the Lincoln Memorial in Washington, D.C.

Four score and seven years ago our fathers brought forth on this continent, a new nation, conceived in Liberty, and dedicated to the proposition that all men are created equal.

Now we are engaged in a great civil war, testing whether that nation, or any nation so conceived and so dedicated, can long endure. We are met on a great battlefield of that war. We have come to dedicate a portion of that field, as a final resting place for those who here gave their lives that that nation might live. It is altogether fitting and proper that we should do this.

But in a larger sense, we can not dedicate—we can not consecrate—we can not hallow—this ground. The brave men, living and dead, who struggled here, have consecrated it, far above our poor power to add or detract. The world will little note, nor long remember what we say here, but it can never forget what they did here. It is for us the living, rather, to be dedicated here to the unfinished work which they who fought here have thus far so nobly advanced. It is rather for us to be here dedicated to the great task remaining before us—that from these honored dead we take increased devotion to that cause for which they gave the last full measure of devotion—that we here highly resolve that these dead shall not have died in vain—that this nation, under God, shall have a new birth of freedom—and that government of the people, by the people, for the people, shall not perish from the earth.

I Have a Dream

Martin Luther King, Jr. delivered a speech which included the following words on August 28, 1963, when more than 200,000 people marched from the Washington Monument to the Lincoln Memorial in Washington, D.C. to protest racial discrimination. Martin Luther King, Jr. won the Nobel Peace Prize in 1964 for leading the black struggle for equality through nonviolent means.

I say to you today, my friends, so even though we face the difficulties of today and tomorrow, I still have a dream. It is a dream deeply rooted in the American dream.

I have a dream that one day this nation will rise up and live out the true meaning of its creed: "We hold these truths to be self-evident; that all men are created equal."

I have a dream that one day, on the red hills of Georgia, sons of former slaves and the sons of former slaveowners will be able to sit down together at the table of brotherhood.

I have a dream that one day even the state of Mississippi, a state sweltering with the heat of oppression, will be transformed into an oasis of freedom and justice.

I have a dream that my four little children will one day live in a nation where they will not be judged by the color of their skin but by the content of their character.

I have a dream today. . .

Symbols of America

The **United States flag** is a symbol of the land, the people, the ideals and the government of the United States.

It was adopted on June 14, 1777. The flag is also known as the Stars & Stripes, the Star-Spangled Banner, and Old Glory.

The stripes stand for the original 13 colonies. The stars stand for the states. There is one for each of the 50 states.
Red stands for hardiness and courage.
White stands for innocence and purity.
Blue stands for vigilance, perseverance and justice.

The **Pledge of Allegiance** is a pledge of loyalty to the United States. It was first said by public school children in 1892.

> I pledge allegiance to the flag of the United States of America and to the Republic for which it stands, one Nation under God, indivisible, with liberty and justice for all.

The **Star-Spangled Banner** is the national anthem. It was written by Francis Scott Key while on a British warship in Chesapeake Bay, Maryland, during the War of 1812. He watched a night-long battle and wrote the song to express his joy at seeing the American flag still flying in the morning. The music was borrowed from an English song composed by John Stafford Smith. The Star-Spangled Banner was officially adopted as the national anthem in March 1931.

> Oh! say, can you see, by the dawn's early light,
> What so proudly we hailed at the twilight's last gleaming?
> Whose broad stripes and bright stars, thro' the perilous fight,
> O'er the ramparts we watched were so gallantly streaming?
> And the rockets' red glare, the bombs bursting in air,
> Gave proof thro' the night that our flag was still there.
> Oh! say, does that star-spangled banner yet wave
> O'er the land of the free and the home of the brave?

The **Liberty Bell** is a symbol of American independence.

It rang on July 8, 1776, to celebrate the adoption of the Declaration of Independence. It was rung every year on the Fourth of July until 1835, when it cracked. It is in Philadelphia, Pennsylvania. The inscription reads: "Proclaim Liberty throughout all the land unto all the inhabitants thereof," (from the Bible— Leviticus 25:10). It weighs over 2,080 pounds.

The **motto** of the United States is "In God We Trust." It was officially adopted on July 30, 1956, and is printed on money.

The **Statue of Liberty** is a symbol of American democracy. It stands on Liberty Island in New York Harbor and is the first thing many early immigrants saw as they came to America. The Statue of Liberty was given to the United States by France on July 4, 1884 as a gift of friendship. It is 151 feet 1 inch high, weighs 450,000 pounds, and has 142 steps inside.

A woman named Emma Lazarus wrote a poem for the Statue of Liberty, which was inscribed on a tablet in the pedestal in 1903. It is called "The New Colossus."

> Not like the brazen giant of Greek fame,
>   With conquering limbs astride from land to land;
>   Here at our sea-washed, sunset gates shall stand
> A mighty woman with a torch, whose flame
> Is the imprisoned lightning, and her name
>   Mother of Exiles. From her beacon-hand
>   Glows world-wide welcome; her mild eyes
>   command
> The air-bridged harbor that twin cities frame.
> "Keep ancient lands, your storied pomp!" cries she
>   With silent lips. "Give me your tired, your poor,
> Your huddled masses yearning to breathe free,
>   The wretched refuse of your teeming shore.
> Send these, the homeless, tempest-tost to me,
>   I lift my lamp beside the golden door!"

Uncle Sam is a symbol for the United States. The name came from the initials U.S. It was first used during the War of 1812 as an unfriendly nickname for the United States government. In 1961, Congress recognized Uncle Sam as a national symbol.

The two major **political parties**, or organized political groups, in the United States are the Democratic and Republican Parties.

The **Great Seal of the United States** is a symbol of the sovereignty of the United States. It was adopted on June 20, 1782.

The American eagle symbolizes self-reliance.
The vertical stripes represent the 13 stripes of the flag.
The blue above the stripes symbolizes the U.S. government.
The olive branch stands for peace and the arrows for war.
The motto, *E pluribus unum*, stands for one (nation) out of many (states).

The **donkey** has been a symbol of the Democratic Party since Andrew Jackson's presidential campaign in 1828, and was used mainly in political cartoons. The Democratic Party is the oldest existing party in the United States. Most historians date its origin from Andrew Jackson's campaign.

The **elephant** was first used as a symbol of the Republican Party in political cartoons in 1874. The party formed in 1854 in opposition to slavery, and Abraham Lincoln was the first Republican president. The Republican Party was nicknamed the G.O.P., or *Grand Old Party,* in the 1880's.

The **bald eagle** is a symbol of American freedom and power. It was adopted as the national bird on June 20, 1782.

Branches of the Government of

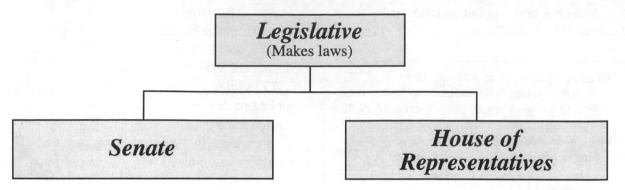

The Senate and the House of Representatives are jointly known as the **United States Congress.**

Membership: 100 members, two from each of the 50 states.

Term: Six years. About one-third of the members are up for reelection every two years. Terms expire in January.

Qualifications:
1. At least 30 years old.
2. U.S. citizen for at least nine years.
3. Legal resident of the state from which elected.

Salary: $133,600

Address: The Senate
Washington, DC 20510

Phone number: (202) 224-3121

Membership: 435 members—one or more from each state based on population. California, the most populous state, has 52 representatives. Seven states have only one representative based on the 1990 census.

Term: Two years. Elections are held in even numbered years. Terms expire in January.

Qualifications:
1. At least 25 years old.
2. U.S. citizen for at least seven years.
3. Legal resident of the state from which elected.

Salary: $133,600

Address: House of Representatives
Washington, DC 20515

The Senate and House of Representatives meet in the United States Capitol Building.

the United States of America

Executive (Enforces laws)	**Judicial** (Interprets laws)
President Vice-President	**Supreme Court**

President: William J. Clinton
Vice-President: Al Gore

Term: Four years. Limited to two terms.

Qualifications:
1. At least 35 years old.
2. Natural born U.S. citizen.
3. Has lived in the U.S. at least 14 years.

Salary: President: $200,000
Vice-President: $166,200

Address: The White House
1600 Pennsylvania Avenue NW
Washington, DC 20500

The Cabinet
Secretary of State
Secretary of the Treasury
Secretary of Defense
Attorney General
Secretary of the Interior
Secretary of Agriculture
Secretary of Commerce
Secretary of Labor
Secretary of Health and Human Services
Secretary of Housing and Urban
    Development
Secretary of Transportation
Secretary of Energy
Secretary of Education
Secretary of Veterans Affairs

Membership: Nine members, appointed by the President, with the advice and consent of the Senate.

Term: Life.

Qualifications: None set in the Constitution.

Salary: Chief Justice: $166,200
Associate Justices: $159,000

Address: United States Supreme Court
1 First Street NE
Washington, DC 20543

Supreme Court Justices
Chief Justice William H. Rehnquist
John Paul Stevens
Sandra Day O'Connor
Antonin Scalia
Anthony M. Kennedy
David H. Souter
Clarence Thomas
Ruth Bader Ginsburg
Stephen Breyer

The President lives and works in the White House.

United States Presidents

Name	Date of Birth	State of Birth	Term	Date of Death
1. George Washington	Feb. 22, 1732	Virginia	1789–1797	Dec. 14, 1799
2. John Adams	Oct. 30, 1735	Massachusetts	1797–1801	July 4, 1826
3. Thomas Jefferson	Apr. 13, 1743	Virginia	1801–1809	July 4, 1826
4. James Madison	Mar. 16, 1751	Virginia	1809–1817	June 28, 1836
5. James Monroe	Apr. 28, 1758	Virginia	1817–1825	July 4, 1831
6. John Quincy Adams	July 11, 1767	Massachusetts	1825–1829	Feb. 23, 1848
7. Andrew Jackson	Mar. 15, 1767	South Carolina	1829–1837	June 8, 1845
8. Martin Van Buren	Dec. 5, 1782	New York	1837–1841	July 24, 1862
9. William H. Harrison	Feb. 9, 1773	Virginia	1841	Apr. 4, 1841
10. John Tyler	Mar. 29, 1790	Virginia	1841–1845	Jan. 18, 1862
11. James K. Polk	Nov. 2, 1795	North Carolina	1845–1849	June 15, 1849
12. Zachary Taylor	Nov. 24, 1784	Virginia	1849–1850	July 9, 1850
13. Millard Fillmore	Jan. 7, 1800	New York	1850–1853	Mar. 8, 1874
14. Franklin Pierce	Nov. 23, 1804	New Hampshire	1853–1857	Oct. 8, 1869
15. James Buchanan	Apr. 23, 1791	Pennsylvania	1857–1861	June 1, 1868
16. Abraham Lincoln	Feb. 12, 1809	Kentucky	1861–1865	Apr. 15, 1865
17. Andrew Johnson	Dec. 29, 1808	North Carolina	1865–1869	July 31, 1875
18. Ulysses S. Grant	Apr. 27, 1822	Ohio	1869–1877	July 23, 1885
19. Rutherford B. Hayes	Oct. 4, 1822	Ohio	1877–1881	Jan. 17, 1893
20. James A. Garfield	Nov. 19, 1831	Ohio	1881	Sept. 19, 1881
21. Chester A. Arthur	Oct. 5, 1829	Vermont	1881–1885	Nov. 18, 1886
22. Grover Cleveland	Mar. 18, 1837	New Jersey	1885–1889	June 24, 1908
23. Benjamin Harrison	Aug. 20, 1833	Ohio	1889–1893	Mar. 13, 1901
24. Grover Cleveland	Mar. 18, 1837	New Jersey	1893–1897	June 24, 1908
25. William McKinley	Jan. 29, 1843	Ohio	1897–1901	Sept. 14, 1901
26. Theodore Roosevelt	Oct. 27, 1858	New York	1901–1909	Jan. 6, 1919
27. William H. Taft	Sept. 15, 1857	Ohio	1909–1913	Mar. 8, 1930
28. Woodrow Wilson	Dec. 29, 1856	Virginia	1913–1921	Feb. 3, 1924
29. Warren G. Harding	Nov. 2, 1865	Ohio	1921–1923	Aug. 2, 1923
30. Calvin Coolidge	July 4, 1872	Vermont	1923–1929	Jan. 5, 1933
31. Herbert C. Hoover	Aug. 10, 1874	Iowa	1929–1933	Oct. 10, 1964
32. Franklin D. Roosevelt	Jan. 30, 1882	New York	1933–1945	Apr. 12, 1945
33. Harry S. Truman	May 8, 1884	Missouri	1945–1953	Dec. 26, 1972
34. Dwight D. Eisenhower	Oct. 14, 1890	Texas	1953–1961	Mar. 28, 1969
35. John F. Kennedy	May 29, 1917	Massachusetts	1961–1963	Nov. 22, 1963
36. Lyndon B. Johnson	Aug. 27, 1908	Texas	1963–1969	Jan. 22, 1973
37. Richard M. Nixon	Jan. 9, 1913	California	1969–1974	Apr. 22, 1994
38. Gerald R. Ford	July 14, 1913	Nebraska	1974–1977	
39. James E. Carter, Jr.	Oct. 1, 1924	Georgia	1977–1981	
40. Ronald W. Reagan	Feb. 6, 1911	Illinois	1981–1989	
41. George H. W. Bush	June 12, 1924	Massachusetts	1989–1993	
42. William J. Clinton	Aug. 19, 1946	Arkansas	1993–	

North America

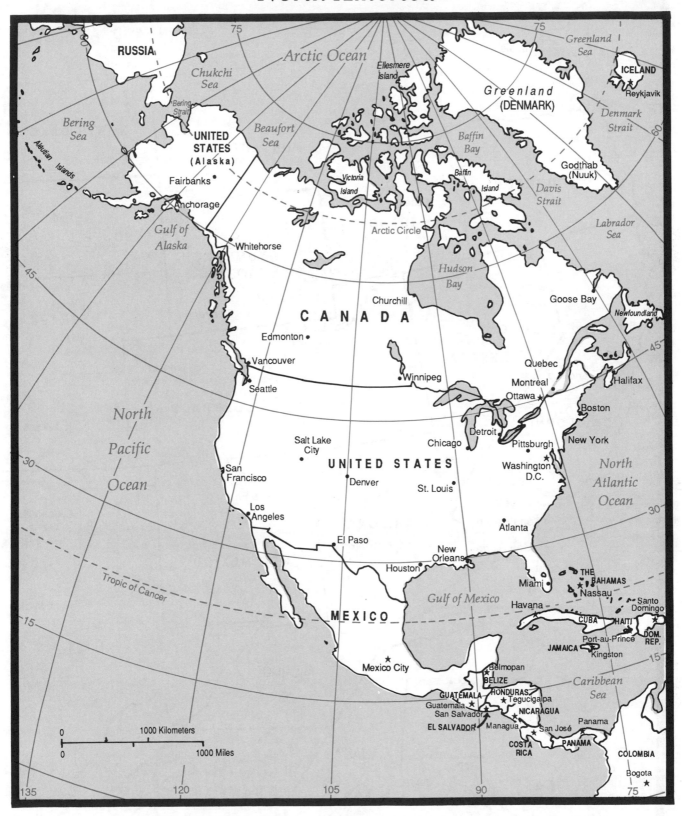

RUSSIA

Chukchi Sea

Arctic Ocean

Ellesmere Island

Greenland Sea

ICELAND

Reykjavik

Greenland (DENMARK)

Bering Strait

Bering Sea

Beaufort Sea

UNITED STATES (Alaska)

Baffin Bay

Baffin Island

Denmark Strait

Godthab (Nuuk)

Aleutian Islands

Fairbanks

Anchorage

Victoria Island

Davis Strait

Labrador Sea

Gulf of Alaska

Whitehorse

Arctic Circle

Hudson Bay

Churchill

CANADA

Goose Bay

Newfoundland

Edmonton

Vancouver

Winnipeg

Quebec

Halifax

Seattle

Montreal

Ottawa

Boston

North Pacific Ocean

Salt Lake City

Chicago

Detroit

Pittsburgh

New York

UNITED STATES

Denver

St. Louis

Washington D.C.

North Atlantic Ocean

Los Angeles

San Francisco

Atlanta

El Paso

New Orleans

Houston

Miami

THE BAHAMAS

Nassau

Santo Domingo

Tropic of Cancer

Gulf of Mexico

Havana

CUBA

HAITI

MEXICO

Port-au-Prince

DOM. REP.

JAMAICA

Kingston

Mexico City

Belmopan

BELIZE

Caribbean Sea

GUATEMALA

HONDURAS

Tegucigalpa

NICARAGUA

Guatemala

San Salvador

Panama

EL SALVADOR

Managua

San José

COSTA RICA

PANAMA

COLOMBIA

Bogota

0 —— 1000 Kilometers

0 —— 1000 Miles

135   120   105   90   75

75   60   45   30   15

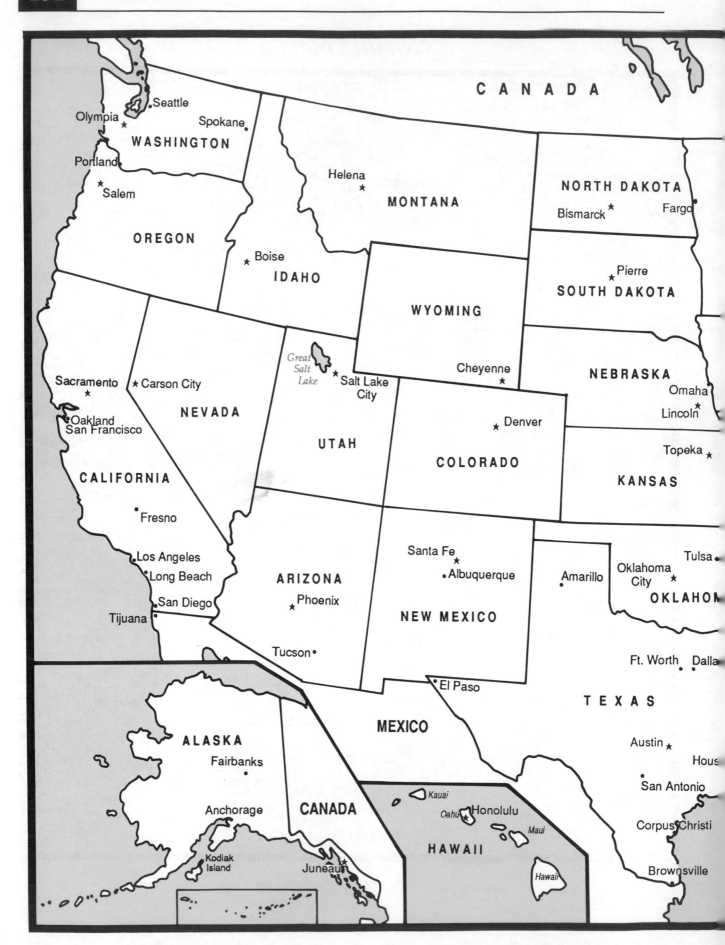

CANADA

Seattle
Olympia ★
WASHINGTON
Spokane •
Portland
Salem ★
OREGON
Boise ★
IDAHO

Helena ★
MONTANA

NORTH DAKOTA
Bismarck ★ Fargo •

Pierre ★
SOUTH DAKOTA

WYOMING

Cheyenne ★

NEBRASKA
Omaha •
Lincoln ★

Great Salt Lake
Salt Lake City ★

Denver ★

COLORADO

Topeka ★
KANSAS

Sacramento ★
Carson City ★
NEVADA
Oakland •
San Francisco

UTAH

CALIFORNIA

Fresno •

Los Angeles •
Long Beach •
San Diego •
Tijuana •

ARIZONA
Phoenix ★

Tucson •

Santa Fe ★
• Albuquerque

NEW MEXICO

El Paso •

Amarillo •

Oklahoma City ★
OKLAHOMA

Tulsa •

Ft. Worth • Dalla •

TEXAS

Austin ★

Hous •

San Antonio •

ALASKA
Fairbanks •

MEXICO

Anchorage
CANADA
Kauai
Oahu ★ Honolulu
Maui
Kodiak Island
Juneau ★
HAWAII
Hawaii

Corpus Christi

Brownsville

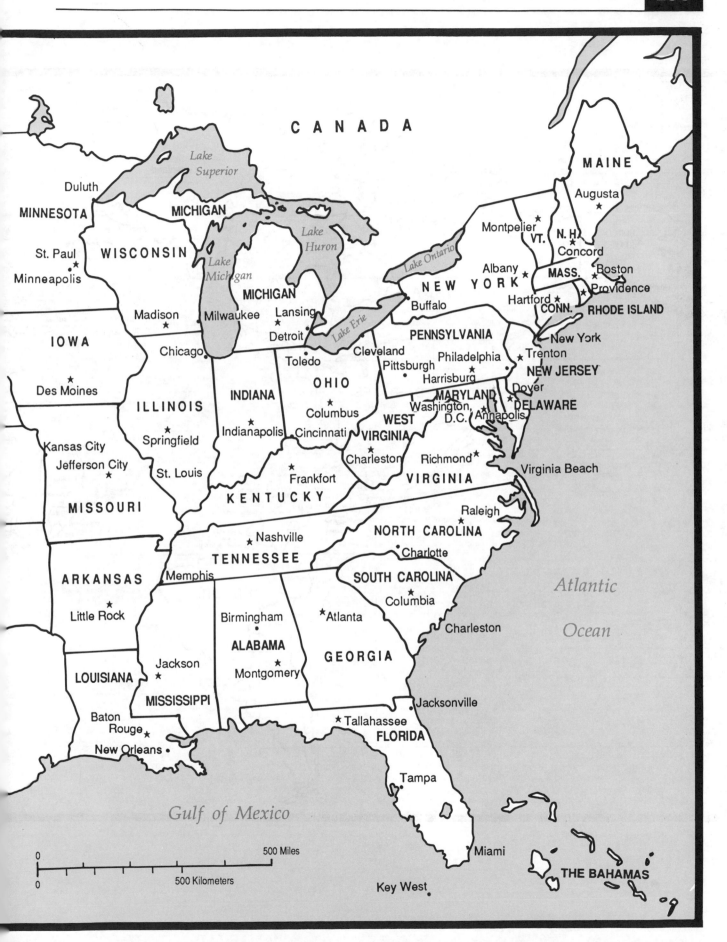

CANADA

MAINE

Augusta ★

MINNESOTA

Duluth

MICHIGAN

Lake Superior

Montpelier ★

N. H.

VT.

Concord ★

St. Paul ★

WISCONSIN

Lake Huron

Albany ★

MASS.

Boston ★

Minneapolis

Lake Michigan

NEW YORK

Hartford ★

CONN.

Providence

Madison ★

Milwaukee

Lansing ★

Buffalo

RHODE ISLAND

IOWA

Chicago

Detroit

Lake Erie

PENNSYLVANIA

New York

MICHIGAN

Toledo

Cleveland

Pittsburgh

Philadelphia

Trenton

Des Moines ★

ILLINOIS

INDIANA

OHIO

Harrisburg ★

NEW JERSEY

Columbus ★

Dover ★

Kansas City

Springfield ★

Indianapolis ★

Cincinnati

MARYLAND

DELAWARE

Washington, D.C.

Annapolis ★

Jefferson City ★

St. Louis

Frankfort ★

WEST VIRGINIA

Charleston ★

Richmond ★

Virginia Beach

MISSOURI

KENTUCKY

VIRGINIA

Raleigh ★

Nashville ★

NORTH CAROLINA

ARKANSAS

TENNESSEE

Charlotte

Memphis

SOUTH CAROLINA

Atlantic

Little Rock ★

Columbia ★

Birmingham

★ Atlanta

Charleston

Ocean

LOUISIANA

Jackson ★

ALABAMA

GEORGIA

Montgomery ★

MISSISSIPPI

Jacksonville

Baton Rouge ★

★ Tallahassee

New Orleans

FLORIDA

Gulf of Mexico

Tampa

0

500 Miles

Miami

0

500 Kilometers

THE BAHAMAS

Key West

165 150 135 120 105 90 75 60 45 30 15 0

Arctic Ocean

—75

Greenland
(DENMARK)

—60

UNITED
STATES
(Alaska)   Arctic Circle

ICELAND

CANADA

—45

IRELAND   UNITED
KINGD

North

Atlantic

PORTUGAL SPAIN   FRAN

Ocean

UNITED STATES

—30

MOROCCO

Tropic of Cancer

Western
Sahara   ALGE

UNITED STATES
(Hawaii)

MEXICO   THE BAHAMAS

CAPE
VERDE   SENEGA

MAURITANIA

MALI

CUBA   DOMINICAN
REPUBLIC   ST. KITTS AND NEVIS
HAITI   ANTIGUA AND BARBUDA

—15

JAMAICA   ST. LUCIA DOMINICA

THE GAMBIA   BURKINA
FASO B

GUATEMALA
EL SALVADOR   BELIZE
HONDURAS
NICARAGUA   ST. VINCENT AND
THE GRENADINES   BARBADOS
GRENADA
TRINIDAD AND TOBAGO   GUINEA-BISSAU   GUINEA

SIERRA LEONE   IVORY
COAST GHAN

COSTA RICA   LIBERIA   TO

PANAMA   VENEZUELA GUYANA
SURINAME   SAO TOME
AND PRINCIP

COLOMBIA   French Guiana
(FR.)

—0 —Equator

ECUADOR

PERU   BRAZIL

—15

BOLIVIA

South   PARAGUAY   *South*

Tropic of Capricorn

Pacific   *Atlantic*

—30

Ocean   CHILE URUGUAY   *Ocean*

ARGENTINA

—45

165 150 135 120 105 90 75 60 45 30 15 0

South
Pacific
Ocean

Prime Meridian

15 30 45 60 75 90 105 120 135 150 165 180

Arctic Ocean

75

Svelbard
(NOR.)

Arctic Circle

60

SWEDEN

FINLAND

ESTONIA
LATVIA
LITHUANIA
POLAND BELARUS
CZECH
SLOV. UKRAINE
AUS. HUNG. MOLDOVA
ROMANIA

R U S S I A

KAZAKHSTAN

MONGOLIA

North

Pacific

Ocean

45

ITALY
BULGARIA
GREECE TURKEY
CYPRUS
LEBANON SYRIA
ISRAEL
JORDAN

GEORGIA
ARMENIA AZERBAIJAN
TURKMENISTAN

UZBEKISTAN

KYRGYZSTAN
TAJIKISTAN

N. KOREA
S. KOREA

JAPAN

IRAQ IRAN AFGHANISTAN

C H I N A

KUWAIT
BAHRAIN
QATAR
U.A.E.

30

LIBYA EGYPT SAUDI
ARABIA

PAKISTAN

NEPAL BHUTAN

Tropic of Cancer

OMAN BANGLADESH

CHAD SUDAN

ERITREA YEMEN
DJIBOUTI

I N D I A

BURMA
LAOS

THAILAND VIETNAM
CAMBODIA

PHILIPPINES

FEDERATED STATES
OF MICRONESIA

MARSHALL
ISLANDS

C.A.R.

ETHIOPIA

SRI
LANKA

MALDIVES

BRUNEI

SEYCHELLES

MALAYSIA

NAURU

Equator 0
KIRIBATI

UGANDA

CAMEROON
CONGO ZAIRE

RWANDA KENYA
BURUNDI

TANZANIA

Indian

Ocean

INDONESIA

PAPUA
NEW GUINEA

SOLOMON
ISLANDS

TUVALU

ANGOLA ZAMBIA

MALAWI

COMOROS

WESTERN
SAMOA

NAMIBIA
ZIMBABWE
MOZAMBIQUE

MADAGASCAR

VANUATU FIJI

15

BOTSWANA

MAURITIUS

TONGA

SWAZILAND

A U S T R A L I A

Tropic of Capricorn

SOUTH
AFRICA
LESOTHO

30

NEW
ZEALAND

45

15 30 45 60 75 90 105 120 135 150 165 180

South America

80 · 60 · 40

Caribbean Sea

North Atlantic Ocean

Barranquilla
Maracaibo · ★ Caracas
VENEZUELA
Georgetown ✦
Medellin **GUYANA** ✦ Paramaribo
★ Bogotá **SURINAME** French Guiana (FR.)
COLOMBIA ✦ Cayenne
Cali Boa Vista
Mitu Macapá

0 — *Equator*
★ Quito Belém São Luis
ECUADOR Fonte Boa Manaus Santarem
Guayaquil
Iquitos **B R A Z I L** Fortaleza
Piura Teresina
Natal
Rio Porto Velho Recife
Trujillo Branco
Huánuco · Porto Nacional Aracaju
PERU Salvador
Lima ★
Ica Cusco Brasilia ★
Trinidad Cuiabá Goiania
Arequipa *Lake Titicaca* **BOLIVIA** Belo
★ La Paz Horizonte
Arica Sucre Santa Vitória
Cruz

South Pacific Ocean

20 — Rio de Janeiro — 20
Antofagasta **PARAGUAY** São Paulo
Tropic of Capricorn Asunción ★ Curitiba
San Miguel
de Tucumán Florianópolis *South Atlantic Ocean*
Resistencia
Porto Alegre
CHILE Córdoba Salto
Valparaiso Mendoza Rosario **URUGUAY**
Santiago Buenos Aires
Concepción **ARGENTINA** Montevideo
Bahia Blanca Mar del Plata

40 — Puerto Montt — 40
San Carlos
de Bariloche

500 Kilometers
Comodoro Rivadavia
500 Nautical Miles

★ Stanley
Strait of Magellan **Falkland Islands**

Ushuaia South Georgia

100 80 60 40 20

Africa

Europe

Greenland (DEN.)

Greenland Sea

Arctic Circle

Norwegian Sea

Hammerfest

Murmansk

Narvik

White Sea

Arkhangel'sk

Reykjavik ★ ICELAND

Oulu

NORWAY   Umeå   FINLAND

Trondheim

SWEDEN

Tórshavn   *Faroe Islands (Den.)*

Lake Onega

Helsinki ★

Lake Ladoga

St. Petersburg

Shetland Islands

Bergen

Gävle

RUSSIA

Oslo

Stockholm ★   Tallinn
ESTONIA

Orkney Islands

Skagerrak

Göteborg

Gotland

Riga ★ LATVIA

Moscow ★

Hebrides

Aberdeen

North Sea

DENMARK

Öland

Baltic Sea

LITHUANIA

Belfast   Glascow

Newcastle

Copenhagen ★   Malmö

Bornholm

Vilnius

Dublin ★ IRELAND   *Irish Sea*   Liverpool   UNITED KINGDOM

RUSSIA

Minsk ★

North Atlantic Ocean

Cardiff   London ★

Amsterdam   Hamburg   Berlin ★

NETH.

Gdansk

BELARUS

Warsaw ★

Poznan

Bonn

GERMANY

POLAND

Kiev ★

Brussels   BEL.

English Channel

Le Havre

LUX.

Frankfurt

Krakow

Lviv ★

UKRAINE

Prague ★

CZECH REP.   SLOVAKIA

Paris ★

Strasbourg

Bratislava ★

MOLDOVA

Odessa

Nantes

Munich

Vienna ★   Budapest ★

Kishiněv ★

FRANCE

SWITZ.   LEICH.

AUSTRIA   HUNGARY

ROMANIA

Bay of Biscay

Bern ★

SLOVENIA

Bucharest ★

Black Sea

Geneva

Venice

CROATIA

Varna ★

Milan   SAN MARINO

BOSNIA AND HERZEGOVINA   Belgrade ★

Bordeaux

Marseille   MONACO

Adriatic Sea   Sarajevo ★   YUGOSLAVIA   BULGARIA

Bilbao

ANDORRA

ITALY

Sofia ★

Istanbul

Porto

Rome ★

Tiranë ★   MACEDONIA

SPAIN

Corsica

Naples

ALB.

TURKEY

PORTUGAL

Madrid ★

Barcelona

Sardinia

Tyrrhenian Sea

GREECE   *Aegean Sea*

Lisbon ★

Valencia

Patrai ★   Athens ★

Balearic Islands

Ionian Sea

Rhodes

Málaga

Mediterranean Sea

Sicily

Crete

Strait of Gibraltar

Gibraltar (U.K.)

Algiers ★

Tunis ★

MALTA

MOROCCO   ALGERIA

| 0 | 200 | 400 Kilometers |
| 0 | 200 | 400 Nautical Miles |

Asia

Arctic Ocean

Wrangel Island
Providéniya
East Siberian Sea
Bering Sea
Anadyr
Cherskiy
Franz Josef Land
Severnaya Zemlya
New Siberian Islands
Evensk
Barents Sea
Novaya Zemlya
Kara Sea
Laptev Sea
Magadan
Petropavlosk-Kamchatskiy
Murmansk
Dikson
Tiksi
Verkhoyansk
Baltic Sea
Arkhangel'sk
Vorkuta
Noril'sk
Arctic Circle
Sea of Okhotsk
Kuril Islands
Riga
Tallinn
LITHUANIA
Vilnius
ESTONIA
LATVIA
St. Petersburg
Kotlas
Urengoy
Yakutsk
Minsk
BELARUS
Moscow
Kirov
Perm
RUSSIA
Lensk
Sakhalin
Kiev
MOLDOVA
Kishiněv
Nizhny Novgorod
Kuybyshev
Sverdlovsk
Bratsk
Komsomol'sk
Khabarovsk
UKRAINE
Volgograd
Orenburg
Chelyabinsk
Omsk
Novosibirsk
Krasnoyarsk
Lake Baikal
Chita
Harbin
Sapporo
Black Sea
GEORGIA
Tbilisi
Caspian Sea
Irkutsk
Vladivostok
Sea of Japan
Yerevan
ARMENIA
AZERBAIJAN
Baku
Aral Sea
KAZAKHSTAN
Semipalatinsk
Ulaanbaatar
Changchun
Shenyang
NORTH KOREA
JAPAN
Tokyo
Tabriz
UZBEKISTAN
Alma-Ata
MONGOLIA
Beijing
P'yongyang
Seoul
SOUTH KOREA
Osaka
TURKMENISTAN
Tashkent
Bishkek
KYRGYZSTAN
Ürümqi
Tianjin
Yellow Sea
Kitakyushu
Teheran
Ashkhabad
Dushanbe
Yinchuan
Jinan
Zhengzhou
Abadan
IRAN
AFGHANISTAN
TAJIKISTAN
Lanzhou
Nanjing
Shanghai
Ryukyu Islands
Persian Gulf
Kabul
Golmud
CHINA
Xi'an
Wuhan
Hangzhou
Nanchang
East China Sea
Naha
Bandar-e Abbas
Qandahar
Islamabad
Lahore
Chengdu
Chongqing
Changsha
Fuzhou
PAKISTAN
New Delhi
Lhasa
NEPAL
BHUTAN
Thimphu
Guiyang
T'ai-pei
TAIWAN
Tropic of Cancer
Karachi
Agra
Kathmandu
Kunming
Guangzhou
Nanning
Hong Kong
Macau
Philippine Sea
Ahmadabad
Varanasi
Dhaka
INDIA
BANGLADESH
Calcutta
BURMA
Mandalay
Hanoi
Hainan Dao
Manila
Bombay
Nagpur
Vishankhapatnam
Yangon
LAOS
Vientiane
PHILIPPINES
Arabian Sea
Hyderabad
THAILAND
VIETNAM
South China Sea
Panaji
Bangkok
CAMBODIA
Tavoy
Phnom Penh
Calicut
Madras
Bay of Bengal
Andaman Islands
Ho Chi Minh City
Jaffna
Andaman Sea
BRUNEI
Laccadive Sea
SRI LANKA
MALAYSIA
Colombo
Nicobar Islands
MALDIVES
Male
MALAYSIA
Kuala Lumpur
Medan
SINGAPORE
Indian Ocean
Equator
INDONESIA

0 500 1000 Kilometers
0 500 1000 Nautical Miles

Australia

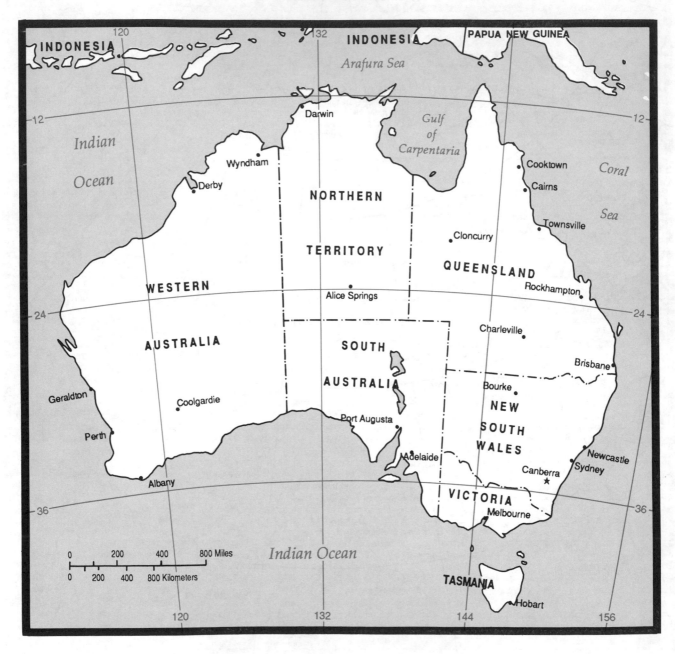

INDONESIA

INDONESIA

Arafura Sea

PAPUA NEW GUINEA

120

132

Indian

Ocean

12

Darwin

Gulf
of
Carpentaria

Coral

12

Wyndham

Derby

NORTHERN

Cooktown

Cairns

Sea

TERRITORY

Townsville

Cloncurry

WESTERN

QUEENSLAND

Rockhampton

24

Alice Springs

24

AUSTRALIA

Charleville

Geraldton

Coolgardie

SOUTH

Brisbane

AUSTRALIA

Bourke

NEW

Perth

Port Augusta

SOUTH

WALES

Newcastle

Adelaide

Canberra

Sydney

Albany

★

VICTORIA

36

36

Melbourne

0   200   400   800 Miles

Indian Ocean

0   200   400   800 Kilometers

TASMANIA

Hobart

120

132

144

156

Libraries

and

Books

The Globe

The **globe** is a model of the earth.

The **North Pole** and **South Pole** are imaginary points. An imaginary line from the North Pole to the South Pole through the center of the earth is the **axis** on which the earth rotates, or spins.

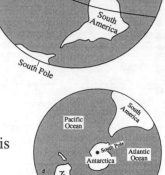

The **equator** is an imaginary line that circles the globe halfway between the North and South Poles. It divides the earth into two halves, called **hemispheres**.

The **northern hemisphere** is the half with the North Pole.

The **southern hemisphere** is the half with the South Pole.

The earth is also divided into eastern and western hemispheres. The imaginary dividing lines are the **prime meridian**, which runs through Greenwich, England, and the **international date line**, exactly halfway around the world from Greenwich. These lines are the basis for time zones.

The **western hemisphere** contains North and South America.

The **eastern hemisphere** contains most of Africa, Asia, Europe and Australia.

Imaginary lines of **latitude** and **longitude** can be used to locate places on the globe.

Lines of latitude, or parallels, tell how far north or south of the equator a place is. The equator is 0° latitude. The North Pole is 90° north latitude (90° N) and the South Pole is 90° south latitude (90° S).

Lines of longitude, or meridians, go around the globe through the North and South Poles. They measure distance east and west of the prime meridian. The prime meridian is 0° longitude. The international date line runs along the 180° longitude line.

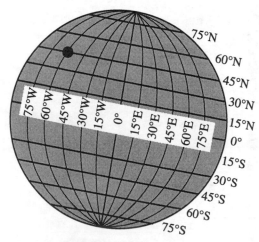

45°N 60°W identifies an exact place on the earth.

Reading Maps

Maps are drawings of the earth's surface that use lines, color and symbols to give information about the location of things. They are more useful than globes because they are easier to carry and store, and because they can show more detail about small areas of the earth than a globe.

Since the earth is round and a map is flat, a map of the world will have distortions. Map makers use different **projections** to "flatten" the earth's surface.

Mercator projection

Robinson projection

Azimuthal Equidistant

Features of a Map

The **title** of a map tells what kind of map it is and what area it covers.

The **compass rose** shows direction. Usually, the top of the map is north, but not always. Direction may also be shown by an arrow pointing north.

The **legend**, or **key**, explains the symbols and colors used on a map.

The **scale of miles** is used to figure the distances on the map. It can be shown three ways:

1. **Fraction.** 1/10,000 or 1:10,000 means one unit on the map equals 10,000 of the same units on the earth.

2. **Graphic Scale.** Each mark represents a certain distance on the earth.

3. **Words and Figures**, such as 1 inch = 20 miles.

An **index** and **map grid** is used to find specific places on the map. For example, if the index says Lorain is at A3, locate A on the left and 3 at the bottom. Find where the imaginary lines meet and look for Lorain in that area.

Atlases and Types of Maps

An **atlas** is a book of maps. Atlases may also contain a variety of other reference information in the front or back. The following kinds of maps may be included in an atlas.

Cities and Counties of Connecticut

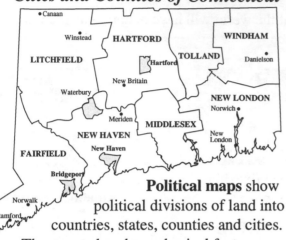

Political maps show political divisions of land into countries, states, counties and cities. They may also show physical features such as lakes and rivers.

Major Rivers of Connecticut

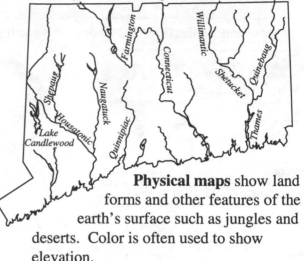

Physical maps show land forms and other features of the earth's surface such as jungles and deserts. Color is often used to show elevation.

Major Highways of Connecticut

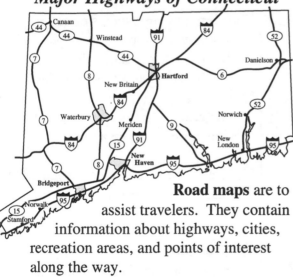

Road maps are to assist travelers. They contain information about highways, cities, recreation areas, and points of interest along the way.

Food Products of Connecticut

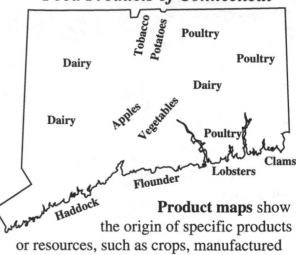

Product maps show the origin of specific products or resources, such as crops, manufactured goods, or natural resources.

Topographical maps are very detailed physical maps which use contour lines to show both elevation and steepness of the land. They are often used by hikers.

Historical maps give specific information about something in history, such as the routes of explorers, the locations of battles, or the changes in political boundaries over time.

Population maps show population density, or people per square mile. **Rainfall maps** use color or shading to show average yearly rainfall of areas on the map. **Temperature maps** use the same techniques to show temperatures. **Weather maps** show weather patterns.

Graphic Aids

Graphs

Pictographs use symbols or pictures of objects and have keys.

Circle graphs, or **pie graphs**, show how parts are related to the whole by percent.

Bar graphs compare items directly.

Line graphs are best used to show changes over time or trends.

Time Line

The American Revolution	

Stamp Act
March 1765

Boston Massacre
March 5, 1770

Boston Tea Party
Dec. 16, 1773

Declaration of
Independence
July 4, 1776

Paul Revere's Ride
April 1775

Victory at
Saratoga
Oct. 17, 1777

Washington's Winter
at Valley Forge
1777-78

British surrender
Oct. 19, 1781

1766 1767 1768 1769 1770 1771 1772 1773 1774 1775 1776 1777 1778 1779 1780 1781 1782

A **time line** shows time spans between historical events. It shows what happened, when it happened, the time between events, and other important things that happened at about the same time.

Diagram

Sailboat

A **diagram** is a drawing that shows how something works or shows the relationship between its parts. Often, there are labels that name the parts and/or arrows to show the direction or movement of the parts.

Table

Most Populous Countries	
Country	Population
1. China	1,191,976,000
2. India	911,576,000
3. United States	260,750,000
4. Indonesia	199,717,000
5. Brazil	155,254,000
6. Russia	147,820,000
7. Japan	125,023,000
8. Pakistan	126,415,000
9. Bangladesh	116,602,000
10. Nigeria	98,091,000

A **table** presents information in columns and rows.

Schedule

Class Schedule	
7:45 - 8:00	Homeroom
8:00 - 8:50	Math
9:00 - 9:50	Physical Ed.
10:00 - 10:50	Geography
11:00 - 11:50	Science
12:00 - 12:50	Lunch
1:00 - 1:50	Band
2:00 - 2:50	English
3:00 - 4:00	Track

A **schedule**, or **timetable**, shows when events are going to occur.

Photographs, **cartoons**, **illustrations**, and **charts** are also graphic aids.

The Library

A library is a place where print and nonprint resources are organized and stored for use by patrons. Resources may include books, periodicals, maps, films and computer software. Since many people share the library, it is important for everyone to be considerate of others by being quiet and by caring for books and materials. The most important library in the United States is the Library of Congress in Washington, D.C. It has about 100 million items in 470 languages. Since 1870, the Library of Congress has received two free copies of every book copyrighted in the United States.

Library Organization

Most libraries have a catalog, stacks of books, a reference section, a periodical section and a vertical file. Libraries have collections of information in many formats, including maps, films, audiotapes, videotapes, microfiche, microfilm and CD-ROM.

The **catalog** is the key to locating books in a library. It contains alphabetical arrangements of **author entries**, **title entries** and **subject entries**. Many libraries have **computers**, **microfiche** or **microfilm** catalogs. Some libraries may have a **card catalog**. When using the catalog, note on a piece of paper the call numbers for any resources you wish to find.

The **author entry** is the main entry in a catalog. **Title entries** and **subject entries** are copies of the author entry. The title entry may be used when the name of the book is known.

Locating information is easier and faster with computer technology. Modern libraries have the catalog and much other information available on computers.

Computer Workstation

Subject entries are useful for finding the materials a library contains on any subject. Never look up a title or subject under the words "a," "an" or "the." Look under the next word in the title or subject.

Cross-reference entries refer the user to another place in the catalog for further information.

Sample Author Entry

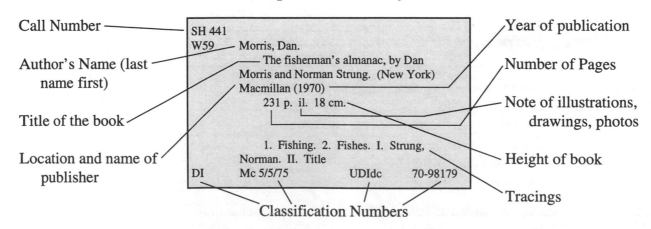

Call Number

Author's Name (last name first)

Title of the book

Location and name of publisher

SH 441
W59 — Morris, Dan.
    The fisherman's almanac, by Dan
Morris and Norman Strung. (New York)
Macmillan (1970)
   231 p. il. 18 cm.

   1. Fishing. 2. Fishes. I. Strung,
Norman. II. Title
DI   Mc 5/5/75   UDIdc   70-98179

Year of publication

Number of Pages

Note of illustrations, drawings, photos

Height of book

Tracings

Classification Numbers

The **stacks** are the shelves of books. Call numbers on the ends of the stacks aid in quickly finding the section with the book you are seeking. Books are shelved from left to right in order by call number. Most libraries have two main sections in the stacks.

a. **Fiction books,** or books about imaginary characters and happenings, are shelved in alphabetical order by the author's last name.

b. **Nonfiction books** are organized by subject using the Dewey Decimal System or the Library of Congress classification system. Most nonfiction is factual rather than imaginary.

The **reference section** consists of encyclopedias, atlases, almanacs, dictionaries and other reference resources. Many libraries do not allow reference books to be checked out.

Stacks

Periodicals such as magazines and newspapers are generally kept together in a special section. Periodical indexes are often kept in the reference section.

The **vertical file** consists of filing cabinets with folders on various subjects. Pamphlets, newspaper articles, brochures, photographs and other materials not sturdy enough for the regular shelf may be filed by subject in the vertical file.

Dewey Decimal System

000–099	General works (encyclopedias, bibliographies, periodicals)
100–199	Philosophy and Related Disciplines (psychology, logic)
200–299	Religion
300–399	Social Sciences (economics, sociology, civics, law, education, vocations, customs)
400–499	Language (language, dictionaries, grammar)
500–599	Pure Sciences (mathematics, astronomy, physics, chemistry, geology, biology)
600–699	Technology (medicine, engineering, agriculture, home economics, business, radio, television, aviation)
700–799	The Arts (architecture, sculpture, painting, music, photography, recreation)
800–899	Literature (novels, poetry, plays, criticism)
900–999	General Geography and History

Library of Congress Classification System

A	General Works
B	Philosophy, Psychology, Religion
C–F	History
G	Geography, Anthropology, Recreation
H	Social Science
J	Political Science
K	Law
L	Education
M	Music
N	Fine Arts
P	Language and Literature
Q	Science
R	Medicine
S	Agriculture
T	Technology
U	Military Science
V	Naval Science
Z	Bibliography and Library Science

Parts of a Book

The main parts of a book are the front matter, the text, and the back matter.

The **front matter** includes the title page, copyright page, dedication, acknowledgments, preface, foreword or introduction, and the table of contents.

An African Journey

A TALE OF DREAMS AND ADVENTURES

Susan C. Anthony

Travel Time, Inc.
NEW YORK

Title Page

The **title** is the name of the book.

The **author** is the person who wrote the book. Some books do not have an author, but instead have an **editor**, a person who has selected and arranged the work of several writers into a book.

The **publisher** is the company which printed the book.

The **place of publication** is where the book was printed. Sometimes several places are listed. The first place listed is generally where the book was published.

Copyright Page

The **copyright notice** tells when the book was published and who owns the rights to the book. If there is more than one date, the most recent one is the most important. A copyright keeps people from legally copying books instead of buying them. It also keeps people from copying and selling the work of another person. In some cases, it is very important to use books with a recent copyright date in order to get the most accurate facts and information available.

© 1987 by Susan C. Anthony

All rights reserved. No part of this work may be reproduced or transmitted in any form or by any means, electronic or mechanical, including photocopying and recording, or by any information storage or retrieval system, except as may be expressly permitted by copyright law or in writing from the publisher. Requests for permission should be addressed in writing to Travel Time, Inc., 5826 First Street, New York, New York 02183.

Dedication. Some authors dedicate their books to someone special in their lives, usually the person who inspired them to write the book or someone in their family. Not all books have a dedication.

Acknowledgments. This is a section to thank people who helped with the book.

Preface/Foreword/Introduction. This is generally background information about the book which readers should know before reading the text.

Contents

Table of Contents

The **table of contents** lists chapters or sections of the book in order and tells the page number of each. Skimming the table of contents can give a reader a good general sense of what is in the book.

Text

The **text** is the main part of the book, the written words with the author's message. The text may contain graphic aids, such as pictures, graphs, etc. as well as words. Some books have chapter titles, headings and subheadings which are part of the text.

CHAPTER 5

The Steaming Jungle

We waited in Bumba, Zaire, for several days for the ferry to Kisingani. It would cut off miles of very bad road, and was supposed to be a highlight of the trip, three days on the Zaire River, formerly known as the Congo, traveling with the local people.

The ferry has no time schedule. It goes up and down the river, arriving when it arrives and not before. Prospects didn't look good. So we arranged an alternative, a two-day excursion out on the Zaire River in the only boat in town available for hire. We could camp on an island and return by a different route. For $6.00 a person, it sounded great!

The **back matter** may contain an appendix, glossary, bibliography, and/or index.

The **appendix** contains any charts, notes, lists, diagrams, maps or tables that the author did not include in the main text.

Appendix: List of Important Gear

Backpack	Small pouch
Daypack	Small towel and washcloth
Small camp stove	Razors
Lighter or matches	Soap and shampoo
Frying pan	Toothbrush

The **glossary** is a list of special words used in the book and their definitions. It is like a mini-dictionary.

Glossary

baksheesh—a tip, gratuity, or alms. It is from an Arab word meaning "share the wealth."
hajj—a pilgrimage to Mecca, the Moslem holy city. Every Moslem is supposed to make this journey once in a lifetime.

The **bibliography** is a list of books with their authors, publishers, and dates of publication. A bibliography may list the books an author referred to while writing the book, or it could list books recommended for further reading.

Bibliography

Ellis, William S. "Africa's Stricken Sahel." *National Geographic* 172 (August 1987): 140.
Grove, A.T. *Africa.* Oxford, N.Y.: Oxford University Press, 1978.

Index

The **index** is a detailed list of information in a book, arranged in alphabetical order with page numbers. To find specific information in a book, think of the key words which describe your subject and look for them in the index.

Index

Beggars, 62-63, 98.	Markets, 61, 77-79.
Camels, desert adaptations, 79, riding, 83-84.	Photography, 25-28, tips for good photos, 7, 10, 63-68, permits, 82. See also FILM.
Cave paintings, 80, 83.	
Cooking, 64-65, 98.	Poaching, 91.
Customs, regulations and pro... exp...	Pygmies, 105-108.

Photography, 25-28, tips for good photos, 7, 10, 63-68, permits, 82. See also FILM.

Dese...	...s, ...0,
Disea... 38... aga... medication, ...5, 94. See also MALARIA.	also ...r. Snakes, ...-...-..., 99, snake charmers, 63-65, safety precautions, 58, 94. See also REPTILES.
Film, availability, 42, 86.	
Languages, phrases, 30, difficulties, 69, 94.	Tamanrasset, 87-90.
Malaria, 98-100.	Theft, 67, 95–98,

The **topic**, "**Photography**," is the main heading.

Subtopics break topics into smaller divisions and are to help the reader more quickly find specific information. The subtopics in this entry are "tips for good photos" and "permits."

A **dash** between page numbers means "through." "25-28" means page 25 *through* page 28.

A **comma** between page numbers means "and." "7, 10" means page 7 *and* page 10.

A **cross-reference** refers the reader to another topic.

Encyclopedia

An **encyclopedia** contains articles on many subjects in alphabetical order. It is useful for brief, general information and may refer readers to other resources for in-depth information. Many encyclopedias are sets of books. **Electronic encyclopedias** are accessed using computers.

The **index** lists all encyclopedia articles that contain information about a subject. It tells the volume and page number for each article, and helps in locating articles other than the main entry which have information on a subject.

Volume numbers help keep the books shelved in order.

Guide letters help in quickly finding the correct volume for any subject.

ADAMS

Adams, John Quincy (1767-1848), was the sixth president of the United States. He also served as Secretary of State from 1817-25 and was an eight-term member of the U.S. House of Representatives.

Early Career. John Quincy Adams was born in Massachusetts, the son of John Adams, the second U.S. president. He was very bright, and at the age of only 14, he was working as a French translator for the U.S. minister to Russia. He was his father's secretary in 1783, during the peace negotiations which ended the American Revolution. He graduated from Harvard College in 1787 and opened a law office in Boston.

He married Louisa Catherine Johnson in 1797, and was elected to the Massachusetts Senate in 1801. Two years later, he was elected to the U.S. Senate.

Secretary of State. In 1817, President James Monroe appointed Adams Secretary of State. Adams worked with Monroe to force Spain to cede Florida and to make a favorable settlement with France on the Louisiana boundary.

President. Adams ran against three other men for president in 1824. None of the candidates won a majority in the electoral college, so the race was decided by the House of

Representatives. Although Adams was chosen, the supporters of the other candidates made it difficult for Adams to get the support he needed from Congress to carry out many of his plans as President. In the 1828 elections, he was overwhelmingly defeated by Andrew Jackson.

John Quincy Adams

Later Congressional Service.
Two years after his term as president ended, Adams was elected to the House of Representatives, where he served eight terms. He was an eloquent speaker. On February 21, 1848, he suffered a stroke on the floor of the House, and died two days later.

Related articles: Presidents of the U.S.

Additional Resources

Hecht, Marie B. *John Quincy Adams: A Personal History of an Independent Man.* Macmillan, 1972.
Lipsky, George A. *John Quincy Adams: His Theory and Ideas.* Harper, 1965.

Addis Ababa, is the capital and largest city of Ethiopia. It is located on a plateau in central Ethiopia and is about 8000 feet above sea level. Its population is approximately 1,412,580.

See also ETHIOPIA.

Addition. See ARITHMETIC.

15

Guide words show the first and last article listed on each set of facing pages. They help in quickly locating articles.

Illustrations are graphic aids.

Sections and **headings** divide longer articles into shorter segments. They may be quickly scanned to locate answers to questions.

Related articles refer the reader to additional encyclopedia articles.

Additional resources are listed at the end of some articles, and refer the reader to other books.

Cross-references refer the reader to an article of a different title.

A **yearbook** may be issued each year to update old encyclopedias. It has information from the past year.

Dictionary

A **dictionary** is a book alphabetically listing words and giving information about each word. An **unabridged dictionary** lists all or nearly all English words. There are more than 600,000 words in English, and such a book is very large. Most dictionaries are **abridged**, and list only words which occur frequently.

Guide words tell the first and last words on the page. They are useful for quickly finding the page on which a word will be listed.

The **entry** is in bold face type. It shows the correct spelling and syllabication of the word.

The **phonetic spelling**, in parentheses, uses letters and symbols from the pronunciation key to show how the word is pronounced. The accent mark shows which syllable(s) to stress when saying the word.

Reprinted by permission from the Random House Dictionary of the English Language, School Edition. ©1984 by Random House, Inc.

Illustrations are pictures.

An abbreviation shows **part of speech**. Many words have more than one part of speech, depending on how they are used.

n.	noun
pron.	pronoun
adj.	adjective
v.	verb
adv.	adverb
prep.	preposition
conj.	conjunction
interj.	interjection

Inflected forms are from the same root but show number and tense (run, ran, running; lid, lids).

The **pronunciation key** tells what sounds are represented by the symbols used in phonetic spellings. This page has a short version of a complete pronunciation key, which would be found at the beginning of the dictionary.

Definitions are explanations of what the word means. Words may have more than one definition and the user must choose the correct one based on how the word was used.

Examples such as sentences or phrases illustrate correct usage of the word.

Some dictionaries also show **etymology**, or the history of the word, as well as synonyms and antonyms. In addition to information on words, a dictionary may have useful general information, such as tables of weights and measures, lists of colleges, maps, and lists of famous people. This information is generally in the front or the back of a dictionary.

Almanac and Thesaurus

An **almanac** is a collection of facts and information such as calendars, statistics, movements of heavenly bodies, and outstanding dates and events. Many almanacs are published once a year with current information. Tables and charts are often used to save space. Specific information in an almanac can be found by using the index.

> *Poor Richard's Almanac* was written and published by Benjamin Franklin yearly from 1733–1758. In each almanac, there were proverbs, many of which are well known today:
> *Haste makes waste.*
> *A penny saved is a penny earned.*
> *God helps them that help themselves.*

A **thesaurus** is a book of synonyms and antonyms. It is helpful to a writer who wants to find exactly the right word or who wants to vary words instead of using the same ones over and over.

Mini Thesaurus

big – large, huge, gigantic, bulky, great, vast, extensive, enormous, immense, colossal

fast – quick, swift, speedy, rapid, hasty, snappy

fly – soar, hover, flit, waft, glide, wing

funny – humorous, amusing, comical, silly, laughable

get – acquire, obtain, secure, procure, fetch, find, win, earn, collect, gather

good – excellent, fine, superior, wonderful, marvelous, splendid, great, grand, superb

happy – pleased, contented, satisfied, delighted, elated, overjoyed, tickled, glad

hate – despise, loathe, detest, abhor, dislike

have – possess, own

hide – conceal, cover, mask, camouflage, screen, shroud, veil

hurry – rush, speed, hasten, bustle

hurt – damage, harm, injure, wound

interesting – fascinating, intriguing, thought-provoking, inspiring, moving, exciting, entertaining, appealing

little – tiny, small, miniature, puny, dinky, microscopic, minute, petite

look – gaze, glance, watch, survey, study, seek, peek, glimpse, stare, contemplate, examine, gape, scrutinize, inspect, behold, observe, view, witness, peer, gawk

place – space, area, spot, region, location, site

quiet – silent, still, soundless, mute, tranquil, peaceful, calm, restful

said – asked, answered, exclaimed, replied, repeated, insisted, roared, protested, remarked, stammered, announced, drawled, stated, echoed, sighed, whispered, murmured, commanded, ordered, demanded, grumbled, muttered, snarled, hissed, growled, snapped, moaned, mumbled, pleaded, whimpered, whined, yelled, screamed, howled, shouted, squeaked, squealed, laughed, chuckled, giggled

scared – afraid, frightened, alarmed, terrified, petrified, paralyzed

slow – unhurried, leisurely, gradual

stop – cease, halt, discontinue, end, finish, quit

walk – plod, creep, crawl, inch, drag, toddle, shuffle, trot, dawdle, jog, plug, trudge, stump, lumber, trail, run, sprint, bound, streak, stride, breeze, rush, dash, dart, bolt, scamper, scurry, scoot, scuttle, scramble, race, hasten, hurry, gallop, lope, wander, roam, trek, slip, glide, slither, saunter, hobble, amble, stagger, slouch, prance, straggle, meander, waddle, wobble, stroll, swagger, lunge, race, spring, dash, flee

Newspaper

A **newspaper** is a daily or weekly publication which is made up of loose pieces of paper folded together. It contains up-to-date news and information on a large variety of subjects of interest. In fact, newspapers contain the most up-to-date information on the widest variety of subjects. Although some newspapers are saved on microfiche for later reference, most are not indexed. The **New York Times Index** can be used to find articles in that newspaper.

Newspapers are generally printed in several **sections**, folded separately.

The **banner** is the place where the newspaper's name is printed. It contains the date the paper was printed and the price.

The **headlines** are printed in large letters over an article and tell what the article is about. Headlines may be scanned to find articles of interest.

The **lead story** is the front page news which the editor feels will be of most interest to most people, so the paper will sell well.

Pictures highlight the important news and contain **captions** which tell briefly what the picture is about.

The **index** is usually found on the first or second page of a newspaper. It tells where to find various features of the newspaper by section and page number.

Rafting the Mighty Matanuska Sports D-1	Anchorage Teachers SPEAK OUT about Education Opinions E-3	How to BEAT the High Cost of Housing Lifestyles F-1

The Susan C. Anthony

Chronicle

December 1984   Anchorage, Alaska   Price: $1.00

Car Demolished by Unmanned Vehicle

December 8, 1983—A beige 1977 Subaru station wagon, owned by Mrs. Susan Anthony, was repeatedly bashed and knocked 45' across a median by an unmanned Eagle in the back parking lot of Chinook Elementary School, where Mrs. Anthony is employed.

The Eagle, owned by PTA Executive Board member Kay Smithe, had been parked across from Anthony's car and left idling in neutral. An 11 year old girl waiting in the car presumably knocked the Eagle into reverse. It took off at a high speed in a tight circle, crashing into the Subaru's door, then circling around and around, hitting it again and again. The Subaru bounced against another car, owned by Mrs. Nancy Brandt-Erichsen, and caused $1500 damage to it.

The child had jumped out of the car and run to "get help." Mrs. Smithe, seeing the situation, panicked and ran to try and stop her car. It was going too fast for her to get in the open door. She was knocked down and her legs were run over. Not seriously hurt, she got up to try again. Finally, after several attempts, she wedged her foot under the tire and brought the car to a stop.

Although the Subaru still ran, body damage was estimated at over $3000.00.

The Eagle sustained slight damage to the rear bumper and a broken taillight.

One onlooker commented, "I guess it really *is* true that American cars are better built."

Another, musing, suggested that the Eagle may have mistaken Anthony's car for a Rabbit.

Anthony's Subaru—Victim of bizarre demolition derby.

Freak Accident Just The Beginning...

December 9—Subaru's body damage estimated at $3000.
December 14—Insurance company refused to pay more than $1950 for the car, deemed totaled.
December 16—Replacement vehicle bought for $1995–blue 1977 Subaru station wagon with 50,000 miles.
January 3—New hood ordered for blue car for $100. (Old hood was buckled.)
February 16—Fuse for headlights burned out. Car was rendered unusable on the big morning of Mrs. Anthony's first inservice presentation to teachers.
March 6—Accelerator stuck and blue car took off. The road was black ice, with cars and a stop sign ahead. The car crashed into a large snowbank, turned on its side and then righted itself, perched atop 5' of snow and ice.
March 7—Mechanics informed Mrs. Anthony that blue car had no compression in one cylinder and needed a valve job.
March 11—Traffic light turned too quickly.
March 22—Driver's Education class taken to cancel traffic ticket.
April 5—Insurance company released a check for $1950. Windshield wiper fell off during a heavy rain.
May—Blue car was sent to Mr. Alton Smith, who agreed to replace the engine for $700. The newly installed engine had no power and backfired. Smith spent four months trying to fix it, taking the engine out and replacing it five times, having it computer analyzed and checked by other mechanics. No luck.
June 20—Gear shift lever on beige car pulled out by the roots on the morning before a planned trip to Fairbanks. Mr. Smith fixed it at no charge, apologizing for the delay on the other car.
September 2—Smith informed Anthony that the blue car was ready for pickup. He had finally given up and bought another engine.
September 7—Blue car was picked up–complete with new engine and new hood.
September 8—Hood latch came loose at 45 mph. New hood flew up and buckled over the top of the car. Car had a flat tire within hours.
September 9—Windshield of beige car was demolished by an unhitched trailer.
September 19—Brand new 1984 Subaru 4wd station wagon purchased, covered by five year warranty and comprehensive insurance. Whew!
(Hopefully NOT "To Be Continued")

INDEX

Classified	H
Dear Suzie	E8
Editorials	K
Lifestyles	C
Opinions	E
Sports	D
Travel	G
Weather	A2
World News	A

WEATHER

Dec. 21—	Sunrise:	9:14 a.m.
	Sunset:	2:45 p.m.
	Daylight:	5 hrs., 28 min.
Average winter temperature: 16° F.		
June 21—	Sunrise:	2:21 a.m.
	Sunset:	9:42 p.m.
	Daylight:	19 hrs., 21 min.
Average summer temperature: 55° F.		
Annual precipitation: 15.2"		

Organization of a Newspaper

Newspapers contain four major types of information: news, opinions, features and advertisements.

A. **News** is factual information about things that have recently happened. Its purpose is to keep readers informed. A news story answers six basic questions in the first paragraph: who, what, where, when, how and why. The rest of the article gives details and more in-depth information. Minor details are saved for last in case the story has to be cut in length to fit in the paper.

   1. **Headline news**
   - a. World and national news is sent by wire services over Teletype machines or directly into computers. The chief wire services in the United States are UPI (United Press International) and AP (Associated Press)
   - b. State and local news is written by reporters of the newspaper

   2. **News which is covered daily**
   - a. Sports
   - b. Weather
   - c. Vital Statistics—births, deaths, engagements, marriages, divorces
   - d. Entertainment—TV guide, movies, plays, symphonies, etc.
   - e. Business—stock market index, foreign currency exchange rates, price of gold and silver
   - f. Crime—police report and court report
   - g. Announcements—community meetings, etc.

B. **Opinions** are written by the editor or others to try to persuade the reader to see and take the point of view of the writer.

   1. **Editorials**

   2. **Letters to the Editor** may be written by anyone. The address for writing to the editor is on the page where these letters are printed.

   3. **Political cartoons**

C. **Features** are articles written to entertain or inform the reader.
   1. Travel
   2. Health
   3. Real Estate
   4. Finance
   5. Food
   6. Lifestyles
   7. Humor
   8. Human Interest
   9. Gardening
   10. Cartoons, Crosswords, Puzzles
   11. Advice Columns

D. **Advertisements** are a major source of income for a newspaper. Companies or individuals pay for ads.

   1. **Display ads** are generally paid for by a business.

   2. **Classified ads**, or want ads, are often paid for by individuals.
   - a. Personals
   - b. Lost and Found
   - c. Jobs
   - d. Services
   - e. For Sale (houses, cars, land, equipment)
   - f. For Rent
   - g. Legal Notices

Periodicals

Periodicals, or **magazines,** are publications that appear regularly but not every day. They contain a variety of articles and stories of current interest, are generally illustrated, and have many advertisements. They are a good source of up-to-date information.

Over 25,000 periodicals are published in the United States. The five which have the largest circulations are Modern Maturity, NRTA/AARP News Bulletin, Reader's Digest, TV Guide, and National Geographic.

Information can be located in a periodical by referring to an **index.** Some indexes, such as those listed below, are in book form. Others are published on microfiche or may be found on computer. Indexes are kept in the reference department of most libraries.

Reader's Guide

The **Reader's Guide to Periodical Literature** is an index to articles published in common magazines. One hardbound book is issued each year and there is a small supplement for each month during the year.

> **ANIMALS**
> Do fish sleep? And what's that
> on your eyelash? D. Stewart.
> il *National Wildlife* v 32
> p50-9 Ap/My '94

Entry. ANIMALS. Entries are alphabetized. Articles are indexed by subject, title and author, with cross references.

Title of article. Do fish sleep? And what's that on your eyelash?

il means the article is illustrated.

Periodical name. *National Wildlife.* Names may be abbreviated to save space. A key is in the front of the index.

Volume, page number. v32 p50-9

Date. Ap/My '94, abbreviation for April/May, 1994.

National Geographic Index

The **National Geographic Index** lists articles published in National Geographic magazine between 1888 and 1988 by author, title and subject. Articles published since 1988 are indexed in small supplements.

> **NEPAL:**
> The Mighty Himalaya: A Fragile
> Heritage. By Barry C. Bishop.
> Photos by William Thompson.
> 624-651, *Nov. 1988*

Entry. NEPAL. Entries are alphabetized. Articles are indexed by subject, title and author, with cross references.

Title of article. The Mighty Himalaya: A Fragile Heritage

Author. Barry C. Bishop

Photographer. William Thompson

Pages. 624-651

Date of magazine. *Nov. 1988*

Telephone Directories

A telephone directory lists names, addresses and phone numbers of individuals and businesses. It also contains advertisements and listings for government agencies.

Most telephone books contain useful information in the front of the book including area codes and rates at various times of the day (it is cheaper to call long distance at night). They also contain white pages, yellow pages, and blue pages. The **white pages** list businesses and individuals alphabetically by last name. They are most useful if you know the name of the person or business you want to call. The **yellow pages** are arranged by subject and contain advertisements. They are most useful if you need a product or service and want to find out where to go. The **blue pages** contain government listings, and are organized by level of government and agency.

The White Pages

Martin R C 280 Maple Ct........428-6915

The Yellow Pages

MUSIC MAN
*Fine Hand Crafted
Instruments*
Discounts and Rentals
See Our Ad at Music Instruction
2890 W 80th Ave...........479-2836

Special Numbers

911 Emergency number. Use only when human life or property is in danger.

0 Operator. The operator can help if you have trouble placing a call, or if you wish to call collect or bill your call to another number.

411 Directory Assistance. This is useful if there is no telephone directory nearby or if the number has just been listed. You may be charged for this service.

1 (Area code) 555-1212 Long distance information. Area codes for places in the United States are generally listed in the front of the phone directory.

Hot Lines

Boys Town Hot Line. 1-800-448-3000. Offers 24-hour crisis counseling and local referrals to kids and families having difficulty.

Runaway Switchboard. 1-800-621-4000. Gives referrals to shelter, counseling, medical help, etc., and sends messages home without revealing a runaway's location.

Child Find of America. 1-800-I-AM-LOST. Help for lost or kidnapped children.

Crime Tips Hot Line, WeTIP. 1-800-78-CRIME. Anonymous tips are relayed to authorities. The purpose is to eliminate major crime and drug trafficking. Arrests will be made only after a full police investigation.

Long Distance Calls and Services

Person-to-person calls may be made if you wish to talk with a certain person. You are not charged if the person is not there.
Station-to-station calls are less expensive than person-to-person calls.

Direct dialed calls are those a person dials without the help of an operator. Direct dialed calls between 11:00 p.m. and 8:00 a.m. on weekdays or anytime on weekends until 5:00 p.m. Sunday are the least expensive calls.

Operator assisted calls are more expensive than direct dialing, but are necessary when you wish to call collect, bill the call to your home number, or have the operator give you time and charges for your call.

Types of Literature

Fiction is literature which originated in an author's imagination. Generally, the characters and events in fiction are not real although they may be based on reality.

Poetry is a form of literature which expresses experiences, ideas or emotions in a powerful, concentrated and imaginative style. Many poems are written with rhyme and rhythm. Poems may also be written in *free verse,* without a set rhythm.

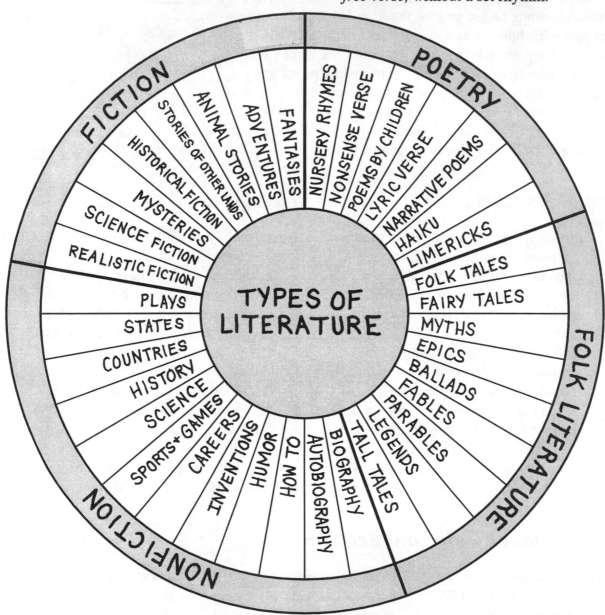

Nonfiction literature is organized by subject. It is generally factual and gives information about real people, places and events. Plays, poetry and folk literature are nonfiction and are classified by subject.

Folk literature is based on the traditional beliefs and stories of a group of people. Most folk literature was passed down by word of mouth from generation to generation before being written down.

Story Elements

Characters

Characters are the people in the story. **Main characters** are the most important people, and generally face a problem which must be resolved. **Minor characters** are people who have little to do with the main action of the story. Authors create characters by describing their looks, speech, thoughts, actions, attitudes and motives.

Setting

Setting is the place and time in which a story takes place. The place could be, for example, in the country, in the city, in outer space, or in a fantasy land. The time may be the time of day, season, or a time in history. A story is always set in the past, the present, or the future.

Style

An author's **style** is his or her unique way of communicating with words.

Plot

The **plot** is the action of a story, or what happens in the story. It is built around a series of **events**, or happenings. A plot generally has four parts:

1. **Exposition**—the background and situation of the story.
2. **Rising action**—events which create suspense in the reader.
3. **Climax**—the highest point of interest, at which time the outcome becomes clear.
4. **Denouement**—the end or conclusion of the story.

Theme

The **theme** is the basic idea or statement about life which the author wishes to convey. For example, a story could show that crime doesn't pay, that standing up for what you believe is worthwhile, or that an individual can make a difference in the world.

Books in Series

The Chronicles of Narnia
by C. S. Lewis
1. *The Lion, the Witch and the Wardrobe*
2. *Prince Caspian*
3. *The Voyage of the "Dawn Treader"*
4. *The Silver Chair*
5. *The Horse and His Boy*
6. *The Magician's Nephew*
7. *The Last Battle*

The Pooh Books
by A. A. Milne
1. *Winnie the Pooh*
2. *House at Pooh Corner*

The Lord of the Rings
by J. R. R. Tolkien
1. *The Hobbit*
2. *The Fellowship of the Ring*
3. *The Two Towers*
4. *The Return of the King*

The Prydain Chronicles
by Lloyd Alexander
1. *The Book of Three*
2. *The Black Cauldron*
3. *The Castle of Llyr*
4. *Taran Wanderer*
5. *The High King*

Little House Books
by Laura Ingalls Wilder
1. *Little House in the Big Woods*
2. *Little House on the Prairie*
3. *Farmer Boy*
4. *On the Banks of Plum Creek*
5. *By the Shores of Silver Lake*
6. *The Long Winter*
7. *Little Town on the Prairie*
8. *These Happy Golden Years*
9. *The First Four Years*

Caldecott Award Winning Books

Both the Newbery and Caldecott awards were established by Frederic G. Melcher. The Caldecott Medal is awarded annually for the most distinguished picture book for children published during the previous year. It was named after Randolph Caldecott, an English illustrator of children's books. The Newbery Medal is given each year for the most distinguished contribution to American children's literature. It was named after John Newbery, an English publisher and bookseller.

The award-winning illustrators, not the authors, are listed below. Look up the title in a library.

Year	Illustrator	Title
1938	Dorothy P. Lathrop	*Animals of the Bible*
1939	Thomas Handforth	*Mei Li*
1940	Ingri & Edgar d'Aulaire	*Abraham Lincoln*
1941	Robert Lawson	*They Were Strong and Good*
1942	Robert McCloskey	*Make Way for Ducklings*
1943	Virginia Lee Burton	*The Little House*
1944	Louis Slobodkin	*Many Moons*
1945	Elizabeth Orton Jones	*Prayer for a Child*
1946	Maude & Miska Petersham	*The Rooster Crows*
1947	Leonard Weisgard	*The Little Island*
1948	Roger Duvoisin	*White Snow, Bright Snow*
1949	Berta & Elmer Hader	*The Big Snow*
1950	Leo Politi	*Song of the Swallows*
1951	Katherine Milhous	*The Egg Tree*
1952	Nicolas Mordvinoff	*Finders Keepers*
1953	Lynd K. Ward	*The Biggest Bear*
1954	Ludwig Bemelmans	*Madeline's Rescue*
1955	Marcia Brown	*Cinderella; or The Little Glass Slipper*
1956	Feodor Rojankovsky	*Frog Went A-Courtin'*
1957	Marc Simont	*A Tree is Nice*
1958	Robert McCloskey	*Time of Wonder*
1959	Barbara Cooney	*Chanticleer and the Fox*
1960	Marie Hall Ets & Aurora Labastida	*Nine Days to Christmas*
1961	Nicolas Sidjakov	*Baboushka and the Three Kings*
1962	Marcia Brown	*Once a Mouse*
1963	Ezra Jack Keats	*The Snowy Day*
1964	Maurice Sendak	*Where the Wild Things Are*
1965	Beni Montresor	*May I Bring a Friend?*
1966	Nonny Hogrogian	*Always Room for One More*

Year	Illustrator	Title
1967	Evaline Ness	*Sam, Bangs, & Moonshine*
1968	Ed Emberley	*Drummer Hoff*
1969	Uri Shulevitz	*The Fool of the World and the Flying Ship*
1970	William Steig	*Sylvester and the Magic Pebble*
1971	Gail E. Haley	*A Story A Story*
1972	Nonny Hogrogian	*One Fine Day*
1973	Blair Lent	*The Funny Little Woman*
1974	Margot Zemach	*Duffy and the Devil*
1975	Gerald McDermott	*Arrow to the Sun*
1976	Leo & Diane Dillon	*Why Mosquitoes Buzz in People's Ears*
1977	Leo & Diane Dillon	*Ashanti to Zulu: African Traditions*
1978	Peter Spier	*Noah's Ark*
1979	Paul Goble	*The Girl Who Loved Wild Horses*
1980	Barbara Cooney	*Ox-Cart Man*
1981	Arnold Lobel	*Fables*
1982	Chris Van Allsburg	*Jumanji*
1983	Marcia Brown	*Shadow*
1984	Alice and Martin Provensen	*The Glorious Flight*
1985	Trina Schart Hyman	*St. George and the Dragon*
1986	Chris Van Allsburg	*The Polar Express*
1987	Richard Egielski	*Hey, Al*
1988	John Schoenherr	*Owl Moon*
1989	Stephen Gammell	*Song and Dance Man*
1990	Ed Young	*Lon Po Po*
1991	David Macaulay	*Black and White*
1992	David Wiesner	*Tuesday*
1993	Emily Arnold McCully	*Mirette on the High Wire*
1994	Allen Say	*Grandfather's Journey*

Newbery Award Winning Books

Year	Author	Title
1922	Henrik Van Loon	*The Story of Mankind*
1923	Hugh Lofting	*The Voyages of Dr. Dolittle*
1924	Charles Hawes	*The Dark Frigate*
1925	Charles Finger	*Tales from Silver Lands*
1926	Arthur Chrisman	*Shen of the Sea*
1927	Will James	*Smoky, the Cowhorse*
1928	Dhan Mukerji	*Gay-Neck, the Story of a Pigeon*
1929	Eric P. Kelly	*The Trumpeter of Krakow*
1930	Rachel Field	*Hitty, Her First Hundred Years*
1931	Elizabeth Coatsworth	*The Cat Who Went to Heaven*
1932	Laura Adams Armer	*Waterless Mountain*
1933	Elizabeth Lewis	*Yung Fu of the Upper Yangtze*
1934	Cornelia Meigs	*Invincible Louisa*
1935	Monica Shannon	*Dobry*
1936	Carol Ryrie Brink	*Caddie Woodlawn*
1937	Ruth Sawyer	*Roller Skates*
1938	Kate Seredy	*The White Stag*
1939	Elizabeth Enright	*Thimble Summer*
1940	James Daugherty	*Daniel Boone*
1941	Armstrong Sperry	*Call It Courage*
1942	Walter D. Edmonds	*The Matchlock Gun*
1943	Elizabeth Janet Gray	*Adam of the Road*
1944	Esther Forbes	*Johnny Tremain*
1945	Robert Lawson	*Rabbit Hill*
1946	Lois Lenski	*Strawberry Girl*
1947	Carolyn Bailey	*Miss Hickory*
1948	William Pène du Bois	*The Twenty-One Balloons*
1949	Marguerite Henry	*King of the Wind*
1950	Marguerite de Angeli	*The Door in the Wall*
1951	Elizabeth Yates	*Amos Fortune, Free Man*
1952	Eleanor Estes	*Ginger Pye*
1953	Ann Nolan Clark	*Secret of the Andes*
1954	Joseph Krumgold	*...And Now Miguel*
1955	Meindert DeJong	*The Wheel on the School*
1956	Jean Lee Latham	*Carry On, Mr. Bowditch*
1957	Virginia Sorensen	*Miracles on Maple Hill*
1958	Harold V. Keith	*Rifles for Watie*
1959	Elizabeth George Speare	*The Witch of Blackbird Pond*
1960	Joseph Krumgold	*Onion John*
1961	Scott O'Dell	*Island of the Blue Dolphins*
1962	Elizabeth George Speare	*The Bronze Bow*
1963	Madeleine L'Engle	*A Wrinkle in Time*
1964	Emily Neville	*It's Like This, Cat*
1965	Maia Wojciechowska	*Shadow of a Bull*
1966	Elizabeth Borton de Trevino	*I, Juan de Pareja*
1967	Irene Hunt	*Up a Road Slowly*
1968	Elaine Konigsburg	*From the Mixed-Up Files of Mrs. Basil E. Frankweiler*
1969	Lloyd Alexander	*The High King*
1970	William H. Armstrong	*Sounder*
1971	Betsy Byars	*Summer of the Swans*
1972	Robert C. O'Brien	*Mrs. Frisby and the Rats of NIMH*
1973	Jean Craighead George	*Julie of the Wolves*
1974	Paula Fox	*The Slave Dancer*
1975	Virginia Hamilton	*M. C. Higgins, the Great*
1976	Susan Cooper	*The Grey King*
1977	Mildred D. Taylor	*Roll of Thunder, Hear My Cry*
1978	Katherine Paterson	*Bridge to Terabithia*
1979	Ellen Raskin	*The Westing Game*
1980	Joan W. Blos	*A Gathering of Days*
1981	Katherine Paterson	*Jacob Have I Loved*
1982	Nancy Willard	*A Visit to William Blake's Inn*
1983	Cynthia Voigt	*Dicey's Song*
1984	Beverly Cleary	*Dear Mr. Henshaw*
1985	Robin McKinley	*The Hero and the Crown*
1986	Patricia MacLachlan	*Sarah, Plain and Tall*
1987	Sid Fleischman	*The Whipping Boy*
1988	Russell Freedman	*Lincoln: A Photobiography*
1989	Paul Fleischman	*Joyful Noise: Poems for Two Voices*
1990	Lois Lowry	*Number the Stars*
1991	Jerry Spinelli	*Maniac Magee*
1992	Phyllis Reynolds Naylor	*Shiloh*
1993	Cynthia Rylant	*Missing May*
1994	Lois Lowry	*The Giver*

Long Time Favorite Books

Year	Title	Author
1883	The Adventures of Pinocchio	Carlo Collodi
600 B.C.	Aesop's Fables	Aesop
1865	Alice in Wonderland	Lewis Carroll
1947	Anne Frank: Diary of a Young Girl	Anne Frank
1908	Anne of Green Gables	L. M. Montgomery
1873	Around the World in 80 Days	Jules Verne
1941	The Black Stallion	Walter Farley
1903	The Call of the Wild	Jack London
1964	Charlie and the Chocolate Factory	Roald Dahl
1952	Charlotte's Web	E. B. White
1855	Fairy Tales	Hans Christian Andersen
1823	Grimm's Fairy Tales	Jacob and Wilhelm Grimm
1865	Hans Brinker, or, The Silver Skates	Mary Elizabeth Mapes Dodge
1881	Heidi	Johanna Spyri
1966	The Hobbit	J. R. R. Tolkien
1961	The Incredible Journey	Sheila Burnford
1902	Just So Stories	Rudyard Kipling
1886	Kidnapped	Robert Lewis Stevenson
1950	The Lion, the Witch and the Wardrobe	C. S. Lewis
1932	Little House in the Big Woods	Laura Ingalls Wilder
1935	Little House on the Prairie	Laura Ingalls Wilder
1868	Little Women	Louisa May Alcott
1934	Mary Poppins	Pamela L. Travers
1946	Merry Adventures of Robin Hood	Howard Pyle
1959	My Side of the Mountain	Jean Craighead George
1904	Peter Pan	James M. Barrie
1719	Robinson Crusoe	Daniel Defoe
1911	The Secret Garden	Frances Hodgson Burnett
1807	Tales From Shakespeare	Charles and Mary Lamb
1697	Tales of Mother Goose	Charles Perrault
1901	Tales of Peter Rabbit	Beatrix Potter
1469	The Death of (King) Arthur	Sir Thomas Malory
1876	Tom Sawyer	Mark Twain
1883	Treasure Island	Robert Lewis Stevenson
1898	War of the Worlds	H. G. Wells
1972	Watership Down	Richard Adams
1969	Where the Lilies Bloom	Vera and Bill Cleaver
1961	Where the Red Fern Grows	Wilson Rawls
1908	Wind in the Willows	Kenneth Grahame
1926	Winnie the Pooh	A. A. Milne
1938	The Yearling	Marjorie Rawlings

The English Language

The Alphabet

An **alphabet** consists of the letters of a language arranged in order. The word comes from the first two letters of the Greek alphabet, *alpha* and *beta*. Long ago, people could communicate only by speaking or making gestures. Early civilizations, including the ancient Egyptians, used a system of **hieroglyphic** writing. Many of the early symbols were **pictographs**. For example, a picture of a man would stand for a man. An **ideograph** was a symbol which stood for an idea. Gradually, the system of writing changed so that certain symbols stood for certain sounds. Then the same symbols could be used to write many different words. Most modern languages have an alphabet. Chinese and languages based on Chinese never developed alphabets, however. The Chinese use about 50,000 **characters**, or symbols, in their writing.

The English language developed over a very long time and each letter has its own history. The Romans changed older letter forms into those we use today, and were the first to use lower-case letters and punctuation in writing. English has 26 letters—19 consonants and five vowels: *a, e, i, o,* and *u.* Two other letters, *y* and *w*, are also sometimes used as vowels. The list on the right below shows the order of frequency of use.

Handwriting Examples

Order of Frequency	
1	E
2	T
3	A
4	O
5	N
6	I
7	R
8	S
9	H
10	L
11	D
12	C
13	U
14	M
15	F
16	P
17	Y
18	G
19	W
20	B
21	V
22	K
23	X
24	J
25	Q
26	Z

Manuscript

Aa Bb Cc Dd Ee Ff Gg
Hh Ii Jj Kk Ll Mm Nn Oo
Pp Qq Rr Ss Tt Uu Vv Ww
Xx Yy Zz

Cursive

Aa Bb Cc Dd Ee Ff
Gg Hh Ii Jj Kk Ll Mm
Nn Oo Pp Qq Rr Ss Tt Uu
Vv Ww Xx Yy Zz

Combinations   br os ve wr

Special Alphabets

Braille is a coded alphabet of raised dots which can be read by touch. It was developed in 1824 by Louis Braille, a 15-year-old blind Frenchman, and is the alphabet used most often by the blind. Numerals are formed by using a special number sign with the first ten letters. An **A** preceded by this sign is 1, **B** is 2, **C** is 3, and so on. **J** is used for the numeral 0.

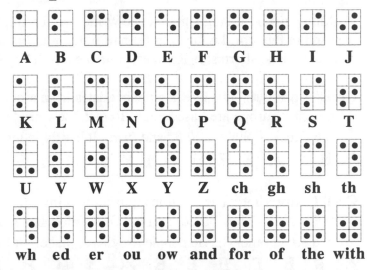

A B C D E F G H I J

K L M N O P Q R S T

U V W X Y Z ch gh sh th

wh ed er ou ow and for of the with

The **phonetic alphabet** is used by the military and by airplane pilots around the world to stand for letters of the alphabet. A pilot whose airplane number is N6837E would say November 6837 Echo.

Sign language is a system of communicating with hand gestures. The American manual alphabet below can be used to spell out words and is generally understood by deaf people.

A B C D E F
G H I J K
L M N O P
Q R S T U
V W X Y Z

Alpha
Bravo
Charlie
Delta
Echo
Foxtrot
Golf
Hotel
India
Juliet
Kilo
Lima
Mike
November
Oscar
Papa
Quebec
Romeo
Sierra
Tango
Uniform
Victor
Whiskey
X-Ray
Yankee
Zulu

A B C D E F
G H I J K
L M N O P
Q R S T U
V W X Y
Z Period Comma
? Start Wait End
Error Understand SOS
1 2 3
4 5 6 7
8 9 0

International Morse code was developed by the inventor of the telegraph, Samuel Morse. It was used extensively in the past to transmit telegraph messages and news.

Alphabets from Other Lands

Many different languages can be written with a single alphabet. Nevertheless, some 65 alphabets are used in the world today, almost half of them in India. The longest alphabet is Cambodian, with 74 letters. The shortest is Rotakas, from the South Pacific, with only 11 letters.

Greek alphabet: The Greek alphabet dates from around 700 B.C. and most of the alphabets in modern Europe are based on it. In fact, the word "alphabet" comes from the first two letters of the Greek alphabet, *alpha* and *beta*. It has 24 letters.

Α Β Γ Δ Ε Ζ Η Θ Ι Κ Λ Μ Ν Ξ Ο Π Ρ Σ Τ Υ Φ Χ Ψ Ω

Cyrillic alphabet: The Cyrillic alphabet was invented by two missionaries, one named Cyril, in the 800's A.D. They based it on the Greek alphabet and the Slavic language. Russian, Bulgarian, and some other Slavic people use this alphabet. It has 33 letters.

А Б В Г Д Е Ё Ж З И Й К Л М Н О П Р С Т
У Ф Х Ц Ч Ш Щ Ъ Ы Ь Э Ю Я

Arabic alphabet: The Arabic alphabet is used throughout the Middle East and northern Africa. Arabic is the language of the religion of Islam. It is read from right to left, and has 28 consonants. Vowels are shown by dots called vowel points written near the letters.

ا ب ت ث ج ح خ د ذ ر ز س ش ص ض ط ظ ع غ ف ق ك ل م ن ه و ي

Hebrew alphabet: Hebrew is the language of the Jewish religion and of the Old Testament of the Bible. It has 32 consonants, and is written from right to left.

ס ן נ ם מ ל ך כ י ט ח ז ו ה ד ג ב א
ע פ ף ץ צ ק ר ש ת ת

Basic Computer Keyboard

A typewriter keyboard is the same as a computer keyboard, except for certain special keys. Most computer keyboards contain a large number of special keys not shown below. The arrangement of the *letters* is always the same.

Abbreviations

Meaning	Abbreviation
anno Domini (in the year of our Lord)	A.D.
ante merediem (before noon)	a.m.
as soon as possible	ASAP
Avenue	Ave.
before Christ	B.C.
before Christian era or before common era (means the same as B.C.)	B.C.E.
Boulevard	Blvd.
care of (in care of)	c/o
cash on delivery	C.O.D.
Central Intelligence Agency	CIA
Chief Executive Officer	CEO
Christian era or common era (means the same as A.D.)	C.E.
Circle	Cir.
Company	Co.
continued	cont.
Corporation	Corp.
Court	Ct.
Department	Dept.
Doctor	Dr.
Drive	Dr.
et cetera (and other things)	etc.
exempli gratia (for example)	e.g.
Federal Bureau of Investigation	FBI
Fort	Ft.
General	Gen.
Governor	Gov.
Heights	Hts.
Highway	Hwy.
hour	hr.
id est (that is to say)	i.e.
I owe you	IOU
Incorporated	Inc.

Abbreviations for:
Days—page 11
Months—page 12
State names—page 101
Parts of speech—page 152
Measurement units—pages 206–207

Meaning	Abbreviation
intelligence quotient	IQ
Internal Revenue Service	IRS
Junior	Jr.
Lane	Ln.
Limited	Ltd.
medicinae doctor (medical doctor)	M.D.
miles per hour	mph
minute	min.
Missus	Mrs.
Mister	Mr.
Miz	Ms.
Mount	Mt.
not applicable	N/A
number	no. (#)
page	pg.
Park	Pk.
Place	Pl.
Point	Pt.
post meridiem (after noon)	p.m.
Post Office	P.O.
postscript	P.S.
President	Pres.
public address	P.A.
respondex, s'il vous plait (answer, if you please)	R.S.V.P.
requiescat in pace (rest in peace)	R.I.P.
Reverend	Rev.
Road	Rd.
Room	Rm.
Route	Rt.
Saint	St.
second	sec.
Senior	Sr.
Square	Sq.
Street	St.
unidentified flying object	UFO
United Kingdom	U.K.
United States of America	U.S.A.
University	Univ.
versus (against)	vs.
very important person	VIP
Vice President	V.P.

Punctuation

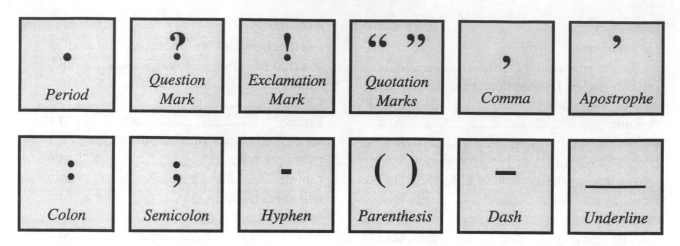

.	?	!	" "	,	,
Period	*Question Mark*	*Exclamation Mark*	*Quotation Marks*	*Comma*	*Apostrophe*
:	;	-	( )	—	_____
Colon	*Semicolon*	*Hyphen*	*Parenthesis*	*Dash*	*Underline*

The marks shown above are to assist readers in recognizing punctuation marks. The rules below are for the punctuation marks most often used. Most dictionaries contain complete rules of punctuation.

Punctuation to End Sentences

1. To end a **statement**, a sentence which tells, use a period (**.**).
2. To end a **question**, a sentence which asks, use a question mark (**?**).
3. To end an **exclamation**, a sentence which expresses strong feeling, use an exclamation point (**!**).
4. To end a **command**, a sentence which tells someone to do something, use a period (**.**).

Uses of Periods (.)

Use periods:
1. To end statements or commands. *Please come here.*
2. In bibliography cards or entries. See page 227 for examples.
3. After initials. *A. R. Smith*
4. After most abbreviations. *A.D., B.C., Mr.* See page 167 for a list of common abbreviations.
5. After numbers or letters of a list.

Uses of Apostrophes (')

Use apostrophes:
1. In contractions, to show letters have been left out. *didn't, o'clock*
2. To show possession. *Mary's book* Use *s'* with plural nouns. *the boys' coats*
3. To pluralize letters and numerals. *A's, 5's*

Uses of Colons (:)

Use colons:
1. After the salutation in a business letter. See page 193 for an example.
2. Between place of publication and publisher in a bibliography entry. See page 227.
3. To introduce a long list of items.

Uses of Hyphens (-)

Use hyphens:
1. In writing numbers from *twenty-one* to *ninety-nine*.
2. To divide words at the end of a line. The rules for correctly dividing words are complicated. Avoid it when possible.

Punctuating Direct Quotations

1. Use quotation marks (" ") to enclose the **exact words** a person says in a direct quotation. Remember to capitalize the first word of a direct quotation.
"This book is interesting," said Jane.
Jane said, "This book is interesting."
"This book," said Jane, "is interesting."

2. Use a comma (,) to set off direct quotations from expressions such as *he said* and *she replied.* See page 153 for words to use instead of "said."

3. Use a period (.) placed inside the quotation marks when the end of a quoted sentence is the end of the written sentence.
Martha said, "I think this is the right way."

4. Replace the period at the end of a direct quotation with a comma (,) when the end of a quoted statement is **not** the end of the sentence. The comma is placed inside the quotation marks.
"I think this is the right way," said Martha.

5. When the quoted sentence is a question or exclamation, use a question mark (?) or exclamation point (!) placed inside the quotation marks even if the end of the quotation is not the end of the sentence.
"Look out!" shouted Jane.
Steven asked, "Where are my skates?"

Parenthetical Phrases

for example	to begin with
for instance	at this point
in fact	at the same time
in one case	in conclusion
furthermore	as a result
in addition	therefore
also	consequently
meanwhile	for this reason
eventually	on the other hand
at last	however
in the meantime	nevertheless

Uses of Commas (,)

Use commas:
1. In direct quotations. See "Punctuating Direct Quotations," to the left.
2. In letters. See pages 191–193.
3. In bibliography cards or entries. See page 227 for examples.
4. Between the day of the week and the date. *Monday, March 4*
5. Between the date and the year. *July 4, 1776*
6. Between city and state. *Tampa, Florida*
7. Between city and country. *London, England*
8. After a person's last name when written before the first name (as in a telephone book or encyclopedia). *Lincoln, Abraham* *Smith, Larry*
9. Between items in a series of three or more. *She can sing, dance, and play the saxophone.*
10. After words which introduce a sentence, such as *yes, no, oh, well, first,* and so on. *Well, I guess so.*
11. Before certain words which end a sentence, such as *etc., too,* and *also. May I come, too?*
12. To separate the name of the person to whom you are talking from the rest of the sentence. *Mom, are you ready to go?* *I understand what you mean, Mr. Jones.* *This, Mike, is for you.*
13. Before such words as *and, but* and *or* in a compound sentence (a sentence made by combining two shorter sentences). *The roads are icy today, and there have been several accidents.*
14. To separate "parenthetical" words or phrases, such as *of course, however.* See the chart to the left for examples. These words and phrases add meaning, but the sentence would be a complete sentence without them. *This book, however, is very useful. You are right, of course.*

Capitalization

Capitalize:

1. The first word in a sentence. *Did you enjoy the show?*
2. The first word in a direct quotation. *John said, "Let's go!"*
3. The first word in a line of poetry. *Swift things are beautiful:*
4. The first word in each part of an outline.
5. The pronoun *I*. *Jeff and I are twins.*
6. The first word and all important words in titles. *Gone With the Wind.* See **Titles** below for more examples.
7. All proper nouns—special names of people, places, animals, things, or groups of people. See **Proper Nouns** below for examples.
8. Titles used before a name or in place of a name, including family titles. *Senator Smith, Mother*
9. Initials and many abbreviations. *B.C., A.D., A. W. Smith*
10. The names of days, months, and holidays, but **not** seasons. *Monday, March, Christmas, spring*
11. Historical documents, events and periods. *Constitution, Civil War, Middle Ages*
12. All words, including pronouns, which refer to God, the Holy Family, or Scripture.

For capitalization in **letter writing**, see pages 192–193.

Titles are the names of:

Books. *Winnie the Pooh*
Magazines. *Reader's Digest*
Newspapers. *New York Times*
Stories. *Jack and the Beanstalk*
Chapters. *Chapter II—The Gypsy Band*
Articles. *Anchorage: A Dream Reborn*
Poems. *Poem of Praise*
Plays. *Camelot*
Television Shows. *Sesame Street*
Movies. *Star Wars*
Songs. *America the Beautiful*
Paintings or other works of art. *The Night Watch*

Proper Nouns are special names of specific people, places, animals, things or groups of people. They include the following:

People, Animals, Groups of People
Names of people (and initials). *Mary Johnson*
Names of pets. *Rover*
Nationalities and languages. *French*
Religions. *Catholic*
Political groups. *Democrats*
Organizations, clubs, societies. *Boy Scouts*
Special groups of people. *Beatles*

Geographical Locations
Continents. *Asia*
Countries. *Brazil*
Geographical Regions (**not** directions). *Middle East*
States and provinces. *Florida*
Cities and towns. *Los Angeles*
Streets, highways, roads, avenues, etc. *Highway 7*
Parks. *Yellowstone Park*

Bodies of Water
Oceans. *Indian Ocean*
Seas. *North Sea*
Bays. *Hudson Bay*
Rivers. *Colorado River*
Waterfalls. *Niagara Falls*
Lakes. *Great Salt Lake*

Land Forms
Mountains. *Mt. Hood*
Valleys. *Bear Valley*
Canyons. *Grand Canyon*
Caves or caverns. *Mammoth Cave*
Forests. *Black Forest*
Islands. *Barter Island*
Deserts. *Sahara Desert*

Heavenly Bodies
Planets. *Jupiter*
Stars. *Alpha Centauri*
Constellations. *Big Dipper*
Earth, *sun* and *moon* are **not** capitalized unless used in a list of other planets or heavenly bodies.

Buildings and Other Structures
Bridges. *Golden Gate Bridge*
Schools. *Deer Park Elementary*
Stores. *Safeway*
Museums. *Western Heritage Museum*
Hospitals. *Memorial Hospital*
Churches. *First Baptist Church*
Hotels, motels, inns. *Ramada Inn*
Libraries. *Library of Congress*
Restaurants. *Dan's Pancake House*

Things
Ships. *Queen Elizabeth II*
Trains. *Midnight Express*
Airplanes. *Boeing 747*
Autos. *Ford Mustang*
Registered Trademarks. *Kleenex*

Do **not** capitalize:
Seasons. *spring, summer, autumn, winter*
Directions. *east, north, southeast*
Names of school subjects—*math, science*—unless they are languages or numbered course titles—*English, Math 201*

Spelling Memory Helps

all right	It's either all right or all wrong.
argument	He lost an **e** in the argument.
beauty	**Be a bea**uty.
believe	Don't be**lie**ve a **lie**.
business	Busy ness.
cemetery	You go to the c**e**met**e**ry with "**e**"s (ease).
familiar	He is a fami**liar liar**.
February	You say "**br**" in Feb**r**uary.
foreign	Kings **reign** in fo**reign** countries.
friend	You'll be my fri**end** to the **end**.
grammar	**Gramma** knows **gramma**r.
hear	You h**ear** with your **ear**.
independent	There is a **dent** in indepen**dent**.
innocent	in no cent
lose	When you use one **o**, you **lose**.
niece	My **nie**ce is **nice**.
parallel	Not **all** lines are par**all**el.
piece	Have a **pie**ce of **pie**.
pleasant	Picnics are pleas**ant** for an **ant**.
prairie	There is **air** on the pr**air**ie.
principle	A ru**le** can be called a princip**le**.
prison	Her **son** is in pri**son**.
receive	**R-E C-E I**s **V**ery **E**asy.
secretary	A **secret**ary can keep a **secret**.
separate	There is **a rat** in sep**a rat**e.
sincerely	You can **rely** on me, since**rely**.
stationery	Use station**e**ry to write a lett**e**r.
together	to get her - They went **together to get her**.
tomorrow	tom or row
weather	We **eat** in all kinds of w**eat**her.
weird	**We** are w**ei**rd.
whether	I wonder wh**ether** they're tog**ether**.
whose	**Wh**ose **hose** is that?

See pages 175–177 for more information on spelling.

Homophones and Confusing Words

Homophones are words with the same pronunciation but different spellings and meanings. This list includes homophones as well as other confusing words. Its purpose is to help readers distinguish between the words. For complete definitions, consult a dictionary.

accept – except
  accept (v) – to receive willingly
  except (prep) – other than
access – excess
  access (n) – right to enter or use
  excess (adj) – more than enough
acts – ax
  acts (v) – behaves, takes action
  ax (n) – a chopping tool
ad – add
  ad (n) – advertisement
  add (v) – to combine by addition
addition – edition
  addition (n) – result of adding
  edition (n) – a version or issue of
    a publication
affect – effect
  affect (v) – to influence
  effect (n) – a result or outcome
allowed – aloud
  allowed (v) – permitted
  aloud (adv) – out loud
are (see **hour**)
ate – eight
  ate (v) – past tense of *to eat*
  eight (adj) – the number 8
ax (see **acts**)
be – bee
  be (v) – to exist
  bee (n) – an insect
bear – bare
  bear (n) – a large animal
      (v) – to carry
  bare (adj) – without covering
beat – beet
  beat (v) – to hit again and again
  beet (n) – a vegetable
berry – bury
  berry (n) – an edible fruit
  bury (v) – to hide beneath the
    earth
blew – blue
  blew (v) – past tense of *to blow*
  blue (adj) – a color
board – bored
  board (n) – a flat piece of lumber
  bored (v) – filled with boredom

break – brake
  break (v) – to split into pieces
  brake (n) – something which
    slows or stops motion
bury (see **berry**)
buy – by – bye
  buy (v) – to purchase
  by (prep) – near or beside
  bye (interj) – short for
    "goodbye"
capital – capitol
  capital (adj) – of most
    importance: *capital city,*
    capital letter
  capitol (n) – the building in
    which Congress meets
ceiling – sealing
  ceiling (n) – opposite of *floor*
  sealing (v) – closing, shutting,
    fastening
cell – sell
  cell (n) – a small room, such as
    in a prison; basic unit of life
  sell (v) – to exchange something
    for money
cent – sent – scent
  cent (n) – a penny
  sent (v) – past tense of *to send*
  scent (n) – a smell
chews – choose
  chews (v) – crushes or grinds
    with the teeth
  choose (v) – to select
clothes – close
  clothes (n) – clothing
  close (v) – to shut
council – counsel
  council (n) – a group of people
  counsel (v) – to give advice
creak – creek
  creak (v) – to make a grating or
    squeaking sound
  creek (n) – a small stream
dear – deer
  dear (adj) – used in letters:
    Dear Jim,
  deer (n) – an animal

desert – dessert
  desert (n) – a dry region
      (v) – to leave or abandon
  dessert (n) – a sweet course at
    the end of a meal
dew – do – due
  dew (v) – moisture in small
    drops
  do (v) – to carry out, finish
  due (adj) – owed and payable
die – dye
  die (v) – to stop living
  dye (v) – to change the color of
    using *dye*
do – due (see **dew**)
edition (see **addition**)
effect (see **affect**)
eight (see **ate**)
except (see **accept**)
excess (see **access**)
fair – fare
  fair (adj) – just and honest
  fare (n) – money paid to travel
    on a bus or train
fir – fur
  fir (n) – a kind of tree
  fur (n) – soft, thick animal hair
flew – flu
  flew (v) – past tense of *to fly*
  flu (n) – a sickness, short for
    influenza
flour – flower
  flour (n) – fine powder: wheat
    flour is used in bread
  flower (n) – a blossom
flu (see **flew**)
forth – fourth
  forth (adv) – forward
  fourth (adj) – 4th, the one after
    third
for – fore – four
  for (prep) – with the purpose of:
    a pencil is *for* writing
  fore (adv) – toward the front of a
    ship, opposite of *aft*
  four (adj) – the number 4
fur (see **fir**)

great – grate
    great (adj) – very good
    grate (v) – to grind into shreds

groan – grown
    groan (n) – a deep sound of pain
    grown (adj) – from the word *grow*

guessed – guest
    guessed (v) – made a guess about
    guest (n) – a person entertained in one's house

hair – hare
    hair (n) – the growth covering people's heads
    hare (n) – an animal like a rabbit

hay – hey
    hay (n) – cut and dried grass for animal food
    hey (interj) – an exclamation to attract attention

heal – heel
    heal (v) – to make healthy again
    heel (n) – the back part of the foot

hear – here
    hear (v) – to hear with the ear
    here (adv) – in this place, opposite of *there*

heard – herd
    heard (v) – past tense of *to hear*
    herd (n) – a group of cattle or large animals

here (see **hear**)

hey (see **hay**)

higher – hire
    higher (adj) – taller, more elevated
    hire (v) – to take on an employee

hole – whole
    hole (n) – a *hole* in the ground
    whole (adj) – complete

hour – our – are
    hour (n) – sixty minutes
    our (adj) – belonging to us
    are (v) – form of "to be" (we are)

its – it's
    its (adj) – belonging to it
    it's – contraction of *it is*

knew (see **new**)

knight (see **night**)

knot (see **not**)

know (see **no**)

knows (see **nose**)

lead – led
    lead (n) – a gray metal
    led (v) – past tense of *to lead*

loose – lose
    loose (adj) – not tight
    lose (v) – to misplace

maid – made
    maid (n) – a girl
    made (v) – past tense of *to make*

mail – male
    mail (n) – letters and packages handled by the Post Office
    male (adj) – man or boy

main – Maine – mane
    main (adj) – the most important
    Maine (n) – a state of the U.S.
    mane (n) – long heavy hair on the neck of some animals

meat – meet
    meat (n) – food
    meet (v) – to come together: to *meet* a person

missed – mist
    missed (v) – failed to hit or felt the absence of
    mist (n) – a haze of water vapor in the air, similar to fog

new – knew
    new (adj) – not old
    knew (v) – understood, past tense of *to know*

night – knight
    night (n) – opposite of *day*
    knight (n) – a military man in the Middle Ages who wore armor

no – know
    no (adv) – opposite of *yes*
    know (v) – to understand

none – nun
    none (pron) – not any
    nun (n) – a religious woman of the Catholic church

nose – knows
    nose (n) – a part of the face
    knows (v) – understands

not – knot
    not (adv) – no
    knot (n) – a fastening made by tying

one – won
    one (adj) – the number 1
    won (v) – past tense of *to win*

oh – owe
    oh (interj) – an exclamation
    owe (v) – to have a debt

our (see **hour**)

pail – pale
    pail (n) – a small bucket
    pale (adj) – without much color

pain – pane
    pain (n) – hurt
    pane (n) – division of a window

pair – pare – pear
    pair (n) – two
    pare (v) – to cut or trim away
    pear (n) – a fruit

passed – past
    passed (v) – did pass
    past (adj) – gone by, ended

patience – patients
    patience (n) – ability to wait without complaining
    patients (n) – two or more people under a doctor's care

pause – paws
    pause (v) – stop temporarily
    paws (n) – feet of some animals

peace – piece
    peace (n) – freedom from war
    piece (n) – a part

peak – peek
    peak (n) – top of a mountain, highest place
    peek (v) – to glance at something without being seen

peal – peel
    peal (n) – a loud ringing of bells
    peel (v) – to cut away the skin or covering of something

piece (see **peace**)

plain – plane
    plain (adj) – simple, ordinary, clear
    plane (n) – short for *airplane*

principal – principle
    principal (n) – first in rank: the school *principal,* or the amount of a debt, not including interest
    principle (n) – a fundamental truth

quite – quiet
    quite (adv) – really
    quiet (adj) – not noisy

rain – rein – reign
    rain (n) – water falling from the sky
    rein (n) – part of a horse's bridle
    reign (v) – to rule: kings and queens *reign*

raise – rays
    raise (v) – to lift
    rays (n) – lines of light which radiate from something bright
rap – wrap
    rap (v) – to tap
    wrap (v) – to wind or fold a covering around something
read – red
    read (v) – past tense of *to read*
    red (adj) – a color
real – reel
    real (adj) – genuine
    reel (n) – a fishing *reel*
rein – reign (see **rain**)
right – rite – write
    right (adj) – correct
    rite (n) – a ceremonial custom or ritual
    write (v) – to *write* a letter
ring – wring
    ring (n) – a circular object such as a wedding *ring*
      (v) – to sound or cause a ringing sound
    wring (v) – to squeeze or twist to get water out
road – rode
    road (n) – a highway
    rode (v) – past tense of *to ride*
rote – wrote
    rote (n) – routine
    wrote (v) – past tense of *to write*
sail – sale
    sail (n) – canvas sheet of a sailboat
    sale (n) – having to do with selling
scene – seen
    scene (n) – scenery
    seen (v) – from *to see:* I have *seen* her.
scent (see **cent**)
sea – see
    sea (n) – a body of salt water, like an ocean
    see (v) – look at
sealing (see **ceiling**)
seam – seem
    seam (n) – the line made by sewing two pieces of cloth together
    seem (v) – to appear
seen (see **scene**)
sell (see **cell**)

sense – since
    sense (n) – ability to think or feel
    since (adv) – from then to now
sent (see **cent**)
sew – so – sow
    sew (v) – to join with a needle and thread
    so (adv) – very: It's *so* good.
    sow (v) – to plant seeds
since (see **sense**)
some – sum
    some (pron) – A certain number *Some* people came early.
    sum (n) – the result of addition
son – sun
    son (n) – a male child
    sun (n) – the *sun* in the sky
stair – stare
    stair (n) – a step in a staircase
    stare (v) – to look fixedly at something
stationary – stationery
    stationary (adj) – not moving
    stationery (n) – writing paper and envelopes
steak – stake
    steak (n) – a thick slice of meat
    stake (n) – a short post: tent *stake*
steal – steel
    steal (v) – to rob
    steel (n) – a kind of metal
tacks – tax
    tacks (n) – small, short nails with broad heads
    tax (n) – money paid to the government
tail – tale
    tail (n) – an animal's *tail*
    tale (n) – story
there – they're – their
    there (adv) – in that place, opposite of *here*
    they're – contraction of *they are*
    their (adj) – belonging to them
threw – through
    threw (v) – past tense of *to throw*
    through (prep) – in one side and out the other
to – too – two
    to (prep) – toward, for, as far as: Go *to* the store.
    too (adv) – more than enough: *too* much; also
    two (adj) – the number 2

toad – towed
    toad (n) – a frog-like animal
    towed (v) – pulled with a rope or chain
toe – tow
    toe (n) – a part of the foot
    tow (v) – to pull with a rope or chain
wade – weighed
    wade (v) – to walk through water
    weighed (v) – past tense of *to weigh*, meaning to find out how heavy something is
waist – waste
    waist (n) – middle part of the body
    waste (v) – to use up needlessly
wait – weight
    wait (v) – to stay in one place and *wait* for something
    weight (n) – the heaviness of something
way – weigh
    way (n) – Examples: the right *way,* clear the *way*
    weigh (v) – to find the heaviness of something with a scale
weak – week
    weak (adj) – not strong
    week (n) – seven days
weather – whether
    weather (n) – rain, storms, etc.
    whether (conj) – Example: *whether* or not
which – witch
    which (pron) – Example: *Which* one?
    witch (n) – an evil woman
whole (see **hole**)
were – we're
    were (v) – past tense of *are*: They *were* gone.
    we're – contraction of *we are*
wood – would
    wood (n) – from trees
    would (v) – from the word *will*: He *would* not say.
won (see **one**)
wrap (see **rap**)
wring (see **ring**)
write (see **right**)
wrote (see **rote**)
your – you're
    your (adj) – belonging to you
    you're – contraction of *you are*

Spelling

Many words in the English language are difficult to spell because sounds can be represented by more than one letter and letters can represent more than one sound. Most "rules" have many exceptions. Some words must simply be memorized. This section includes one method for studying spelling, a list of rules which have few exceptions, and a list of frequently misspelled words. See page 171 for some spelling **mnemonics**, or memory helps, for difficult words.

How to Study Spelling

Once a method for studying new words is learned, all words can be practiced using it. Here is one possible method:

1. Make sure you know the meaning, use and pronunciation of the word.
2. Read the word aloud.
3. Spell the word aloud as you point to each letter, then read it.
4. Write the word on a piece of paper as you spell and read it.
5. Check the model. Point to each letter.
6. Check and correct the word you wrote. Point to each letter.
7. Cover the word you wrote. Repeat steps 4–6 two more times.
8. Close your eyes and visualize the word. Spell the word aloud and say it.

Repeat the procedure as many times as necessary to master the word. Generally, it takes at least 60–75 practices to master a new spelling word. Use the word in your writing.

Long ago in England, people spelled words the way they sounded. There was no one correct spelling for a word. In fact, some people took pride in creative spelling. William Shakespeare spelled his name several different ways. Some of the common ways to spell *cliff* were: *clif, clief, cleove, cleo, cluf, clive, clef* and *cleve*. The idea of "correct" spelling came with the printing of books and the dictionary.

Spelling Rules

The following rules in English spelling have very few exceptions:

1. The letter *q* is always followed by a *u* in English words. *(question, quite)*

2. English words do not end with the letter *v*. *(gave, have)*

3. When a one-syllable word ends with a short vowel and a single consonant, double the final consonant before adding a suffix beginning with a vowel. *(swim + -ing* is *swimming)*
In a two-syllable word, double the final consonant only if the word is accented on the last syllable. *(begín + -ing* is *beginning* but *ópen + -ing* is *opening)*

4. When a word ends in silent *e,* drop the *e* before adding a suffix beginning with a vowel. *(make + -ing* is *making)*
Keep the silent *e* before adding a suffix beginning with a consonant. *(time + -ly* is *timely)*

5. When a word ends in a consonant and *y,* change the *y* to *i* before adding a suffix, unless the suffix begins with *i.* *(happy + -ly* is *happily,* but *hurry + -ing* is *hurrying)*
When a word ends in a vowel and *y,* do not change the *y* to *i.* *(play + -ed* is *played)*

Frequently Misspelled Words

absence	awful	completely	disappoint	experience	happier
absorb	beautiful	concentrate	discipline	extremely	happiest
accept*	beauty	conscientious	discuss	familiar	happily
accidentally	because	conscience	discussion	families	happiness
accommodate	before	conscious	disease	fascinate	hear*
accompany	beginning	continue	dissatisfy	fasten	height
accuse	believe	continuous	doctor	fatigue	here*
ache	benefit	control	does	favorite	heroes
achieve	bicycle	convenience	doesn't	February	history
acquaintance	biscuit	convenient	dropped	fiction	hoping
acquire	boundary	corner	dropping	fictitious	hospital
address	brake*	counterfeit	during	field	humor
affect*	break*	countries	easier	finally	humorous
afraid	Britain	courage	easiest	first	hungry
against	brilliance	courageous	easily	forecast	hurrying
aggression	brilliant	courteous	effect*	forehead	identify
aggressive	bureau	cried	eighth	foreign	imagine
all right	business	cries	either	foresee	immediate
almost	calendar	criticism	embarrass	forest	immediately
a lot	captain	criticize	enemy	foretell	immensely
already	career	curiosity	enough	formerly	incident
always	carrying	debt	entertain	forty	independence
amateur	cemetery	deceive	envelope	fourth*	independent
ambition	certain	decide	environment	fragile	Indian
among	challenge	decision	equipment	freight	innocent
answer	character	definite	equipped	friend	instead
apology	chief	definitely	escape	front	intelligence
apparent	children	descend	especially	fulfill	intelligent
appearance	chocolate	describe	etc.	further	interest
appeared	chosen	description	everybody	genius	interpret
appreciate	Christian	desert*	everything	getting	interrupt
appreciation	cinnamon	desperately	everywhere	government	introduce
approach	climb	dessert*	exaggerate	governor	its*
arctic	climbed	destroy	exceed	grabbed	it's*
argument	climbing	develop	excellence	grammar	jealous
article	clothes	diarrhea	excellent	grateful	judgment
associate	colonel	dictionary	except*	group	knew*
athlete	college	didn't	excited	guarantee	know*
athletic	column	different	excitement	guard	knowledge
attendance	coming	difficult	exciting	guess	laboratory
attendant	commercial	dinner	existence	guest	laid
attitude	committee	dining	expense	handsome	later
author	complete	disappear	experiment	happen	laughed

*These words may be confused with other English words. See *Homophones and Troublesome Words*, pages 172–174.

Frequently Misspelled Words

leisure	occasion	practically	remember	stepped	trouble
library	occur	prairie	rendezvous	stepping	truly
lightning	occurred	precede	repetition	stopped	two*
literature	occurrence	preferred	repellent	stopping	unique
lonely	occurring	prejudice	reservoir	stories	unnecessary
loose*	often	preparation	restaurant	straight	until
lose*	omitted	pretty	rhyme	strengthen	unusual
lying	opinion	principal	rhythm	stretch	usually
magazine	opportunity	principle	ridiculous	studied	vaccinate
magnificent	opposite	prison	running	studies	vacuum
many	original	privilege	safely	studying	vegetable
marriage	other	probably	safety	succeed	very
mathematics	pageant	procedure	Saturday	success	village
maybe	paid	proceed	scene*	successful	villain
meant	pamphlet	profession	scent*	sugar	weather*
medicine	parallel	professor	schedule	suggest	Wednesday
millionaire	parents	pronunciation	scissors	summarize	weight*
miniature	parliament	prophecy	search	summary	weird
minute	particular	psychologist	secret	superintendent	went
miscellaneous	passed*	psychology	secretary	suppose	were
mischievous	pastime	pursue	seize	surprise	we're
misspell	peculiar	pursuit	semester	suspense	where
model	perform	quantity	sense*	suspicion	whether*
modern	period	quiet*	sentence	swimming	which*
month	permanent	quite*	separate	synagogue	whole*
mosquito	persuade	raspberry	separation	temperament	who's*
motor	phenomenon	realize	sergeant	their*	whose*
mountain	physical	really	servant	themselves	witch*
muscle	piece*	receipt	shepherd	there*	woman
mystery	pilot	receive	shining	therefore	women
narrative	plain*	receiving	similar	they	wonder
necessary	plane*	recess	since*	they're*	wonderful
neighbor	planned	recognize	sincerely	thief	would*
nervous	planning	recommend	soldier	thorough	wreck
niece	pleasant	reference	something	thoroughly	write*
night	pneumonia	referred	sophomore	thought	writer
nineteen	poem	referring	spaghetti	through	writing
ninety	poison	rein*	speak	tobacco	written
notice	possess	reign*	speech	together	wrote*
noticeable	possessed	relative	sponsor	tomorrow	yacht
nuisance	possession	relief	squirrel	too*	yolk
obedience	possible	religion	stationary*	tragedy	your*
obstacle	practical	religious	stationery*	tried	you're*

*These words may be confused with other English words. See *Homophones and Troublesome Words*, pages 172–174.

Greek and Latin Word Roots

Word roots from Greek and Latin are helpful in figuring out the meanings of unfamiliar words. Experts estimate that about 60% of common English words come from Latin or Greek.

Root	*Meaning*	*Examples*	*Root*	*Meaning*	*Examples*
-aqua-	water	aquarium	-pel-	drive	compel, repel, expel
-audi-	hear	audience, audition	-pend-	hang	depend, pendulum
-biblio-	book	bibliography	-phil-	love	philosophy
-cede-	go	recede, precede	-phobia-	fear	claustrophobia
-ceed-	go	exceed, proceed	-phon-	sound	phonics, telephone
-cept-	take	intercept, reception	-phot-	light	photography
-chrom-	color	monochrome	-phys-	nature	physics, physical
-chron-	time	chronic, synchronize	-plex-	network	complex, perplex
-cide-	kill	suicide, decide	-pod-	foot	tripod, podiatrist
-clud-	close	seclude, include	-port-	carry	portable, transport
-cred-	believe	incredible, credit	-poten-	power	potent, potential
-dent-	tooth	indent, dentist	-press-	press	impress, depress
-derm-	skin	epidermis	-psych-	mind	psychology, psychic
-dict-	say	dictator, contradict	-rupt-	break	disrupt, interrupt
-duct-	lead	conduct, product	-scien-	knowledge	science, conscience
-fide-	faith	fidelity, confidence	-scend-	climb, go	ascend, descent
-flamm-	fire	flammable	-scop-	see, look	microscope, telescope
-flex-	bend	flexible, reflex	-scri-	write	describe, prescription
-flor-	flower	florist, florid	-sect-	cut	dissect, intersection
-flu-	flow	fluent, influence	-serv-	protect	conserve, observe
-gramm-	letter	telegram, grammar	-spect-	look, see	inspect, spectator
-graph-	writing	autograph, telegraph	-stell-	star	constellation
-gress-	walk	progress, congress	-stig-	goad, prick	instigate, stigma
-homo-	alike	homonym	-struct-	build	construct, structure
-ject-	throw	eject, reject, inject	-tact-	touch	intact, tactile
-jour-	day	journey, adjourn	-tain-	hold	maintain, retain
-junct-	join	junction, conjunction	-tend-	stretch, pull	pretend, tendency
-leg-	law	legal, legislature	-therap-	treatment	psychotherapy
-loc-	place	locate, locus	-therm-	heat	thermometer, thermal
-man-	hand	manufacture, manual	-tim-	fear	timid, intimidate
-miss-	send	missionary, dismiss	-tort-	twist	distort, torture, extort
-mit-	send	transmit, admit	-tract-	draw, pull	tractor, subtract
-mort-	death	mortal, mortician	-ven-	come	convention, intervene
-nov-	new	novice, novelty	-vert-	turn	convert, divert
-pan-	all	panacea, panorama	-vis-	see	visible, supervise
-pan-	bread	pantry, company	-vit-	life	vitality, vitamin
-path-	suffering	sympathy, pathology	-viv-	alive	survive, revive
-ped-	foot	pedal, pedestrian	-voc-	voice	vocal, vocation

Prefixes

A **prefix** is a word part that can be added to the beginning of a base word to change its meaning or to form a new word.

Prefix	Meaning	Examples
ab-	away, off	abnormal, absent
ad-	toward, to	admit, advance
aero-	air	aerobatics, aerospace
ante-	before	antedate, anteroom
anti-	against	antiseptic, antiaircraft
anthropo-	human	anthropology
astro-	star	astronomy, astronaut
auto-	self, own	autograph, automatic
bi-	two	bicycle, biweekly
bio-	life	biography, biology
centi-	hundred	centigram, centipede
circum-	around	circumference
co-	together	cooperate, coordinate
com-	together	combine, compete
con-	together	connect, conversation
contra-	against	contradiction
cosmo-	universe	cosmonaut, cosmic
counter-	against	counteract
de-	from, down	defrost, depress
deca-	ten	decade, decagon
deci-	ten	decimal, decibel
dis-	not	disagree, dishonest
	opposite of	disappear, disconnect
en-	put into	entangle, enjoy
	cause to be	enlarge, enable
equi-	equal	equator, equilateral
ex-	out, from	explode, extend
ex-	former	ex-teacher
extra-	outside of	extraordinary
fore-	before	forewarn, forefathers
geo-	earth	geology, geography
hydro-	water	hydroelectric
hyper-	too much	hyperactive
il-	not	illegal, illogical
im-	not	impossible, impolite
in-	not	incorrect, invisible
	in, into	inject, include
infra-	below	infrared, infrasonic
inter-	between	interrupt, intercept
ir-	not	irregular
mal-	bad	malfunction
mega-	great	megaphone, megaton
micro-	small	microscope, microbe
mid-	middle	midnight, midsection
milli-	thousand	millimeter, millipede
mini-	small	miniskirt
mis-	wrong, bad	misspell, mistrust
mono-	one	monotone, monopoly
multi-	many	multicolored
non-	not	nonstop, nonsense
ob-	toward	object, obtain
omni-	all	omnivore, omniscient
out-	more than	outnumber, outdo
over-	too much	oversleep, overflow
poly-	many	polygon, polychrome
post-	after	postscript, postdate
pre-	before	prefix, preschool
pro-	for	pronoun, prolabor
quadr-	four	quadruplet, quadrant
re-	back	refill, repay
	again	rebuild, reconsider
retro-	behind	retroactive, retrospect
semi-	half	semicircular, semisoft
sub-	below	submarine, subzero
super-	above	superpower, superior
sym-, syn-	together	sympathy, synonym
tele-	far off	telephone, television
trans-	across	transport, transect
tri-	three	tricycle, triangle
ultra-	beyond	ultrasonic, ultraviolet
un-	not	unlucky, unsafe
	opposite of	unplug, uncover
under-	below	underground
	not enough	undercooked
uni-	one	universe, uniform
up-	up	uplift, uphill

Suffixes

A **suffix** is a word part that is added after a base word to change its meaning or form a new word.

Suffix	Meaning	Examples	Part of Speech
-able, -ible	capable or worthy of being	washable, reversible	adjective
-al	pertaining to	frontal, educational	adjective
-an	one born or living in	American, African	noun, adjective
-ance, -ancy	a thing that is	inheritance	noun
-ant	a person or thing that	accountant	noun
	causing, showing or being	radiant, observant	adjective
-ary	pertaining to, connected with	dictionary, imaginary	noun, adjective
-ate	to become or cause to become	activate, evaporate	verb
	filled with	proportionate	adjective
-dom	state of being	wisdom	noun
-ed	past tense	liked, wanted	verb
-eer	person having to do with	engineer, mountaineer	noun
-en	become, cause to be or have	darken, brighten	verb
	made of	wooden, woolen	adjective
-er	more	taller, wider	adjective
	a person or thing which	miner, roller	noun
-ery	the act of	robbery	noun
-ese	native of, language of	Chinese, Japanese	adjective
-ess	female	lioness, actress	noun
-est	most	biggest, highest	adjective
-ful	full of, having	colorful, careful	adjective
-fy	make or cause to become	simplify, glorify	verb
-hood	condition of	childhood, likelihood	noun
-ian	someone who	musician, politician	noun
-ing	continuous action	listening, running	verb
-ion, -tion	result of, state of being	correction, action	noun
-ish	like, somewhat	childish, foolish	adjective
-ist	person who	novelist, artist	noun
-ity, -ty	state of being	possibility, difficulty	noun
-ize	cause to be	modernize, finalize	verb
-less	without	helpless, restless	adjective
-logy	science of	geology, biology	noun
-ly	like, in a manner that is	friendly, loudly	adverb
-ment	result of being	punishment, pavement	noun
-ness	quality or state of being	happiness, sickness	noun
-ous	full of, having	humorous, dangerous	adjective
-or	person who	actor, sailor	noun
-s, -es	more than one	boys, boxes	noun
-y	like, full of	dusty, wavy	adjective

Grammar and Parts of Speech

Note: It would be impossible to include a thorough explanation of our complex English language in a short space. This section is intended to provide a simplified framework from which learning can progress, and is not intended to be comprehensive.

Nouns

Definition: A **noun** names a person, place, thing, quality, act or feeling: *girl, city, desk, honesty, sadness*
Nouns may be made up of more than one word: *Dr. Smith, Pikes Peak*

Proper nouns and common nouns:
> A **proper noun** names someone or something in particular and is capitalized: *Mary* (See pages 170–171.)
> A **common noun** is any noun that is not a proper noun: *girl, city, river*

Singular nouns and plural nouns:
> A **singular noun** names <u>one</u> person, place, thing, quality, act or feeling: *hat*
> A **plural noun** names more than one: *hats*
> **Rules for pluralizing words:**
> 1. To form the plural of most nouns, add *-s: dogs*
> 2. For nouns ending in *-s, -x, -z, -sh,* or *-ch,* add *-es: buses, foxes, bushes, scratches*
> 3. For nouns ending in *-o,* add *-s* or *-es: radios, potatoes*
> 4. For nouns ending with a vowel and *-y,* add *-s: toys, monkeys*
> For nouns ending with a consonant and *-y,* change the *y* to *i* and add *-es: berries, babies*
> 5. Some nouns form irregular plurals, including the following:

moose – moose	*child – children*	*mouse – mice*
deer – deer	*man – men*	*goose – geese*
fish – fish	*woman – women*	*foot – feet*
sheep – sheep	*person – people*	*tooth – teeth*

Possessive nouns
> **Possessive nouns** show ownership: <u>*Mike's*</u> *book*
> **Rules for forming possessives:**
> 1. To form the possessive of most singular nouns, add *'s: Mary* becomes *Mary's* — *Mary's new car is red.*
> 2. To form the possessive of a plural noun that ends in *-s,* add *': boys* becomes *boys'— The boys' mothers were all at school.*
> 3. To form the possessive of a plural noun which does not end in *-s,* add *'s: children* becomes *children's — The children's hats were gone.*

Pronouns

Definition: A **pronoun** is a word that takes the place of a noun.

Personal pronouns
> A **personal pronoun** refers to a specific person or thing.
> Singular pronouns refer to one person, plural pronouns to more than one.
> First person pronouns refer to the person speaking or writing.
> Second person pronouns refer to the person being spoken or written to.
> Third person pronouns refer to any other person or object.
> Subject pronouns replace a noun in the subject of the sentence (person or thing doing the action).
> Possessive pronouns replace a possessive noun.
> Object pronouns replace a noun which is receiving the action of a sentence.

Indefinite pronouns do not refer to a specific person or thing.

anybody	*anyone*	*anything*	*whatever*
everybody	*everyone*	*everything*	*whoever*
somebody	*someone*	*something*	*one*
nobody	*no one*	*nothing*	*you*

Reflexive pronouns refer back to the subject.

myself	*ourselves*
yourself	*yourselves*
himself	*themselves*
herself	
itself	

Chart of Personal Pronouns

	Singular			Plural		
	Subject	Object	Possessive	Subject	Object	Possessive
First Person	*I*	*me*	*my* *mine*	*we*	*us*	*our* *ours*
Second Person	*you*	*you*	*your* *yours*	*you*	*you*	*your* *yours*
Third Person	*he* *she* *it*	*him* *her* *it*	*his* *her(s)* *its*	*they*	*them*	*their* *theirs*

Adjectives

Definition: An **adjective** describes, or modifies (limits the meaning of), a noun or pronoun: *Three angry people were arguing. She was happy to come home.*

Articles. The **articles** are *a, an,* and *the.*
> Use *a* before singular nouns beginning with a consonant: *a dog*
> Use *an* before singular nouns beginning with a vowel sound: *an egg, an hour*
> Use *the* before any noun, to refer to a specific noun: *the milk, the moon*

Comparative and superlative adjectives.
> **Rules for forming comparative and superlative adjectives:**
> 1. For most adjectives of one or two syllables, add *-er* or *-est* to form comparative and superlative adjectives.
>   > *John is tall.*
>   > *Janet is taller than John.*
>   > *Mike is the tallest of the three.*
> 2. For longer adjectives, use *more* or *most* to form comparative and superlative adjectives.
>   > *Monica is discouraged.*
>   > *I am more discouraged than Monica.*
>   > *Mrs. Miller is the most discouraged of all.*
> 3. A few common adjectives form irregular comparatives and superlatives.
>   > *good, better, best*
>   > *bad, worse, worst*
>   > *many, more, most*
>   > *little, less, least*

Contractions	
Contractions are formed with nouns or pronouns and auxiliary verbs or verbs which express a state of being or having.	*I would - I'd* *you would - you'd* *he would - he'd* *she would - she'd* *it would - it'd* *we would - we'd* *they would - they'd*

I am - I'm *you are - you're* *he is - he's* *she is - she's* *it is - it's* *we are - we're* *they are - they're*	*I will - I'll* *you will - you'll* *he will - he'll* *she will - she'll* *it will - it'll* *we will - we'll* *they will - they'll*	*is not - isn't* *are not - aren't* *was not - wasn't* *were not - weren't* *will not - won't* *would not - wouldn't* *can not - can't* *could not - couldn't* *should not - shouldn't* *has not - hasn't* *have not - haven't* *had not - hadn't* *does not - doesn't* *do not - don't* *did not - didn't*
I have - I've *you have - you've* *he has - he's* *she has - she's* *it has - it's* *we have - we've* *they have - they've*	*I had - I'd* *you had - you'd* *he had - he'd* *she had - she'd* *it had - it'd* *we had - we'd* *they had - they'd*	

Verbs

Definition: A **verb** expresses action, either physical or mental, or it expresses a state of being.
> Examples of action verbs: *sing, think, like, make, do*
> Examples of verbs to express a state of being: *am, is, are, was, were, be, being, been*

Verb phrases are made up of a main verb and one or more helping or auxiliary verbs. The main verb is the last verb in the phrase. *Mr. Jones might hire me tomorrow. They could have been on vacation.*
> The main auxiliary verbs are forms of *have, be, can, may, must, do, shall,* and *will.*
> Forms of the verbs *do, be,* and *have* are often used as auxiliary verbs: *She has been working a lot.*

Verb tenses show different time, or tense.
Present tense:	*I look.*
Past tense:	*I looked.*
Future tense:	*I will look.*

The **present participle** is used in progressive forms to show continuing action.
Present progressive tense:	*I am looking.*
Past progressive tense:	*I was looking.*
Future progressive tense:	*I will be looking.*

The **past participle** shows finished action. It is used in the passive voice.
Present tense:	*It is being drawn.*
Past tense:	*It was drawn.*
Future tense:	*It will be drawn.*

Perfect tenses show when an ongoing action started. They consist of forms of the word and the past participle.
Present perfect tense:	*I have looked.*
Past perfect tense:	*I had looked.*
Future perfect tense:	*I will have looked.*

Principal parts of verbs are the verb, the present participle, the past and the past participle.

Regular verbs are verbs which form the past and past participle by adding *-ed.*
Present	*walk*
Present Participle (add *-ing*)	*walking*
Past (add *-ed*)	*walked*
Past participle (add *-ed*)	*walked*

Spelling rules for forming the parts of regular verbs:
1. For words ending in silent *e,* drop the *e* before adding *-ed* or *-ing. (live, lived, living)*
2. For words ending in a short vowel and a single consonant, double the final consonant before adding *-ed* or *-ing. (drop, dropped, dropping)*

Irregular verbs form the past and the past participle in a variety of ways. The present participle is formed the same as for regular verbs. See the Chart of Irregular Verbs for examples.

Chart of Irregular Verbs

Present	Past	Perfect	Present	Past	Perfect
beat	beat	beaten	let	let	let
begin	began	begun	lie	lay	lain
bend	bent	bent	lose	lost	lost
bite	bit	bitten	make	made	made
blow	blew	blown	meet	met	met
break	broke	broken	put	put	put
bring	brought	brought	raise*	raised*	raised*
build	built	built	read	read	read
burst	burst	burst	ride	rode	ridden
buy	bought	bought	ring	rang	rung
catch	caught	caught	rise	rose	risen
choose	chose	chosen	run	ran	run
come	came	come	say	said	said
cost	cost	cost	see	saw	seen
cut	cut	cut	sell	sold	sold
dig	dug	dug	set	set	set
dive	dived, dove	dived	shake	shook	shaken
do	did	done	shoot	shot	shot
drag*	dragged*	dragged*	show	showed	shown
draw	drew	drawn	shrink	shrank	shrunk
drink	drank	drunk	sing	sang	sung
drive	drove	driven	sink	sank	sunk
eat	ate	eaten	sit	sat	sat
fall	fell	fallen	sleep	slept	slept
feel	felt	felt	slide	slid	slid
fight	fought	fought	speak	spoke	spoken
fit	fit	fit	spend	spent	spent
fly	flew	flown	spread	spread	spread
forget	forgot	forgotten	spring	sprang	sprung
freeze	froze	frozen	stand	stood	stood
get	got	gotten	steal	stole	stolen
give	gave	given	sting	stung	stung
go	went	gone	swear	swore	sworn
grow	grew	grown	sweep	swept	swept
hang	hung	hung	swim	swam	swum
have	had	had	swing	swung	swung
hear	heard	heard	take	took	taken
hide	hid	hidden	teach	taught	taught
hit	hit	hit	tear	tore	torn
hold	held	held	tell	told	told
hurt	hurt	hurt	think	thought	thought
is/are	was/were	been	throw	threw	thrown
keep	kept	kept	understand	understood	understood
know	knew	known	wear	wore	worn
lay	laid	laid	win	won	won
lead	led	led	wind	wound	wound
leave	left	left	wring	wrung	wrung
lend	lent	lent	write	wrote	written

*These words are regular but are often mistaken for irregular verbs.

Adverbs

Definition: An **adverb** modifies (qualifies or limits the meaning of) a verb, adjective or another adverb. Adverbs usually tell *where, when, how,* or *to what extent.* Adverbs may consist of more than one word.

Examples: Where: *here, inside, nearby, somewhere*
When: *tomorrow, earlier, frequently, lately*
How: *quietly, quickly, well, carefully*
(Many adverbs that tell how end in *-ly.*)
To what extent (these may also be called intensifiers): *extremely, very, quite, so*

Prepositions

Definition: A **preposition** shows a relationship between a noun or a pronoun and another word in the sentence. A preposition is often more than one word.

about	*beside*	*near*
above	*besides*	*next to*
according to	*between*	*of*
across	*beyond*	*on*
after	*by*	*onto*
against	*down*	*over*
ahead of	*during*	*through*
along	*except*	*throughout*
among	*for*	*to*
around	*from*	*toward*
at	*in*	*under*
because of	*in back of*	*until*
before	*in front of*	*up*
behind	*instead of*	*with*
below	*into*	*within*
beneath	*like*	*without*

Conjunctions

Definition: Conjunctions are used to connect words, phrases or sentences: *and, but, or, however, therefore, so, if, when, except, because, though, although, unless*

Interjections

Definition: Interjections are special words which often express emotion, or serve as fillers or attention-getters. The word "interjection" comes from Latin and means "thrown in between." Most interjections are followed by commas or exclamation points.

> *Ouch! Whew! Oh! Hey!*
> *Why, I know what you mean!*
> *Well, I guess I'd better go.*
> *Say, I have an idea.*
> *Oh, I suppose it's all right.*

Word Usage in Standard English

bring, take — *Bring* means to carry or lead someone or something **here**. *Please bring the newspaper to me. Take* means to carry or lead someone or something **there**. *Please take this with you to school tomorrow.*

can, may — *Can* shows the ability to do something. *She can play tennis well. May* asks or gives permission to do something. *May I use your telephone?*

did, done — *Did* is the past tense of *do. We did our work. Done* is used after a form of *have. They have done their chores. She has learned a lot.*

doesn't, don't — *Doesn't* is used with *he, she* and *it. Janet doesn't like ice cream. Don't* is used with *I, you, we* and *they. We don't have to leave until 9:00.*

good, well — *Good* describes something or someone. *That is a good apple. Well* describes an action. *He writes well.*

in, into — *In* means a location inside of something. *We drove in a car. Into* means motion or direction to a place within. *We drove into a car.*

lay, lie — *Lay* means to put or place something down. *Lay the books on the table, please. Lie* means to put or place yourself down. *I think I'll lie down and rest.*

learn, teach — *Learn* means to acquire or get knowledge. *He wants to learn French. Teach* means to give or impart knowledge. *The professor teaches history.*

leave, let — *Leave* means to go away. *They have to leave now. Let* means to permit. *He let me borrow a car.*

lend, borrow — *Lend* means to allow another person to use something of yours with the understanding that it be returned. *She will be happy to lend you a pen. Borrow* means to take something belonging to another person with the understanding that it will be returned. *May I borrow your hammer?*

raise, rise — *Raise* means to cause something to move upward. *It's time to raise the flag. Rise* means to move upward. *The sun will rise at 5:38 a.m. today.*

set, sit — *Set* means to place or put something in a certain position. *Please set the table. Sit* means to put yourself in a sitting position. *I will sit on the bench.*

Writing, Music and Art

Writing Process

1.

Think of an
Idea
Use your imagination
and experience.

2.

Then
Brainstorm
List, cluster, map,
make an outline.

3.

Write a
Rough Draft
Double space.
Revise as you write.

4.

Read and Revise
Read your work aloud and
revise it. Draw lines
through what you change
rather than erasing. You
may later want to recover a
word or an idea.

Most good writers revise
their work again and again
throughout the writing
process, improving it each
time. Revising means:
1. Adding words.
2. Taking out words that
   aren't needed.
3. Changing words to make
   your meaning more
   clear.
4. Rearranging words.
5. Changing or combining
   sentences.

5.

Share
your writing with someone.
Is the meaning clear?
Are there questions or
suggestions?
Revise if needed.

6.

Edit
Check correctness of:
1) Spelling
2) Punctuation
3) Capitalization
4) Form

7.

Prepare a
Final Draft
Use your best handwriting.

8.

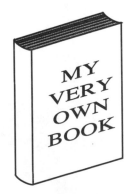

MY
VERY
OWN
BOOK

Finally
Publish
Share with an audience.

To Write

advertisements
advice columns
animal stories
announcements
apologies
autobiographies
awards

beauty tips
bedtime stories
biographies
book jackets
book reviews
books
bumper stickers

campaign speeches
cartoon captions
cereal boxes
character sketches
codes
comic strips
comparisons
complaints
congratulations
conversations
crossword puzzles

definitions
descriptions
dialogues
diaries
diets
directions
directories
dramas
dream scripts

editorials
epitaphs
essays
exaggerations
explanations

fables
fairy tales
fantasies
folk tales
fortunes

game rules
get well notes
good & bad news
greeting cards
grocery lists
gossip

headlines
horoscopes

inquiries
interviews
introductions
invitations

jokes
journals

labels
legends
letters
lies
lists

magazine articles
memories
menus
messages
monologues
movie reviews
mysteries
myths

newscasts
newspapers
notebooks
notes

observations
opinions
orders

persuasive letters
plays
poems
post cards
posters
predictions
problems
problem solutions
product descriptions
puppet shows
puzzles

quizzes
questionnaires
questions
quotations

ransom notes
realistic fiction
rebus writing
recipes
reports
requests
research papers
riddles

sales notices
schedules
science fiction
secrets
self descriptions
signs
silly sayings
soap operas
songs
speeches
spook stories
sports stories
stories
superstitions

tall tales
thank you notes
tongue twisters
travel folders
TV commercials
TV guides
TV programs

want ads
wanted posters
warnings
wills
wishes
weather reports

Before beginning to write, think about your **purpose** and your intended **audience**. Your audience may be yourself, your friends, a teacher, the readers of a newspaper or someone else. Your **purpose** may be one of the following:

to report	to inspire
to evaluate	to prove learning
to summarize	to clarify thoughts
to explain	to record
to share	to question
to inform	to create
to persuade	to discover yourself

Prewriting

Thinking is the most important part of good writing. Thinking of a good topic is the first challenge. It may help to close your eyes and imagine possible topics until you find one that interests you and that you can write about. Some writers make a list of possible topics just before writing. Others keep an ongoing "idea notebook" in which they write possible topics whenever they think of them. This provides a "bank" of ideas to review and choose from when it is time to write.

After choosing a topic and before beginning a rough draft, note as many ideas as possible about the topic. This helps with two important steps:

1. Capturing specific ideas on paper and clarifying them.
2. Organizing thoughts.

Each writer eventually discovers his/her own best methods for prewriting. The following are some suggestions to try.

Clustering

1. Write the topic in a big circle in the middle of a page.
2. As you think about the topic, write one or two words to remind you of each idea or thought about it.
3. When writing, group related ideas as much as possible. Circle and connect ideas that have something in common.

Bubbling

Bubbling is similar to clustering, but the circles are not connected. After writing all ideas, go back and use color to highlight and group ideas which belong together.

Mapping

Mapping is a form of outlining.
1. Write the topic in a circle in the middle of the page.
2. Write main ideas on lines connected to the circle.
3. Write supporting ideas on lines connected to the main ideas.
4. Write details connected to supporting ideas.
5. When finished, go back and number the main ideas, supporting ideas, and details to indicate a sequence to use for writing.

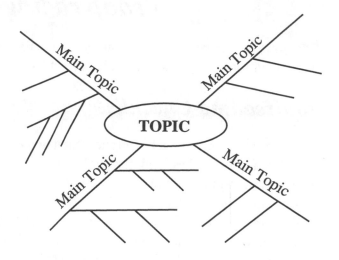

Outlining

An outline is a formal map. Other prewriting activities can help organize thoughts into an outline.

The **title** of the outline is the main subject.
Roman numerals are used for the main headings, which may be sections of a report or topics of paragraphs. The first ten Roman numerals are: I, II, III, IV, V, VI, VII, VIII, IX, and X.
Capital letters show subheadings:
A, B, C, D, E, F, etc.
Arabic numerals show the details about the subheadings:
1, 2, 3, 4, 5, etc.
Small letters can be used under Arabic numerals to show details about details: a, b, c, d, e, etc.

Either phrases or sentences may be used in outlines, but the structure should be kept consistent. Generally, if there is a **I.**, there must be a **II.** If there is an **A.**, there must be a **B.**, and so on.

Title of Outline	*Poisonous Snakes of the United States*

I. Main Heading
  A. Subheading
    1. Detail
      a. Sub-detail
      b. Sub-detail
    2. Detail
  B. Subheading
  C. Subheading
II. Main Heading
  A. Subheading
  B. Subheading
	I. Pit vipers
	  A. Rattlesnake
	    1. Characteristics
	      a. Size
	      b. Rattle
	    2. Range
	  B. Water mocassin
	  C. Copperhead
	II. Coral snakes
	  A. Eastern coral snake
	  B. Western coral snake

Listing

1. Write all the ideas you can think of about the topic in a list.
2. Go back through the list and group related ideas. You might use color to highlight ideas which belong together, or use another sheet of paper and rewrite by main topic.

Using Cards

1. Use 3x5 index cards and write one idea per card.
2. When finished, group cards with related ideas into piles. Name each group of cards (these will be main topics).
3. Put the cards within each group in order.

Proofreading and Editing

The purpose of proofreading and editing is to prepare a piece of writing for a final draft or for publication by making sure it is correct in all details.

Proofreading Checklist

1. Is the first word of each sentence capitalized?
2. Are margins straight and correct?
3. Are paragraphs indented?
4. Are all words spelled correctly? See pages 176–177, *Frequently Misspelled Words*, or use a dictionary.
5. Are homophones and confusing words spelled correctly? See pages 172–174, *Homophones and Confusing Words*.
6. Do all sentences end with correct punctuation?
7. Is all other punctuation correct? See pages 168–169, *Punctuation*.
8. Are words capitalized correctly, including proper nouns and titles? See pages 170–171, *Capitalization*.
9. Are correct verb forms used? See page 183, *Chart of Irregular Verbs*.
10. Are all sentences complete? Are there any run-on sentences?

Proofreaders' Marks

Proofreaders' marks show changes that must be made in the proof, or rough draft. The short essay on the bottom left shows the use of proofreaders' marks.

✗	delete (take out)
/	delete
∧	insert
⊙	insert period
∧	insert comma
∨	insert apostrophe
∨	insert quotation marks
#	insert a space
⌢	delete a space
∽	transpose
⊏	move left
⊐	move right
‖	straighten
¶	begin a new paragraph
≡	capitalize
lc	use lower-case letters
sp	spell out
?	check to see if correct
stet	let it stand the way it was before it was marked

Alaska is the largest state of the U.S. in size, but in many other ways most people don't realize. It is emmense, more than twice as large as Texas and larger than allbut 17 of the world's countries! Although most people know that Mt. Mckinley is the highest peak in North america, few realize that the 16 highest peaks in the national are in Alaska, all over 14,500 feet.

Alaska's Coastline nearly is as long as thatof the entire continental United States. The Yukon river is the third longest in the country and is part of Alas ka's more than 20,000 square miles of inland water. That's more water than seven of the 50 states haveland!

Most remarkable of all, perhaps, is thefact that Alaska still has more bears than people!

Letter Form

A **letter** is a written message addressed to a person or organization and most often sent through the **postal system**. There are two types of letters: friendly letters and business letters.

	Friendly Letter	*Business Letter*
Sent to	Friends Relatives Pen Pals	Companies Editors Government officials
Purpose	Keep in touch Make friends (pen pals) Say thank you Say congratulations Apologize Send birthday or holiday greetings	Express an opinion Make a complaint Praise something good Ask for information Request materials Order a product
Writing	Usually handwritten.	Usually typed.
Return address	Sometimes is not included.	Often is part of printed letterhead stationery.
Date	May be abbreviated.	Never abbreviated.
Inside address	Never included.	Always included. Use the exact address which will be on the envelope.
Greeting	Follow with a comma (,). Normally use the person's first name.	Follow with a colon (:). Use a person's title and last name. If unknown, use *Dear Sir or Madame:* or *To Whom It May Concern:*
Body	Indent the first line of each paragraph.	Skip lines between paragraphs. Paragraphs may not be indented.
Closing	*Your friend,* *Love,*	*Sincerely,* *Sincerely yours,* *Yours truly,*
Signature	Sign with first name only, or first and last name.	Always sign in ink with both first and last names.
Typed name	Not included.	Always included in typewritten business letters. Usually, it is four spaces below the closing.

Friendly Letter

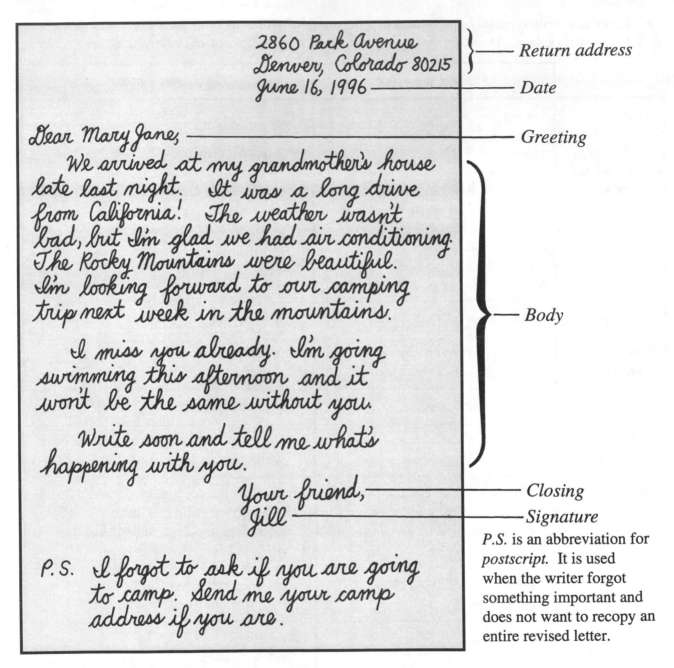

2860 Park Avenue
Denver, Colorado 80215 — Return address
June 16, 1996 — Date

Dear Mary Jane, — Greeting

We arrived at my grandmother's house late last night. It was a long drive from California! The weather wasn't bad, but I'm glad we had air conditioning. The Rocky Mountains were beautiful. I'm looking forward to our camping trip next week in the mountains.

I miss you already. I'm going swimming this afternoon and it won't be the same without you.

Write soon and tell me what's happening with you.

Your friend, — Closing
Jill — Signature

— Body

P.S. is an abbreviation for *postscript*. It is used when the writer forgot something important and does not want to recopy an entire revised letter.

P. S. I forgot to ask if you are going to camp. Send me your camp address if you are.

Finding a Pen Pal

Letters are a good way to make new friends from almost anywhere in the world. To be matched with a pen pal overseas or in another state, send a self-addressed, stamped envelope requesting an application to: Student Letter Exchange, 630 Third Avenue, New York, New York 10017. Indicate the countries or states in which you are most interested. For a $6.00 fee, you will be matched with up to four pen pals. The fee can be sent with the completed application. Once you have found a pen friend, make your letters interesting. Include such things as photographs, newspaper clippings, or stamps. Write often enough to stay in touch!

Business Letter

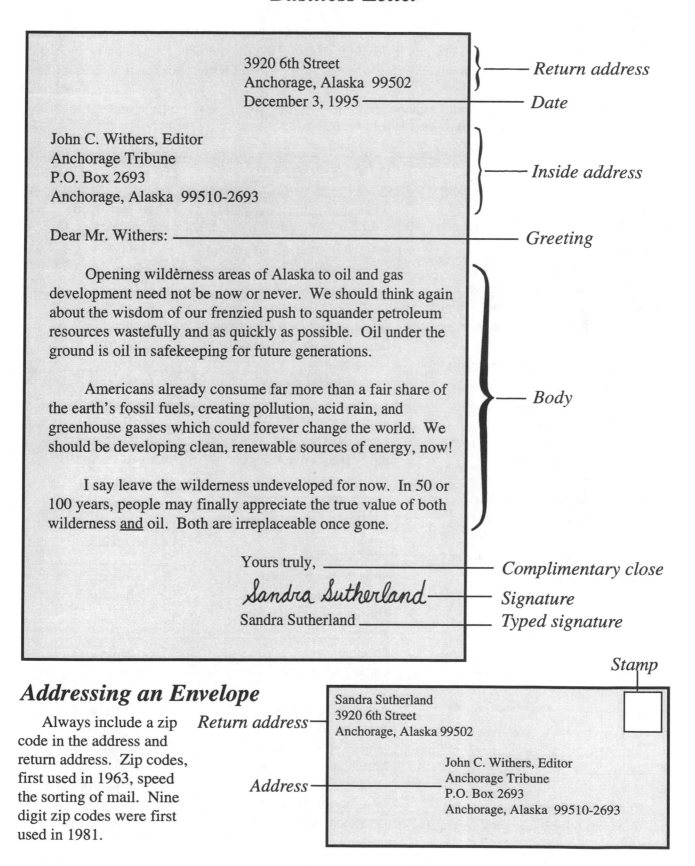

3920 6th Street
Anchorage, Alaska 99502
December 3, 1995 — *Date*

}—— *Return address*

John C. Withers, Editor
Anchorage Tribune
P.O. Box 2693
Anchorage, Alaska 99510-2693

}—— *Inside address*

Dear Mr. Withers: ——————— *Greeting*

Opening wilderness areas of Alaska to oil and gas development need not be now or never. We should think again about the wisdom of our frenzied push to squander petroleum resources wastefully and as quickly as possible. Oil under the ground is oil in safekeeping for future generations.

Americans already consume far more than a fair share of the earth's fossil fuels, creating pollution, acid rain, and greenhouse gasses which could forever change the world. We should be developing clean, renewable sources of energy, now!

I say leave the wilderness undeveloped for now. In 50 or 100 years, people may finally appreciate the true value of both wilderness <u>and</u> oil. Both are irreplaceable once gone.

}—— *Body*

Yours truly, ——————— *Complimentary close*

Sandra Sutherland —— *Signature*

Sandra Sutherland ——————— *Typed signature*

Addressing an Envelope

Always include a zip code in the address and return address. Zip codes, first used in 1963, speed the sorting of mail. Nine digit zip codes were first used in 1981.

Return address —

Sandra Sutherland
3920 6th Street
Anchorage, Alaska 99502

Stamp

Address —

John C. Withers, Editor
Anchorage Tribune
P.O. Box 2693
Anchorage, Alaska 99510-2693

Daily Writing

Writing every day can help you think, learn, remember and clarify your thoughts. Write in a special notebook often, every day if possible. Be sure to note the date of each entry. Occasionally, read back through what you've written in the past and write your thoughts about that!

Whenever possible, write about today or right now. When you have more time or want to write about something else, consider the ideas below.

Today or Right Now

places you went
people with whom you spent time
things you did
things people said
things you bought or were given
special events at home, school, work
first impressions about someone or
    something new
stories in the news and your reaction
things you learned today

Observations of nature
    temperature, weather, the first
    robin, the first snow

What you see, hear, smell or feel at
    this moment

Today's feelings, thoughts, goals,
    problems, opinions, ideas,
    decisions, accomplishments

Lists

Make lists of:
    things you love or dislike
    things for which you are thankful
    things about which you wonder
    things which hurt
    things which don't make sense
    things to which you look forward

About Yourself

what your name means and
    how you got that name
what you know about your
    ancestors
events and memories of
    your childhood
stories people tell about you
things you want to do or be
    someday
your parents' work

your appearance
your good or bad habits
the best or worst things
    about you
things about which you are
    proud

your interests
your daily or weekly
    schedule
chores or your job
sports
hobbies
clubs

places you've lived
pets you've had
people you admire
things you've lost or found

birthdays or holidays
dreams or nightmares

Best and Worst

When were you:
    happiest
    saddest
    sickest
    silliest
    angriest
    guiltiest
    loneliest
    laziest
    most afraid
    most grateful
    most disgusted
    most determined
    most envious
    most courageous
    most cowardly

Opinions

On: advice
       cheating
       divorce
       haircuts
       homework
       lying
       smoking
       stealing
       teenagers
       unfair rules
       war
       being your age
       crying
       writing

Descriptions

Describe the people in your life. Write about their appearance, feelings, clothing, actions, beliefs. What do they say? How do they talk? What do others say about them?

Write about family, friends, teachers, famous people.

Describe the places in your life. Write about:
your room
the view from your window
your house
your neighborhood
your classroom
your school
Draw floor plans or maps of some of the places.

Feelings

What are your feelings about:
how you look
getting your way
getting pushed around
getting up early
making mistakes
failing or losing
growing older
being ignored
being teased
being cheated
being tricked
being bothered
succeeding or winning
not being invited
not being understood
love, happiness, kindness
friendship, trust, death

Favorites

Your favorites and why:
activity
animal
article of clothing
birthday
book
cartoon character
color
day of the week
dessert
flower
food
holiday
invention
movie
music
person
place
pet
restaurant
school subject
sport
story
time of the year
TV commercial
TV program

If Only

if you had $10,000…
if you had three wishes…
if you had a time machine…
if you had three minutes on television…
if you could go anywhere…
if you could keep only five things …
if you could change the world…
if you lived in the past…
if you lived in the future…
if you were… someone else
something else
the boss

Experiences and Memories

Firsts. Write about:
your first day of school
your first haircut
your first home run
your first memory
your first performance
your first report card
your first speech
your first swimming lesson

Experiences. Write about:
being homesick
being in trouble
dressing up
getting something new
going to the doctor or dentist
losing a friend
making a friend
riding the bus
the beach
a camping trip
the circus
parades
parties
plays
vacations

Special events. Write about:
a big storm
a disaster
an encounter with a dangerous animal
a time you felt understood
a time you got revenge
a time you helped someone
a phase you went through
a wish which came true
a special celebration
an adventure

Music

Music consists of sounds and silences arranged and combined in patterns. **Sound** is produced by the vibrations of an object. All music has five basic elements.

Elements of Music

1. **Pitch** is the highness or lowness of a sound and is based on the **frequency**, or speed, of the vibrations. The faster an object vibrates, the higher the pitch. Pitch is shown with **notes**.

2. **Rhythm** is the regular arrangement of strong and weak sounds and **rests**, or silences. It is measured in **beats**.

3. **Melody** is the **tune**, or order of sounds and silences.

4. **Harmony** is the sounding of two or more notes at the same time. Three or more notes sounded together are a **chord**.

5. **Tone color** is the quality of a musical sound. The difference in sound between a trumpet and a violin playing the same note is tone color.

Musical Notation

Music is written using **musical notation**, symbols for notes and rests on a **grand staff**. The grand staff is a combination of the **treble clef** for high notes and the **bass clef** for low notes. A **clef** consists of five lines and the four spaces between them.

Pitch in Musical Notation

Each line or space on the clef represents a certain pitch. The notes are named using the letters A through G.

The distance between two notes with the same name is an **octave**. On a piano, the keys which are an octave apart look the same. Notes raised one-half tone form a **sharp**, shown with the symbol ♯. Notes lowered one-half tone are **flat**, shown with the symbol ♭. A **natural** ♮ cancels a sharp or flat. The **key signature** shows which sharps or flats are always played.

Rhythm in Musical Notation

Rhythm is the beat of the music. It is shown by the shape of the notes and by **rests**, which are silences with the same time value as the notes.

Whole Note	Half Note	Quarter Note	Eighth Note
Whole Rest	Half Rest	Quarter Rest	Eighth Rest

A whole note or rest has the same **duration**, or time value, as two half notes, four quarter notes, or eight eighth notes.

Notes and rests are grouped into **measures**, which are evenly spaced units of time. **Bar lines** separate the measures.

A **time signature** is a fraction. The numerator, or top number, shows how many beats are in a measure and the denominator, or bottom number, shows which kind of note (quarter note, half note, eighth note) receives one beat.

Expression in Musical Notation

Composers also note "expression," or their ideas about how the music should be performed. Some of the terms used to show expression and dynamics are:

adagio	slow	*allegro*	fast
piano	soft	*forte*	loud
legato	smooth	*staccato*	abrupt
crescendo ...	growing louder	*diminuendo*	growing softer

Musical Instruments

Musical instruments are grouped according to the source of the sound vibration. Some examples of each type are given.

A. **Chordophones** are stringed instruments.
1. Bowed — violin, viola, cello, bass
2. Plucked — guitar, harp, banjo
3. Keyboard — piano, harpsichord

B. **Aerophones** are wind instruments.
1. Woodwind — recorder, flute, reed instruments such as clarinet and oboe
2. Brass — horn, trumpet, trombone, tuba
3. Keyboard — pipe organ

C. **Membranophones** are some of the percussion instruments.
1. Drums
2. Tamborines

D. **Idiophones** are also percussion instruments.
1 Cymbals
2. Gongs

E. **Electrophones** have electrically produced sounds.
1. Synthesizer
2. Electronic keyboard

Vocal Music

Vocal music is produced by the vibration of people's vocal chords in song. Voices are classified by the **range** of tones, high to low, which a person can sing. **Lyrics** are the words of a song. **Accompaniment** is the instrumental part played with a song.

soprano	highest female voice
alto (contralto)	lowest female voice
tenor	high adult male voice
baritone	middle male voice
bass	lowest male voice

Art and Color

Art is the use of skill and creativity in the making of beautiful objects. Some of the **fine arts** are drawing, painting and sculpture. **Graphic arts** include printing, etching and photography.

Principles of Art

Rhythm
Balance
Unity
Variety
Emphasis

Elements of Design

Line
Shape
Color
Texture
Form

The Spectrum

A **prism**, which is a triangular piece of glass, divides light into a **spectrum** of colors. Visible light has in it all of the colors of the rainbow in this order: red, orange, yellow, green, blue, indigo and violet. **Ultraviolet** light is beyond violet and **infrared** is beyond red. People cannot see these colors but some animals can.

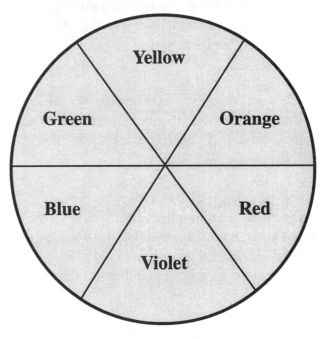

The Color Wheel

Primary colors are yellow, blue and red.

Secondary colors are orange, violet and green. They are made by mixing the primary pigments. **Pigment** is the coloring material in paint.

Complementary colors are opposite each other on the color wheel, such as green and red.

Adjacent colors are next to each other on the color wheel, such as yellow and green.

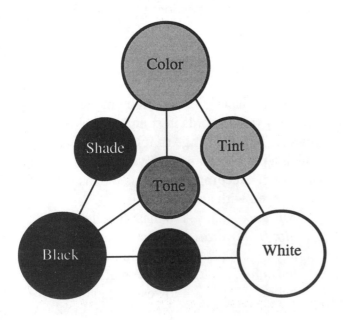

Tints and Shades

A **shade** is made by mixing any color and black.

A **tint** is made by mixing any color and white.

Gray is the result of mixing black and white.

A **tone** is made by mixing a color with both black and white.

Math
and
Numbers

Mathematics

Mathematics is the science of numbers. **Arithmetic** is a branch of mathematics which deals with numbers and computation. **Geometry** is another branch of mathematics, dealing with points, lines, angles, surfaces and solids. Some other branches of mathematics are **algebra**, **calculus** and **trigonometry**.

A **number** is an amount. A **numeral** is the symbol we use to show that amount. Although most places in the world use our numeration system, with 0, 1, 2, 3, 4, 5, 6, 7, 8, and 9 as the numerals, some systems are different. For example, people in Egypt use the following symbols for the numerals 1 to 9:

Roman Numerals

Roman numerals were widely used until the 1500's. They are occasionally used now on the faces of clocks, in outlines, and to record dates on monuments.

$$I = 1$$
$$V = 5$$
$$X = 10$$
$$L = 50$$
$$C = 100$$
$$D = 500$$
$$M = 1000$$

Addition rule: Add the values for the symbols from left to right: **XVII** = 10+5+1+1 = 17

Subtraction rule: When a symbol for a smaller number is written to the *left* of a symbol for a larger number, subtract the smaller number from the larger one just to its right and add the result as usual:
IV (1 before 5) = 5 – 1 = 4
XXIX (1 before 10) = 10+10+(10–1) = 29

Common Math Symbols

+	plus (addition)	>	greater than
−	minus (subtraction)	<	less than
X	times (multiplication)	%	percent
÷	divided by (division)	$	dollars
/	divided by (keyboard)	¢	cents
=	equals	∞	infinity
≠	does not equal		

Suggestions for Solving Math Word Problems

1. **Read** the problem carefully. What does it ask you to find?
2. **Think** about the problem. Try using these strategies.
   - Visualize what is happening in your mind.
   - Draw a picture or diagram.
   - Restate the problem in your own words.
   - Make a list or chart to organize the facts.
   - Act out the problem.
3. Notice any **key words**.
   Key words which may signal addition are:
   total, in all, all together, sum, together
   Key words which signal subtraction are:
   how many more, how many less, difference, greater than, fewer than, left, more than, less than, change
4. **Decide** how to solve the problem and put the facts into a number sentence, such as 18 x 45 = _____.
5. **Solve** the number sentence.
6. **Label** the answer.
7. **Check** the math for accuracy. Then think again. Does the answer make sense?

Place Value

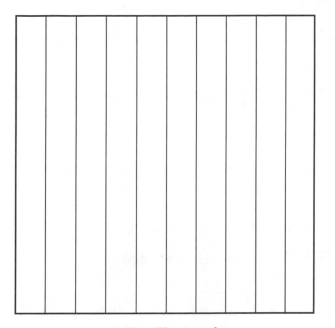

Ten Thousand
10 thousands

Thousand
10 hundreds

Hundred
10 tens

Ten
10 ones

One

Base 10

Our number system is based on ten. Each place is worth ten times more than the place just to its right.

	Trillion			Billion			Million			Thousand			Units		
	Hundred Trillions	Ten Trillions	One Trillions	Hundred Billions	Ten Billions	One Billions	Hundred Millions	Ten Millions	One Millions	Hundred Thousands	Ten Thousands	One Thousands	Hundreds	Tens	Ones
	3	8	7	0	9	6	4	2	7	1	8	0	3	5

3 8,7 0 9,6 4 2,7 1 8,0 3 5

This number would be read *thirty-eight trillion, seven hundred nine billion, six hundred forty-two million, seven hundred eighteen thousand, thirty-five.*

Number	Zeros
Thousand	3
Million	6
Billion	9
Trillion	12
Quadrillion	18
Quintillion	21
Sextillion	24
Septillion	27
Octillion	30
Nonillion	33
Decillion	36
Google*	100

Number Prefixes

uni-	....	one
bi-	....	two
tri-	....	three
quadri-	....	four
quinti-	....	five
sexti-	....	six
septi-	....	seven
octi-	....	eight
noni-	....	nine
deci-	....	ten

A hundred seconds is 1⅔ minutes.
A thousand seconds is about 17 minutes.
A million seconds is more than 11½ days.
A billion seconds is over 31½ years.
A trillion seconds is 31,710 years!

*At one time, there was no name for a one with 100 zeros after it. An American mathematician, Edward Kasner, asked his nine-year-old nephew to name it. He called it a "googol" and that is what mathematicians call it today!

```
0 +  0 =  0      1 +  0 =  1      2 +  0 =  2      3 +  0 =  3      4 +  0 =  4      5 +  0 =  5      6 +  0 =  6
0 +  1 =  1      1 +  1 =  2      2 +  1 =  3      3 +  1 =  4      4 +  1 =  5      5 +  1 =  6      6 +  1 =  7
0 +  2 =  2      1 +  2 =  3      2 +  2 =  4      3 +  2 =  5      4 +  2 =  6      5 +  2 =  7      6 +  2 =  8
0 +  3 =  3      1 +  3 =  4      2 +  3 =  5      3 +  3 =  6      4 +  3 =  7      5 +  3 =  8      6 +  3 =  9
0 +  4 =  4      1 +  4 =  5      2 +  4 =  6      3 +  4 =  7      4 +  4 =  8      5 +  4 =  9      6 +  4 = 10
0 +  5 =  5      1 +  5 =  6      2 +  5 =  7      3 +  5 =  8      4 +  5 =  9      5 +  5 = 10      6 +  5 = 11
0 +  6 =  6      1 +  6 =  7      2 +  6 =  8      3 +  6 =  9      4 +  6 = 10      5 +  6 = 11      6 +  6 = 12
0 +  7 =  7      1 +  7 =  8      2 +  7 =  9      3 +  7 = 10      4 +  7 = 11      5 +  7 = 12      6 +  7 = 13
0 +  8 =  8      1 +  8 =  9      2 +  8 = 10      3 +  8 = 11      4 +  8 = 12      5 +  8 = 13      6 +  8 = 14
0 +  9 =  9      1 +  9 = 10      2 +  9 = 11      3 +  9 = 12      4 +  9 = 13      5 +  9 = 14      6 +  9 = 15
0 + 10 = 10      1 + 10 = 11      2 + 10 = 12      3 + 10 = 13      4 + 10 = 14      5 + 10 = 15      6 + 10 = 16

7 +  0 =  7      8 +  0 =  8
7 +  1 =  8      8 +  1 =  9
7 +  2 =  9      8 +  2 = 10
7 +  3 = 10      8 +  3 = 11
7 +  4 = 11      8 +  4 = 12
7 +  5 = 12      8 +  5 = 13
7 +  6 = 13      8 +  6 = 14
7 +  7 = 14      8 +  7 = 15
7 +  8 = 15      8 +  8 = 16
7 +  9 = 16      8 +  9 = 17
7 + 10 = 17      8 + 10 = 18

9 +  0 =  9     10 +  0 = 10
9 +  1 = 10     10 +  1 = 11
9 +  2 = 11     10 +  2 = 12
9 +  3 = 12     10 +  3 = 13
9 +  4 = 13     10 +  4 = 14
9 +  5 = 14     10 +  5 = 15
9 +  6 = 15     10 +  6 = 16
9 +  7 = 16     10 +  7 = 17
9 +  8 = 17     10 +  8 = 18
9 +  9 = 18     10 +  9 = 19
9 + 10 = 19     10 + 10 = 20
```

Addition

Addition tells the total when two or more sets, or groups of things, are put together.

♣♣♣♣♣♣♣♣♣♣♣ **11** addend
♣♣♣♣♣♣♣♣   **+ 8** addend
            19 sum

Check addition by doing the problem again, perhaps with the addends in a different order. The two answers should be the same.

> Addition and subtraction facts can be grouped. For example:
>
> 5 + 8 = 13   8 + 5 = 13
> 13 − 5 = 8   13 − 8 = 5

```
0 -  0 =  0      1 -  1 =  0
1 -  0 =  1      2 -  1 =  1
2 -  0 =  2      3 -  1 =  2
3 -  0 =  3      4 -  1 =  3
4 -  0 =  4      5 -  1 =  4
5 -  0 =  5      6 -  1 =  5
6 -  0 =  6      7 -  1 =  6
7 -  0 =  7      8 -  1 =  7
8 -  0 =  8      9 -  1 =  8
9 -  0 =  9     10 -  1 =  9
10 -  0 = 10    11 -  1 = 10

2 -  2 =  0      3 -  3 =  0
3 -  2 =  1      4 -  3 =  1
4 -  2 =  2      5 -  3 =  2
5 -  2 =  3      6 -  3 =  3
6 -  2 =  4      7 -  3 =  4
7 -  2 =  5      8 -  3 =  5
8 -  2 =  6      9 -  3 =  6
9 -  2 =  7     10 -  3 =  7
10 -  2 =  8    11 -  3 =  8
11 -  2 =  9    12 -  3 =  9
12 -  2 = 10    13 -  3 = 10
```

Subtraction tells how many are left when some of a set, or group of things, is taken away.

  19 minuend
            − 8 subtrahend
            11 difference

Check subtraction by adding the difference and the subtrahend. The answer should equal the minuend.

Subtraction

```
4 -  4 =  0      5 -  5 =  0      6 -  6 =  0      7 -  7 =  0      8 -  8 =  0      9 -  9 =  0     10 - 10 =  0
5 -  4 =  1      6 -  5 =  1      7 -  6 =  1      8 -  7 =  1      9 -  8 =  1     10 -  9 =  1     11 - 10 =  1
6 -  4 =  2      7 -  5 =  2      8 -  6 =  2      9 -  7 =  2     10 -  8 =  2     11 -  9 =  2     12 - 10 =  2
7 -  4 =  3      8 -  5 =  3      9 -  6 =  3     10 -  7 =  3     11 -  8 =  3     12 -  9 =  3     13 - 10 =  3
8 -  4 =  4      9 -  5 =  4     10 -  6 =  4     11 -  7 =  4     12 -  8 =  4     13 -  9 =  4     14 - 10 =  4
9 -  4 =  5     10 -  5 =  5     11 -  6 =  5     12 -  7 =  5     13 -  8 =  5     14 -  9 =  5     15 - 10 =  5
10 -  4 =  6    11 -  5 =  6     12 -  6 =  6     13 -  7 =  6     14 -  8 =  6     15 -  9 =  6     16 - 10 =  6
11 -  4 =  7    12 -  5 =  7     13 -  6 =  7     14 -  7 =  7     15 -  8 =  7     16 -  9 =  7     17 - 10 =  7
12 -  4 =  8    13 -  5 =  8     14 -  6 =  8     15 -  7 =  8     16 -  8 =  8     17 -  9 =  8     18 - 10 =  8
13 -  4 =  9    14 -  5 =  9     15 -  6 =  9     16 -  7 =  9     17 -  8 =  9     18 -  9 =  9     19 - 10 =  9
14 -  4 = 10    15 -  5 = 10     16 -  6 = 10     17 -  7 = 10     18 -  8 = 10     19 -  9 = 10     20 - 10 = 10
```

0 x 0 = 0	1 x 0 = 0	2 x 0 = 0	3 x 0 = 0	4 x 0 = 0	5 x 0 = 0	6 x 0 = 0
0 x 1 = 0	1 x 1 = 1	2 x 1 = 2	3 x 1 = 3	4 x 1 = 4	5 x 1 = 5	6 x 1 = 6
0 x 2 = 0	1 x 2 = 2	2 x 2 = 4	3 x 2 = 6	4 x 2 = 8	5 x 2 = 10	6 x 2 = 12
0 x 3 = 0	1 x 3 = 3	2 x 3 = 6	3 x 3 = 9	4 x 3 = 12	5 x 3 = 15	6 x 3 = 18
0 x 4 = 0	1 x 4 = 4	2 x 4 = 8	3 x 4 = 12	4 x 4 = 16	5 x 4 = 20	6 x 4 = 24
0 x 5 = 0	1 x 5 = 5	2 x 5 = 10	3 x 5 = 15	4 x 5 = 20	5 x 5 = 25	6 x 5 = 30
0 x 6 = 0	1 x 6 = 6	2 x 6 = 12	3 x 6 = 18	4 x 6 = 24	5 x 6 = 30	6 x 6 = 36
0 x 7 = 0	1 x 7 = 7	2 x 7 = 14	3 x 7 = 21	4 x 7 = 28	5 x 7 = 35	6 x 7 = 42
0 x 8 = 0	1 x 8 = 8	2 x 8 = 16	3 x 8 = 24	4 x 8 = 32	5 x 8 = 40	6 x 8 = 48
0 x 9 = 0	1 x 9 = 9	2 x 9 = 18	3 x 9 = 27	4 x 9 = 36	5 x 9 = 45	6 x 9 = 54
0 x 10 = 0	1 x 10 = 10	2 x 10 = 20	3 x 10 = 30	4 x 10 = 40	5 x 10 = 50	6 x 10 = 60

7 x 0 = 0	8 x 0 = 0
7 x 1 = 7	8 x 1 = 8
7 x 2 = 14	8 x 2 = 16
7 x 3 = 21	8 x 3 = 24
7 x 4 = 28	8 x 4 = 32
7 x 5 = 35	8 x 5 = 40
7 x 6 = 42	8 x 6 = 48
7 x 7 = 49	8 x 7 = 56
7 x 8 = 56	8 x 8 = 64
7 x 9 = 63	8 x 9 = 72
7 x 10 = 70	8 x 10 = 80

9 x 0 = 0	10 x 0 = 0
9 x 1 = 9	10 x 1 = 10
9 x 2 = 18	10 x 2 = 20
9 x 3 = 27	10 x 3 = 30
9 x 4 = 36	10 x 4 = 40
9 x 5 = 45	10 x 5 = 50
9 x 6 = 54	10 x 6 = 60
9 x 7 = 63	10 x 7 = 70
9 x 8 = 72	10 x 8 = 80
9 x 9 = 81	10 x 9 = 90
9 x 10 = 90	10 x 10 = 100

Multiplication

Multiplication of 6 x 3 tells how many total there would be in 3 sets, or groups, of 6 each.

3 times

♥ ♥ ♥ ♥ ♥ ♥
♥ ♥ ♥ ♥ ♥ ♥
♥ ♥ ♥ ♥ ♥ ♥

6 in each group

```
    6   multiplicand
  x 3   multiplier
 ―――
   18   product
```

Check multiplication by doing the problem again. Perhaps reverse multiplicand and multiplier. The two answers should be the same.

> Multiplication and division facts can be grouped. For example.
>
> 7 x 9 = 63   9 x 7 = 63
> 63 ÷ 9 = 7   63 ÷ 7 = 9

Division of 14 ÷ 4 tells how many sets, or groups, of 4 are in 14, and how many are left over.

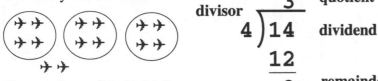

There are 3 sets of 4 with 2 left over.

```
         3    quotient
divisor
      4)14    dividend
        12
        ――
         2    remainder
```

Check division by multiplying the quotient by the divisor, then adding the remainder if there is one. The answer should equal the dividend.

Division

0 ÷ 0 = I	0 ÷ 1 = 0
1 ÷ 0 = M	1 ÷ 1 = 1
2 ÷ 0 = P	2 ÷ 1 = 2
3 ÷ 0 = O	3 ÷ 1 = 3
4 ÷ 0 = S	4 ÷ 1 = 4
5 ÷ 0 = S	5 ÷ 1 = 5
6 ÷ 0 = I	6 ÷ 1 = 6
7 ÷ 0 = B	7 ÷ 1 = 7
8 ÷ 0 = L	8 ÷ 1 = 8
9 ÷ 0 = E	9 ÷ 1 = 9
10 ÷ 0 =	10 ÷ 1 = 10

0 ÷ 2 = 0	0 ÷ 3 = 0
2 ÷ 2 = 1	3 ÷ 3 = 1
4 ÷ 2 = 2	6 ÷ 3 = 2
6 ÷ 2 = 3	9 ÷ 3 = 3
8 ÷ 2 = 4	12 ÷ 3 = 4
10 ÷ 2 = 5	15 ÷ 3 = 5
12 ÷ 2 = 6	18 ÷ 3 = 6
14 ÷ 2 = 7	21 ÷ 3 = 7
16 ÷ 2 = 8	24 ÷ 3 = 8
18 ÷ 2 = 9	27 ÷ 3 = 9
20 ÷ 2 = 10	30 ÷ 3 = 10

0 ÷ 4 = 0	0 ÷ 5 = 0	0 ÷ 6 = 0	0 ÷ 7 = 0	0 ÷ 8 = 0	0 ÷ 9 = 0	0 ÷ 10 = 0
4 ÷ 4 = 1	5 ÷ 5 = 1	6 ÷ 6 = 1	7 ÷ 7 = 1	8 ÷ 8 = 1	9 ÷ 9 = 1	10 ÷ 10 = 1
8 ÷ 4 = 2	10 ÷ 5 = 2	12 ÷ 6 = 2	14 ÷ 7 = 2	16 ÷ 8 = 2	18 ÷ 9 = 2	20 ÷ 10 = 2
12 ÷ 4 = 3	15 ÷ 5 = 3	18 ÷ 6 = 3	21 ÷ 7 = 3	24 ÷ 8 = 3	27 ÷ 9 = 3	30 ÷ 10 = 3
16 ÷ 4 = 4	20 ÷ 5 = 4	24 ÷ 6 = 4	28 ÷ 7 = 4	32 ÷ 8 = 4	36 ÷ 9 = 4	40 ÷ 10 = 4
20 ÷ 4 = 5	25 ÷ 5 = 5	30 ÷ 6 = 5	35 ÷ 7 = 5	40 ÷ 8 = 5	45 ÷ 9 = 5	50 ÷ 10 = 5
24 ÷ 4 = 6	30 ÷ 5 = 6	36 ÷ 6 = 6	42 ÷ 7 = 6	48 ÷ 8 = 6	54 ÷ 9 = 6	60 ÷ 10 = 6
28 ÷ 4 = 7	35 ÷ 5 = 7	42 ÷ 6 = 7	49 ÷ 7 = 7	56 ÷ 8 = 7	63 ÷ 9 = 7	70 ÷ 10 = 7
32 ÷ 4 = 8	40 ÷ 5 = 8	48 ÷ 6 = 8	56 ÷ 7 = 8	64 ÷ 8 = 8	72 ÷ 9 = 8	80 ÷ 10 = 8
36 ÷ 4 = 9	45 ÷ 5 = 9	54 ÷ 6 = 9	63 ÷ 7 = 9	72 ÷ 8 = 9	81 ÷ 9 = 9	90 ÷ 10 = 9
40 ÷ 4 = 10	50 ÷ 5 = 10	60 ÷ 6 = 10	70 ÷ 7 = 10	80 ÷ 8 = 10	90 ÷ 9 = 10	100 ÷ 10 = 10

Fractions

A **fraction** is an equal part of a whole.

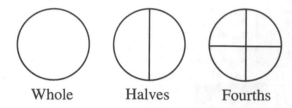

Whole   Halves   Fourths

The **numerator** tells how many parts are being counted or referred to.

$$\frac{1}{2}$$ Numerator

Denominator

The **denominator** tells into how many equal parts the whole is divided.

Equivalent fractions are different ways of naming the same amount.

$$\frac{1}{2} = \frac{2}{4} = \frac{3}{6}$$

To change a fraction to an equivalent fraction, multiply both numerator and denominator by a common multiple. To change to lowest terms (**simplify**), divide both numerator and denominator by a common factor.

Factors Chart

1 1	**29** 1 29
2 1 2	**30** 1 2 3 5 6 10 15 30
3 1 3	**31** 1 31
4 1 2 4	**32** 1 2 4 8 16 32
5 1 5	**33** 1 3 11 33
6 1 2 3 6	**34** 1 2 17 34
7 1 7	**35** 1 5 7 35
8 1 2 4 8	**36** 1 2 3 4 6 9 12 18 36
9 1 3 9	**37** 1 37
10 1 2 5 10	**38** 1 2 19 38
11 1 11	**39** 1 3 13 39
12 1 2 3 4 6 12	**40** 1 2 4 5 8 10 20 40
13 1 13	**41** 1 41
14 1 2 7 14	**42** 1 2 3 6 7 14 21 42
15 1 3 5 15	**43** 1 43
16 1 2 4 8 16	**44** 1 2 4 11 22 44
17 1 17	**45** 1 3 5 9 15 45
18 1 2 3 6 9 18	**46** 1 2 23 46
19 1 19	**47** 1 47
20 1 2 4 5 10 20	**48** 1 2 3 4 6 8 12 16 24 48
21 1 3 7 21	**49** 1 7 49
22 1 2 11 22	**50** 1 2 5 10 25 50
23 1 23	**75** 1 3 5 15 25 75
24 1 2 3 4 6 8 12 24	**100** 1 2 4 5 10 20 25 50 100
25 1 5 25	
26 1 2 13 26	
27 1 3 9 27	
28 1 2 4 7 14 28	

Factors of a number divide into it evenly.

Common factors are any factors two numbers have in common.

The **greatest common factor** is the largest factor two numbers have in common.

A **prime number** has only itself and 1 as factors.

A **composite number** has factors other than itself and 1.

Common multiples are any multiples two numbers have in common.

The **least common multiple** is the smallest multiple two numbers have in common.

Multiples Chart

1	2	3	4	5	6	7	8	9	10
2	4	6	8	10	12	14	16	18	20
3	6	9	12	15	18	21	24	27	30
4	8	12	16	20	24	28	32	36	40
5	10	15	20	25	30	35	40	45	50
6	12	18	24	30	36	42	48	54	60
7	14	21	28	35	42	49	56	63	70
8	16	24	32	40	48	56	64	72	80
9	18	27	36	45	54	63	72	81	90
10	20	30	40	50	60	70	80	90	100

Decimal Fractions

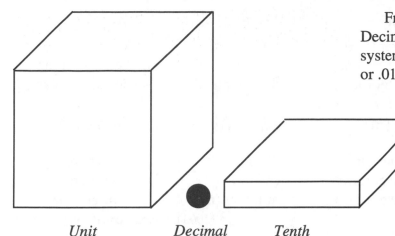

| Unit | Decimal Point | Tenth | Hundredth | Thousandth | Ten Thousandth |

Fractions may be written as decimals. Decimal fractions are used in our money system. A penny is worth one hundredth, or .01, of a dollar.

Place Value

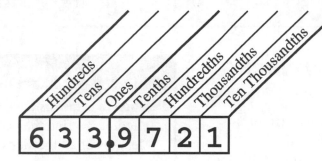

The decimal point is read as "and." The number above would be read *six hundred thirty-three and nine thousand, seven hundred twenty-one ten thousandths.*

Beyond Ten Thousandths:
Hundred Thousandths
Millionths
Ten Millionths
Hundred Millionths
Billionths
Ten Billionths
Hundred Billionths
Trillionths

Fraction Decimal Equivalents

$\frac{1}{2}$ = .5	$\frac{3}{4}$ = .75	$\frac{4}{5}$ = .8	$\frac{3}{8}$ = .375	$\frac{3}{10}$ = .3
$\frac{1}{3}$ = .333*	$\frac{1}{5}$ = .2	$\frac{1}{6}$ = .167*	$\frac{5}{8}$ = .625	$\frac{7}{10}$ = .7
$\frac{2}{3}$ = .667*	$\frac{2}{5}$ = .4	$\frac{5}{6}$ = .833*	$\frac{7}{8}$ = .875	$\frac{9}{10}$ = .9
$\frac{1}{4}$ = .25	$\frac{3}{5}$ = .6	$\frac{1}{8}$ = .125	$\frac{1}{10}$ = .1	*Approximate

Metric Measurement

	Prefix	Length	Volume	Weight
x 1000	kilo-	kilometer (km)	kiloliter (kl)	kilogram (kg)*
x 100	hecto-	hectometer (hm)	hectoliter (hl)	hectogram (hg)
x 10	deca-	decameter (dam)	decaliter (dal)	decagram (dag)
Basic Unit		**Meter** (m)	**Liter** (l)	**Gram** (g)
x .1	deci-	decimeter (dm)	deciliter (dl)	decigram (dg)
x .01	centi-	centimeter (cm)	centiliter (cl)	centigram (cg)
x .001	milli-	millimeter (mm)	milliliter (ml)	milligram (mg)

*1000 kilograms equal one metric ton.

Metric ruler

English Measurement

Length

12 inches (in. or ")	=	1 foot (ft. or ')
3 feet (ft.)	=	1 yard (yd.)
5,280 feet (ft.)	=	1 statute mile (mi.)
3 statute miles (mi.)	=	1 league
1.15 statute miles	=	1 nautical mile

Volume

3 teaspoons (tsp.)	=	1 tablespoon (tbsp.)
2 cups (c.)	=	1 pint (pt.)
4 cups (c.)	=	1 quart (qt.)
2 pints (pt.)	=	1 quart (qt.)
2 quarts (qt.)	=	1 half-gallon
4 quarts (qt.)	=	1 gallon (gal.)
8 quarts (qt.)	=	1 peck (dry measure)
4 pecks (pk.)	=	1 bushel (bu.)

Weight

16 ounces (oz.)	=	1 pound (lb.)
2000 pounds (lb.)	=	1 short ton (t.)

Using Measurement

Perimeter is the distance around a geometric figure. To find the perimeter, add the lengths of all the sides.

Area is the number of square units that cover a geometric figure. To find the area:
Rectangle: length x width (l x w)
Triangle: ½ base x height (½ b x h)
Some units of English measurement are used only for area:

1 acre	=	43,560 square feet
1 section	=	640 acres
1 section	=	1 square mile
1 township	=	36 square miles

Volume is the number of cubic units that fill a three-dimensional solid. To find the volume of a rectanglar solid, multiply: length x width x height (l x w x h)

English ruler

Conversion Charts

English to Metric

When you know	Multiply by	To find
inches (in.)	2.54	centimeters (cm)
feet (ft.)	30.48	centimeters (cm)
yards (yd.)	0.9	meters (m)
miles (mi.)	1.6	kilometers (km)
teaspoons (tsp.)	4.93	milliliters (ml)
tablespoons (tbsp.)	14.79	milliliters (ml)
cups (c.)	0.24	liters (l)
pints (pt.)	0.47	liters (l)
quarts (qt.)	0.95	liters (l)
gallons (gal.)	3.8	liters (l)
ounces (oz.)	28.35	grams (g)
pounds (lb.)	0.45	kilograms (kg)
short tons (t.)	0.9	metric tons (T)

Metric to English

When you know	Multiply by	To find
millimeters (mm)	0.04	inches (in.)
centimeters (cm)	0.4	inches (in.)
meters (m)	3.3	feet (ft.)
meters (m)	1.1	yards (yd.)
kilometers (km)	0.6	miles (mi.)
liters (l)	2.1	pints (pt.)
liters (l)	1.06	quarts (qt.)
liters (l)	0.264	gallons (gal.)
grams (g)	0.035	ounces (oz.)
kilograms (kg)	2.2	pounds (lb.)
metric tons (T)	1.1	short tons (t.)

Note: Conversions are approximate.

Temperature Conversions

Fahrenheit to Celsius — subtract 32, multiply by 5 and divide by 9. To estimate, subtract 30 and divide by 2.

Celsius to Fahrenheit — multiply by 9, divide by 5 and add 32. To estimate, double the Celsius reading and add 30.

Temperature

The Celsius, or Centigrade, temperature scale is part of the metric system, and is used in most parts of the world today. The Fahrenheit scale is still more common in the United States.

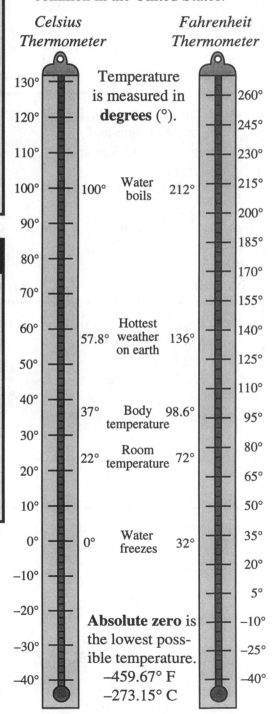

Celsius Thermometer   *Fahrenheit Thermometer*

Temperature is measured in **degrees** (°).

Celsius		Fahrenheit
100°	Water boils	212°
57.8°	Hottest weather on earth	136°
37°	Body temperature	98.6°
22°	Room temperature	72°
0°	Water freezes	32°

Absolute zero is the lowest possible temperature. –459.67° F –273.15° C

Geometric Terms

point: a location in space with no dimensions; points are named with letters •A Symbol: **A**	**line:** a line in geometry extends infinitely (forever) in two directions Symbol: $\overleftrightarrow{SP}$	**line segment:** a part of a line which has two endpoints C——————D $\overline{CD}$
ray: a part of a line which has one endpoint and extends infinitely in one direction Symbol: $\overrightarrow{AB}$	**angle:** a figure formed by two rays with the same endpoint, or *vertex* Symbol: ∠R ∠NRT ∠TRN	**right angle:** an angle which forms a square corner (measures 90°)
acute angle: an angle which measures less than 90°	**obtuse angle:** an angle which measures more than 90°	**congruent:** matching exactly. The figures below are congruent.
intersect: cross. The two lines below intersect one another.	**parallel lines:** lines in a plane which do not intersect	**perpendicular lines:** lines which intersect at a right angle

Geometric Figures

Triangles (3-sided figures)

equilateral triangle: all sides are congruent, all angles are congruent

isosceles triangle: two sides are congruent, two angles are congruent

right triangle: one angle of the triangle is a right angle (90°)

scalene triangle: no sides or angles are congruent

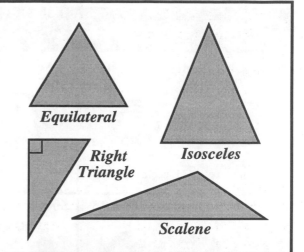

Quadrilaterals (4-sided figures)

parallelogram: a quadrilateral with opposite sides parallel

rectangle: a parallelogram with four right angles

square: a rectangle with four congruent sides

rhombus: a parallelogram with four congruent sides

trapezoid: a quadrilateral with two sides parallel

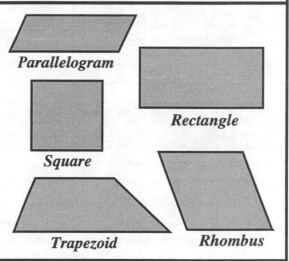

Circles

Pi (π) is a number used with circles. It equals about 3.14.

radius: the distance from the center to the circle

diameter: distance across the circle through the center

circumference: distance around the circle ($2\pi r$)

area: square units inside (πr^2)

A **protractor** is used to measure angles. Circles are divided into 360 **degrees** (°), of which a protractor shows half (180°).

Protractor

United States Money

Coins

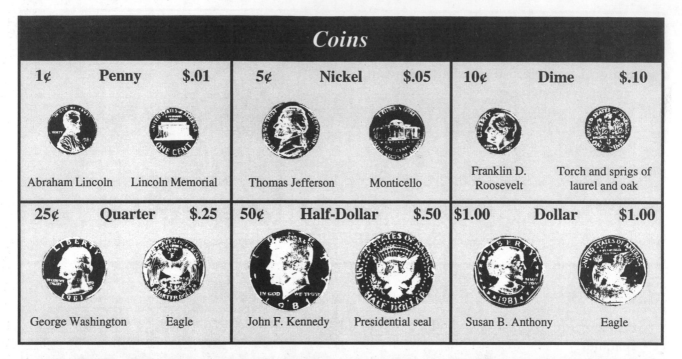

1¢   **Penny**   **$.01**

Abraham Lincoln   Lincoln Memorial

5¢   **Nickel**   **$.05**

Thomas Jefferson   Monticello

10¢   **Dime**   **$.10**

Franklin D. Roosevelt   Torch and sprigs of laurel and oak

25¢   **Quarter**   **$.25**

George Washington   Eagle

50¢   **Half-Dollar**   **$.50**

John F. Kennedy   Presidential seal

$1.00   **Dollar**   **$1.00**

Susan B. Anthony   Eagle

Bills

$1.00   George Washington

$2.00   Thomas Jefferson

$5.00   Abraham Lincoln

$10.00   Alexander Hamilton

$20.00   Andrew Jackson

$50.00   Ulysses S. Grant

$100.00   Benjamin Franklin

$500.00   William McKinley

$1,000   Grover Cleveland

$5,000   James Madison

$10,000   Salmon P. Chase

$100,000   Woodrow Wilson

Note: The Susan B. Anthony dollar, the $2.00 bill, and bills worth more than $100.00 are not currently being produced.

Handbook

First Aid

First aid is emergency treatment for injury or sudden illness which is given before regular medical care is available. Correct knowledge and action by the first person on the scene of a major medical emergency can save a life. Knowing what *not* to do is as important as knowing what to do. Mistakes can make things much worse. The best trained person available should take charge in an emergency. *Because blood may carry infectious diseases, always wear rubber gloves when helping a person who is bleeding.* This section is a short guide to first aid for major emergencies. It may be used as a guide if well-trained persons or first aid books are not available.

What to Do in Every Emergency

1. Stay calm. Call or send for help. In most places, call 911.
2. Go to the victim only if it is safe. Do not put yourself in danger. Wear rubber gloves as a precaution.
3. Check for breathing. See *Breathing*.
4. Stop heavy bleeding. See *Bleeding*.
5. Prevent further injury. In general, *do not* move a person who may have broken bones, especially of the back or neck. Move other victims only as much as is necessary to treat them.
6. Treat the injury. Only do as much as you know is right.
7. Treat for shock in *all* major medical emergencies. See *Shock*.

Bleeding

1. Apply direct pressure to the wound with a sterile dressing or a piece of clean cloth for at least ten minutes.
2. If the cloth becomes soaked with blood, put a new cloth on top of it. Do not remove the old cloth.
3. If there is no reason to suspect broken bones, a wounded arm or leg may be raised to help slow bleeding.
4. Treat for shock and make sure help has been called.

Breathing

1. If a victim is not breathing, quickly call or send for help.
2. Place the victim on his back with his face to the side. Kneel beside his head.
3. Listen for breathing. *Do not* give artificial respiration to a person who is breathing.
4. Clear the mouth with your fingers.
5. Clear the airway. Using two fingers on the forehead and two fingers under the chin, tilt the head back to clear the airway. The tongue should not be blocking the throat.
6. Listen again for breathing. Clearing the airway may allow the person to breathe on his own. If it does, *do not* give artificial respiration. If it does not, continue.
7. Pinch the nose and blow into the person's mouth until the chest rises.
8. When the chest rises, stop blowing. Turn your head to the side and listen for the air to be exhaled while you breathe.
9. Repeat. Give one breath every five seconds for adults, and a smaller breath every three seconds for young children.
10. Continue artificial respiration until the victim breathes for himself or is pronounced dead by a doctor.

It is recommended that everyone receive first aid training and that all homes and businesses have a complete up-to-date first aid handbook. For information, contact your local chapter of the American Red Cross.

Broken Bones

1. If broken bones are suspected, a victim should *not* be moved.
2. Use ice packs to reduce pain and swelling.
3. Get help and treat for shock.

Burns

1. Wash your hands with soap and water before treating a burn. Burns are easily infected.
2. Put the burned part in a pan or sink of cold water for at least five minutes. Do not use ice.
3. Do not touch a serious burn or put ointment on it.
4. Put a sterile dressing or clean sheet over the burn if medical help will not be coming quickly. This may help prevent infection.
5. Treat for shock. All serious burns will cause shock, and more deaths result from the shock than from the burns themselves.
6. Make sure help has been called.

Drowning

1. Call for help.
2. *Never* swim to a drowning person unless you are certified in lifesaving.
3. Toss a rope, or push a board, oar or towel to the person and pull her to shore.
4. Give artificial respiration if needed. (See *Breathing*.)
5. Treat for shock and make sure help is coming.

Electric Shock

1. Disconnect the plug or turn off the electric current. *Do not* touch the victim if there is a live current.
2. If it is not possible to turn off the electricity, use a dry stick to push apart the victim and the wire. Be sure your hands are dry and you are standing on a dry surface.
3. Once the person is away from the current, check for breathing. Give artificial respiration if necessary. (See *Breathing*.)
4. Treat the burned areas. (See *Burns*.)
5. Treat for shock and make sure help is coming.

Poisoning

1. Look for the poison. If there is a container, read the label for directions.
2. Call a doctor, 911, or the Poison Control Center.
3. If the victim is unconscious, do not give liquids.
4. If the victim is conscious, dilute the poison by having her drink water or milk.
5. Watch the victim's breathing. If she stops breathing, give artificial respiration. (See *Breathing*.)
6. Treat for shock and make sure help is coming.

Shock

Shock is a result of poor blood circulation caused by the body's reaction to a severe injury. Shock can cause death even when the injuries are not life-threatening. Remember, do not move a person if bones may be broken.

1. Treat the injury first.
2. Keep the victim lying down on his back.
3. Keep the victim warm but not hot. Cover him with a blanket or coat.
4. Help the victim get comfortable. Loosen tight clothing.
5. In general, do not give the victim anything to drink unless for treatment.
6. Talk calmly to the victim and reassure him that help is coming.

Etiquette

Etiquette is another word for manners, or being polite. Knowing the basic rules of etiquette will help you know what to do in situations with other people, such as eating out and meeting new people. The purpose for manners is to show courtesy and consideration for others. People generally enjoy being around a person with good manners, and are poorly impressed with bad manners. The most important rules of etiquette are to be thoughtful about how your words and actions will affect other people, and to treat others as you would like to be treated.

Very Important Words

Please. Say *Please* when you are asking for something.

Thank You

Say *Thank you*
- when others are courteous or helpful to you.
- when you receive praise or a compliment.
- when you receive a gift.
- when you've enjoyed a good time with someone.
- when you've been to someone's home.

Excuse Me or I'm Sorry

Say *Excuse me* or *I'm sorry*
- when you bump someone.
- when you interrupt.
- when you spill or break something.
- when you are late.
- when you yawn.
- when you forget something.
- when you must leave a group.
- when you don't hear or understand something.
- when you have hurt or embarrassed someone.

May I*

Say *May I?*
- when you are asking permission. *May I borrow your pencil, please?*
- when you are asking someone to pass something to you at the table. *May I please have some more potatoes?*

*May I? asks permission. *Can I?* asks if you are able. For example: *Can I drive your car?* asks if you know how to drive. *May I drive your car?* asks if the person will allow you to borrow it.*

Introductions

Always make introductions when two or more people are meeting for the first time. The best introductions lead easily into conversations. Think of what interests or experiences people might have in common and mention them in the introduction.

Introducing Others

1. Say: *Mrs. Smith, this is John.* Or, more formally: *Mrs. Smith, this is my cousin, John. John, this is my neighbor, Mrs. Smith.*

2. It is best to tell something about the people so it is easy for them to begin a conversation. For example: *John is visiting us this week from California.*

3. Remember:
   - Say a woman's name before a man's.
   - Say an adult's name before a child's.
   - Say a more important person's name before a less important person's.

Introducing Yourself

1. Say: *Hello, my name is _____.*
2. Ask the other person's name.
3. Begin a short conversation.

When You're Introduced

1. Stand if the other person is standing.
2. Look at the person and smile. Shake hands.
3. Say: *Hello. How are you?* or *Nice to meet you.*
4. Say the other person's name and make sure you are pronouncing it correctly.
5. Use the person's name and try to remember it. If you forget, say: *I'm sorry, could you tell me your name again?*
6. Young people should use an adult's title and last name unless asked to do otherwise. For example, *Mr. Johnson* not *Dick.*

Conversations

Beginning a Conversation

1. Say something about what's going on around you.
2. Ask a general question.
3. Give an honest compliment.
4. Ask a question or make a comment about something the person has said or something you've noticed about them.

Having a Conversation

1. Take turns talking and listening.
2. Listen and pay attention to the other person. Don't let your eyes or mind wander.
3. Ask questions, but don't ask about things which are none of your business, such as personal affairs or finances. If someone asks you a question you don't want to answer, say: *I'm sorry, but I'd rather not talk about that.*
4. Find things you both have in common and talk about them.
5. Talk about your interests and experiences, especially those which seem to interest the other person.

6. Don't interrupt. If you must interrupt for some reason, say: *Excuse me for interrupting, but _____.*
7. Don't brag or exaggerate.
8. Don't criticize others or say untrue or unkind things.
9. Don't whisper to someone in front of someone else.
10. Don't talk or laugh so loudly that people outside the conversation are disturbed.

Ending a Conversation

1. Say something like:
   It's been great talking with you.
   Well, have a good afternoon.
   Take care of yourself.
2. Smile, say goodbye, and leave.

Telephone Etiquette

Making a Call

1. Don't call when the other person is likely to be sleeping or having a meal.
2. Let the phone ring at least seven times.
3. When someone answers, say: *Hello, this is _____. May I speak to _____, please?*
4. Speak clearly and loudly enough to be heard. Talk right into the phone.
5. Keep calls short. Someone else may need to use the phone.
6. If you want to have a long conversation, ask the person if he has time to talk.
7. When finished, say something like: *It was nice to talk with you.*
8. If you reach an answering machine, leave a short message that you called.
9. If the person you want isn't there, ask to leave a message or say you'll call back later.
10. If you think you've reached a wrong number, ask: *Is this 342-9168?* If not, say: *I'm sorry to have bothered you.*

Receiving a Call

1. Say: *Hello.*
2. **If** the person asks for someone else, say: *Just a moment, please.* Put the receiver down quietly and go to get the person, or cover the receiver and call her to the phone.
3. **If** the person asks for someone who is not there, say: *I'm sorry. She's not here right now. May I take a message?*
4. **If** the person is busy and can't come to the phone for *any* reason, or if a young person doesn't want the caller to know he's home alone, say: *I'm sorry. She can't come to the phone right now. May I take a message or have her call you back?* Don't tell the caller the reason the person can't come to the phone.
5. **If** someone calls when you have company, say: *I'd love to talk to you, but I have a guest. May I call you back later?*

Table Manners

There are many rules for good table manners. The most important thing is to be considerate of others. If you don't know what to do, watch your host or hostess and do as they do.

Before a Meal

1. Wash your hands and face before coming to the table. Washing hands vigorously for thirty seconds with soap and water will remove most harmful bacteria.
2. Be on time.
3. Put the napkin on your lap.
4. Sit up straight at the table. Don't slouch or tilt the chair.

Serving

1. Pass the whole serving dish.
2. Use the serving spoon or fork, not your own.
3. Don't reach in front of someone to get a serving dish. Ask the person nearest it to pass it.
4. If you don't like some of the food, take a small amount or say: *No, thank you.* Always take some of the main dish.
5. If you don't know if you'll like something, take a small amount and try it. If you like it, take more later.
6. Don't take so much of something you like that there isn't enough left for the other people.
7. Wait until everyone is served to begin eating. Wait until the host or hostess begins.
8. Compliment the cook or say nothing. Do not say anything negative or critical to the host or hostess.

Eating

1. Chew with your mouth closed.
2. If food is too hot, let it cool. Don't blow on it.
3. If you take a bite of something which is too hot, quickly drink some water and say nothing.
4. Don't put too much food in your mouth at once.
5. Don't drink anything when your mouth is full. Use the napkin before taking a drink to avoid getting food on the glass.
6. Don't talk with your mouth full.
7. Avoid distasteful conversation.
8. Don't make loud eating noises.
9. If you find something in your food, such as a hair, try to put it aside without being noticed and say nothing.
10. If you must sneeze or cough, turn your head away from the table and cover your nose and mouth with the napkin.
11. If you spill some food, scoop it up with a knife or spoon and put it on the side of your plate. If someone has noticed, say *I'm sorry.*

12. If you must take something out of your mouth, take it out the same way you put it in. For example, take olive pits out with your fingers, but fish bones out with your fork. Put these things on the side of your plate.
13. Don't comb your hair, pick your teeth, or otherwise groom yourself at the table.
14. If you must leave the table, say: *Excuse me, I'll be right back.* Don't explain your reasons.

After a Meal

1. Leave the utensils on the plate.
2. Lay the napkin on the table next to your plate. Don't crumple or fold the napkin.
3. Thank the host and hostess.
4. Ask to be excused if you need to leave the table before everyone leaves together.

Saying "No"

Sometimes people ask you to do things which are wrong. It is important to be assertive—to be able to say "no" and keep your friends, have fun and stay out of trouble.

1. **Ask questions.** Be sure you know exactly what the person has in mind.
2. **Name the trouble.** "You mean you want me to go with you to steal something?"
3. **Identify the consequences.** "If I do that, I could get caught and arrested!"
4. **Suggest an alternative.** "Why don't we see if we can earn some money and buy what we want? My dad needs some help in his shop, and I bet he'd pay us."
5. **Move away.** Begin moving away from the person and the situation while still talking. Don't give them a chance to argue.
6. **Sell your idea.** "Dad's shop is great, and it would be fun working with you."
7. **Leave the door open.** "I'll be at the shop in about an hour. Come on over!"

Parties

Planning a Party

1. What type of party will you have? You could have a birthday party, surprise party, holiday party, costume party, or picnic.
2. Where will it be held? Places to consider are your house, the backyard, or a park.
3. When will it be? What day, date and time of day?
4. How many people will come and who? Make a guest list. Don't leave out one or two people who are part of a group. Pass out invitations privately to avoid hurting the feelings of anyone not included.
5. What refreshments will be served?
6. What activities or entertainment will there be? Consider games, contests or music.
7. What decorations are needed?
8. Who will help set up and clean up?

Invitations

Invite people in person, by telephone or in writing a week or so ahead of time. Be sure guests know your name, the date and time of the party, the location of the party and anything special, such as what to bring or wear.

At the Party

1. Greet the guests at the door.
2. Take their hats and coats.
3. Make introductions.
4. Make sure that everyone has a good time and that no one is left out.
5. Walk people to the door when they leave.
6. Say: *Thank you for coming.*

After the Party

1. Be sure to clean up and take down any decorations.
2. Send thank you notes for any gifts and thank anyone who helped you.

Problem Solving

1. **Define the problem.** Put the problem in words. Whose problem is it, really? Is it within your power to change?

2. **Research the problem.** Get all the information available.

3. **Brainstorm solutions.** Think of as many ideas as possible. Don't judge them at all at this stage. The wilder the ideas, the better.

4. **Analyze solutions.** Which ideas are possible? Think about the possible outcomes of each solution. Who might be hurt or helped? What are the pros and cons of each idea? Combine and change ideas while searching for the best solution.

5. **Choose a solution.** What seems most likely to work? Choose the best alternative.

6. **Make a plan.** Follow through on your plan.

7. **Evaluate** whether the solution is working after some time has passed. If not, think about trying another solution.

Discussions

The leader:
1. Introduces the topic.
2. Makes sure everyone has a chance to speak.
3. Closes by summarizing what was said.

Participants:
1. Ask questions.
2. Answer questions.
3. Tell personal experiences.
4. Restate what someone else has said.
5. Summarize what others have said.
6. Tell ideas.
7. Introduce other topics.
8. Retell what was read.
9. Tell feelings.
10. Give examples.
11. Read or give supporting evidence.
12. Relate the discussion to other learning.

Courtesy in Discussions

1. Move to the discussion area quickly and quietly.
2. Listen as others speak and do not interrupt.
3. Look at the speaker.
4. Keep your mind on the discussion.
5. Speak clearly.
6. Talk about the topic.
7. Respect others who have ideas different from yours.
8. Tell others when and why you like what they said.
9. Let others have a turn to speak.
10. Summarize and participate well.

Reading Orally

1. Stand straight and face the audience.
2. Read loudly enough for everyone to hear.
3. Speak clearly and use correct pronunciation.
4. Hold the book down so the audience can see your face.
5. Hold your head up so your voice will not be blocked. Speak so your voice will project.
6. Look up often and make eye contact with someone in the audience.
7. Read smoothly and use good expression.

Preparing a Speech

A. Decide on the purpose of the speech.
1. To entertain. You may want your audience to simply enjoy themselves.
2. To inform. You may want the audience to learn or understand something.
3. To create a feeling. You may want your audience to feel inspired, angry, or enthusiastic.
4. To convince. You want the audience to change their minds to agree with you.
5. To move to action. You want your audience to do something, such as vote for someone.

B. Think about the audience and the occasion.

C. Choose and narrow the subject.
1. Choose a subject about which you already know something and in which you are interested.
2. Think about what will be interesting to the audience.
3. Know the time limit of your speech and narrow the subject to fit.

D. Gather material, such as facts, stories or examples.
1. Think about your personal experience.
2. Talk to or interview other people.
3. Read and study to find out more about your subject than anyone in your audience will know.
4. Consider gathering maps, pictures, charts, models, or other visual aids.

E. Organize your material into an outline.
1. Introduction.
    a. Give the subject of the speech.
    b. Get the attention of your audience, perhaps with humor or a surprising fact.
2. Body.
    a. List your three or four main points.
    b. Note details or examples for each.
3. Conclusion.
    a. Summarize the main ideas.
    b. Recommend action if you want your audience to do something.

F. Prepare the speech.
1. Write the speech or practice giving it from the outline.
2. Make sure you know the correct pronunciation of words you plan to use.
3. Practice the speech again and again until you feel very comfortable with it. Write the outline on a card and carry it with you to practice when time allows. Practice in front of family members, friends or a mirror.
4. Review the outline in detail shortly before delivering the speech.

Delivering a Speech

Before you stand up, take a deep breath and imagine yourself doing an excellent job of delivering your speech. Picture your audience responding just as you want them to respond.

1. Stand tall and straight.
2. Speak loudly, clearly, and slowly enough for everyone to hear and understand you.
3. Talk in a lively, conversational way.
4. Make eye contact with people in the audience.
5. Use movements and gestures.
6. Avoid unnecessary movements.
7. Use your outline and reference notes as a guide but do not read from them.
8. Pay attention to your audience. Watch their reactions.

Presenting a Formal Play

A. Make basic planning decisions.
1. Who will present the play? How many people will be involved?
2. Who will be the audience?
3. Who will be the director?
4. Is there a theme or special occasion?
5. Should the play be serious or humorous? Is a musical appropriate?
6. How long should the play be?
7. How much time is available for practice?
8. Where can the play be held? Is there a stage, curtains or lighting?
9. How much money can be spent?

B. Locate potential scripts.
1. Check with a librarian.
2. Write your own script.

C. Select a script. Keep these questions in mind while reading scripts:
1. How many characters are required?
2. Are speaking parts distributed?
3. Is the play interesting?
4. Are vocabulary and subject matter suitable for the cast and the intended audience?
5. Can the set, costumes, and props be done with the time, space and money?
6. Are the stage directions clear?

D. Conduct a first reading.
1. Make sure there is a highlighted copy of the script for each character.
2. Read through the script, taking parts.
3. Discuss the characteristics of each character.

E. Cast the play.
1. Have tryouts and select main characters first, then the minor characters.
2. Choose understudies if needed.
3. Choose a stage crew and prompters.

F. Characters begin to memorize lines. Here are tips for memorizing:
1. Read the play several times and know the order of events.
2. Say your character's cues and lines again and again, out loud and in your mind. Visualize the play. Once in a while, rest and do something else, then repeat the lines to yourself again.
3. Practice while relaxed, such as just before sleeping.
4. Have someone read the other parts, especially your cues, while you practice your lines with expression.

G. Plan the setting.
1. Decide what different scenes or backgrounds are needed.
2. Sketch possible stage arrangements and backdrops.
3. Plan for a backstage area, if needed.
4. Decide how to change scenes.
5. Begin work on the backdrops.

H. Plan costumes.
1. Consider the time period and place in which the play takes place.
2. Begin gathering and making costumes.

I. Walk through the play, reading the scripts.
1. Speak loudly, slowly and distinctly.
2. Face the audience as much as possible.

J. Rehearse from memory.
1. Practice entrances, exits, speech, actions, gestures, expressions.
2. Practice sound effects and use of props.

K. Advertise and make programs.

L. Perform the play for the audience and enjoy the results of all your work.

Interviewing a Person

An **interview** is a meeting with a person for the purpose of asking about his knowledge, ideas, or experiences. A reporter or writer may interview a person to get information for a story. A job applicant may be interviewed. Sometimes the best way to find information on a subject is to interview an expert in the field. Here are guidelines for setting up and conducting an interview.

A. Know your purpose. Choose the best person to interview based on your purpose.

B. Make arrangements in person or by telephone.
1. Introduce yourself.
2. Ask for an interview and tell your purpose for doing the interview.
3. Tell the person how long you expect the interview to take. Generally, interviews should last no longer than an hour.
4. Set a time and place to meet that is convenient for the person you will interview.
5. If you would like to use a tape recorder or video camera at the interview, ask permission in advance.

C. Read background information on the person and the topic of the interview. Use what you learn to help prepare questions.

D. Write questions that you want to have answered during the interview.
1. Avoid yes/no questions. Write open-ended questions which will lead the person into talking about what you are interested in learning. An example of an open-ended question is, "What do you think about...?"
2. Avoid personal questions or questions about things which are none of your business.
3. List the questions in some order and mark the most important ones. If you notice that you are running short of time, skip the less important questions. Plan to finish on time.

E. Beginning the interview.
1. Be on time and be prepared. Have with you your questions, a notebook and a pencil.
2. Smile, shake hands, introduce yourself and thank the person for taking time to talk with you.
3. Talk with the person for a few minutes before beginning the questions so you will both feel more comfortable, but don't waste too much time.

F. Conducting the interview.
1. Ask your questions one at a time.
2. Listen carefully and show interest.
3. Take notes on what the person says. See page 222, *Taking Notes.*
4. Don't keep to the list of questions so closely that the interview is stiff and uncomfortable.
5. Don't allow the person to wander *too* far from the subject.

G. Ending the interview.
1. Toward the end of the time planned, say, "I have one last question." Then ask it.
2. Before finishing, ask if the person has any final comments or suggestions for you.
3. Close the interview by thanking the person again.

H. After the interview.
1. As soon as possible, read your notes and fill them in.
2. **Always** send a thank you note within ten days.

Taking Notes

Notes are words, phrases and numbers written quickly for the purpose of assisting or jogging the writer's memory. A person may take notes on reading materials, speeches, films, or his own thoughts.

With practice, note taking becomes easy and natural. The following ideas may help as you find your own best way of taking notes.

1. Date your notes and write the source. Write the name of a speaker, the title of a film, or bibliographic information on reading material. Bibliographic information includes the author, title, and copyright date of the book. See page 227, *Bibliographic Form*.

2. Leave large margins so more can be written to fill in the notes later.

3. Write key words and phrases. Do not use complete sentences. Leave out words which are unimportant. When deciding what to write, ask yourself, "Is this really important?"

4. Use abbreviations you understand. Some common ones are **+** for "and," **@** for "at" or "around," **#** for "number," **%** for "percent," and **w/** for "with."

5. Write clearly enough that you can read the notes later, but don't waste time trying to use your best handwriting.

6. Write numbers, statistics, and important facts. These are especially hard to remember without notes.

7. Skip a line between major ideas.

8. Underline or put a star by the most important points.

9. Respect copyright laws. Do not copy words exactly without using quotation marks and giving credit to the author.

10. If possible, read over your notes soon after taking them and fill them in while your memory is fresh.

Organizing Notes and Papers

It is important to organize your notes so that you can locate information when you need it. Different systems work for different people. Here are some suggestions:

1. Give each school subject a different color. Make sure all spiral notebooks or folders for that subject are the same color.

2. Use a separate spiral notebook for each subject. Use a new page for each new day and be sure to write the date.

3. Use loose leaf paper and a folder. One advantage to this system is it is easy to keep handouts with your notes. The disadvantage is papers may get lost or out of order.

4. Use a three-ring binder to keep notes for all subjects together. Use dividers to separate the subjects. Keep the notebook neat and don't tear papers out.

Homework and Studying

Nearly all students will be required to study on their own or do homework while attending school. Successful students make a habit of studying regularly, and know how to use their time well. It is very important to learn to pay attention and **concentrate,** or focus your mind, on what you are attempting to learn. It's easier for most people to study in a quiet environment away from distractions such as television. Some people are able to study successfully with friends, but only when everyone concentrates and avoids casual conversation. Here are some suggestions which may help as you work to find your own best methods of studying.

A. Set up a place for studying.
1. Find a quiet spot where you will not be interrupted.
2. Make sure there is enough light, a good chair, a desk or table, and a clock.
3. Gather study materials and keep them together in a desk, drawer or box. At least have paper, pencils and pens. General reference books, such as a dictionary, a thesaurus, and *Facts Plus Almanac* are also good to have.

B. Choose a regular time for homework and study based on your schedule and preferences.

C. Know what you are doing.
1. Pay attention in class and ask questions if something is not clear.
2. Write down all assignments when they are given. Include page numbers, special requirements, and dates due.
3. Put assignment notes and books you will need at home in a backpack or special place immediately so they will not be forgotten at the end of the day.

D. Use your study time wisely.
1. Get into a good frame of mind. Focus your attention.
2. Plan your time. Learn to estimate how long each assignment will take.
3. Begin your study time with a review of what you've already learned.

4. Study reading materials, such as textbook chapters.
   a. Survey the chapter quickly. Read the title, headings, chapter summary, and questions. Look at the illustrations.
   b. Have a purpose for reading. What do you need to learn?
   c. Read the chapter section by section. Concentrate.
   d. After each section, review in your mind the important points. Later, review again by paging through and trying to remember important points. Review again within 24 hours. The more often you review, the better. Always review before tests.
5. Do daily assignments.
   a. Work carefully and neatly.
   b. Put completed assignments and books in a backpack or special place immediately so they will not be forgotten in the morning.
6. Work on long term projects or assignments.
   a. List all of the small jobs which need to be done and keep the list up to date.
   b. Make a time line for yourself and set goals.
   c. Do a little on the project each day.
7. Congratulate yourself at the end of each study time. Reward yourself for progress toward your goals.

Improving Your Memory

Memory is the ability to recall information after a period of time during which you were not thinking about it. To have a good memory, you must be able to get information into your mind, store it in your memory, and then be able to get it out when you need it.

Getting the information. You must "get" it before you can forget it (or remember it). The amount you learn depends directly on the amount of time you spend learning. You must practice or rehearse new knowledge again and again, or it will be forgotten. Generally, people forget 40% of what they learn within 20 minutes, and more than half of it within an hour. Repeat new information to yourself at least seven times in a row, then take a break and come back to it. Check yourself a lot at first, then gradually increase time between practices. For best long-term memory, keep reviewing long after you think you know something perfectly. Use times when your mind is free to practice, such as when you're washing up, waiting for a bus, or waiting in line. For best results, practice a little at a time and often.

Storing the information. You must store what you learn in some organized and meaningful way or it will be difficult or impossible to recall. Your mind is like a huge library. If information is not organized and stored, it is like having all of the books in a pile on the floor. To store information, you connect it to things you already know. The more connections, the better.

Finding and retrieving the information. Unless knowledge is completely mastered and used a lot, this will mean scanning your memory. As in a library, you may look through several categories before finding what you want. Practice finding and retrieving information.

Tips for Better Memory

A. Keep notes, lists, calendars and diaries to jog your memory.

B. Decide what is most important to remember. Always look for main ideas.

C. Classify information and make categories. Things can be classified by:
   1. **Time.** Winter: snow, cold, storms.
   2. **Place.** School: office, classroom, gym.
   3. **Similarities.** Hat, cap, bonnet.
   4. **Differences.** Mountains, valleys.
   5. **Wholes to parts.** Horse: hoof, mane.
   6. **Scientific groups.** Birds: robin, eagle.

D. Look for patterns. For example, the first letters of the five Great Lakes spell **H O M E S**, **H**uron, **O**ntario, **M**ichigan, **E**rie, **S**uperior. Sometimes you can make a sentence mnemonic which will remind you of the first letters of words you need to remember in order. For example, the lines on the treble clef from bottom to top are **E G B D F**, **E**very **G**ood **B**oy **D**oes **F**ine.

E. Associate new learning with what you already know. If there is no association, make one up. For example, you might picture a person whose name is Bailey bailing out a sinking boat.

F. Make up a rhyme or use rhythm. Rhythm is probably how you learned the alphabet.

G. Visualize the information in your mind. Make bright, exaggerated and interesting pictures that get your attention.
   1. See it clearly and in vivid color.
   2. Exaggerate and enlarge things.
   3. See it in three dimensions.
   4. Put movement and action in the picture.
   5. Put yourself in the picture.

H. Create a story about the information to link it together and give it meaning.

I. Use the information. Relate it to new things you see and learn. Imagine yourself needing it in a funny or unusual situation.

Taking Standardized Tests

Standardized tests are tests which have been used and revised many times until they give consistent results. Generally, they are **norm-referenced**. This means the test was given to a large group of people before being published to find a norm, or average standard of achievement. In most cases, standardized tests are scored by the publishers of the tests, who then compare your results with the norm. The results are often given as **percentiles**, which compare your scores with the norm for your age group. The 50th percentile is average. Below the 50th percentile is below average and above the 50th percentile is above average. If the test is very good, half of the people who take the test will score below the 50th percentile and half will score above.

It is important to do your best on standardized tests to show what you truly know and what you still need to learn. Here are suggestions for doing your best.

A. Before the test.
1. Know the purpose of the test.
2. Get a good night's sleep.
3. Eat breakfast.
4. Don't drink many fluids.
5. Get into a good frame of mind. Picture yourself as calm, confident and successful.
6. Get to the testing location on time. Plan to avoid stress and rushing.
7. Have two sharp #2 pencils with good erasers.
8. Get drinks and go to the restroom before or between tests, so that the testing time will be uninterrupted.
9. Make sure you are seated comfortably and can see the clock.

B. During the test.
1. Concentrate. Focus your mind.
2. Do not talk or make distracting noises.
3. Listen carefully. Ask questions if the directions are not clear.
4. Watch the time and know when the test will end. Pace yourself but don't worry too much about not finishing.
5. Work through all the questions in order. If a question is especially hard, skip it and come back to it when you have finished the test. Be sure to skip the answer space if you do this.

6. Read all of the possible answers for each question before choosing an answer.
7. Quickly discard any answers which are clearly wrong and choose from the others. Words like "always" and "never" often signal that an answer is false.
8. Make your best guess if you don't know. If you have a strong hunch, you may be right.
9. If questions are based on a reading passage, it is best to read the questions, then the passage. Then try to answer the questions. Scan back through the passage again to make sure your answer is correct.
10. When you finish, go back through the test a second time and check all answers for careless mistakes. Change answers only if you are *sure* they were wrong or if you have a very strong feeling they were wrong.
11. Do the hard questions you skipped the first time through. Don't be afraid to guess. Even a wild guess has a chance of being correct.
12. Use all of the time allowed to check and recheck your work. Congratulate yourself for having done your best when the test is over.

Library Research Report

The **library research report** is a common school assignment which provides experience in locating and organizing information. There is no single correct way to do such a report. With practice, people find what works best for them. Here are some suggestions.

A. Choose a topic
 1. List several topics, then choose one.
 2. Make sure the topic is not too broad. *The United States* is an example of a topic which is too broad.
 3. Make sure enough information is available about the topic. Only limited information may be available about a topic such as *Multnomah Falls* in a school library.

B. Think about the topic.
 1. Write what you already know about the topic.
 2. Write what you would like to learn.
 3. Begin thinking of categories of information. For a report on a country, for example, you might think of categories such as the land, the people, and the government.

C. Locate information and begin a bibliography.
 1. Think of key words which would describe the topic.
 2. Go to the card catalog. Write titles and call numbers, then locate the books and choose those which seem the most valuable.
 3. Use the encyclopedia and almanac for general background information.
 4. Check atlases, periodical indexes, and the vertical file.
 5. Make a bibliography card for every book or source of information. See page 227 for examples of bibliography entries.

D. Select and gather information. Take notes. Notes are brief written records. See page 222, *Taking Notes.*
 1. Write only as much as you need in order to remember the ideas.
 2. Do not write complete sentences.
 3. Write in your own words. Do not copy. Copying words written by someone else and representing them as your own violates copyright and is a crime known as **plagiarism**.
 4. Notes may be taken on notebook paper, but it may be easier to organize them on 3x5 cards. Write only one idea, or "note" on each card.

E. Organize the information and begin an outline.
 1. Think about the information and how it fits together.
 2. Think of a title which tells the topic.
 3. Put note cards into piles by category. The names of the categories are the **main headings** of the outline.
 4. Put the cards in each pile into a sequence, or order, which makes sense. The information on the cards may be **subheadings** or **details** of the outline.
 5. Write an outline. See page 189 for other ideas for organizing information and an example of complete outline form.

F. Write the report.
 1. Write a rough draft. Skip lines on the paper to leave room for revisions. Each main heading on the outline should be a new paragraph.

2. Read your work and revise as you write. Revising means adding words, taking out unnecessary words, moving words or combining sentences to make your writing communicate better.
3. Edit the report for spelling, punctuation, capitalization and sentence sense.
4. Write a final draft. Include such things as maps, diagrams and pictures.
5. Make a cover, title page, table of contents and bibliography. The main part of the report should come between the table of contents and the bibliography.

G. Presenting the report orally.
1. Study the information and know it well. Begin the report with some fascinating facts or information.
2. Do not read the report to your audience. Use the outline and notes to talk about it.
3. Stick to the subject. Follow the outline so you can end on time.
4. Speak loudly and clearly. Look at the audience.
5. Use visual aids such as maps and pictures to interest the audience.
6. See *Making a Speech*, page 219, for more suggestions.

Bibliographic Form

A **bibliography** is a list of books and other materials on a specific subject which have been used by a writer. When doing a library research report, it is important to keep track of sources of information by recording the author, title, place of publication, name of publisher, and copyright date of each source. The bibliography, or list of sources, should be alphabetized and listed at the end of the report. If bibliography cards have been kept, they can be alphabetized and copied in order.

Punctuation is very important in a bibliography, and different types of reference materials have slightly different bibliographic forms. If a piece of information, such as the author's name, is not available, leave it out and write the next piece of information.

Bibliography

Quarteroni, Bob. "Awful Handwriting." Saturday Evening Post 265 (May 1993):16.

Little Soldier, Lee M. "Handwriting." The World Book Encyclopedia. 1994.

Book

Duvall, Betty. Writing Right: A Guide to Improving Handwriting. Spokane, WA: Ten Speed Press, 1979.

Author. Title. Place of Publication: Publisher, Date.

Magazine Article

Quateroni, Bob. "Awful Handwriting." Saturday Evening Post 265 (May 1993): 16.

Author. "Title of Article." Periodical Name Volume (Month and Year): Page Number.

Encyclopedia

Little Soldier, Lee M. "Handwriting." The World Book Encyclopedia. 1994.

Author. "Title of Article." Name of Encyclopedia. Date.

Science Projects

A science project is generally done to present at a **science fair**. Its purpose is to give students a chance to practice being scientists by using scientific skills and processes to investigate a problem or question. The final product is a display which includes a written report.

Skills of Scientists

1. **Observing** is using the senses of sight, hearing, smell, taste or touch.
2. **Classifying** is identifying and arranging things by similarities or differences.
3. **Measuring** is finding such things as length, weight, temperature, pressure or time.
4. **Communicating** means telling or writing data, such as numbers or words.
5. **Predicting**, or **hypothesizing**, means making an educated guess about what will happen before an experiment takes place.
6. **Inferring** is suggesting reasons, causes or explanations for what happened. It is done after the experiment.
7. **Experimenting** is setting up a way of testing a hypothesis in order to answer a question. It is important to test only *one* thing at a time—one variable. All other variables must stay the same. In most experiments, there should be a **control**, or one sample which is not tested. The tested samples can then be compared to it.

Types of Science Projects

1. **Collection.** The student gathers and arranges objects, such as rocks.
2. **Model.** The student builds a model, or example, of something to show a scientific fact or idea such as a model of a volcano.
3. **Demonstration.** The student shows how something works, often using a **working model**, or model with moving parts. For example, a homebuilt model of a simple electric motor could be used to demonstrate how a motor works.

4. **Experiment.** The student investigates a problem using the scientific method. An experiment could be set up, for example, to see which colors absorb the most light.

Doing a Science Project

1. Choose a topic and form a question.
2. Do background reading and talk to others.
3. Develop a hypothesis, or educated guess, based on the background information.
4. Decide on methods and procedures.
5. List and then gather materials.
6. Do the experiment and collect data.
7. Organize the data using tables, graphs or charts.
8. Draw conclusions. Was your hypothesis correct?
9. Write the report. Include your question, hypothesis, list of materials, methods used, results, conclusions, and a bibliography of books and other sources.
10. Design and construct your exhibit. It should be freestanding, neat and uncluttered. Use photographs, drawings, charts or graphs. In front of the standing backboard, show samples, results or measuring devices.

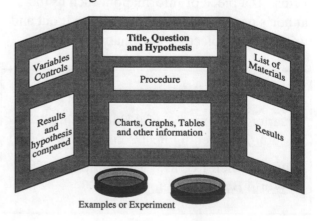

Examples or Experiment

Sources and Notes

p. 12 — Since 1972, scientists have adjusted the **atomic clock**, accurate to a billionth of a second a day, by 19 **leap seconds**. These compensate for the gradual slowing of the earth's rotation.

p. 13 — "**B.C.E.**" may also be called "before Christian era."

p. 13 — Holidays in the **Islamic calendar** move through the seasons on a 32 year cycle.

pp. 15, 16 — The **speed of light** in a vacuum is 186,282.42 ± 0.2 miles per second, according to the General Assembly of the International Scientific Radio Union. In air on a standard day, it is about 52 miles per second slower than in a vacuum.

p. 15 — **Distances to stars** varied greatly from source to source. These figures are from the World Book Encyclopedia. **Galaxies** which may be seen without a telescope are the Andromeda Nebula and the Small and Large Magellanic Clouds.

p. 16 — **Rotation of sun** varies by latitude because the sun is a ball of gas. 22 days is an average.

p. 17 — The **earth's rotation period** is actually 23 hours and 56 minutes as measured by fixed stars. This is the *sidereal day*. Because of the earth's motion around the sun, the time from noon to noon is 24 hours.

p. 17 — In the chart of **Planets of the Solar System**, both **distance from sun** and **speed in orbit** vary because orbits around the sun are eliptical, not circular. The *aphelion* is the point furthest from the sun. For earth, it is 94.5 million miles; for Pluto, 4,571 million miles. The *perihelion* is the point closest to the sun. For earth it is 91.4 million miles; for Pluto, 2,748 million miles. Fastest speeds are at the perihelion.

p. 18 — 27⅓ days is the *sidereal month,* the time it takes for the moon to revolve around the earth in relation to fixed stars. 29½ days is the *synodic month,* the period from one new moon to the next new moon.

p. 24 — The **speed of sound** depends on the substance through which the sound waves travel. No sound can be heard in a vacuum because there is no medium. The speed of 1,116 feet per second is for air on a standard day (59° F at sea level with barometric pressure of 29.92). The speed increases as air temperature rises. Through water at 77°, sound travels about 4,908 feet per second; through steel, 17,100 feet per second.

p. 25 — The **fastest winds** not in a tornado were recorded at Mt. Washington in New Hampshire on April 12, 1934. The wind speed was 231 miles per hour.

p. 28 — The lengths and beginnings of **geological periods** are scientific estimates which overlap and vary to some degree from source to source. The **Pennsylvanian** and **Mississippian** periods may be called the **Carboniferous**.

p. 31 — Although the **Richter Scale** is still used for smaller earthquakes, the largest earthquakes are now measured with a newer system called moment magnitude. The measurements for specific earthquakes are from Kanamori in *The Journal of Geophysical Research,* July 10, 1977. Sources vary.

p. 33 — The **decibel scale** was compiled from several sources with the assistance of an audiologist at Gallaudet College in Washington, D.C. The true intensity of a sound depends on distance from the source. Although 0 to 15 dB is considered the threshold of normal hearing, some people can hear sounds in the –15dB range. Continuous exposure to sounds of 90dB or higher can cause hearing loss.

Impact sounds such as gunshots are most likely to cause damage.

p. 34 — The **number of known elements** varies by source. According to Dr. Glenn Shaw at the Geophysical Institute at the University of Alaska Fairbanks, atoms with atomic numbers higher than 107 are so unstable that it is hard to isolate them.

p. 35 — **Plasma** is a fourth state of matter found mostly in space. It seldom occurs naturally on earth (lightning is plasma). Plasmas form when great heat or a flow of electricity strips electrons from the atoms of a gas.

p. 35 — **Steel** is an **alloy** of iron and other materials. **Stainless steel** contains about 8% nickel, 18% chromium and 74% iron.

p. 36 — Scientists now classify living things into five **kingdoms**: Animalia (animals), Plantae (plants), Fungi (mushrooms, molds, lichens), Protista (algae), and Prokaryotae (bacteria).

p. 38 — The **speeds of animals** are not easily tested and recorded. Speeds listed are mostly estimates for short distances, not speeds that can be sustained. The cheetah's speed is often *estimated* at 70 mph. It is *documented* at 63 mph.

p. 38 — The 188dB **sound** of a blue whale carries 530 miles in *water.* It would not travel so far in air.

pp. 43–45 — The **recommended daily allowances** for vitamins and minerals are generally the highest given, except for sodium. Consult an in-depth source for recommendations based on age and sex.

p. 46 — The **outline of drugs** is based on the classifications shown in *The Encyclopedia of Drug Abuse,* by Dr. Robert O'Brien and Dr. Sidney Cohen. **Anabolic steroids** are derivatives of testosterone, a natural male hormone.

p. 48 — **Depth and pressure chart.** A column of salt water one inch square and 33 feet deep weighs the same as a column of the atmosphere at sea level (14.7 pounds). Fresh water weighs less—a column *34* feet deep weighs 14.7 pounds. The pounds per square inch on the depth and pressure chart include the weight of both air and sea water. About half of the weight of the atmosphere is in the 18,000 feet nearest the earth. Mountain climbers at 18,000 feet experience only about 7.4 pounds of pressure.

p. 48 — Irrigation has caused the **Aral Sea** in Russia to shrink to 60% of its former size.

p. 49 — The heights of **waterfalls** are for total drops, not single drops.

pp. 53–70 — **Countries of the World.** For languages, the CIA's *World Factbook 1993* was used. The *Wall Street Journal* 10/10/94 was the source of currencies. Areas, capitals, populations, population growth rates, population densities, per capita GNPs, average life expectancies, infant mortality rates and locations are from the *1994 World Population Data Sheet*, compiled by the Population Reference Bureau, Inc. World statistics from the same sources are listed below:

Area: 196,683,760 sq. mi.
139,252,100 sq. mi. water (70.8%)
57,431,657 sq. mi. land (29.2%)
Population: 5,606,989,000
Population Growth Rate: 1.6%
Population Density: 98
Per capita GNP: $4,340
Average life expectancy: 65
Infant Mortality Rate: 63

— **Countries. Germany** was united on October 2, 1990. **Yemen** was united on May 22, 1990. The **Soviet Union** was dissolved on December 26, 1991. **Slovenia, Croatia, Bosnia-Herzegovina,** and **Macedonia** declared independence from **Yugoslavia** in 1992. Serbia and Montenegro united as the Federal Republic of Yugoslavia on April 27, 1992.

Czechoslovakia split into the **Czech Republic** and **Slovakia** on December 31, 1992. **Eritrea** became independent from **Ethiopia** on May 24, 1993.

— **Capital cities. Germany:** Many government offices are still in the in the old West German capital of **Bonn. Amsterdam** is the official capital of **The Netherlands;** the seat of government is **The Hague. Quezon City** was the capital of the **Philippines** from 1948–1976. **Nigeria** may soon move its capital to **Abuja. Tanzania** will move its capital to **Dodoma** in the 1990's. The de facto capital of **Benin** is **Cotonou. South Africa** has three capitals: legislative, executive and judicial. Other countries may have more than one capital; the one listed is most frequently cited.

— **Areas** are land areas, not total areas, as published by the United Nations Food and Agricultural Organization.

— **Populations of capital cities** are 1995 estimates for urban areas of the largest 94 cities in the world. The source was the *Statistical Abstract,* 1993. For a definition of "urban area," see notes for p. 105.

— **Languages** include official languages and others most commonly used. Hundreds of separate languages and dialects are spoken in some countries.

— **Currency** shows basic units of currency, including currencies new countries have announced plans to introduce soon.

— **Populations** are 1994 mid-year estimates. More than half of the world's people live in just six countries. See table on page 145.

— **Population growth rates** shown are rates of natural increase—the birth rate minus the death rate. They show rates of population growth without counting net immigration or emigration.

— **Population density** is population divided by land area. The figures are rounded to the nearest whole number. Countries with high

densities can be thought of as more crowded than those with low densities. The type of land influences how many people can live in a place. Fewer people can live in a desert, for example, than on fertile farmland.

— **Per capita GNP** are per capita gross national products based on 1994 estimates by the World Bank, in equivalent U.S. dollars. The GNP is the value of all goods and services produced within a country, plus income earned abroad, minus income earned by foreigners within the country. This is *not* the per capita income. Average people do not earn this much. Income is distributed unevenly. Poor people would have a much lower per capita income than this figure indicates.

— **Average life expectancy** is the average number of years a newborn infant can expect to live under current mortality levels. These figures are a combined average for both sexes. Women generally have a longer life expectancy than men.

— **Infant mortality rate (IMR)** is the number of deaths of infants under one year of age in a given year per 1000 live births occurring in the same year. It is considered an important indicator of the general health of a society. If a country has an IMR of 50 or more, it indicates a societal problem of hunger and starvation. Figures are rounded.

— **Location** reflects new U.N. geographical definitions. Russia is now classified by the U.N. as an Eastern European country because its population is predominantly European. More than 75% of its land mass is in Asia.

pp. 72–77 — The **time line of history** is intended to be a simplified general outline or overview of history. Eras and civilizations did not suddenly start or stop in the years indicated on the time line, but gradually grew and declined.

pp. 78–83 — **Notable people** were chosen to highlight individual contributions from a wide variety of people of different races and backgrounds. Those listed have articles written about them in standard encyclopedias. In the short space of six pages, many notable people cannot be listed.

pp. 84–87 — **Inventions and discoveries** were chosen on the basis of both importance and understandability.

p. 88 — **Bridges** included in the chart have the longest main spans in the world. The longest total length, including bridge and approaches, is the Rio-Niterói Bridge in Brazil, at 45,604 feet. The main span is 984 feet. It is a plate and box girder construction. The longest cable-stayed bridge is the Alex Fraser near Vancouver, British Columbia, with a main span of 1,526 feet. The longest continuous truss bridge is the Astoria in Oregon/Washington, at 1,232 feet. KRK in Croatia is the longest concrete arch bridge, with a main span of 1,280 feet.

p. 90 — **Heights of skyscrapers** are heights to the roof. The total height may be quite a bit more. The information was verified by telephone with building owners.

pp. 94–101 — **States of the Union.** Information is from the Council of State Governments *Book of the States, 1990–91,* the U.S. Bureau of the Census, the U.S. Bureau of Economic Analysis, and the U.S. Geological Survey. For comparison purposes, here in information on the United States as a whole from those sources:
Population: 248,708,873
Population density: 66
Area: 3,787,425 sq. mi.
Per capita income: $17,596
Highest point: 20,320 ft.
Lowest point: –282 ft.

— **Populations of capital cities** are official 1990 census figures for the cities themselves, not the metropolitan areas.

— **Nicknames.** Some states have more than one. The first listed is the one most often used.

— **Populations** are official 1990 census figures.

— **Population density** is population divided by area and rounded to the nearest whole number.

— **Per capita income** is from the U.S. Bureau of Economic Analysis for 1992. These figures refer to before tax income, and are not the same as per capita GNP.

— **Areas** include both land and inland water areas. The U.S. Census Bureau is using a new computer mapping system and including water areas not previously counted, so the figures for areas have changed.

pp. 103–105 — **Largest cities of the United States.** Official 1990 census figures and areas are from *Summary Population and Housing Characteristics* issued by the U.S. Census Bureau.

p. 105 — **Largest urban areas of the world.** These are mid-1995 estimates from the 1993 *Statistical Abstract.* For this list, urban areas are defined as population clusters of continuous built-up area with a population density of 5,000+ persons per square mile. Political and administrative boundaries were disregarded in determining populations. The most densely populated city in the world is Hong Kong, with 247,000 persons per square mile. Mexico City grew by an average of 83 people per hour between 1989 and 1990.

pp. 106–109 — Many parks first entered the **National Park System** as national monuments. Others were authorized several years before they were established. The date given is the date *established.* Most parks have had numerous boundary changes. The acreages given are those of September 30, 1994. Some parks have changed their names. The date given is the date established under *any* name. Haleakala National Park was

separated from Hawaii Volcanoes National Park on September 13, 1960.

pp. 110–111 — Information about **Indians** is to provide a *general* framework for studying traditional native American cultures. Not all tribes in a group are listed, and not all information given about a group applies to each tribe. Tribes listed have individual articles in standard encyclopedias. Information on food, clothing, shelter, and transportation is for traditional and customary use before the adaptation of modern ways, and will generally not apply to the present day. Many tribes no longer live in their traditional homelands. **Staple foods** are foods most constantly and generally eaten. Information on **Indians of the Plains** reflect the lifestyle after Europeans came to the Americas. Before that time, Indians did not have horses. They farmed corn, beans and squash, and men generally hunted deer and elk. Buffalo were difficult to hunt on foot. The lifestyle of following buffalo herds and hunting on horseback lasted only about 200 years. The great buffalo herds disappeared by about 1890, the year of the Battle of Wounded Knee, the last battle with the Sioux Indians.

p. 142 — There are 60 nautical miles (69 statute miles) between **lines of latitude**. At the equator, there are 60 nautical miles between **lines of longitude**.

p. 164 — The **frequency of letters** given was based on letter counts from the following six sources: (a) press reporting, (b) religious writing, (c) scientific writing, (d) general fiction, (e) 15 categories of text totalling over a million words, (f) the order used by Samuel Morse based on quantities of type in a printer's office.

p. 209 — **Pi:** $\pi = 3.14159265$. The diameter of a circle multiplied by pi equals its circumference.

Selected Bibliography

Caney, Steven. *Steven Caney's Invention Book.* New York: Workman Publishing, 1985.

Chase's Annual Events, 1994. Chicago: Contemporary Books, Inc., 1993.

Conlin, Joseph R. *The Morrow Book of Quotations in American History.* New York: William Morrow & Company, Inc., 1984.

Council of State Governments. *The Book of the States, 1994-95.* Lexington, Kentucky: The Council of State Governments, 1994.

Council of State Governments. *State Administrative Officials Classified by Function, 1993-94.* Lexington, Kentucky: The Council of State Governments, 1993.

Crystal, David. *The Cambridge Encyclopedia of Language.* New York: Cambridge University Press, 1987.

Encyclopedia Americana, 1993 edition. Danbury, Connecticut: Grolier Incorporated, 1993.

Ensminger, Audrey H. and others, *Foods and Nutrition Encyclopedia.* Clovis, California: Pegus Press, 1983.

Europa World Year Book 1993. London: Europa Publications Limited, 1993.

Guide to Places of the World, A Geographical Dictionary. London: Reader's Digest Association, 1987.

The Guinness Book of World Records 1994. New York: Facts on File, Inc., 1993.

Gunston, Bill and others. *The Guinness Book of Speed Facts and Feats.* Enfield, Middlesex: Guinness Superlatives, 1984.

Hatch, Jane M. *The American Book of Days, 3rd edition.* New York: H.W. Wilson Company, 1978.

Hurlbut, Cornelius S., Jr., *The Planet We Live On, An Illustrated Encyclopedia of the Earth Sciences.* New York: Harry N. Abrams, Inc., 1976.

The Incredible Machine. Washington, D.C.: National Geographic Society, 1986.

Jenkins, Francis A. and Harvey E. White. *Fundamentals of Optics, 4th edition.* New York: McGraw-Hill Book Company, 1976.

Lide, David R. *Handbook of Chemistry and Physics, 75th edition, 1994-95.* Boca Raton, Florida: CRC Press, Inc., 1994.

Merit Student's Encyclopedia. New York: Macmillan Educational Company, 1988.

The New Encyclopædia Britannica. Chicago: Encyclopædia Britannica, Inc., 1994.

New York Public Library Desk Reference. New York: Prentice Hall General Reference, 1993.

The 1994 Information Please Almanac. Boston: Houghton Mifflin Company, 1994.

O'Brien, Robert and Sidney Cohen, M.D. *The Encyclopedia of Drug Abuse.* New York: Facts on File, Inc., 1984.

Simpson, J. A. and E. S. C. Weiner. *The Oxford English Dictionary.* Oxford: Clarendon Press, 1989.

Population Reference Bureau. *1994 World Population Data Sheet.* Washington, D.C.: Population Reference Bureau, 1994.

Ridpath, Ian. *Illustrated Encyclopedia of Astronomy and Space.* New York: Crowell, 1979.

Sebel, Peter and others. *Respiration, The Breath of Life.* New York: Torstar Books, 1985.

Small Inventions That Make a Big Difference. Washington, D.C.: National Geographic Society, 1984.

The Statesman's Year-Book, 1994-95, 131st edition. New York: St. Martin's Press, Inc., 1994.

U.S. Central Intelligence Agency. *The World Factbook 1993.* Washington, D.C.: U.S. Government Printing Office, 1993.

U.S. Congress. *1993-1994 Congressional Directory, 103rd Congress.* Washington, D.C.: U.S. Government Printing Office, 1993.

U.S. Department of Commerce, Bureau of the Census. *Statistical Abstract of the United States: 1993, 113th edition.* Washington, D.C.: U.S. Government Printing Office, 1993.

U.S. Department of Commerce, Bureau of the Census. *World Population Profile 1989.* Washington, D.C.: U.S. Government Printing Office, 1989.

U.S. Department of the Interior, National Park Service. *The National Parks Index 1993.* Washington, D.C.: U.S. Government Printing Office, 1993 and unpublished data.

Washington Information Directory, 1994-1995. Washington, D.C.: Congressional Quarterly, Inc., 1994.

Webster's New Geographical Dictionary. Springfield, Massachusetts: Merriam-Webster, Inc., 1984.

Whitford, H. C. *A Dictionary of American Homophones and Homographs.* New York: Teachers College Press, 1966.

Willoughby, David P. "Running and Jumping," *Natural History,* (March 1974), pp. 69-72.

The World Almanac and Book of Facts, 1994. New Jersey: Funk & Wagnalls Corp., 1994.

World Book Encyclopedia, 1994 edition. Chicago: World Book, Inc., 1994.

Wulffson, Don L. *Extraordinary Stories Behind the Invention of Ordinary Things.* New York: Lothrop, Lee & Shepard Books, 1981.

Index

Pyrite, 32
Python, 39

Qatar, 65, 70, *137*
Quadrilaterals, 209
Quartz, 32
Quasars, 15
Quaternary Period, 28
Quayle, J. Danforth, 82
Quebec Bridge, 88
Queens, 123
  See Cleopatra
Quezon City, Philippines, 230
Quito, Ecuador, 57, *136*
Quotations, 124, 18
  punctuation/capitalization, 169, 170
  in note taking, 222
Qur'an
  See Koran

Rabat, Morocco, 63, *137*
Rabbi, 91
Rabbit, 37, 38, 39, 111
  Easter bunny, 9
  See also Hare
Rabbit Hill, 161
Racicot, Marc, 97
Radio, 86
Radium, 34
Radon, 34
Railroad engineers
  See Jones, Casey
Railroad tunnels, 89
Railroads, 3, 77
  See also Locomotive, steam
Rain, 22-25, 26, 31
Rain dance, 111
Rainbow, 198
Rainfall map, 144
Raleigh, North Carolina, 98, 102, *133*
Raleigh, Sir Walter, 82
Ramadan, 92
Ramses II, 82
Rangoon, Burma, 55, *139*
Raphael, 82
Raskin, Ellen, 161
Rat, 13
Rawlings, Marjorie, 162
Rawls, Wilson, 162
Rays (animal), 37
Reader's Digest, 156
Readers' Guide to Periodical
  Literature, 156
Reading, 218
  See also Books
Reagan, Ronald W., 130, 82
Reaper, 86
Recommended Daily Dietary
  Allowances, 44-45, 229
Record-player
  See Phonograph
Recreation Areas, National, 109
Red Cross
  See Barton, Clara
Red Sea, 49, *137*
Redwood National Park, 108
Reed instruments, 197
Reed, Walter, 82
Reference books and materials,
  144-157, 223
  in research report, 226-227

Reformation, 76, 92
  See also Luther, Martin; Calvin, John
Refrigerator, 33
Regions of the world, 70
Rehnquist, William H., 129
Reincarnation, 91
Relativity, Theory of, 84
Religion, 91-92
  holidays, 8-10
  calendars, 13
  history of, 72-77
  freedom of, 119 (Amendment 1)
  library classification, 147
  See also Mount Fuji (sacred
    mountain in Japan); Ganges River
    (sacred river in India)
Rembrandt, 82
Remington, Frederic, 82
Renaissance, 75-76
  See also Da Vinci, Leonardo;
    Michelangelo; Raphael
Renoir, Pierre, 82
Report, 226-228
Representative democracy, 123
Reptiles, 37-38, 28
  endangered, 39
Republic (form of government), 123
Republican party, 127
Research report, 226-227
Respiratory system, 41
  See also Breathing
Resurrection of Christ, 9
  See also Christianity
Réunion, 25
Revere, Paul, 82, 145 (time line)
Revising, 186, 227
  See also Mini Thesaurus;
    Parenthetical phrases
Revolution of earth and heavenly
  bodies (orbits), 14, 16, 18
  See also Copernicus, Nicolaus; Year
    (of planets)
Revolutionary War
  See American Revolutionary War
Revolver, 86
Reykjavik, Iceland, 59, *138, 131*
Rhine River, 50
Rhinoceros, 39
Rhode Island, 99, 101, 102, 76, 113,
  122, *133 (R.I.)*
Rhodesia
  See Zambia; Zimbabwe
Rhythm, 196-197
  in poetry, 158
  as a memory aid, 224
Ribbon Falls, 49
Riboflavin, 44
Rice, 43, 45, 111
Richmond, Virginia, 100, 102, *133*
Richter scale, 31, 229
Rickenbacker, Eddie, 82
Rickets, 44, 45
Ride, Sally K., 20, 82
Ridge, Thomas, 99
Rifles for Watie, 161
Riga, Latvia, 61, *138*
Rigel, 15
Ring of Fire, 27
Rio de Janeiro, Brazil, 105, *136*
Rio Grande River, 50
  See also Big Bend National Park

Rio Niterói Bridge, 231
Ritty, James, 85
Rivers, 50, 23, 31, 72
  in National Parks, 106-109
  national, 109
  of Connecticut, 144
Riyadh, Saudi Arabia, 65, *137*
Road maps, 143, 144
Robin, 37, 94, 97, 100
Robin Hood, 82
Robin Hood, Merry Adventures of,
  162
Robinson Crusoe, 162
Robinson, Jackie, 82
Robinson projection, 143
Rock, 32, 23, 27-32
  in space, 16, 18
Rock and roll band, 33
Rockefeller, John D., 82
Rocket, 87
  See also Von Braun, Wernher
Rockwell, Norman, 82
Rocky Mountain National Park, 108
Rocky Mountains, 52, 28, 30, 108,
  110-111
Roemer, Olaus, 84
Roentgen, Wilhelm, 82, 84
Rogers, Will, 82
Rogers Pass Tunnel, 89
Rogun Dam, 90
Rojankovsky, Feodor, 160
Rokko Tunnels, 89
Roll of Thunder, Hear My Cry, 161
Roller skates, 87
Roller Skates, 161
Roman Catholic Church, 75, 76, 92
  See also Pope Gregory XIII
Roman Empire, Ancient, 73-74
  alphabet, 164
  See also Latin; Roman gods; Roman
    numerals
Roman gods, 8, 11, 13
Roman numerals, 189, 200
Romania, 65, 70, *138*
Rome, Italy, 60, *138*
  See also Roman Empire, Ancient
Romer, Roy, 94
Roosevelt, Eleanor, 82
Roosevelt, Franklin D., 130, 82, 124,
  210
Roosevelt, Theodore, 130, 82, 109,
  124
Rooster Crows, The, 160
Roots of plant, 36, 31, 110, 111
Roots, word, 178
Rose, 12, 95, 96, 98
Rose hips, 44
Roseau, Dominica, 57
Ross, Betsy, 82
Rotation, 11, 3, 16, 142, 229
  of hurricane winds, 24
  See also Days (of planets)
Rowland, John, 94
Royal Gorge, 50
Rubber bands, 87
Rubber, vulcanized, 87
Ruby, 12, 32
Rulers, English and metric, 206
Rumania
  See Romania

Runaway Switchboard, 157
Ruppel's vulture, 38
Russia, 65, 20, 49, 70, 75, 105, 110,
  145 (table), 230, *138, 139, 131*
  alphabet, 166
  See also Catherine the Great;
    Nicholas II
Russian Orthodox Church
  See Orthodox Church
Rust, 35
Ruth, Babe, 82
Rutherford, Ernest, 84, 34
Rwanda, 65, *137*
Rylant, Cynthia, 161

Sabbath, 91
  See also Creation
Sabine-Neches Waterway, 88
Sacagawea, 82
  See also Shoshone Indians
Sacramento, California, 104, 94, 102,
  132
Safety pin, 86
Sahara Desert, 51
Sailboat, diagram of, 145
Saint Augustine, Florida, 76
Saint Christopher-Nevis
  See Saint Kitts and Nevis
Saint George and the Dragon, 160
Saint George's, Grenada, 58
Saint Gotthard Tunnel, 89
Saint Helens, Mount, 30
Saint John's, Antigua & Barbuda, 53
Saint Kitts and Nevis, 65, *134*
Saint Lawrence River, 50
Saint Lawrence Seaway, 88
Saint Louis, Missouri, 105, *133*
Saint Lucia, 65, *134*
Saint Patrick's Day, 8, 7
Saint Paul, Minnesota, 97, 102, *133*
Saint Valentine, 8
Saint Vincent & the Grenadines, 65,
  134
Saints
  See Joan of Arc
Salad oil, 43, 44
Salamander, 37
Salaries, federal government, 128-
  129
Salem, Oregon, 99, 102, *132*
Salisbury, Zimbabwe
  See Harare
Saliva, 42
Salk, Jonas, 82, 87
Salmon, 37, 108, 110
Salt, 32, 35, 45
Salt Lake City, Utah, 100, 102, *132*
Sam, Bangs, and Moonshine, 160
Samoa
  See Western Samoa
Samoset, 82
Samuelson, Ralph, 87
San Andreas Fault, 30
San Antonio, Texas, 105, *132*
  See also Cisneros, Henry Gabriel
San Bernardino Tunnel, 89
San Diego, California, 105, *132*
San Francisco, California, 105, 31,
  88, 89, 3, 132
San Francisco-Oakland Bay Bridge,
  88

Check your local stores for these items or order direct:

	Quantity	Extended Cost

Materials to Help Students Learn Reference

Facts Plus: An Almanac of Essential Information ©1995, 250 pages,
   ISBN 1-879478-10-2 Item 102 $15.95
   Item 10D, $11.96 when 25 or more almanacs are ordered.
Facts Plus Activity Book* ©1995, 182 pages, ISBN 1-879478-11-0
   Item 110 $19.95
Encyclopedia Activity for use with *The World Book Encyclopedia**
   ©1994, Item 129 $9.50

Materials to Help Students Learn Spelling

Spelling Plus: 1000 Words Toward Spelling Success* Item 048 $19.95
Dictation Resource Book for use with *Spelling Plus* Item 137 $12.95
Homophones Resource Book* Item 145 $15.95
Personal Dictionary Masters* Item 153 $9.50

Materials to Help Students Learn Handwriting

Manuscript Handwriting Masters* Item 161 $8.50
Cursive Handwriting Masters* Item 17X $10.50

Materials to Help Students Learn Math

Addition Facts in Five Minutes a Day* Item 056 $11.95
Subtraction Facts in Five Minutes a Day* Item 064 $11.95
Multiplication Facts in Five Minutes a Day* Item 072 $13.95
Division Facts in Five Minutes a Day* Item 080 $11.95
Casting 9's: A Quick Check for Math Computation* Item 099 $6.00
Base 10 Blocks, set of 120 units, 22 tens, 2 hundreds Item B10 $12.00

*contains reproducible masters

Total _____

Shipping (2.50 for first book,
   .50 for each additional book) _____

Total enclosed _____

Instructional Resources Company
3235 Garland
Wheat Ridge, CO 80033
       or
Instructional Resources Company
P.O. Box 111704
Anchorage, AK 99511-1704
907-345-6689

Credit card orders only: 800-356-9315

Name _____

Organization _____

Address _____

_____

Phone number _____

❐ Teacher   ❐ Home School   ❐ Library   ❐ Other